Blackening Europe
The African American Presence

CROSSCURRENTS IN AFRICAN AMERICAN HISTORY
Graham Russell Hodges, Series Editor

Blackening Europe
The African American Presence

Edited by
Heike Raphael-Hernandez
With a Foreword by Paul Gilroy

ROUTLEDGE
NEW YORK AND LONDON

Published in 2004 by
Routledge
29 West 35th Street
New York, NY 10001
www.routledge-ny.com

Published in Great Britain by
Routledge
11 New Fetter Lane
London EC4P 4EE
www.routledge.co.uk

Printed in the United Stated of America on acid-free paper.

10 9 8 7 6 5 4 3 2 1

Library of Congress Cataloging-in-Publication Data
Raphael-Hernandez, Heike.
    Blackening Europe : the African American presence / Heike
Raphael-Hernandez.
        p. cm.
    ISBN 0-415-94398-1 (alk. paper) — ISBN 0-415-94399-X (pbk. : alk.
paper)
    1.   Blacks—Europe—Social conditions.   2.   Europe—Ethnic relations.
    3.   Europe—Race relations.   4.   African American jazz musicians—Europe.
    5.   Blacks—Europe—Public opinion.   I.   Title.
        D1056.2.A7R36   2003
        305.896′07304—dc21
2003009695

Contents

Acknowledgments

Many people showed their genuine interest in the fundamental ideas of *Blackening Europe: The African American Presence* and participated with challenging discussions at many different sites and occasions. I owe thanks to all of them. Because it is not possible to include all, I would like to name some in particular whose ideas contributed to the final product in very different but wonderful ways. Graham Hodges encouraged me to (actually insisted that I) turn an idea into reality. Denise Sokolowski, head librarian at the University of Maryland University College in Europe, has been awarded the title "Research Wizard" for locating material that seemed to be unlocatable. Pirjo Ahorkas established the initial contact with Pekka Jalkanen in Finland. Lene Johannessen, Roy Goldblatt, Anastasia Stefanidou, María Frías, Maria Sternkvist Proitsaki, Jaroslav Kusnir, Elisabetta Marino, Peter Gardner, and their students participated in a longer discussion about the European-wide MTV impact on youth culture. Many people read parts of the manuscript, but I would like to thank in particular Susan E. Tomlison, Frank Lay, Rocio Davis, Heide Weidner, and Thomas DeFrantz. Rareş Beuran offered several pictures from his rich collection of contemporary Roma life. Vikram Mukhija, Jaclyn Bergeron, and Karen Wolny were a great team to work with at Routledge.

My biggest thanks goes to my homefront—Don and Markus, Jakob, and Jonathan—an incredible bunch full of humor, support, and love. That this project is realized is also due to them.

Migrancy, Culture, and a New Map of Europe

PAUL GILROY

In the mid-1950s, Aimé Césaire examined the condition of Europe amid the aftershock of the 1939–45 war and in the grip of anticolonial conflicts. He pronounced a grim and memorable judgment: European civilization was decadent and dying. In failing to answer the reasonable demands made by its colonial peoples for liberation, it had proved incapable of justifying itself, either in terms of reason or in terms of conscience. He argued that this compound failure revealed European civilization to be incapable of solving the two major problems to which its modern existence had given rise: the problem of the proletariat and the colonial problem.[1]

Our judgment may be less categorical than his. It must necessarily be more alive to the ludic, cosmopolitan energy and the democratic possibilities so evident in the postcolonial metropolis. However, it is true that the big issue which we must now address in order to evaluate the health of Europe's cultural and political institutions, has arisen right at the intersection of the items that composed Césaire's inventory. Race and class have been articulated together, and profound questions concerning the depth and character of European democracy and unity are being posed by nationalist and racist responses to the claims of old settlers, new migrants, refugees, and asylum seekers. That list of aliens has been recently supplemented by the addition of other shadowy, infra-human figures: bodies without rights or recognition detained exceptionally in the course of the ongoing "war against terror."

Very few of these vulnerable people were postcolonial settlers. New inflow from those quarters had been shut out long ago. Simple exclusionary mechanisms have ensured that Europe's twenty-first-century retirement benefits will be paid for by Poles and Slovaks rather than Nigerians, Jamaicans, and Somalis. Happily, in some places, the grandchildren of the 1950s settler-citizens are negotiating their right to belong with some success, and not all of the latest incomers are actively racialized though many are, of course, demonized as Islamic terrorists in waiting.

This welcome volume rests upon the implicit demand to consider what the supposedly intrusive presence of strangers and the correspondingly punitive treatment dished out to them by various governments suggests about the condition of European civilization. It stands today, militarized once again and heavily fortified against the encroachments by its proliferating enemies, within and without. The war against asylum seekers, refugees, and economic migrants offers a chance to consider not just changing patterns of governmentality, commerce, and labor but to examine the cultural and ethical contours of Europe where the notion of public good and the practice of politics seem to be in irreversible decline—undone by a combination of consumer culture, privatization, and the neoliberal ideology.

This collection affirms that the peculiar synonymity of the terms European and white cannot continue. And yet, against a wealth of detailed historical and cultural evidence, all across Europe, identity, belonging—and consequently the imperiled integrity of national states—are being communicated through the language and symbols of absolute ethnicity and *racialized* difference. The telltale mixture of ethnicity and identity was identified long ago as essential to the workings of culturalist racism that had succeeded the cruder, obviously biological varieties in the second half of the twentieth century.[2] Two practical consequences follow from this historic combination of circumstances. Firstly, historians of Europe's repressed, denied, and disavowed blackness must be willing to say the same things over and over again in the hope that a climate will eventually develop in which we will be able to find a hearing, and secondly, we must be prepared to step back boldly into the past. This should be done not only in order to establish where the boundaries of the postcolonial present should fall, but to enlist Europe's largely untapped heterological and imperial histories in the urgent service of its contemporary multiculture and its future pluralism. The little-known historical facts of Europe's openness to the colonial worlds it helped to make, might then be employed to challenge fantasies of the newly embattled European region as a culturally bleached or politically fortified space, closed off to further immigration, barred to asylum-seeking, and willfully deaf to any demand for hospitality made by refugees and other displaced people.

I've associated the cultural turn in race-thinking with the midcentury mass migration of formerly colonial peoples to Europe. It is also connected to the settlement of guest workers from various extraneous sources, another influx that ended long ago. But the old "new racism" exerts an influence even as it fades and cedes its dubious authority to emergent genomic and bio-social explanations. Its distinctive tones are still audible in the anthropological subtleties and evasions characteristic of the racializing discourse to which it gives enduring expression. Europe's common-sense racism now speaks the language of cultural difference blandly and fluently. Even the tacit islamophobic belligerence of the post–September 11th environment is not usually inclined to be overt. The crudest expressions of racial antipathy are redolent of imperial and colonial domination. They are usually regarded as unsavory, indiscrete, disreputable and offensive. But the old codes remain alive. They have been buried inside forms of nationalism and patriotism that are seldom judged harshly. At least when viewed from above, those varieties of solidarity are welcomed as desirable features of social and political life. They are supposed to endow Europe's various national communities with a necessary strength and a positive confidence. Under these respectable banners, which have become far more symbolically important since official politics started to be boring and the idea of public good fell into disrepute, the standard of what counts as acceptable commentary has been sharply altered. Arranged reverently around their national flagpoles, the mean-spirited people who only a short time ago sounded like old-style nativists, racists, ultranationalists and neofascists turn out instead to be populist, postmodern patriots and anxious, pragmatic liberals insulated by the warm glow of a newly invented cultural homogeneity. Defending the simple hierarchies engineered during the nineteenth century is no longer their principal concern. Instead, emphasis falls on the wider dimensions of cultural and more recently civilizational difference. Those divisions are just as intractable and fundamental as the natural hierarchies they have partly replaced, but they have acquired extra moral credibility and additional political authority by being closer to cultural nationalism and more remote from bio-logic of any kind. As a result, we're informed not only that the mutually exclusive cultures of indigenes and incomers can be incompatible, but also that their mistaken attempts to mix or even dwell[3] peaceably together will bring only destruction. From this angle, exposure to otherness was always going to be risky. That type of contact promotes ontological jeopardy. Predictably, the resulting dangers are acute for those with the most to lose in a tumble from the giddy heights of their natural and cultural superiority. These themes have now supplied the staple content of various European racial nationalisms all the way from Sweden to Rome.[4]

The feral beauty of postcolonial culture, literature, and art of all kinds can be used to complicate this picture, but they cannot provide an antidote to the problems that make culture and ethnicity so widely and automatically resonant. Something larger, bolder, and more imaginative is called for. We need to be able to see how the presence of strangers, aliens, and blacks and the distinctive dynamics of Europe's imperial history have combined to shape its cultural and political habits and institutions. These dynamics cannot be understood as external to the workings of European political culture. They do not represent the constitutive outside of its modern and modernist life. They can be shown to be alive in the interior spaces and mechanisms through which Europe has come to know and interpret itself. This volume suggests that they are already contributing to the making of a new European culture.

Most polite, mainstream interests recoil in horror from that prospect. They start off by registering their distaste in the anthropological tongue and then move without apparent effort through the sham wisdom of incommensurable cultural difference, contending civilizations, opposed religions, and untranslatable customs. These volkish themes are anxious emanations from a brittle culture that is in deep denial about the global dimensions of its imperial history and the compromised morality of its colonial historicity. All this culture-talk[5] is comfortably contained by the idiom of populist racism with its litany of hatred against bogus asylum seekers, aggressive beggars, and devious thieves: the latest vectors of danger, dirt, disease, and crime. However archly innocent they may strive to be, the patterning of these thoughts associates them with the oldest xenophobic impulses. Europe's congested metropolitan spaces stage puzzling confrontations with unblinking alien alterity. The strange and threatening groups in question turn out to be the very ones that were already well known and fixed under the sign of race. The old hierarchies produced by race-thinking's excursions into political anatomy are then recycled and endorsed for the test of absolute culture that they provide. In other words, Europe's culture-talk draws renewed power from the specifications of racial difference that are smuggled inside it.

2.

Critics and historians of this period must be alert to the oblique connections that have made Europe's cultural history into a new battleground. If it is to be intellectually as well as politically productive, any critical work must be ready to confront the culture of imperial denial and the flourishing revisionism that supports it. Effective opposition to racism, nationalism, and ethnic absolutism must be able to resignify the complicated discursive figures that have made tacitly race-coded common-sense an attractive and compelling option for confused and anxious European folk and for their increasingly cynical and manipulative political leaders as both groups confront the perils of globalization.[6]

The wider ethical climate in which for Europe, fervent governmental or popular racism can be made to hark back to the Third Reich, must surely be taken into account. But as the history of that genocidal conflict is also mystified and forgotten, the corrective power of shame at complicity cannot be relied upon to supply ethical orientation. It bears repetition that the biopolitical commitments that were previously mandated by old-style racial hierarchy persist in the form of common sense even after the languages of absolute cultural difference and gene-determinism start to take hold. The residual traces of imperial racism combine easily with mechanistic notions of culture and a deterministic organicism to form a deadly cocktail. These operations are no longer being exclusively conducted by the neofascists and the ultraright. They have also been attractive to the aspirations of the social democratic left. Indeed the populist metaphysics of "race," nation and identity fudges those increasingly fluid categories.

Once, not racism, but the legitimate fear of the host community is identified as a substantive object of government and statecraft, race will have acquired the power to reconfigure the political field by revealing unforeseen connections that operate across the formal divisions of ideology and party. These developments are clearly visible through the prisms provided by counterhistories of race, racism, and culture. Thus the critical study of those formations can contribute to the task of generating a new, antiracist cartography of Europe addressed to the quality and character of the continent's postcolonial predicament.

The convenient argument that some cultural differences are so profound that they cannot be bridged has become commonplace. It can be explained by the way that nationality gets blurred once "race" has becomes a matter of culture. The absence of clarity is telling and symptomatic; it suggests that anyone who makes a fuss about European racism, past or present, is getting things out of proportion, engaging in witch hunts, practicing empty moralism, or indulging in the immature outlooks of "loony leftism" and above all, "political correctness." From this perspective, the conceptual and semantic interconnections that have been established between the forms of language which produce race, nation, and culture not as networked but as interchangeable terms, are irrelevant.

Because "race" *ought* to be nothing, it *is* immediately of no consequence whatsoever. Racism either disappears or lingers on as a marginal issue, an essentially prepolitical event that should not be addressed by government worthy of the name. To even suggest that it might be worthwhile to approach

Europe's racism politically, threatens a debasement of government and a travesty of justice. There is, in fact, no substantive problem here because racism requires no specific intervention beyond the worn-out rubrics of generic liberalism. Any fool knows that real, grown-up governments cannot legislate the emotions of their populations. Any attempt to do so points them toward totalitarianism.

Arrayed against that type of argument is another disabling script. It bears the deep imprint of conditions and struggles over race and racism in North America. Those conflicts have been routinely invoked as part of Europe's future problems in this area of social life. This orientation answers the culture of denial by saying that "race" is not nothing but everything: a permanent and apparently inescapable structuring feature of social relations. This assertion is not a tactical response to the complacent liberal and conservative voices that regularly deny the most obvious manifestations of racial division and hierarchy. This position does not aim to promote recognition of the unstable potency of racism in economic, social, and political relations. It is more concerned to argue that any aspiration to live outside of racialized bonds, codes and structures of feeling is naïve, misplaced, foolish, or devious. Before making a stand against the patience required by politics and turning instead toward fatalism and resignation, this approach insists rightly that there is a racial ordering of the world, that we must comprehend it historically and endeavor to represent it analytically with an epistemological valency and rigor comparable to those more usually found in critical projects centered on class and gender.

You should note that this Americo-centric discourse is animated not by a confrontation with racism(s) or even racialized hierarchy but by its extreme attachments to a reified notion of race. Race becomes above all an experiential and therapeutic question that identifies a zone of feeling and being considered to be emphatically prior to all merely political considerations. In this setting, a totemic concept of race is present but abstract. Sometimes it specifies visible differences lodged in or discovered on and around the body but this attention to what can be seen does not exhaust it. In other moments, race becomes a signifier for generic problems of cultural plurality and translation.

The remarkable contributions that follow demonstrate that neither of these depressing but popular options is satisfactory. The first is complacent and essentially indifferent to the sufferings of those whose lives are still conditioned by western imperial and colonial power. The second is equally unsatisfying because it refuses the prospect of race as politics and opts instead to stay comfortably inside the safer areas where critical analysis is unnecessary and narcissistic expressions of feeling will always be sufficient. As far as the articulation of race with culture is concerned, these warring positions or tendencies are equally comfortable with absolutist notions of cultural particularity and diversity.

That shared focus is being put to diametrically opposed political uses. The essays below answer it by exploring the detailed unfolding of a dynamic cultural complex. Read together, they do not construct a history of simple hybridity to offset against the achievements of the homogenizers and purity seekers. Instead, they contribute to a counter-history of cultural relations and influences from which a new understanding of Europe will doubtless emerge. They discover and explore some of the emancipatory possibilities that are at stake in cultural workings that remain complex and unpredictable.

3.

An ordinary, spontaneous antiracism has emerged intermittently from these cultural developments but that small triumph counts for little once invasive immigration has been constructed as a simple problem with national dimensions. At that point, hybrid urban culture and creolized history go out of the window and we get transported into the frozen realm of mythic time shaped around the master analogy of immigration as a form of warfare. This unhappy, archaic domain is populated by the timeless, iconic ciphers of Europe's postcolonial melancholia: criminals, spongers, and their numberless alien offspring. It manifests a racial order that presents the problematic diversity that black settlers and strangers have inserted into Europe's political bodies as an effect of their unchanging and alien ways. Complexity, on the other hand, like history and indeed like the momentum of European development itself, is the apparent monopoly of those who are in possession of a very precious solidarity that derives from cultural unanimity. Justifying their pessimistic responses to the nightmare of multiculture, leads policy-makers to opine that it is "easier to feel solidarity with those who broadly share your values and way of life"[7] as if the assimilation of interwar Germany's Jews provided an obstacle rather than an incentive to their murder. If that strand of European history offers any insights into the present moment which can be characterized by resurgent ultranationalism and neofascism, it might suggest that much of the time, the anger and hatred that racisms promote can be triggered even by modest success in attempts at sharing "values and ways of life" across the leaky barriers of race and absolute ethnicity.

Antiracists are now obliged to judge where acceptable national feeling ends and xenophobic racism commences. We must find the courage to reflect on the history of political nationalism that has been entangled with the ideas of race, culture, and civilization, and to understand how Europe's imperial and colonial dominance brought racisms and nationalisms together in ways that still impact upon present conditions. These essays suggest that analysis of the syncretic cultures prompted, but never regulated by postcolonial settlement, now affords many opportunities to join a joyful enterprise in critical counter-history. That exercise in postcolonial culture-building encompasses several additional confrontations. The first of these is aimed at the realization of a more worthwhile liberalism, one that would, for example, be prepared to be profaned by systematic reflections upon its own colonial habits and implications[8] and might also be able to confront the habits which specify racial, ethnic, and national divisions in subtle patterns as potent as they are inferential. The second involves an assault upon the pragmatic formulae that place both racism and antiracism outside of the political field, leaving them to be essentially private issues, matters of taste, preference and ultimately, of consumer or lifestyle choice. The third confrontation would perhaps culminate in a revised account of European modernisms and their complex relationship with colonial and imperial experiences at home and abroad. The fourth would be directed toward understanding the impact of black literature, culture, art, and music on European life, and in particular seeing how during the latter half of the twentieth century an appetite for various African American cultures was part of how Europe recomposed itself in the aftermath of fascism.

These interpretative puzzles have been rendered more difficult to solve because the ground on which the ramshackle edifice of political antiracism was erected—largely, we should remember, by immigrants and their supporters—has dwindled. That notable contribution to Europe's civic well-being and political health passes unremarked upon by those who babble instead about an endless oversimple conflict between solidarity and diversity. Hasn't antiracism demanded more solid and supple forms of democracy? Couldn't dynamic solidarity be articulated around the noble desire that racism should have no place in Europe's political cultures?

Anyway, with hybrid culture on our side and postcolonial counterhistory at our disposal, antiracism can move out of its defensive and apologetic postures. Its aims are being annexed by corporate interests that are a good deal less squeamish than governments about feeding the popular hunger for a world purged of racial conflicts. However, the market-driven pastiche of multiculturalism that is manipulated from above by commerce, only appears compelling and attractive in the absence of governmental action and political initiatives organized from below.[9] Most corporate attempts at ventriloquizing the desire to live lives that are not amenable to race-coding have been ham-fisted. The betrayal of that utopia is obvious where racial types are reinscribed in the service of commercial reach rather than abolished in the name of human freedom. Meanwhile, the nonracial ideal is more likely to beat risk of being rendered banal by the carnival of hetero-culture now at large in the metropolis.

As the implications of these large changes begin to dawn, we should ac-knowledge that the routinization of that cultural plurality does not mean that the work of antiracism is over. That project must go on because the wholesome, democratic cadences of nonracial nationalism are not being heard either as loudly or as frequently as their advocates had anticipated they would be. In many instances, it would appear that the mere presence of new "waves" of immigrants is enough to silence the cheerleaders of tol-erance, negative or positive.

Faced with this degree of inertia, another battle ensues. It requires us to be alert to the workings of political racism and able to apprehend "race" as a process of relation, of imaginary kinship and real narration rather than some badge worn on, or lodged deep inside, the body. Without making any concessions to the reification of "race" and ethnic identity, we must try to find ways to take the divisive dehumanizing power of race-thinking more se-riously than has been done in the past. In other words, we must be prepared to identify European racism as a specific and significant object, to compre-hend it as a part of a web of discourse, to see that it has a knowable history and to appreciate its social implication in the exercise of bio-political powers that have damaged European democracy before and can still compromise it.

4.

This collection shows that taking race discourse and cultural intermixture seriously involves scholarly as well as political tasks. It demonstrates that there can be no excuses for failure to become intimate with the history of Europe's modern invention and projection of humanity in racially divided, antagonistic, and hierarchical encampments. And yet, these essays also re-veal that there is new value in telling and retelling the story of racism's ratio-nal irrationality, in seeing where its alchemical blends of knowledge and power have contributed significant cultural, ethical, and political resources to ailing European democracy, particularly where Europe has struggled to make adequate responses to the suffering racism still creates.

A command of that contested domestic history is all the more impor-tant as the living memory of the Third Reich dies out and ceases to form the constellation under which critical, oppositional, reflexive work on the developing lore that brings the dismal and destructive power of "race" to life can take place. The automatic assumption that European history will be told best and most powerfully when it is made to coincide with the fixed borders of its national states will also have to be disposed of.

In drawing the new map of Europe we will need to accomplish these tasks, we must be prepared to make detours into the imperial and colonial zones where the catastrophic power of race-thinking was first institutionalized and its distinctive anthropologies put to the test, above all, in the civilizing storms of colonial war. Making that long-forgotten history co-extensive with the moral lives of European nations is essential, but a viable antiracism cannot end with the sense of shame that story ought to produce. That redemptive movement must be able to pass beyond a compensatory acknowledgment of Europe's imperial crimes and the significance of its colonies as places of governmental innovation and experiment. The empires were not simply out there—distant terminal points for trading activity where race consciousness could grow—in the torrid zones of the world at the other end of the colonial chain. Imperial mentalities were brought back home long before the immigrants arrived and altered economic, social, and cultural relations in the core of Europe's colonial systems. This shift in standpoint makes those imperial dynamics much more significant in the constitution of national states than they have been allowed to be before. It sets a number of challenges before historians of the postcolonial present.

The principled opposition to nationalism that was so important to socialist and feminist traditions has faded away with the ashes of the Cold War. Scholastic orthodoxy is now keen to reinterpret the xenophobia, nationalism, and ethnic absolutism of today's racists in benign ways. If their hateful responses are not immediately intelligible as a grumbling anticapitalism, then they must be heard as a new anxiety induced by the experience of de-industrialization, or downward mobility or the growing inequality that has been prompted by turbo capitalism's merciless destruction of Europe's once-proud welfare states. We've already seen that some scholastic voices argue that for Europe racism is not a substantive issue. Others say that culturalist and nationalist racism is not proper racism after all but rather a veiled protest against the rupture of Europe's post-1945 settlement by mass immigration. The either/or-ism of these shallow explanations is itself deeply problematic. A more useful approach would seek to understand why it is through the political language of race that these destabilizing statements of dissent and fear become expressible.

Faced with strangers seeking entry to Europe's fortress, today's civic and ethnic nationalisms reply negatively in one hostile voice. If we are to situate, interpret, and then to answer that uniform rejection, we must be extra careful about returning to what we can call migrancy problematic. The mistaken choice involved in centering our work on migrancy introduces a risk of collusion with the cheap consensus that ties immigration and social policy to the nebulous discussions of diversity, multiculturalism, and "political correctness" I have already criticized. At worst, this new orthodoxy stipulates that multiculturalism is actually bad for Europe, its national states and its suprastate system. This particular interpretative language is neither innocent nor inevitable. Recent postcolonial conflicts in Southern Africa have reminded us that "immigrant" does not sound at all like "settler"—the word that was used to fix the precarious predicament of adventurous Europeans at the other end of the colonial chain. The sharp contrast between these terms helps to show why the migrant label will always be a badge of secondariness and marginality if not of rejection.

The figure of the immigrant is part of the very intellectual mechanism that holds us—postcolonial Europeans, black and white—hostage. Its prominence returns our discourse, against our will, to the idea that immigration and its discontents contain the key to understanding all the bids for recognition, belonging and autonomy that have been made recently by not-white Europeans. This should not mean, of course, that the history of migration is to be abandoned before it has even been produced. But fascination with the figure of the migrant must be made part of Europe's history rather than its contemporary geography. The postcolonial migrant needs to be recognized as an anachronistic figure bound to the lost imperial past. We need to conjure up a future in which black Europeans stop being seen as migrants. Migrancy becomes doubly unhelpful when it alone supplies an explanation for the conflicts and opportunities of this transitional moment in the life of Europe's polities, economies, and cultural ensembles. I prefer to say that if there must be one single concept, a solitary unifying idea around which the history of postcolonial settlement in twentieth-century Europe should revolve, that place of glory should be given not to migrancy but to racism. The racisms of Europe's colonial and imperial phase preceded the appearance of migrants inside the European citadel. It was racism, not diversity, that made their arrival into a problem. This is more than just a question of perspective. There are significant political interests at stake. Where migrancy supplies the decisive element, the door gets opened to patterns of explanation that ultimately present immigrants as the authors of their own misfortune. The violence and hostility regularly directed against them by their reluctant hosts can then be excused.

These pieces show how we can answer this depressed and depressing view with a different kind of analysis to which culture is central. This approach is premised upon a commitment to make modern racism part of the moral landscape through which today's political processes must move. I feel strongly about these matters because I am a European but not an immigrant. We do need a new map but, at this point, to try and orient ourselves through the idea of migrancy seems a big and potentially tricky step. It promotes an unnecessary retreat from the claim to be insiders and would carry debate onto ground that our enemies have carved out for us. We are forced onto political territory in which we are always and only interlopers. At best, our constitutional exteriority to the mysterious inner life of Europe's decaying national states means we will be "negatively" tolerated rather than admitted with a smile. Our belonging is still pending and we will be desperately vulnerable while our local affiliations are on trial. We can be rapidly removed to where we really belong by the stroke of a governmental pen or the flash of nongovernmental knife.

Migrants, let me remind you, are people who are required to occupy an intermediate but juridically second-class position. So far, the best that the left can come up with to challenge this negative diagnosis is a desperate plea that incomers should be welcomed because they can be set to work as the fortuitous answer to Europe's falling fertility rates. That will never be enough. Searching for a more robust and complex position than that, I don't think that migrancy can remain intact at the center of our thinking. To leave it there undisturbed is a vestige of the mid-twentieth century that promotes an implicit agreement to stay in the twilight, to remain on the threshold peering into the cosy but forbidden space of the national hearth, ever-mindful of the dubious benefits of being somewhere else. We do need that new map, but I know that the Europe we are writing, the Europe that we need to bring into being, is not an entity which identifies us with that nether world, with the migrant lives of our parents' and grandparents' post- and anticolonial generation, never mind the bolder claims that might be made on the basis of even older intimacies with the European mother country than theirs.

Notes

1. Aimé Césaire, *Discourse on Colonialism*, trans. Joan Pinkham (New York: Monthly Review Press, 1972).
2. Martin Barker, *The New Racism* (Toronto: Junction Books, 1981).
3. Bob Rowthorn, "In Defense of Fortress Europe," *Prospect* (February 2003): 24–31; John Lloyd, "Poor Whites," *Prospect* (June 2002): 44–48.
4. Giles Tremlett, "Immigrants provoke ire in Catalonia," *Guardian*, 1 March 2001, n.p.. <www.guardian.co.uk/Archive/>; Rory Carroll, "Italy orders anti-fascist snatch squads at Lazio," *Guardian*, 2 February 2000, n.p.. <www.guardian.co.uk/Archive/>.
5. Mahmood Mamdani, ed., *Beyond Rights Talk and Culture Talk* (New York: St. Martin's Press, 2000).
6. At a May Day rally in Paris, Jean-Marie Le Pen told his dwindling band of followers, "Globalisation and its Trojan horse, a federal Europe, are leading France to its death." Jon Henley, "Europe's far right loses its way," *Guardian*, 2 May 2000, n.p.. <www.guardian.co.uk/Archive/>.
7. Alan Wolfe and Jytte Klausen, "Other People," *Prospect* (December 2000): 28–33.
8. James Tully, *Strange Multiplicity: Constitutionalism in an Age of Diversity* (Cambridge, UK: Cambridge University Press, 1995).
9. Slavoj Žižek, "Multiculturalism, or, the Cultural Logic of Multinational Capitalism," *New Left Review* 225 (September/October 1997), 28–51.

Making the African American Experience Primary

HEIKE RAPHAEL-HERNANDEZ

A forced African diaspora in Europe originated as early as Roman times, and with a significant number of slaves from North African shores, southern Europe experienced its first blackening in some areas. Another wave of African influence that had a tremendous impact on southern Europe was the Moorish occupation of the Iberian Peninsula for several centuries. Europe's blackening in this specific case of voluntary African diaspora, which ended in 1492 when the last Moorish troops were expelled from Spain, can still be observed today in Spanish culture in such diverse fields as architecture and music. However, the roots for a significant blackening of contemporary Europe go back to the late Middle Ages. In 1444, the first captured Africans from West Africa were brought to Lagos in Portugal; their shipment can be considered the start of the forced African diaspora in modern Europe. Because the majority of western and central European nations were involved in the transatlantic slave trade or in slave-owning colonies during the subsequent centuries, the presence of Africans in European countries became an established fact. Over the centuries, a few free Africans—or later, free African Americans—lived or stayed in Europe, but the majority of African diasporic people in Europe were slaves. During later centuries, nations even as far away as Russia started their own process of being blackened. A small number of Africans already lived in Russia at the beginning of the eighteenth century, and a growing number of African Americans went to Russia during the second half of the nineteenth century because Russia offered something unique to them: a chance to gain a prosperous life devoid of discrimination based on their color.

After transatlantic slavery in its various national forms had been abolished, the number of black people in Europe grew tremendously. In the twentieth century, because of different postcolonial and postimperial immigration laws, one could observe a particularly large increase in the number of Africans and African diaspora members in many different European countries. While this form of late-nineteenth-century and twentieth-century voluntary black migration to Europe has had a significant impact on the blackening of Europe, the twentieth century brought additional and specifically new forms of blackening. For example, during and after both world wars, large numbers of African American soldiers came to Europe; many of them were stationed for longer periods in a variety of countries throughout Western Europe, thus influencing the socioeconomic and cultural fabric in many different areas. Furthermore, the African diaspora in Europe received another organized impulse for growth during the Cold War: The countries that were members of the Warsaw Pact invited large numbers of Africans and members of the African diaspora to their countries as either guests for a short time or as students for several years. Although the reasons for these invitations likely involved the notion of honest desire for international solidarity and support, they often also served the purpose of "demonstrating" U.S. capitalist oppression and gaining intellectual territory in African nations by educating prospective leaders. In addition, the media have increasingly played a leading role in the blackening of Europe in the twentieth century. During the first half of the century, radio stations brought jazz to faraway corners such as northern Finland, and the role of TV stations in bringing "African Americanness" to Europe has steadily grown during the last fifty years. The volume discusses, for example, the tremendous impact of MTV on an ongoing European-wide process of blackening youth culture.

The volume presents a collection of seventeen essays that deal with the idea of how African American influences—stemming from fields as diverse as history, literature, politics, social studies, art, film, dance, music, and jazz—have either changed Europe directly or enabled a revision of certain aspects in Europe. It is perfectly clear that a blackening of Europe is related to a variety of geographical influences—be they African or African diasporic, such as African Caribbean or African American—but this collection focuses primarily on the African American influence. *Blackening Europe: The African American Presence* is seen as an invitation to take African America as the starting point for a discussion about the blackening of Europe in general. As reflected in many essays in this collection, often the European "product" is the complex result of African American aspects traveling to Europe, meeting there with already existing black influences, and with these factors influencing some "white" aspects. For example, Felicia McCarren shows in her essay that French hip-hop culture is a product of obvious African American roots meeting Maghrebian first- or second-generation immigrants, for whom Africa represents a problematic origin quite different from the Africa idealized in U.S. hip-hop culture and French state-supported youth culture. Paul Gilroy has already argued in his *Black Atlantic: Modernity and Double Consciousness* (1993) that Africans in the diaspora on both sides of the Atlantic have influenced one another, an argument Kobena Mercer takes up for Britain in his *Welcome to the Jungle: New Positions on Black Cultural Studies* (1994). In light of this ongoing scholarly discussion, *Blackening Europe: The African American Presence* echoes Gilroy's and Mercer's theories but develops their thoughts toward a black American/black diasporic, European/white European hybridity.

The volume's invitation to focus on African American influences as a starting point is motivated by the fact that traditionally, scholars have looked at African American studies through the lens of European theories. Gradually, influenced by Afrocentric approaches, the interpretation of African American texts with the help of "European theories" was rejected. African American intellectuals, among them Cornel West and bell hooks, for example, have claimed that Eurocentric theories, particularly Eurocentric (post)modernism, have often "minoritized" and "secondarized" the African American experience and the African American contributions to culture and cultural critique—contributions that enshrine the materiality and specificity of African American life. Yet, still, even with claims such as West's and hooks's, the majority of scholarship undertaken in regard to African America and Europe follows this traditional one-way street, as one recent publication, *Beyond the Color Line and the Iron Curtain: Reading Encounters between Black and Red, 1922–1963* by Kate A. Baldwin (2002), shows: The author sees as the book's focus "the impact of the Soviet Union on African Americans."[1]

Against this backdrop, the idea for this collection was born: What about the other way around? How have African American ideas traveled to Europe, and how much have they actually changed some traditional European structures? How much is so-called "white" Europe actually very much based on and connected to a "black" Europe? How much do they become theory applied to Europe, thus helping us understand certain problems in Europe? These questions take up critiques, such as the above-mentioned West/hooks argument, about making the African American experience secondary and turn African American aspects into primary contributions to culture and cultural critique. And the time is indeed "ripe" for this approach as, for example, the African American theorist Karla Holloway has already pointed out. In

2000, in her keynote address for the Second Conference of the Society for Multi-Ethnic Studies: Europe and the Americas (MESEA) in Orleans, France, Holloway called on European scholars in African American studies in particular to apply African American knowledge the other way across the Atlantic.[2]

A wealth of excellent and fundamental scholarship has already been done in regard to the African or African American presence in Europe. I name a few as representative of all. Foremost, one has to mention J. A. Rogers's quite thorough study *Sex and Race: The Old World (Vol. 1)* (1941), but also Hans Werner Debrunner's *Presence and Prestige: Africans in Europe: A History of Africans in Europe before 1918* (1979). Other scholars have dealt with African Americans' experiences with specific countries, such as Allison Blakely in his *Russia and the Negro: Blacks in Russian History and Thought* (1986) and *Blacks in the Dutch World* (1993), or David McBride and Leroy Hopkins in their *Crosscurrents: African Americans, Africa, and Germany in the Modern World* (1998). Significant and abundant country-specific scholarship has been done by Michel Fabre and Genevieve Fabre for France and by David Dabydeen for Great Britain. In addition, jazz scholarship often recognized African American influences in Europe. Essays about African American encounters with Europe are included in collections such as in Maria Diedrich and Werner Sollors's *Black Columbiad* (1994), and in general, one can find essays in many journals and anthologies about African Americans and Europe.

Yet, again, the majority of these studies do not focus on the African American influence on Europe, but rather on the idea of African Americans' or Africans' encounter with Europe. *Blackening Europe* is the first book-length collection of scholars from different academic fields on both sides of the Atlantic coming together in a discussion and claiming a unique thesis with a European-wide validity—African American knowledge as primary knowledge for Europe.

Blackening Europe: The African American Presence also serves another interest of contemporary scholars: For some time now, critical interest in transatlantic studies on both sides of the Atlantic has grown. For example, in 2002 alone, Europe hosted several academic conferences with a transatlantic focus: the European Association for American Studies (EAAS) in Bordeaux, France; the Society for Multi-Ethnic Studies: Europe and the Americas (MESEA) in Padua, Italy; the Maastricht Center for Transatlantic Studies in Maastricht, Netherlands; and the Transatlantic Studies Association in Dundee, Scotland. The Dundee Transatlantic Studies Conference simultaneously launched its journal, the *Journal of Transatlantic Studies*. And in 2004, another transatlantic journal will be launched—MESEA's *Atlantic Studies,* with a specific focus on ethnic studies theory. *Blackening Europe* plays a fitting part in this emerging dialogue. At the same time, it offers its unique focus—the African American influence on Europe—because although these afore-mentioned transatlantic conferences and essay collections include ethnic studies and, consequently, studies about the African American experience, this collection, again, is the first essay collection that discusses specifically the primary knowledge African America has to offer Europe.

Blackening Europe is divided into three parts. Scholars from both sides of the Atlantic discuss the thesis that one can indeed claim a strong African American influence on Europe in general, be it the former USSR, Roma-nia, Britain, the Netherlands, Germany, France, Spain, Portugal, Italy, or Hungary.[3]

Part I: Creating a Foundation deals with African American aspects that directly influenced or changed some European cultural constructions dur-ing the twentieth century. It covers topics that are familiar to scholars in a discussion about African American influences in Europe and that come immediately to mind, such as the arrival of jazz, Josephine Baker, Kather-ine Dunham, or Europe's concept of modernism and primitivism. The inclusion of such familiar themes in a volume like *Blackening Europe* is es-sential as one cannot claim a thorough discussion of African American in-fluences by omitting the familiar or the obvious. Yet, all essays in this part also undertake the task of discussing familiar ideas from new perspectives, thus adding fresh insight to these themes.

Jed Rasula claims that jazz has only recently been acknowledged as rele-vant to the study of modernism. Yet, completely overlooked is the extent to which something called "jazz" was absorbed into the modernist avant-garde, particularly in Europe. Therefore, Rasula documents the absorption of jazz by the artistic and literary vanguard throughout Europe, an attempt that has been consistently overlooked in the otherwise abundant jazz-modernism scholarship.

Samir Dayal shows that Josephine Baker has sometimes been maligned for being ridiculous on stage, reinforcing stereotypes about black perfor-mance, but has also been hailed by some for being a performer who sub-verted the conventions of the stage. Dayal argues that neither of these views adequately captures the complex and subtle shades of her performa-tive as a black woman in Europe. According to him, Baker inhabited black-ness as a "symptom" of whiteness itself: In her performance of blackness, or in her performative as a black woman, one can read, inversely, the modalities of the consolidation of white subjectivity.

Dorothea Fischer-Hornung demonstrates the impact Katherine Dun-ham had on her German post–World War II and post-Holocaust audience during her tour throughout Germany in 1954, both in the public performance sphere as well as for individual Germans and Afro-Germans. Fischer-Hornung's discussion so far has been nonexisting and not dared in the otherwise large field of Dunham scholarship.

Irina Novikova analyzes the power of subversive and countercultural jazz in the former Soviet Union, a society that attempted to regulate leisure and entertainment by state-owned institutions in charge of developing socialist aesthetic tastes among the masses. She shows how jazz, however, was able to carve out its own countercultural chronotope, with black music becoming an expression of yearnings for white freedom in the USSR and its satellite countries.

Part II: Accompanying Europe into the Twentieth-first Century treats the ongoing fascination with African American themes and all things black in general throughout Europe. For example, the topic that comes to mind immediately is the impact of MTV on youth culture and its spreading of African American music to even the most remote little village in Europe—be it the very north of Norway or Sweden or Finland, or the very south of Greece or Spain or Italy. Everyone from all the countries surveyed for this volume in regard to MTV's blackening of Europe reported the same.[4] Yet, as all the essays in Part II show, this ready acceptance of and fascination with African American, African Caribbean, and African influences among the young in Europe does not reveal that these younger generations have grown in their understanding of black issues in comparison with all the generations discussed in Part I of this volume. Even if one looks at "more mature generations" or more intellectual groups, as, for example, Johanna C. Kardux does in her discussion of the slavery monument movement in the Netherlands, all essays in Part II show that current black fascination often also carries some problematic forms of extreme naïveté toward African American issues. Still, as all the chapters in this part also strongly argue, even with the accompanying problems, current African American contact with European structures differs from the earlier influences described in Part I in regard to depicting relationships in which Europeans show high respect for African Americans and operate on terms of a sense of equally high accomplishments.

Johanna C. Kardux explicates how paper monuments such as Toni Morrison's *Beloved*, gave rise to movements with the goal of constructing slavery memorials of a more material kind. In her essay, Kardux discusses two of the memorial projects that came out of the new public awareness of a shared history of slavery, which spread from African America to diasporic communities throughout the Atlantic world: the Middle Passage Monument of the U.S.-based Homeward Bound Foundation and the National Monument for the Remembrance of the Slavery Past in the Netherlands.

P. A. Skantze conducts an interview with African American choreographer Bill T. Jones about his influence on a new, young generation of European choreographers, who seem to have begun to import Jones's "language" as a language with which to speak about the issue of immigration in Europe—about nationalism and open borders for immigrants, about contemporary multinational identity questions and formations, and about tensions of race in place.

André Lepecki reclaims Josephine Baker as a contemporary critical voice when he analyzes a contemporary choreographic reflection by Portuguese choreographer Vera Mantero on current European racism and European forgetting of its quite recent colonialist history. He argues that Europe's contemporary problematic fascination with blackness is caused partly by its "haunted melancholia" about the colonial past.

María Frías focuses on the blackening of the art form that is specifically Spanish: flamenco. She argues that twentieth-century flamenco has been influenced by African American music to such an extent that contemporary musicologists talk about flamenco blues or new flamenco to refer to this fusion/blending.

Felicia McCarren, when asking how the specific African American youth cultural form of hip-hop is translated into French and what it means when the same form is transferred from the New York vacant lot to a Paris dance studio, discusses the many figures of the crossover of a popular cultural form originating in the United States, imported into and diffused in France, and developed into an art form with funding from national and local structures.

Cathy Covell Waegner offers some reasons for the striking phenomenon that for young people in Germany, "black" is undeniably "in." Waegner, with an eye to German television programming, provides an analysis of the powerful hip-hop marketing mechanisms that prepare the way for the outline of a theory of "cultural adulation"—an attempt to account for young Germany's double-edged fascination with all things black as well as to point out the risks involved in their foregrounding of blackness.

Along the same lines of blackening youth culture, Éva Miklódy shows that American "blackness" is not incorporated into cultural creations in a uniform way in Europe. This is of particular interest when considering the African American cultural influence on countries of the former Eastern Bloc, as Miklódy depicts in her discussion of Hungarian rap music.

Ch. Didier Gondola argues that France's immense interest in and seemingly color-blind treatment of black Americans throughout the twentieth century and its simultaneous xenophobic and racist treatment of Africans allowed the French to have a vicarious, "sanitized" African experience, affording engagement with so-called "African primitive culture" without that uncomfortable intimacy. The presence of African Americans in France enabled an officially sanctioned discourse proclaiming the absence of race discrimination and negrophobia and connecting any mistreatment of Africans not to race but simply to immigration.

Alan Rice turns to Jackie Kay's and Caryl Phillips's fiction to interrogate the interaction of a black British literature imbued with knowledge of a sustained historical tradition that is always dovetailed, however, with a fascination with the sophisticated African cousins across the sea in America. Rice argues that diasporan Africans in Britain possess a fascination with African American culture because it has displayed an exoticism and dynamism that have been in marked contrast to their own more liminal presence on European shores.

Part III: Turning into Theory for Europe presents a departure from the usual emphasis in African American/European studies. It illustrates Karla Holloway's challenge explored in her keynote address mentioned earlier—the stipulation that instead of applying European theories to African American studies, the latter becomes the theory or the lens through which one looks at Europe, thus making African American knowledge primary instead of the usual other way around.

In her essay, Sabine Broeck moves toward a partial rereading of John Locke's *Two Treatises* of 1689. She claims that Locke's rather local act of political theorizing propelled a European post–seventeenth-century discursive tradition in which "freedom" became an object of negotiation always already in relation to "slavery." Any rebuttal of "slavery" in a Lockean conception had nothing to do with a universal rejection of slavery, but, on the contrary, became a motor of the Atlantic slave trade *and* of early modern bourgeois emancipation in tandem.

Applying current African American feminist theory and Harriet Jacobs's *Incidents in the Life of a Slave Girl* as theoretical instruments, Peter Gardner examines one group of current immigrants: foreign prostitutes in Italy. He contends that the representation of the enslaved foreign prostitute is a rhetorical construct that fissures along the color line. In addition, he proves how the rhetorical construct of the enslaved immigrant prostitute is a displaced discourse that diverts attention away from the widespread exploitation of a large number of immigrants to a small number of women who have been forced into prostitution.

Mihaela Mudure compares the historical situation of African Americans and Roma in Romania—two groups that were enslaved until mid-nineteenth century and that started their way to emancipation around the same time and in somewhat similar ideological circumstances. Since she claims that the situation of African Americans today is much more improved than that of the Roma, she reads the situation of contemporary

Roma through the African American lens, thus hoping to point to some possible solutions for the still very problematic position of the Roma community in Romanian society.

In my own essay, I compare two groups of young people from two completely different backgrounds that seem at first sight not to be comparable: African American youth in low-income urban communities and right-wing youth in former East German small towns and rural areas. However, I claim that when dealing with both groups, one can easily detect similarities that allow such a comparison, such as both being social products of economically heavily disadvantaged communities and of their governments' failure or unwillingness to develop responsible youth policies. Analyzing the sophisticated discourse of protest and of attempts to remedy the U.S. situation, and "turning the discourse into possible theory," I claim that the East German situation will get worse if the current official discourse stays at its self-limiting and "just-enough-to-stay-out-of-the-international-media" level.

At a time when a myriad of social, political, religious, and economic differences continues to divide races and ethnic groups or, in some cases, even hardens disparate positions, a text like *Blackening Europe* presents a significant attempt to show the increasing hybridization of our societies, be they "Old" or "New" World—an attempt that may encourage people to coexist in mutual respect and peace. In short, the book is a starting point for further discussions, or, in the words of one scholar of American Studies who read about its concept, a "daisy cutter" (if such negative military image from the Vietnam War is permitted for a positive idea here)—a ground-clearing for many more landings and a launching pad for future explorations.

Notes

1. Kate A. Baldwin, *Beyond the Color Line and the Iron Curtain: Reading Encounters between Black and Red, 1922–1963* (Durham, N.C.: Duke University Press, 2002), advertisement flyer.
2. See Karla F. C. Holloway, "The Consequences of the Race for Theory," in *Literature on the Move: Comparing Diasporic Ethnicities in Europe and the Americas*, ed. Dominique Marçais, Mark Niemeyer, Bernard Vincent, and Cathy Covell Waegner (Heidelberg, Germany: Winter Verlag, 2002), 347–54.
3. I would like to thank Pekka Jalkanen, who, in an extensive E-mail correspondence with me, has explained the impact of Black America for Scandinavia throughout the twentieth century. Originally, we had planned to include Jalkanen's thoughts as an essay of its own in *Blackening Europe* as the Scandinavian part of our discussion, but for a variety of reasons, this wonderful idea did not work out. For a blackening of Finland, Jalkanen points to the special importance of African American music for several musical genres for twentieth-century Finnish music. Like in most other European countries, the first Finnish contact with African America happened with the arrival of jazz, just after World War I. And after the 1960s, even the traditional African American blues found its equivalent in Finnish traditional music, and both in combination created a new genre—the minor-key popular

song. Like the African American blues, Finnish music had already a tradition of its own of a musical representation of anguish: the descending fifth (sol-do) and the oppressive *katabasis* figure defined in the Baroque doctrine of affections, which had been adopted in secular songs in the nineteenth century as the symbol of negative emotions and events such as deceit, jealousy, separation, and pain. Between the opposing poles of Finnish traditional music and the African American blues, the Finnish minor-key popular song has proved its persistence, its prevailing moods being anguish and nostalgia. And even today's Finnish heavy metal, rock, and rap groups display this distinguishing feature of a unique combination of African American and traditional popular Finnish music. This is why, for instance, one can hear clearly African American musical traces and at the same time the minor key or even la pentatonic melodies in the music of such internationally celebrated and most appreciated rock, rap, and techno bands like HIM, BOMFUNC, M'C', and DARUDE. Jalkanen is professor of musicology at the University of Tampere, Finland, and the composer of two operas, three concertos, and several works for orchestras, among many other works. For more information about the influence of African American music on popular Finnish music, see Pekka Jalkanen, "Popular Music," in *Finnish Music*, ed. Kalevi Aho, Pekka Jalkanen, Erkki Salmenhaara, and Keijo Virtamo (Keuruu, Finland: Otava, 1996), 206–38.

4. I have had the pleasure of an ongoing discussion at many different sites about MTV's influence on youth culture throughout Europe since the idea of *Blackening Europe* was born, yet I would like to thank the following people in particular for sharing with me their observations, their experiences, and in many cases, even their own students, whom they involved in this survey: Lene Johannessen (Norway), Roy Goldblatt (Finland), Anastasia Stefanidou (Greece), María Frías (Spain), Maria Sternkvist Proitsaki (Sweden), Jaroslav Kusnir (Slovakia), Elisabetta Marino (Italy), and Peter Gardner (Italy).

PART I
Creating a Foundation

1

Jazz as Decal for the European Avant-Garde

JED RASULA

Jazz has only recently been acknowledged as relevant to the study of modernism. A title one might have expected long before now, *Jazz Modernism: From Ellington and Armstrong to Matisse and Joyce* by Alfred Appel Jr., was not published until 2002, and its selection of canonized musicians, artists, and writers to represent the spirit of "jazz modernism" is at once understandable and disappointing. Completely overlooked in Appel's account is the extent to which something called "jazz" was absorbed into the modernist avant-garde, particularly in Europe. The Parisian setting in which jazz achieved its first notoriety in vanguard circles has often been studied, but Paris is only one piece of the historical puzzle. The following essay, documenting the (decidedly one-sided and opportunistic) absorption of jazz by the artistic and literary vanguard throughout Europe, attempts to establish the importance of jazz for any further consideration of the historical avant-garde.

It is described as "*an art of living and enjoying*"; it is "nonchalant, fantastic, playful, nonheroic, and erotic": "Nothing but joy, magic, and everybody's optimistic faith in the beauty of life. Nothing but the immediate data of sensibility. Nothing but the art of wasting time. Nothing but the melody of the heart. The culture of miraculous enchantment." What is this "sweetness of artificiality and . . . spontaneity of feelings" that "calls for the free mind of a juggler of ideas"? Much as it sounds like other celebrations of jazz of the 1920s, what's being extolled here by Karel Teige is his program for poetism,[1] "the art of living in the most beautiful sense of the word, a modern Epicureanism"—but, he stresses, "Poetism *is not an art*, that is, art in its current romantic sense of the word." Rather, it has the potential to "*liquidate existing art categories*," Teige declares, because poetism not only has film at its disposal, but also "avionics, radio, technical, optical, and auditory inventions (optophonetics), sport, dance, circus and music hall, places of perpetual improvisation." *Improvisation* is the major lesson, and "Clowns and Dadaists taught us this aesthetic skepticism."[2] Teige's list of contributing elements is itself an improvisational variation on what was (in 1924) an ensemble of modern enchantments consistently cited in vanguard declarations across Europe. Jazz and Charlie Chaplin were routinely mentioned, invariably associated with sports, dancing, music hall, and circus, those "places of perpetual improvisation" valued precisely for the fact that they were unpretentious and, above all, *not art.*

The antiartistic tendencies of the avant-garde helped prepare this reception of jazz before it appeared in Europe. The prototype of avant-garde movements in the early twentieth century, Italian futurism, was inaugurated in 1909 as an assault against cultural conservatism, pillorying officious institutional efforts to insulate art from modernity. Filippo Tommaso Marinetti's polemical strategies closely resembled (and to some extent preceded) the entrepreneurial outlook of mass media moguls: Keep the product before the public eye (bad press being better than none at all). The anti-art posture of Dada, benefiting from Marinetti's precedent as vanguard impresario, enabled such venues as Cabaret Voltaire in Zurich to amalgamate shock to entertainment, a decisive precursor in turn for the appearance of jazz a few years later. In the early USSR, the anti-art position established by futurism and Dada was transformed into an ideological repudiation of bourgeois values, and the art-for-life insistence of constructivism spread far beyond the Soviet Union, validating a more general sense that modernity could result in a unified practice of daily life—"to consolidate a common front against 'the tyranny of the individual' in art"[3]—in which the arts would be thoroughly integrated to social needs without being made a fetish.

To raise the specter of the fetish, however, suggests precisely what was at stake in the enthusiasm for jazz, and how precarious was its footing in the developing European wish for a rational epicureanism. The enthusiasm with which jazz was received in Europe can be precisely correlated to the passion for primitivism fueling the avant-garde from cubism through surrealism. Because of its mobility as a generic signifier of modernism as such,[4] jazz was affixed to pronouncements and activities of the avant-garde like a decal on a traveler's bag, in the process becoming inseparable from fashion cycles affecting the absorption of jazz in social circles. Robert Goffin noted the paradox that "In New Orleans and in Chicago at this time jazz was the preserve of the dregs of the population. In Paris the cream of society went to hear [Louis] Mitchell."[5]

The role of Paris in sponsoring negrophilia in the arts and fashion is well known and thoroughly documented.[6] For Blaise Cendrars—Swiss poet, editor of *Anthologie nègre* (1921), and collaborator with Darius Milhaud and Fernand Léger on *Le Creation du monde* (1923)—"*Le jazz hot* is not an art but a new way of living."[7] Given Parisian fashion cycles, it was not new for very long. Bernard Gendron argues that "one must recognize the primary role played by the avant-garde and its allies in the commodification of everything that was called 'negro,' "[8] a charge that particularly applies to Jean Cocteau—a cultural "pimp" according to Hans Stuckenschmidt[9]—"who without much musical knowledge managed to turn his consumption of jazz into the well-recognized emblem of his own brand of avant-garde practice."[10] On the other hand, the brief season of enthusiasm for jazz on the part of Cocteau and members of Les Six may not warrant Gendron's claim that "jazz became seriously implicated in the depoliticization and the upscaling of the avant-garde."[11] Jody Blake more accurately recognizes that "jazz, which was condemned for breaking all the rules and dismissed for not being music at all, was the musical counterpart of dada's own anti-art activities."[12] The "blackening of Europe," at any rate, cannot be adequately assessed with reference to Parisian fashions, not least because negrophilia there had been integrated into both the avant-garde and fashionable society long before jazz arrived as yet another installment.

As for negrophilia, the grip of fashion could never quite dispel a question put to the issue by an American writer confronting cubism in 1908. Having reflected on his adventures "mus[ing] over the art of the Niger and Dahomey . . . gaz[ing] at Hindu monstrosities, Aztec mysteries and many other primitive grotesques," Gelett Burgess pondered the consequence: "Men had painted and carved grim and obscene things when the world was young. Was this revival a sign of some second childhood of the race, or a true rebirth of art?"[13] For many Europeans in the 1920s, a replenishing juvenility and an artistic renaissance were equally compelling. Insofar as the avant-garde was in pursuit of the same goals, jazz was destined to become part of its arsenal of affiliations. The link was made explicit by Cocteau: "If you accept the Jazz Band you should also welcome a literature that the intelligence can savour like a cocktail."[14] Of course, the analogy betrays a recreational disposition that many, including Cocteau, would soon repudiate ("a certain decor, a certain racket, a certain Jazz-bandism" as he derisively put it[15]); Milhaud, also announcing its demise, was more kind in observing that jazz was "like a salutary storm after which the sky is purer."[16] In similar terms of disdain, Anglo-American scholarship has often regarded the European avant-garde as adolescent high jinks unrelated to the serious work of culture, but as literary historians as well jazz historians now concede, the appearance of frivolity often masked a salutary desperation.

While Dada is still far from being adequately understood by Anglo-American critics, the Cabaret Voltaire has settled into place as a perfunctory citation, much the way Storyville serves in jazz history. Both sites share pertinent features of primitivist regeneration. New Orleans' Mardi Gras has no civic corollary in Zurich, but within the confines of Hugo Ball's cabaret, carnival was a nightly occasion. "The Cabaret Voltaire was a six-piece band. Each played his instrument, i.e. himself, passionately and with all his soul," Hans Richter recalled.[17] Richard Huelsenbeck "was obsessed with Negro rhythms. . . . His preference was for the big tomtom, which he used to accompany his defiantly tarred-and-feathered 'Prayers.' "[18] Huelsenbeck "pleads for stronger rhythm (Negro rhythm)," Ball observed. "He would prefer to drum literature into the ground."[19] The walls of Cabaret Voltaire were covered with modern art in the primitivist mode, including Marcel Janco's masks ("zig-zag abstracts," Jean Arp called them[20]), and the performances included music-hall piano, recitations of *Lautgedichte* (sound poetry, which readily struck listeners as faux-Africaine), and the relentless boom of Richard Huelsenbeck's drumming ("banging away nonstop on the great drum, with Ball accompanying him on the piano, pale as a chalky ghost"[21]). It was specifically and most imposingly drums that heralded the arrival of jazz in Europe during the next few years, even to the extent that many took "the jazz" to be drums as such. In England drum kits were called "jazz-sets," and in Germany they became known as "the jazz." Leo Vauchant complained of Parisians that they "didn't know that jazz band meant an orchestra."[22]

In a telling glimpse of the backdrop against which jazz made its prodigious Parisian splash, Jean Cocteau noted that "Impressionist music is outdone . . . by a certain American dance which I saw at the Casino de Paris."[23] In a footnote he pinpointed the mesmeric impact of the drummer, "a barman of noises under a gilt pergola loaded with bells, triangles, boards, and motor-cycle horns. With these he fabricated cocktails, adding from time to time a dash of cymbals."[24] Little wonder that Cocteau took up drumming, as did the painter Francis Picabia and the composer Milhaud. Expatriate American artist Man Ray set himself up as a one-man band, personifying what the French called "l'homme orchestre." Michel Leiris captures the dominant impression of Europeans, for whom any exposure to jazz "was dominated almost from beginning to end by the deafening drums."[25] For combat veterans, of course, drums connoted other sorts of bombs. Francesco

Berger, reporting on a jazz concert for *Monthly Musical Record* in 1919 (calling the drummer a "'utility' man"), likened the aftermath of a performance to a battlefield: ". . . when, after the final crash of a Piece, you look round for the *débris*, and are preparing to count the dead and wounded on the ground, you find the players mentally, if not physically, as cool as cucumbers, tuning their instruments for their next encounter, or exchanging with one another critical remarks on Puccini or Debussy."[26] Nor was the martial evocation confined to drums. Cocteau described a performance by the dance team Pilcer and Deslys as a "hurricane of rhythm and beating of drums . . . which left them quite intoxicated and blinded under the glare of six anti-aircraft searchlights."[27] The martial context persisted long after the hostilities ceased, as in Albert Jeanneret's review of Billy Arnold's band in *L'Esprit nouveau* (1923): "This percussion, an arsenal which entirely unlocks the rhythm. Synesthesia. The entrails are stimulated."[28]

Stirring the entrails was a prerogative traceable to Pablo Picasso (among others), particularly in his consideration that *Les Demoiselles d'Avignon* was a "canvas of exorcism."[29] Picasso's prescient exorcism preceded the Great War, whereas for others the Roaring Twenties and the Jazz Age were needed to achieve a comparable purgative. The acoustic transition from war to peacetime was heralded not only by drums but by brass: "the echoes of the last bugle were being drowned out by the music of innumerable jazz bands."[30] Fittingly, James Reese Europe—who had pioneered the era of modern dance in tandem with Vernon and Irene Castle, and whose military unit introduced dozens of European cities to the potential of "ragging" and "the jazz"—concluded a 1919 Chicago performance with a sonic depiction of trench warfare called "On Patrol in No Man's Land," for which the house lights were extinguished to accentuate the acoustic menace.[31] This synaesthetic tactic was precisely what the Italian futurists had pioneered, evoking combat with vocal extemporizing and noise machines (*intonorumori*). The combat precedent for jazz was not lost on English writer R. W. S. Mendl, whose 1927 book, *The Appeal of Jazz*, pointedly characterizes it as "musical alcohol" meant to relax soldiers on leave from the trenches. Mendl attributes to early jazz "a reflection of the elemental instincts of war fever."[32]

The prewar vanguard—whether that of Italian futurism or French simultaneism—sponsored *modernolatria*, idolatry of the modern, the new. By the end of the war, modernity had arrived in the form of Americans, bearing within them like a Trojan horse the germ of jazz. Postwar European *modernolatria* therefore took modernity to be indistinguishable from Americanism. Edmund Wilson was among the earliest Americans to notice the phenomenon. In the February 1922 issue of *Vanity Fair*, Wilson addressed "The Aesthetic Upheaval in France: The Influence of Jazz in

Paris and the Americanization of French Literature and Art." Wilson noted
the irony that Americans in Paris "discover that the very things they have
come abroad to get away from—the machines, the advertisements, the elevators and the jazz—have begun to fascinate the French at the expense of
their own amenities."[33] He went on to excoriate vanguard enthusiasts,
whom he identified as Dadaists, for their tepid attempts to replicate as cultural shock those aspects of modernity incarnated in New York ("electric
signs in Times Square make the Dadaists look timid"[34]):

> Our skyscrapers may be monstrous but they are at least manifestations of
> force; our entertainments may be vulgar but they are at least terrifyingly alive.
> That is why we find French Dadaism—a violent, rather sophomoric move-
> ment—laying hold on our advertisements, with their wild and aggressive
> make-up, as models for the pictures and text of their manifestos and tracts.[35]

Wilson was wrong to attribute Dada typography to American advertisements, but he accurately diagnosed the paradox of Europeans self-
consciously emulating American *lack* of self-consciousness—and jazz, for
many Europeans, epitomized this paradoxical condition. Furthermore,
residual stereotypes of negrophilia reinforced the specter of spontaneity and
untutored talent. Wilson nowhere discussed jazz in his article, despite its
title, but to evoke "the influence of jazz" on Europeans accurately registered a
conceptual slippage pervasive in Europe (and, to a lesser extent, in America)
because "jazz" meant "American," and America meant modernity.

Americans were perceived as agents of modernity in Europe before the
arrival of jazz, of course. In 1916, Hugo Ball noted in his diary: "Art must
not scorn the things that it can take from Americanism and assimilate
into its principles; otherwise it will be left behind in sentimental romanti-
cism."[36] Americans were harbingers of radical change and were therefore
suitable emblems of a cultural avant-garde with which the artistic vanguard struggled to keep pace. T. S. Eliot, for instance, made his initial vanguard mark in England not as a poet but as a proponent of Americanism in
a college debate at Oxford in 1914:

> I pointed out . . . how much they owed to Amurrican culcher in the drayma
> (including the movies) in music, in the cocktail, and in the dance. And see, said
> I, what we the few Americans here are losing while we are bending out energies
> toward your uplift . . . we the outposts of progress are compelled to remain in
> ignorance of the fox trot.[37]

Understandably, Eliot would later assimilate jazz as a flourish of his verbal
calling card, assuring an English friend in 1920 that, in future visits, "it is a
jazz-banjorine that I should bring [to a soiree], not a lute."[38] As David
Chinitz rightly perceives of this incident, "to have any truck with jazz at all

around 1920 was not only to participate in a particular discourse but to take sides in an ideological battle over the significance and value of modernity."[39]

The battle was not raged exclusively in Europe, nor was modernity the unilateral prerogative of America. Richard Sudhalter offers speculative evidence linking Dada to the Indiana University milieu of Hoagy Carmichael. Citing Hoagy's chum William Moenkhaus, who had studied in Switzerland during the Great War, Sudhalter speculates that Moenkhaus may have brought the Dada germ directly to the Book Nook, famed hangout for Hoagy's gang in Bloomington: "In this context the Book Nook's metamorphosis from simple hangout to scene of overheated discussion and spontaneous, often outrageous behavior (with hot jazz as both soundtrack and counterpoint) makes it seem a middle-American adaptation of the Cabaret Voltaire spirit."[40] This was during the time (1924) when Carmichael's Collegians and Bix's Wolverines played regularly at university and other functions. Sudhalter further speculates that

> To watch [Hoagy], pale and intense in a yellow slicker, bobbing and jerking like a marionette at the keyboard, was to behold a man possessed by a purity of expression wholly consonant with the "manifesto" of Cabaret Voltaire days. It takes no great leap of imagination to see him as a Hugo Ball figure in Moenkhaus's mind, pounding away as the high-spirited japery of this midwestern "playground for crazy emotions" guggled and plashed around him.[41]

It may, of course, be such a leap on Sudhalter's part—provoked, perhaps, by a certain physical resemblance between Carmichael and Ball. But the link is made plausible by the New Orleans Rhythm Kings' hit "That Dada Strain."[42]

With jazz, music became a medium in a quasispiritualist sense, or in the sense of that phase in surrealism called "enter the mediums," heralding automatic writing by way of "sleeping fits." Some previously alien dimension of experience was being channeled through music. Ramón Gómez de la Serna recognized in jazz a human voice not human.[43] Jazz was widely felt as a wake-up call ("Jazz woke us up," declared the composer Georges Auric as early as 1920, but "from now on let's stop our ears so as not to hear it"[44]), as the replenishment of war-torn souls (George Antheil: "Negro music made us remember at least that we still had bodies which had not been exploded by shrapnel"[45]), and as vitalizing accompaniment to gay times (in F. Scott Fitzgerald's various renditions). These social uses rendered jazz transitory, whereas, for the avant-garde, jazz was a transit, a mediumistic excursion to another world altogether. In more or less concurrent scenarios across Europe, Eliot substitutes banjo for lute, Man Ray photographs himself at a drum set, Alexander Rodchenko in the USSR uses a photo of a saxophone in a collage (for Vladimir Vladimirovich Mayakovsky's book *Pro Eto [About This]*), and a journal appears in Belgrade bearing the title *Dada Jazz.* Susan Cook, surveying the German scene, notes that

> [T]he avant-garde, in particular, felt the need to justify their interest and the logical necessity of drawing on these new idioms. It becomes quite clear in these passionate and divergent accounts that jazz had become a symbol of something much larger than the music itself. For the avant-garde, it represented the very spirit of modernism, freedom, and experimentation.[46]

The impact of jazz on classical composers exemplifies the full range of possible responses. Milhaud's *Le Creation du monde* was a calculated immersion in the replenishing bath of primitivism. Igor Stravinsky's samplings of ragtime served to emancipate him from abject dependency on Russian folk themes. Aaron Copland and Antheil absorbed jazz elements as signature effects in their bad-boy phases, exciting the public with a sense that ruffian modernity could invade the concert hall. But these are all familiar examples—too familiar, in fact, to do justice to other possibilities harbored by jazz. For some composers, it represented a precise technical challenge, whereas for others, jazz was not strictly musical. The career of Prague composer Erwin Schulhoff provides an instructive example. Moving to Germany in 1919, Schulhoff composed numerous dadaist works—including "Sonata Erotica," a five-minute orgasm for female soloist, and "Wolkenpumpe," based on Hans Arp's poem. By 1921 he was integrating jazz into such pieces as his *Suite for Chamber Orchestra* (1921), *Piano Concerto* (1923), the ballet *Die Mondsüchtige* (1925), and solo piano works like *Esquisses de Jazz* (1927). Schulhoff's interests were typical of the time in their seamless transition from Dada to jazz—and, like so many other classical composers (Stravinsky, Paul Hindemith, Bohuslav Martinu, Francis Poulenc, Milhaud), from jazz to neoclassicism. Jazz marked a ritual threshold over which avant-garde composers had to pass, to pass *as* avant-garde.

In the establishment of an ascertainable threshold of modernity, jazz was added to an ensemble that also included TSF, cubism, and "sex-appeal." TSF was the universalized French abbreviation for radio transmission (*telegraphie sans fils*), and these enigmatic capital letters commonly perch at the margins of poems, collages, and paintings throughout the 1920s—even figuring in the title of Jaroslav Seifert's 1925 collection of poems, *Na vlnách TSF* (*On the Waves of TSF*). "Sex appeal" was one of the numerous loans from American English, which began infiltrating European vocabulary after the Great War. Rarely translated, "sex appeal" and "cocktail" and "jazz" formed an incipient Esperanto for a floating international stylistic currency. Cubism, having preceded the war, had been sufficiently diffused by 1919 that it served as a general carrier, a principle of applied social locomotion, for all the other elements of modernity. Reviewing *Parade* in its 1919 London performance, F. S. Flint wondered what to call it: "Cubo-futurist? Physical *vers-libre?* Plastic jazz? The decorative grotesque?"[47] Terminological indeterminacy was characteristic among those documenting current events. At the Cabaret Theatre Club in London, the Turkey Trot and Bunny Hug were thought of as "Vorticist dances" in 1914, in a milieu described by Osbert Sitwell as "a super-heated vorticist garden of gesticulating figures, dancing and talking, while the rhythm of the primitive forms of ragtime throbbed through the wide room."[48]

The editor of the immense *Encyclopédie des arts décoratifs et industriels modernes au XXème siècle* (an accompaniment to the major *Exposition des arts décoratifs et industriels modernes* of 1925) evoked a milieu in which, "Tired of curves, having used up the joys of a timid naturalism and stylized flora and fauna which their predecessors had abused, the designers of 1925 have developed a capricious geometry."[49] This "capricious geometry" resonated well with the jazz that accompanied it in the public's association, inasmuch as jazz (in addition to its "jungle" rhythms) was thought to transmit the spirit of the machine age, or to embody the dynamism of a machine aesthetic. Cubism as such was not at issue: "In the press, 'Cubism' sometimes came to represent anything anti-naturalistic, abstract, or geometric."[50] Armand Lanoux characterized the Charleston as "the Cubist dance par excellence,"[51] an image that fittingly appears in the 1926 film *Emak Bakia* by Man Ray. In the dissemination of cubist-inspired geometries, Sonia Delaunay was among the more influential figures in fabric, clothing, and decor, and it seems fitting that her son, Charles Delaunay, would become doyen of hot jazz discography. "Clothing is not made for standing still," writes Richard Martin in *Cubism and Fashion*, "and fashion immediately took to Cubist theory and form that engaged movement. . . . As ready as Futurism was to spring into action, Cubism was a perpetual motion machine, moving with every facet. For fashion, the energy was only exacerbated."[52] Jazz, too, was a perpetual motion machine, supplementing the already "exacerbated" energy of cubist fashion. Robert Goffin's initial response to jazz in 1920 was to write poetry, with visual cubist accompaniment: "Possessed immediately by a sort of frenzied lyricism, I wrote *Jazz Band*, a collection of poems in praise of the new music [to which a] great cubist artist contributed four woodcuts, to illustrate it."[53] In many quarters, cubism was the name for whatever seemed fashionably modernist. Not surprisingly, jazz became one of the more eye- (and ear-) catching symptoms of this phenomenon, as it was assimilated into European life along with an allied American vocabulary ("flirt," "sex appeal," and "cocktail"). Skyscrapers, chewing gum, comic strips, sports cars, Gillette razors, and short haircuts for women were among the other fashionable accessories of the jazz-and-cubist atmosphere.

Jazz was central to the Bauhaus environment. Given the Bauhaus's self-appointed role in synthesizing modern art and design, students and faculty were keenly sensitive to contemporary forms of cultural practice. In 1925, Oskar Schlemmer described a scene convulsively dedicated to "the latest, the most modern, up-to-the-minute, Dadaism, circus, *variété*, jazz, hectic pace, movies, America, airplanes, the automobile. Those are the terms in which people here think."[54] "Nightlife at the Bauhaus claims the same importance as daytime activities," one student reported. "One must know how to dance." "Of course the credit goes to Arnold Weininger," he adds. "He organized the Bauhaus band. Jazz band, accordion, xylophone, saxophone, bombast, revolver."[55] Five years later, jazz still prevails, and "People are either reserved, straightforward, and cerebral, or they are simply sexual in an unsublimated way. People either pray according to German industrial standards or listen to phonograph records of American jazz hits twanging about sentimental voluptuousness."[56] Shortly before joining the Bauhaus staff, Laszlo Moholy-Nagy drafted "Dynamics of a Metropolis: A Film Sketch" (1921–22). All the urban paraphernalia of modernity are here, including a traffic jam, factory work, a football match, pole vaulting, dance, and two visuals straining at the limits of silent film: radio antennae on rooftops and a "Jazz-band, *with its sound.*"[57]

Contemporaneous with the founding of the Bauhaus, an avant-garde collective in Prague published *The Revolutionary Anthology of Devetsil*, with articles on various aspects of modern life. Charlie Chaplin (Charlot) was the emblem of modernity for the Czechs as for so many other Europeans. Chaplin's acrobatic movements were rendered accessible to the populace at large by way of dance—and dance was invariably an extension of jazz. Jan K. Celis emphasizes that, for the Devetsil group, jazz was not strictly a musical phenomenon, but a symbol of popular pastimes from over the ocean.[58] In "The Joys of the Electric Century," Artus Cerník evoked

> The bar, the place of modern dances: the shimmy, the one-step, the two-step, the boston, the fox-trot—of modern music, the jazz band—of the half-waltz, the half-ballad, the polka. These dances are not bad dances, after all. They are acrobatics, madness of youth, a wealth of moves, harmony. Hatred of them is absurd, and time will disarm their enemies. The cossack, the csardás, the trasák, the mazurka, the savoy—all are merely dance forms of the past. The time of futurism and music-halls is perkier, and we have a reason to rejoice over dances that make the blood circulate, that require presence of mind, physical ability, and confidence. . . . And the jazz-band! Listen to it just once—no, better yet, several times—so that you can locate its flavor. In it, there is the screaming of automobile horns, electric bells, and

sirens—there are rough low notes which offend the overly refined ear, there is thunder with colorful flashes, gunshots, a ruckus encapsulated in some beautiful song of battle or triumph.[59]

As for "beautiful song," European poets plentifully availed themselves of references to popular dance, jazz, and the atmosphere of bars in their evocations of contemporary life. Juliette Roche, sitting out the war in New York with her husband Albert Gleizes, captured the euphoria of the early jazz age: "the woodwinds of the Jazz-Bands / the gin-fizzes / the ragtimes / the conversations / contain every possibility."[60] The Italian futurist Fillia, in his poem "Mechanical Sensuality," evoked the "polydimensional . . . tactile visual olfactory supersenses"[61] of a bar, including this approximation of the jazz ensemble:

ta ta km barambarà

ta ta km barambarà

ssssss (Jazz-Band)   barambarà

AAAAAHH!   la pum barambarà

LA PUM BARAMBARA

Dadaists made a point of brandishing the term "jazz" as a typographic feature in their placards. The ad for a 1920 Dada ball in Geneva deploys a single capital "A" to emphasize the vowel shared by the three words "Jazz," "Band," and "Dada." Dragan Aleksic issued two journals from Belgrade in 1922, *Dada Tank* and *Dada Jazz*, with advertising support from local bars where jazz was played (Figure 1). A Merz matinee in Berlin in 1923, featuring Kurt Schwitters and Raoul Hausmann, makes reference to "Wang Wang Blues" (Figure 2). Mexican poet Manuel Maples Arce's poem, "T.S.F.," appeared in the Belgian journal *Manomètre*, celebrating the mysteries of radio transmission, including the heart attentive to the distant broadcasts of New York jazz: "Heart / attentive to the distance, it's / a New York / jazz band."[62]

Jean Cocteau's Parisian Jazz Band (with Auric and Poulenc) played at the opening of an exhibition of work by Picabia at Galerie La Cible in 1920, that precarious moment when the various factions of Parisian Dada were splitting up. (Given the context, the repudiation of jazz issued soon afterward by Auric and Cocteau may have been misconstrued by historians: "Plus de jazz" *also* meant no more Dada.) In 1922 Jacques Povolozky, owner of La Cible, published *L'Homme cosmogonique* by Nicolas Beauduin, a Whitmanian epic, excerpts of which had appeared in most of the leading journals of the European avant-garde. Beauduin makes the obligatory reference to "Le JAZZ-BAND"—with a parenthetical note: "*frénétique*"—howling its electric fever into the music hall atmosphere, charged with alcoholic delirium (a characterization pervasive in poetry throughout this period):

respekt pred romandadom dobiva pp. pub. nakon što će izići **II.** knjiga „MOĆI TUĆI" biblioteke : t. j. dragan aleksić (dada teške težine) nuđa roman „DETEKTIV ROMB" (kolosalan šundroman, o koga su se otimala tri poduzeća „albatros" — beograd, „zt" Zagr., „reflektor" Zagreb—Karlovac, vlaška ul. 111. roman ulaz bez traga mirnoće).

ELEKRO BIFTEKI 3 sjajan naslov treće KNJIGE radova na- šeg slislicrtača M. S. P E T R O V A koji je izvanredan opunomoćenik za celi orient do carigrada. On frapira svojom programskom apstrakcijom i lepo će vam dati pojam o najopasnijim stvarima jevropstva [za

4 g. stranac Melchior Vischer daće vam ro- man pod ovim velikim brojem biblioteke i naslovom „SEKUNDA KROZ MOZAK" (naj- bolji prevodilac preveo: g. M. Reich).

Fig. 1 Local bars' advertisements in Belgrade, 1922.

Fig. 2 A Merz matinée in Berlin, 1923.

The JAZZ-BAND blares   (*frenzied*)
Into the air spreads an electric fever
so strong that suddenly the music halls
seem, charged with delirium and alcohol,
blazes of terrible joy which explode
in the wild night ripped open by their finale.[63]

Marinetti singled out Beauduin as the exemplar of jazz literature as such in his 1924 survey of futurism around the world: "singer of jazz-band paroxysm and the international Grand Express."[64]

References to jazz abounded in avant-garde manifestos as well, albeit often perfunctory, like a daub of Day-Glo paint on a poster: "America lock skyscrapers wide-mind SELF-SHIP . . . Jazz band Zenithist music. Thirty-six soda-bottles—Bruit."[65] In Barcelona, Salvador Dalí and two associates published "Yellow Manifesto (Catalan Antiartistic Manifesto)," declaring the purgative virtues of sports, cinema, rapid transit, modern inventions like the phonograph, and, of course, "the popular music of today: jazz and today's dances."[66] In the Rumanian journal *75HP* (*75 Horsepower*), the editor wrote, in place of a manifesto, an "aviogram" in bold red and black (Figure 3), which read:

LIKE WINDOWS THE CONCERT OF THE CENTURY BEGINS
ELEVATORS RINGS INTER-BANK CLOWN-LIKE JAZZ
HORN
F FLAT
D
F FLAT
IN
PAJAMAS
FOOTBALL[67]

Ilarie Voronca envisions words "run[ning] through the faubourg wrapping themselves in the jazz of vertiginous sentences,"[68] anticipating Jack Ker-

COBOARĂ CA BAROMETRE ARDE COLIERUL DE FARURI EUROPA
ARE CRAMPE INGHITE STÂLPII COMUNALI INUTIL CÂT POȚI CONFORTABIL
INFINITUL IN PANTOFI DE CASĂ ANUNȚĂ
BISEXUALITATE ATLET URMĂREȘTE DISCURSUL RECIPROC GAZETELE SE DESCHID
CA FERESTRE INCEPE CONCERTUL SECOLULUI
ASCENSOR SUNĂ INTERBANCAR JAZZ SALTINBANC CLAXON

**FABEMOL
RE
FABEMOL
IN
PIJAMA
FOOTBALL**

ILARIE VORONCA

Fig. 3 *"Aviogram" in Rumanian journal 75HP, 1924.*

ouac's enthusiasm for "bop prosody"—or what, much earlier, Berlin Dadaist Walter Mehring envisioned as "an international lingual work of art, the language-ragtime"[69]—affirming the widespread Dada aspiration to "rediscover the evangelical concept of the 'word' (logos) as a magical complex image."[70] Following in the wake of Marinetti's "parole in libertà," or words in freedom, Ball envisioned a further step: "We tried to give the isolated vocables the fullness of an oath, the glow of a star."[71] The sense of liberating pledge links the *logos* of Dada (nurtured by vocables emancipated by sheer sound values) with the bruit affirmations of jazz. "Touching lightly on a hundred ideas at the same time without naming them, this sentence [renovated by Dada] made it possible to hear the innately playful, but hidden, irrational character of the listener; it wakened and strengthened the lowest strata of memory."[72] Skimming lightly over a parade of associations, jazz too sought out the primal layers of consciousness long buried under European cultural amnesia.

In the variable shorthand by which factions of the European vanguard advanced their positions, the present was affirmed (and much of it denounced) by blending primitivist regeneration with futurist longing. The paradox of an urban jungle emerged, often under the sign of jazz, which solicited a transfiguration of "psychophysiology," as in the manifesto of integralism (1925): "We definitely live under the sign of the urban. *Filter-intelligence, surprise-lucidity. Rhythm-speed.* Simultaneous balls—atmospheres giving concerts—billions of saxophones, telegraph nerves from the equator to the poles—strikes of lightning . . . New psycho-physiologies are growing."[73] Drawing on the polymathic anarchism of Dada and the utopian program of constructivism,[74] integralism, as its name suggests, was meant to integrate not only art forms but forms of life: "Poetry, music, architecture, painting, dance, all step forward integrally linked towards a definitive and lofty scale."[75] The contributing form of music, presumably, is jazz (explicitly so for Prague's poetism: "*Poetry for HEARING:* the music of loud noises, jazz, radiogenics."[76] Four months before the publication of *Integral*, the allied avant-garde journal *Contimpuranul* held an art exhibit. At its opening, a scholar discoursed on the African influence on modern art, but his lecture was "suddenly sundered by a drum roll":

> The lights that then erupted revealed on the podium, behind the master of ceremonies, a jazz-band, replete with Negro musicians. The sound of strings, sirens and drums. The perplexed multitude attempted without much success to advance at the podium. Did the directors of the exhibition pre-plan perhaps this general first impression, this bewildering amalgam of tones like a gigantic collection of colored butterflies? Because at least as far as the intervention of the jazz band is concerned it is certain that we were not only dealing with an effect of stage direction but with a veritable modernist ritual, of Dadaist manifestation.[77]

Responding to the same exhibition, another commentator concluded, "In fact, everything can be contained in a single word: musicalization!"[78]

In light of the conceptual and sometimes pragmatic overlap between jazz and the avant-garde sketched above, it is not surprising that European studies of jazz that began appearing in the 1920s bear concrete traces of the link. When the editor of *Esquire* wrote his introduction to Robert Goffin's *Jazz from the Congo to the Metropolitan* (1944), he declared Goffin to be "the first serious man of letters to take jazz seriously enough to devote a book to it."[79] This striking piece of misinformation seems to have led to a notable lack of awareness on the part of jazz historians ever since. In fact, Goffin was but one of several "men of letters" who wrote books on jazz, and his 1930 *Aux Frontières du Jazz* was one of the later publications. Preceding it were *Das neue Jazzbuch* by Alfred Baresel (1925), *Le Jazz* by André Coeuroy and André Schaeffner (1926), *Jazz, eine musikalische Zeitfrage* by Paul Bernhard (1927), *Jazz* by E. F. Burian (1928), and *Jazz Band* by A. G. Bragaglia (1929). There was also an intriguing 1927 jazz novel (simply called *Jazz*) by Hans Janowitz, who had studied in Prague and known Franz Kafka, Max Brod, and Karl Kraus and who, before writing *Jazz*, had been scriptwriter for *The Cabinet of Dr. Caligari*.[80] These European authors of books on jazz all had some connection with the avant-garde. Coeuroy and Schaeffner in Paris, like Baresel and Bernard in Germany, had links with the new music (Milhaud, Stravinsky, Hindemith, etc.). Burian performed with a jazz band in a Prague cabaret and, as a composer, wrote "Cocktails" for voice and jazz band (1926), a jazz opera *Bubu of Montparnasse*, and *Jazz-Requiem* (both 1928). He went on to become one of Prague's most important theater directors. *Jazz* was published in Prague by Aventinum, a leading publisher of Czech authors associated with poetism and surrealism. Burian's epigraph is from Karel Teige, the leading Czech theorist of the avant-garde:

> Music, just like theater, has no idea how to keep up with the times and with the other arts. Concerts and recitals are indeed stale waters of a small fish pond . . . the revival of music . . . happens only from external, secular stimuli. Though dead in the concert halls, music is alive in the world at large. Passion for living reality . . . you can hardly fear or refuse a music whose instruments and performers are still taboo—Jazz![81]

Bragaglia's book also came with distinct avant-garde provenance in that he was a pioneer of futurist photography. As author of one of the key early manifestos of the movement, "Futurist Photodynamism" (1911), Bragaglia established a protocol of syncopation for photography that has clear affinities with jazz. He later became deeply involved in theater, and his monograph on jazz was one of a number of studies on the arts, including dance (1928), film (1929), and the stage (1926, 1929, 1930). In fact, *Jazz Band* is less about the music than about its impact in these other fields, particularly its antiromanticism. Despite its salutary impact, Bragaglia recognized that by the end of the 1920s, jazz was on the way out, "already, for us, the face of nostalgia for our time."[82]

As jazz changed with subsequent decades, and as critics and historians began to document the changes, the residual (if long dormant) associations between jazz and the artistic avant-garde were called on to lend a force of analogy. Ralph Ellison, attempting to place the significance of Minton's Playhouse in the bebop revolution, said that it "is to modern jazz what the Café Voltaire in Zurich is to the Dadaist phase of literature and painting."[83] Robert Goffin contended that "Jazz was the first form of surrealism."[84] He summons a host of writers and painters (including Cendrars, Guillaume Apollinaire, James Joyce, Giorgio de Chirico, René-François-Ghislain Magritte, Max Ernst, and Dalí) to make the case that giving "free play to the spontaneous manifestations of the subconscious" was a goal shared alike by jazz musicians and the avant-garde.[85] Reflecting back on the readiness with which Europeans greeted jazz, Eric Hobsbawm observed "jazz had the advantage of fitting smoothly into the ordinary pattern of *avant-garde* intellectualism, among dadaists and surrealists, the big city romantics, the idealizers of the machine age, the expressionists and their like."[86] As Hobsbawm recognized, there was more than analogy at work. In fact, it may be asserted that the greatest difference between European and American responses to jazz (apart from the historical fact that jazz derived from racially denigrated Americans) is that the avant-garde was a pervasive phenomenon across Europe when jazz appeared, whereas it had played almost no role in the United States.

The heyday of the European avant-garde was from 1910 to 1930, after which it was overtaken by political circumstances that dissipated the utopian energies characteristic of futurism, surrealism, constructivism, and even (in its own way) Dada. Jazz was invariably associated, throughout the world, with high spirits and good times, and although it obviously did not dissolve during the 1930s, its "season" as an emblem of modernism was decidedly past. Clive Bell's 1920 diatribe against jazz (as the manner of modernism in general) was premature in its assumption that jazz music was a passing fancy, and similar Parisian pronouncements a few years later were also premature. But in 1931, when Gómez de la Serna published his book-length survey *Ismos* in Madrid, it made sense that "Jassbandismo" would appear alongside "Apollinerismo," "Picassismo," "Futurismo," "Negrismo," "Klaxismo," "Simultaneismo," "Charlotismo," "Dadaismo" and "Suprarrealismo." In a prescient forecast, Gómez de la Serna suggested that *jazzbandism* had provided the present with a forceful image of apocalypse, of a world of the dead resurrected in the carnivalesque image of jazz[87]: a distinctly Spanish vision (and Spain had long since embarked on its own blackening of Europe—its Moorish and Gypsy *duende* inspiring Federico García Lorca's affirmation of "all that has dark sounds"[88]). Whatever the outcome, it is fitting to regard jazz tumbling with a retinue of other *isms* into the cauldron of Europe's midcentury fate. When avant-gardes emerged again along with jazz, they had independent histories of their own and would never again be casually (and opportunistically) conflated.

"Whether you look at futurism, cubism, imagism, or surrealism," writes Geoffrey Jacques, "modernist culture is conspicuous with jazz feelings and references, which suggests that jazz was more than a fad or a 'craze,' as a then-popular word would have it. But if jazz was modern art, it was modernist with a difference."[89] To explore that difference would take us beyond the scope of this essay, and, in any case, it is the subject of a recent book with a title so obvious it's a wonder no one thought of it before—*Jazz Modernism*—in which Alfred Appel Jr. deftly blends anecdote and observation to make Louis Armstrong and Duke Ellington stand shoulder to shoulder with Matisse and Joyce. After nearly a century, of course, generic distinctions are blurred in the pantheon, so why shouldn't Duke and Pops be accorded the status of exemplary modernists? But there was a time, especially in Europe during the heyday of the avant-garde, when "jazz" did not bring proper names to mind, when it served to mark a time and place and mood with indelible succinctness:

> Eyes tumbling into shots of absinthe
> fog horn
>
> bleating ship
>
> a saxophone.[90]

Notes

1. Karel Teige, "Poetism," in *Between Worlds: A Sourcebook of Central European Avant-Gardes, 1910–1930*, ed. Timothy O. Benson and Éva Forgács, trans. Alexandra Büchner (Los Angeles: County Museum of Art and Cambridge, Mass.: The MIT Press, 2002), 581.
2. Ibid., 581.
3. Stephen Bann, ed., *The Tradition of Constructivism* (New York: Viking, 1974), xxv.
4. Charles S. Johnson, writing in the Negro journal *Opportunity* in 1925, was somewhat distressed to find jazz becoming an all-purpose term for "things typically American . . . the gogetters want to 'jazz up' business, modern expressionism in art is jazz art. We have jazz bands, jazz murderers, jazz magazines!" (Lewis Porter, *Jazz: A Century of Change* [New York: Schirmer, 1997], 123). Back in 1920, long before F. Scott Fitzgerald broke the champagne of his prose over the official hull of *The Jazz Age*, Clive Bell had conflated modernism in the arts as such with jazz. Eliot and Stravinsky were Bell's exemplars of jazz poetry and music composition, and he professed some admiration for Virginia Woolf, Cocteau, and Cendrars, but he was dismissive of Joyce, who "rags the literary instrument" with "talents which though genuine are moderate only" (Clive Bell, *Since Cézanne* [New York: Harcourt, Brace, 1928], 224). Dismissive of immediate gratification and sensationalism, Bell seized on the term "jazz" to signify any cultural phenomenon that was superficially exciting but

lacked staying power: "Jazz art is soon created, soon liked, and soon forgotten. It is the movement of masters of eighteen" (216). As this was written when Duke Ellington and Louis Armstrong were eighteen, there were no examples of longevity from which to draw any other conclusion.

5. Robert Goffin, *Jazz from the Congo to the Metropolitan* (Garden City, N.J.: Doubleday, 1944), 74.

6. See Jody Blake, *Le Tumulte Noir: Modernist Art and Popular Entertainment in Jazz-Age Paris, 1900–1930* (University Park: Pennsylvania State University Press, 1999); Bernard Gendron, *Between Montmartre and the Mudd Club: Popular Music and the Avant-Garde* (Chicago: University of Chicago Press, 2002); Glenn Watkins, *Pyramids at the Louvre: Music, Culture, and Collage from Stravinsky to the Postmodernists* (Cambridge, Mass.: Harvard University Press, 1994).

7. Gendron, *Between Montmartre and the Mudd Club*, 112.

8. Ibid., 107.

9. Susan C. Cook, *Opera for a New Republic: The* Zeitopern *of Krenek, Weill, and Hindemith* (Ann Arbor: University of Michigan Research Press, 1988), 52.

10. Gendron, *Between Montmartre and the Mudd Club*, 95.

11. Ibid., 99. Gendron's charge is a variant of Adorno's claim that, in jazz, "all the elements of 'art,' of individual freedom of expression, of immediacy are revealed as mere cover-ups for the character of consumer goods" (Theodor Adorno, *Essays on Music*, ed. Richard Leppert, trans. Susan H. Gillespie [Berkeley: University of California Press, 2002], 498). In any event, Francocentrism was so imposing in Paris that even the cosmopolitan Milhaud could not see beyond it. Writing in *Modern Music* in 1925, he recalled that "During the winter of 1921–1922 in America, the journalists regarded me with scorn whenever I made out a case for jazz. Three years later jazz-band concerts are given in New York, there is talk of a jazz opera at the Metropolitan, banjo classes are organized in the conservatories. Jazz is comfortably installed with official sanction." But he added, "Here it is finished" (Darius Milhaud, "The Day after Tomorrow," *Modern Music* 3, no. 1 [November–December 1925], 22–23). In fact, jazz education in the United States was decades in the future, and if jazz appeared "finished" in Paris, in Germany it was thriving: the Hoch Conservatory in Frankfurt began offering instruction in jazz in January 1928. Such developments prompted Adorno to prophesy the end of jazz: having "become stabilized as a pedagogical means of 'rhythmic education' . . . the last muted trumpet, if not unheard, will soon die away without a shock" (Adorno, *Essays on Music*, 496). Eric Hobsbawm (who, unlike Adorno, was a real enthusiast of jazz) also noted the compromises likely to follow from institutionalization: "Jazz is important in the history of the modern arts because it developed an alternative way of creating art to that of the high-culture avant-garde, whose exhaustion has left so much of the conventional 'serious' arts as adjuncts to university teaching programmes, speculative capital investment or philanthropy. That is why the tendency of jazz to turn itself into yet another avant-garde is to be deplored" (Eric Hobsbawn, *Uncommon People: Resistance, Rebellion and Jazz* [London: Weidenfeld & Nicolson, 1998], 263). Hobsbawm's reasons for deploring the avant-garde may be found in his *Behind the Times: The Decline and Fall of the Twentieth-Century Avant-Gardes* (London: Thames & Hudson, 1998).

12. Blake, *Le Tumulte Noir*, 60.

13. Mark Antliff and Patricia Leighten, *Cubism and Culture* (New York: Thames & Hudson, 2001), 25.

14. John Willett, *Art and Politics in the Weimar Period: The New Sobriety 1917–1933* (New York: Pantheon, 1978), 59.

15. Frederick Brown, *An Impersonation of Angels: A Biography of Jean Cocteau* (New York: Viking, 1968), 200.

16. Gendron, *Between Montmartre and the Mudd Club*, 94.

17. Hans Richter, *Dada: Art and Anti-Art*, trans. David Britt (New York: Oxford University Press, 1965), 27.

18. Ibid., 20.

19. Hugo Ball, *Flight Out of Time: A Dada Diary*, ed. John Elderfield, trans. Ann Raimes (New York: Viking, 1974), 51.

20. Richter, *Dada: Art and Anti-Art*, 46.

21. Jean Arp, *Arp on Arp: Poems, Essays, Memories*, ed. Marcel Jean, trans. Joachim Neugroschel (New York: Viking, 1972), 234.

22. Chris Goddard, *Jazz Away from Home* (London: Paddington Press, 1979), 16.
23. Jean Cocteau, *A Call to Order*, trans. Rollo H. Myers (London: Faber & Gwyer, 1926), 13.
24. Ibid., 13.
25. Michel Leiris, *Manhood*, trans. Richard Howard (San Francisco: North Point, 1984), 108.
26. Francesco Berger, "A Jazz Band Concert," in Lewis Porter, *Jazz: A Century of Change* (New York: Schirmer, 1997), 129.
27. Cocteau, *A Call to Order*, 13–14n.
28. Cook, *Opera for a New Republic*, 54. Jeanneret, a musician, was the brother of Le Corbusier. *L'Esprit nouveau* was the flagship journal for postwar French purism. Jody Blake outlines the extent to which purism assimilated primitivism and jazz to its own agenda, "The purists . . . regarded jazz-inspired rhythms as a means of eliminating coloristic elaboration and achieving the formal economy that was their goal in art as well as in music" (Blake, *Le Tumulte Noir*, 141).
29. E. H. Gombrich, *The Preference for the Primitive: Episodes in the History of Western Taste and Art* (London: Phaidon, 2002), 217.
30. Armand Lanoux, *Paris in the Twenties*, trans. E. S. Seldon (New York: Golden Griffin/Essential Encyclopedia Arts, 1960), 30.
31. The battlefield atmosphere can be distantly gleaned through the static in James Reese Europe's 1919 recording of the tune, with Noble Sissle taking the vocal. The tune was included by Sissle and Eubie Blake in their 1921 musical *Shuffle Along*, which launched the careers of Florence Mills, Josephine Baker, and Paul Robeson, among others. "On Patrol in No Man's Land" can be heard in *Shuffle Along* (New World Records NW260, released in 1976).
32. R. W. S. Mendl, *The Appeal of Jazz* (London: Philip Allan, 1927), 95.
33. Edmund Wilson, "The Aesthetic Upheaval in France: The Influence of Jazz in Paris and the Americanization of French Literature and Art," *Vanity Fair* (February 1922): 49.
34. Ibid., 100.
35. Ibid., 49.
36. Ball, *Flight Out of Time*, 53.
37. T. S. Eliot, *The Letters of T. S. Eliot, Volume I: 1898–1922*, ed. Valerie Eliot (San Diego: Harcourt Brace Jovanovich, 1988), 70.
38. Ibid., 357.
39. David Chinitz, "A Jazz-Banjorine, Not a Lute: Eliot and Popular Music before *The Waste Land*," in *T. S. Eliot's Orchestra: Critical Essays on Poetry and Music*, ed. John Xiros Cooper (New York: Garland, 2000), 10.
40. Richard M. Sudhalter, *Stardust Melody: The Life and Music of Hoagy Carmichael* (New York: Oxford University Press, 2002), 57.
41. Ibid., 60.
42. As Francis Naumann documents, "Da Da Strain" was recorded by Mamie Smith in 1922, the first of half a dozen renditions of the song in the next six months. "Although it is tempting to speculate that the title of this song was inspired by reports of Dada that had appeared in the American press, it is more likely that the syncopation and rhythmic beat of the sound 'dada' lent itself naturally to musical adaptations, particularly to the rhythm and tempo of jazz. Nevertheless, it is compelling to note that some thirty years later, when [Marcel] Duchamp was asked to organize a Dada retrospective for the Sidney Janis Gallery in New York, he chose to exhibit a copy of the original 78 rpm recording of this tune in a vitrine alongside other documents of the New York Dada period" (Francis Naumann, *New York Dada 1915–23* [New York: Abrams, 1994], 242 n. 2). Ishmael Reed incorporates "That Dada Strain" into the phenomenon of "Jes Grew" in *Mumbo Jumbo*: "UPON HEARING ETHEL WATERS SING 'THAT DA-DA-STRAIN' AND A JAZZ BAND PLAY 'PAPA DE-DA-DA' EUROPEAN PAINTERS TAKE JES GREW ABROAD" (Ishmael Reed, *Mumbo Jumbo* [New York: Macmillan, 1972], 105).
43. Ramón Gómez de la Serna, *Obras Completas*, vol. II (Barcelona: AHR, 1957), 1054.
44. Francis Steegmuller, *Cocteau: A Biography* (Boston: Little, Brown, 1970), 259.
45. George Antheil, "The Negro on the Spiral," in *Negro: An Anthology*, ed. Nancy Cunard (London: Wishart, 1934), 218.
46. Susan C. Cook, "Jazz as Deliverance," *American Music* 7, no. 1 (Spring 1989), 37.
47. Alan Young, *Dada and After: Extremist Modernism and English Literature* (Manchester: Manchester University Press, 1981), 49.

48. William C. Wees, *Vorticism and the English Avant-Garde* (Toronto: University of Toronto Press, 1972), 49.

49. Kenneth Wayne, "Cubism and Modern French Design," in *Picasso, Braque, Léger and the Cubist Spirit 1919–1939* (Portland, Me.: Portland Museum of Art, 1996), 39.

50. Ibid., 44.

51. Lanoux, *Paris in the Twenties*, 49.

52. Richard Martin, *Cubism and Fashion* (New York: The Metropolitan Museum of Art, 1998), 53.

53. Goffin, *Jazz from the Congo to the Metropolitan*, 73.

54. Oskar Schlemmer, *The Letters and Diaries*, ed. Tut Schlemmer, trans. Krishna Winston (Middletown, Conn.: Wesleyan University Press, 1972), 185.

55. Farkas Molnár, "Life at the Bauhaus," trans. John Bákti, in Benson and Forgács, *Between Worlds*, 464.

56. Ernö Kállai, "Ten Years of Bauhaus," trans. Wolfgang Jabs and Basil Gilbert, in Benson and Forgács, *Between Worlds*, 640.

57. Laszlo Moholy-Nagy, "Dynamics of a Metropolis: A Film Sketch," in *Moholy-Nagy*, ed. Richard Kostelanetz (New York: Praeger, 1970), 121.

58. The passage is worth quoting in full: "The affinity with the other arts, with dance, poetry and film, is one of the reasons for the enthusiastic reception of jazz and its stylistic impact on the compositions of Bohuslav Martinu, J. Jezek, E. Schulhoff and Emil Burian, author of one of the first studies of jazz in Europe. Jazz was perceived not just as the musical realization of the rhythm of modernity, but also as a symbol of popular entertainments from across the ocean. Jazz responded to the aesthetic 'of the streets' as advocated by the members of Devetsil, incorporating their aspirations for an activity both playful and optimistic" (Jan K. Celis, "Devetsil," *Prague 1900–1938: Capitale secrète des avant-gardes* [Dijon, France: Musée des Beaux-Arts, 1997], 172). My translation.

59. Artus Cerník, "Radosti Elektrického století" ["The Joys of the Electric Century"], *Revolucní sborník Devetsil*, ed. Jaroslav Seifert and Karel Teige (Prague: Vortel, 1922), 141. For this translation, I am grateful to Lara Glenum and Josef Horácek.

60. Juliette Roche, "Etat . . . . . . Colloidal . . . ," in *Demi Cercle* (Paris: Éditions d'Art 'La Cible', 1920), unpaginated. My translation.

61. Fillia, "Sensualità meccanica [Mechanical Sensuality]," in *Futurism and Its Place in the Development of Modern Poetry: A Comparative Study and an Anthology*, ed. Zbigniew Folejewski (Ottawa: University of Ottawa Press, 1980), 178.

62. Manuel Maples Arce, "T.S.F.," *Manomètre* 4 (August 1923): 68. My translation.

63. Nicolas Beauduin, *L'Homme Cosmogonique* (Paris: Jacques Povolozky, 1922), 74. This extract translated by Tim Conley.

64. F. T. Marinetti, "Le Futurisme Mondial," in *Manifesti e Documenti Teorici del Futurismo 1909–1944*, ed. Luciano Caruso (Milan: SPES, 1980), unpaginated.

65. Ljubomir Micic, "Shimmy at the Latin Quarter Graveyard," trans. Maja Starcevic, in Benson and Forgács, *Between Worlds*, 508.

66. Salvador Dalí, *Collected Writings*, ed. and trans. Haim Finkelstein (Cambridge, England: Cambridge University Press, 1998), 61.

67. Ilarie Voronca, "Untitled Statement," trans. Monica Voilescu, in Benson and Forgács, *Between Worlds*, 537.

68. Ibid., 537.

69. Beeke S. Tower, "Jungle Music and Song of Machines: Jazz and American Dance in Weimar Culture," in *Envisioning America: Prints, Drawings, and Photographs by George Grosz and His Contemporaries, 1915–1933* (Cambridge, Mass.: Busch-Reisinger Museum, 1990), 90.

70. Ball, *Flight Out of Time*, 68.

71. Ibid., 68.

72. Ibid., 68. Tracing the precursors of Dada, Ball acknowledges Arthur Rimbaud as "the patron of our many poses and flights of fancy," specifying the racial subconscious opened by the French poet: "Rimbaud's discovery is the European as the 'false Negro' " (Ball, *Flight Out of Time*, 68).

73. "Man," trans. Monica Voiculescu, in Benson and Forgács, *Between Worlds*, 554.

74. Marcel Janco's prominence in the Bucharest avant-garde of the 1920s made Dada a more concrete genealogical factor than in some other outposts of constructivism. Of the six original founders of Cabaret Voltaire, Janco and Tristan Tzara were Rumanian, although Tzara

headed west to Paris after the war, where his presence gave rise to those Dada factions that eventuated in surrealism.

75. Ilarie Voronca, "Surrealism and Integralism," trans. Julian Semilian and Sanda Agalidi, in Benson and Forgács, *Between Worlds*, 556.

76. Karel Teige, "Poetism Manifesto," trans. Alexandra Büchner, in Benson and Forgács, *Between Worlds*, 600.

77. Tudor Vianu, "The First *Contimpuranul* International Exhibition," trans. Julian Semilian and Sanda Agalidi, in Benson and Forgács, *Between Worlds*, 540.

78. Oscar Walter Cisek, "The International Exhibition Organized by the Magazine *Contimpuranul*," trans. Julian Semilian and Sanda Agalidi, in Benson and Forgács, *Between Worlds*, 552.

79. Arnold Gingrich, "Introduction," in Goffin, *Jazz from the Congo to the Metropolitan*, ix.

80. Jurgen Grandt suggests that "the narrative voice in Janowitz's *Jazz* is also, in a way, jazz music itself, creating and reinventing itself in the moment" (Jurgen Grandt, "Kinds of Blue: Toni Morrison, Hans Janowitz, and the Jazz Aesthetic," unpublished manuscript, 7). Certainly Janowitz openly declares his right to play fast and loose with narrative conventions by appealing to the laws of jazz: "A jazz-novel has the right to fade softly in the middle of a motif's repetition and simply come to an end. To safeguard this inalienable right in the first jazz-novel having unfolded according to the laws of jazz music—well, this should naturally be granted to me" (Hans Janowitz, *Jazz*, ed. Rolf Rieß [Bonn: Weidle Verlag, 1999], 112, translation by Jurgen Grandt in "Kinds of Blue").

81. Karel Teige, epigraph in E. F. Burian, *Jazz* (Prague: Aventinum, 1928). Translation by Lara Glenum and Josef Horácek.

82. A. G. Bragaglia, *Jazz Band* (Milan: Edizioni 'Corbaccio,' 1929), 9.

83. Ralph Ellison, *Shadow and Act* (New York: Random House, 1964), 206.

84. Goffin, *Jazz from the Congo to the Metropolitan*, 3.

85. Ibid., 5, 3.

86. Francis Newton [Eric Hobsbawm], *The Jazz Scene* (Boston: Monthly Review Press, 1960), 244.

87. Gómez de la Serna, *Obras Completas*, vol. II, 1062.

88. Federico García Lorca, *Deep Song and Other Prose*, ed. and trans. Christopher Maurer (New York: New Directions, 1980), 43.

89. Geoffrey Jacques, "Listening to Jazz," in *American Popular Music*, ed. Rachel Rubin and Jeffrey Melnick (Amherst: University of Massachusetts Press, 2001), 75.

90. Vítezslav Nezval, "Diabolo: A Poem of the Night," *Antilyrik & Other Poems*, trans. Jerome Rothenberg and Milos Sovak (Los Angeles: Green Integer, 2001), 106.

2

Blackness as Symptom

Josephine Baker and European Identity

SAMIR DAYAL

Whatever white people do not know about Negroes reveals,
precisely and inexorably, what they do not know
about themselves.
—James Baldwin

Paris audiences in the 1920s and 1930s were fascinated by a strange figure "who walks with bended knees . . . and looks like a boxing kangaroo. . . . Is this a man? Is this a woman? Her lips are painted black, her skin is the color of a banana, her hair, already short, is stuck to her head as if made of caviar, her voice is high-pitched, she shakes continually, and her body slithers like a snake."[1] This was Josephine Baker, whose *Danse Sauvage* was described as "barbaric . . . naughty . . . a return to the customs of the dark ages" and a "silent declaration of love by a simple forward movement of her belly . . . and the quiver of her entire rear."[2] Was Baker, in these early years, naively confirming white stereotypes about blacks? Was she self-aware about racial and gender clichés? Was she a sellout to white fantasies, or parodic, resistant, subversive? Interpretations typically have been polarized at either extreme. Baker, who was born Josephine MacDonald on 3 June 1906 in St. Louis, Missouri, and died on 12 April 1975 in Paris may have been constructed as representative of blacks in early-twentieth-century Europe. I argue, however, that the range of her performance and of her performative was wider than either detractors or defenders readily acknowledge. Unlike most commentators and biographers, I highlight both Baker's market orientation—her ability to merchandize herself—and the subtly subversive agency that she was occasionally able to access even through her self-commodification.

Baker's case provides an opportunity to appreciate the role of blacks as alien artists and intellectuals in Europe *and* the self-construction of white Europeans who sought to differentiate themselves from those they construed as their civilizational "others." Yet most of the existing critical commentary on Baker has been on her stage performances. Drawing on speech-act theory as mediated by Judith Butler's provocative emphasis on the "performative" aspect of self-construction, my particular interest is to foreground Baker's performative as an instance of divided black subjectivity (divided between conflicting self-representations).[3] Among other things, my approach calls attention to the possibilities of minoritarian performance—and on the performatives of minoritarian identity that push beyond the familiar categories of identity politics. More generally, it can help to broaden the discussion of the challenges of and prospects for diasporic representational practices and minoritarian political agency. The complexities of the role of blacks in Europe require us to attend to both the abjection of cultural "others" and their emancipatory possibilities. Commentators have generally underappreciated the range of Baker's stage or indeed film performance and of her performatives of identity.[4]

What is new about the argument I offer here is an emphasis on the particular and complex ways in which Baker embodied blackness as a symptom of the modern European subject, most remarkably in her early Paris years. Baker both played and undercut (and not always simultaneously) the language games of racism and sexism in which her performance and performative were constructed. Besides, as the epigraph from James Baldwin suggests, Baker's self-presentation can be situated within a long tradition inaugurated by black slaves. It is a tradition in which the slaves performed parodies that subtly undermined the presumptive superiority of the white master, but in which the white masters themselves did not quite cotton on to the fact that the joke was on them, that their own sense of self was dependent on the black slaves' occupying a role that confirmed the master's place in a presumed hierarchy of humanity. The tradition is marked on the one side by a kind of bitter humor, and on the other side by the kind of indignation registered by Sethe in Toni Morrison's *Beloved*, where Schoolteacher lists Sethe's human characteristics on the one side of the page and her "non-human" characteristics on the other. What the whites did know about "Negroes" revealed what they did not see about themselves, and whiteness itself was constituted in part by establishing blackness as its other. To put it the terms of my title, blackness functions as the symptom of whiteness.

Much has been written about opportunities afforded to African American and other expatriates in Europe—particularly the "lost generation"— from the 1920s until well after World War II, as contrasted with the restrictions placed on them "at home," but there is much less about their impact on European culture. Toni Morrison has astutely glossed a certain glossing-over of blackness in the self-consolidation of the white European self. This essay takes to heart Morrison's civilized lesson to refuse the well-bred instinct to pretend that one does not notice race:

> [I]n matters of race, silence and evasion have historically ruled literary discourse. Evasion has fostered another, substitute language in which the issues are encoded, foreclosing open debate. The situation is aggravated by the tremor that breaks into discourse on race. It is further complicated by the fact that the habit of ignoring race is understood to be a graceful, even generous, liberal gesture. To notice is to recognize an already discredited difference. To enforce its invisibility through silence is to allow the black body a shadowless participation in the dominant cultural body. According to this logic, every well-bred instinct argues against noticing and forecloses adult discourse.[5]

The key issue here is the function of the black man or woman in a majoritarian white society, whether in the United States or in Europe. For African American expatriates, including W. E. B. Du Bois, Europe meant greater personal freedom, richer artistic and intellectual opportunity.[6] Yet, as Baker herself sang, they felt torn "*entre deux amours*"—Europe and America. The 1920s witnessed a resurgence of a debate about modernity, with high modernism's greatest writers producing their major works: T. S. Eliot, Ezra Pound, W. B. Yeats, and James Joyce all wrote about modernity and contemporary life. Themes of cultural difference thoroughly infiltrated these writings. Baker's status as an icon of culturally unfamiliar influences pointed to a symptomatic modernist anxiety about the integrity of European cultural identity, about "the fate of the Western tradition of art. Was Greece to bow before Africa?" Or could these insurgent influences help Europeans "define themselves again—this time by appropriating what they needed of what they imagined the black soul to be"?[7] Embodying an uncivilized or unrepressed, natural self that had been occluded by the culture of modernity, blacks functioned as the original, incomplete germ of humanity against which the modern European could measure, humanize, or culturally regenerate himself. They were at once intimate and abjected—extimate others. In the context of modernist debates, Baker functioned not only as an anthropological and erotic projection, as Sander Gilman might put it, but also a constitutive symptom that consolidated the self-image of the European subject.[8]

Such a symptomatic interpretation complicates identitarian theories by means of a specific theoretical displacement. It contributes to a project of rethinking the aporia between identity politics and poststructuralist deconstructions of identity. Identity politics tends to slide into undignified essentialism. On the other hand, abstract theories of "ambivalence," "hybridity," or the abyss of identity frustrate many from those relatively disenfranchised constituencies most urgently seeking justice, access to institutional recognition, and political agency based on "authentic" ethnic or group identity. Such constituencies are understandably impatient with the deconstruction of identity constructs. This impasse between essentialism and politically debilitating abyss of identity obscures the range of possible identifications in contexts in which performances or performatives require a historically and materially specific identity to be presented for public consumption.

Scholars such as Paul Gilroy have sought alternatives to the impasse.[9] My essay seeks to build on such contrapuntal scholarship, embracing the corrective agenda of cultural studies and postcolonial critique: to debunk Enlightenment modernity's cultural exclusivism, its universalizing claims that entrench the white male as normative subject/citizen.[10] The loci of the "other's" abjection have to be reimagined as sites of resistance. Contemporary cultural studies and postcolonial theory have sought to redress the presumption that "Euro-America" is civilization's summit. This teleology drives Eurocentric discourse without acknowledgment that Europe's cultural and material success would have been impossible without its African and Asian colonies. Europe's putative superiority provided the impetus and justification for nineteenth-century imperialism and today lingers as a neoimperialist universalism paired with an exceptionalism based on the myth of the West's disarticulation from the relatively poor non-West. The "clash of civilizations" meets the end of history. It's the West versus the rest, "McWorld" against "jihad." The challenge of combating such bellicose discourse is a more urgent imperative of transnational cultural studies, and more delicate, after 1989 and especially after 11 September 2001. Baker's reception must be situated within a discursive regime with roots reaching into and before colonialism. That reception entailed, for instance, a dynamic of deliberate misrecognition (*méconnaissance*) of the African American as representative of "the African"—onto whom ambivalent modernist fantasy as well as colonial guilt could be cathected in an attempt to come to terms with colonialism and its ethical implications for European self-understanding.

When *La Revue Nègre* opened on 2 October 1925, Baker danced her *Danse Sauvage* to the cry of "*Quel cul elle a!*"—"What an ass she has!" She was a fetishized curiosity, the object of male erotic fantasy, but finally too "other."

A significant antecedent for this ambivalent response is traceable in the famous example of the Khoisan slave Saartje Baartmann. She was exhibited
in London in 1810, then in France as "the Hottentot Venus" (she was the first
of a series of "Hottentot Venuses")—this, at a time when Britain was de-
bating prohibition of slavery and America the entitlements of free blacks.[11]
Dying at age twenty-five in 1815, she remained at the *Musée de l'Homme* in
Paris until returned to South Africa in 2002, following years of appeals to
restore some of her dignity. Audiences fixated on her steatopygia or pro-
truding buttocks, interpreted as sign of simultaneously overdeveloped and
primitive sexuality.[12] Upon Baartmann's death, the museological rationale
grew stunningly direct and crude. She was dissected, and her genitalia
(particularly the nymphae and clitoris) were presented as a phantasmagoric
aggregate, fascinating yet horrifying, of sexual parts, metonymy for her whole
black body: raw female sexuality in its extreme state of overdevelopment and
primitivity.

Baker's performative holds the mirror up to white Europe's fetishizing of
an eroticized but dehumanized black woman, to (unconscious) white fantasy projected onto the black "other." This fantasy is not epiphenomenal; it
reveals its significance only in the context of the project of modernity. Europeans "re-cognized" their own evolution, their modernity, by contrasting it
with the relative cultural underdevelopment and sexual hypertrophy of
nonwhites, and most particularly of the Hottentot (structurally the lowest
of the low). Indeed, as James Clifford writes, "the orders of the West were
everywhere present in the Musée de l'Homme, except on display."[13]

This dominant discourse of modernity borrowed support from the
anthropological speculations of Immanuel Kant and Georg Wilhelm
Friedrich Hegel—and from the pseudoscientific theories of eugenics and
polygenesis—to which scientists of Samuel Morton's and Louis Agassiz's
caliber subscribed.[14] David Krell shows how Enlightenment modernity
turned on invidious associations of race and sex, the abjection of the European's raced and gendered other.[15] Modernity depended, furthermore, on
an association between the raced primitive and femininity. In the history
of European representational practice, non-Western people have long been
accorded a specific discursive/structural function and positioned at the
conjuncture of "nature" *and* "sexuality."[16] In Enlightenment thought in
particular, the black man was the "other" of the normative European, but
was paradoxically also feminized *within* the broader category of the primitive as oversexed. At the beginning of the twentieth century, Sigmund
Freud's (in)famous description of adult female sexuality as the "dark continent" of psychology similarly conflated female sexuality with "the image
of contemporary colonialism and thus to the exoticism and pathology of

the Other."[17] In a footnote to *Three Essays on Sexuality* (1905) added in 1920, Freud opined that the female genitalia are more *primitive* than the male. The association of blacks with concupiscence, writes Gilman, dates at least from the Middle Ages and was a fixture of popular culture by the eighteenth century.[18] In extreme form, it is troped as a visual equation: "blacks' identity is *as surrogate genitals.*"[19] The black *is* her buttocks or her labia or vagina; the black *is* the penis. Even in less egregious expressions, raced others are often hypersexualized in modern Western representations that betray contradictory impulses. The "primitive" is attractive and repellent at once.[20] The frisson of this simultaneous attraction and repulsion, Freud emphasized, is a token of the uncanny. What I am arguing here is that the uncanny irruption of the primitive elements within European culture—the *Unheimlich* within the *Heimlich*—partly explains the historically specific frisson attached to the nonimmigrant black performer in Europe.[21]

The "blackening of Europe," one might say, consists in precisely this insistence on uncovering the "blackness" that has so often remained covered, unacknowledged, in the makeup of European identity. Baker's story, like Baartmann's, is of geographical and cultural exile. In her, "the primitive" was "musealized" (to adapt Andreas Huyssen's term). The black represented, in the present, Europe's temporally and culturally remote past. Coded as the embodiment of the primitive,[22] the figure furnished the antithetical antecedent for the narrative of psychological development, recapitulating the logic of cultural development. As Huyssen reminds us, the emergence of museum culture in the West can be traced back to the time of the French Revolution and its institutionalization of the Louvre: The museum culture was really part and parcel of the "*querelle des anciens et des modernes*"[23]—a quarrel in which the discourse of the raced and sexualized primitive was critical. This discourse of musealization was, therefore, already entrenched in Europe into the 1920s through to World War II, during the time of Baartmann, as well that of Baker and others of the "lost generation." The project of modernity emphasized a recognition of the self, as well as rationalized the imperialist dehumanization of the "other."[24] Baker must be understood within such a museal framing. As the enshrined symptom of European subjectivity, she allowed Europeans to "re-cognize" themselves via an inversion. There was an increasing imperative to justify colonialism's "*mission civilisatrice*" and a corresponding need to fix in place markers against which Europe could define and refine its self-image. Modernity meant incessant change, and the past seemed increasingly ephemeral, fugitive; this imperiled tradition and threatened the deracination of the European subject. Besides, the presence of blacks in the metropolitan heart of Europe precipitated a moral panic.[25] The nation-state, in the now familiar phrase, may be an "imagined community."[26] But "it can nonetheless call on a range of geographical sites, monuments and symbols to create a powerful visual rhetoric of nationality,"[27] often to exclude what threatens its perceived national identity. Musealization assured the black body's hypervisibility precisely at the conjuncture of the medical, racial, gendered discourses and national discourse in which that body was rendered invisible.

In modernity's contradictory logic, blacks were simultaneously threateningly hypersexualized and "infantilized"[28]—and therefore rendered insupportable or invisible as subjects. Nineteenth-century theories of cultural difference habitually constructed the West's "others" as children.[29] Baker seemed to fit the "pornotrope"[30] of the wild, polymorphously perverse child: the goofy grin, the elastic legs, and the maddening derriere wiggling uncontrollably in a provocative dance, topless, in a banana skirt. But when Baker tried to present herself in Vienna in 1929, she was deemed "too lascivious" by the officials and simultaneously "glorified, totally without irony, by her supporters . . . as 'that beautiful black child.'"[31] Even in the African American context Baker would have been familiar with the chain of associations according to which, for the white majorities, "the laughter of the black evokes the unself-consciousness attributed to black sexuality."[32]

Yet it was the liberatory promise of an unrepressed—polymorphously perverse—sexuality that also galvanized an overcultivated European society, their lives ironically straitened by their repression of their more primal urges and fantasies. Combining animal sexuality with glamour, Baker was the stranger within who introduced Europeans to a "lost" strangeness within themselves, to be recuperated as a fanstasmatic *objet a* that perfected the European subject himself by simultaneously reaffirming his superior completeness and licensing his temporary departures from civilized propriety into the fantasy of erotic abandon. Thus Europe was "blackened," but only to reaffirm ultimately its whiteness. If propriety—the repression of rude physicality—was for Europeans marked as civilized behavior, then abandon was its opposite and therefore aligned with blackness. Through Josephine's own sensual abandon, they could discover that strange, arational "dark continent," their internal Africa, within themselves, although of course it would be a breach of civilized comportment to be defined by that arational blackness as "real" blacks were. Fantasy allowed the European to indulge the desire to shake off the strictures of propriety—the desire for "blackness" as symptom of one's own animal being—while retaining the security of being able to return from the darkness of that radical negation of civilization's sustaining fictions. The encounter with blackness was an encounter with both the limit of whiteness and its transgression. The owner of a Paris sculpture gallery where modernist composers enthusiastic about African American music met (Paul Guillaume) spoke for many when he opined that "the spirit of modern man—or of modern woman—needs to be nourished by the civilization of the negro."[33] Blackness promised both freedom from the repression of the wildness that made civilization possible and the limited condition of whiteness itself, that dangerous border of civilization beyond which white man was no longer himself, a border that he must therefore never allow to be breached. Those who transgressed this border went native like Joseph Conrad's Kurtz, and instead of freedom from repression encountered the "horror"—what Jacques Lacan conceptualizes as the real.[34] It is to illuminate this double move of self-consolidation and self-abandon that I stress a psychoanalytic optics. To highlight the symptomatic fetishization of the black woman is, in short, a way of revealing much about Europeans' psychic life.

If the black was the emblem of the human before the awakening to *reason*, Baker was recognized as embodying a complementary "perfection" *of the black body*—just as Charles-Pierre Baudelaire was enchanted with the physical perfection of Jeanne Duval (*"le serpent qui danse"*) in his *Fleurs du Mal*.[35] With her dancing body, Baker seemed to answer sexual fantasy, but in her racial otherness, she seemed to present to a racialist society an insuperable barrier to intimacy or companionship while modeling the perfect, Platonic ideal of the body. Yet the racial exotic who answers the sexual fantasy remains always a strange bedfellow; the ideal remains remote, excessive.[36] The white man discovered in her the animal secret of his own hidden self, his own internal blackness, but she was at the same time—and thankfully—too "other" to ever seriously make the most intimate demand, the demand of the erotic partner in an equal relationship. The white man could give free rein to at least his fantasy of erotic fulfillment with the dark *objet a*, but he would never have to commit himself to acknowledging her claim on him as a fully equal human being and citizen of European society. This was the key to the doubleness of blackness as symptom. It was a doubleness that did not require the white European to acknowledge its duplicity, its self-canceling dynamic. For the European subject, it was not necessary while performing civilized behavior to acknowledge the dark continent within; neither was it necessary to surrender civilization entirely while finding release in discovering the pleasures (the *jouissance*?) of blackness. One pleasure could be enjoyed without self-reflexive acknowledgment of the other.

But for Baker, for the black woman herself, the stakes were quite different. If my argument were to halt at the point that Baker was the black symptom of the white subject, it would run the risk of being underinterpreted or misinterpreted: If the black woman is a symptom, one might argue, surely that position is a denial of full subjectivity and agency. Would she not function as an instrument of the white man's pleasure and in so doing effectively deny her own agency? Or would she refuse the status of the unequal, abject "other" and assert her own proper and resistant subjectivity, even as she lent herself to the dynamic of this symptomatology? How self-reflexive was Baker about performing this overdetermined, excessive blackness into which she was interpellated, given the conditions that obtained in Europe at the time? We know that the history, or rather genealogy, of the interpellation of blackness in Europe was already deep and complex. Kant had already established the key philosophical precedent in conceptualizing blackness as structurally the antithesis of civilization. Hegel followed in this tradition to argue, as Krell puts it, that "the African is the undeveloped unity of nature—he or she is entirely natural" but unable to reflect on this closeness to nature.[37] Critical self-reflexivity, according to this tradition of thinking, is the prerogative of Western masculinity, rationality, and modernity. For black performers, such as Katherine Dunham and Alvin Ailey, this idea of self-reflexivity about identity construction is crucial.[38] It has been an equally central question for African Americanists ranging from W. E. B. Du Bois to Henry Louis Gates Jr. and Michael Borshuk.[39]

Because my concern is precisely with the question of the degree to which Baker was self-reflexive about the historicized symptom of her performative and to the performance and musealization of blackness, I want to draw attention to the tendency of even sympathetic and attentive critics to fail to register the range of Baker's self-presentation on- and offstage. Although I do not wish to single him out, and even though I agree with much of what he does say about Baker, Michael Borshuk is a good example of this tendency because he ascribes too narrow a scope to Baker's performances. Borshuk does acknowledge that Baker herself spoke explicitly about the difference between the way she presented herself onstage and offstage: "Since I personified the savage on the stage, I tried to be as civilized as possible in daily life."[40] Yet, he suggests that her performances were almost always self-reflexively "parodic," "strategic" subversions of white stereotypes about blacks.[41] This is intended as a defense of Baker against commentators who have "lambasted Baker for her ostensible pliancy and the supposed ease with which she allowed these constructions to advance."[42]

What we need is, first, a distinction between programmatic parody or subversion and self-reflexivity about stereotypes of race, gender, or sexuality. Self-reflexivity does not necessarily imply parody nor exclude the performer's capitalizing on received opinions and entrenched images of black sexuality. Stereotypes "ambivalently" reference an " 'otherness' which is at once an object of desire and derision."[43] Baker knew both how to indulge and exploit white stereotypes of the black woman, at once desirable, repellent, and pathological. She was not always parodic or oppositional. Even in a strategic calculus, exoticized sexuality sells.

We also need a sustained distinction between performance and performativity. Performance refers to the artistic representations—stage shows and films. Judith Butler influentially defines performativity, by contrast, as the engendering on the body's surface of a putative "essence or identity" by "acts, gestures, enactments" responding to various *contingencies* and *desires*; performatives are "*fabrications* manufactured and sustained through corporeal signs and other discursive means."[44] Conflations of *performance* and *performative* confuse different registers of self-construction and occlude the material contingencies and psychic desires that produce performances. "Race" (or ethnicity) and gender are performatives—discursive constructs. Although the histories of slavery, colonialism, imperialism, and racism in general should in no way be conflated, the experiences of different cultures with such evils shows that discourses about "race" and gender are not only historically coproduced[45] but reinforce and feed on each other.[46] These imbricated categories are almost fungible in the sense that racially subordinate groups are sometimes discursively constructed as "effeminate" in a translation of discourses common in colonial contexts. Thomas Laqueur presents copious historical evidence of such "translation."[47] And Marjorie Garber makes the point about the fungibility of Baker's particular raced performative of gender even more strongly when she describes her as a "female female impersonator" whose "identity as a transvestite begins with race as well as with class and gender."[48]

Borshuk does cite Butler's conceptualization of performativity in the specific context of drag—"In imitating gender, drag implicitly reveals the imitative structure of gender itself"[49]—but he pays only lip service to Butler's argument and omits a key clause from the sentence he quotes from Butler. Butler's original sentence reads as follows: "In imitating gender, drag implicitly reveals the imitative structure of gender itself—as well as its contingency." In omitting the phrase "as well as its contingency" Borshuk obscures the contextual and situational frame within which a performative of identity is enacted—a serious glossing over of the pragmatic dimensions of performance. Perhaps sensing he risks overinterpreting the evidence, Borshuk vacillates, admitting that it was necessary for Baker to "adopt an 'accommodating' guise at times." But in the same breath, he asserts that Baker's "utilization of the animal/primitive stereotype was a deceptively clever parody that spoke concession while it whispered rebuttal."[50] So which was it? Was it "an act that intended its affectation to be conspicuous" or "a deceptively clever parody that spoke concession while it whispered rebuttal"? Borshuk asserts that Baker "became the 'always almost' object of the colonial fantasy, a calculated fraud that exposed the whole order as a sham."[51] But exactly how much of Baker's show was "fraud" and "sham"? When she was in public, was she not also "performing"? How should audiences distinguish between show and sham in Baker's on- and offstage performative? Besides, would "conspicuous" subversion not have made it difficult for the performance to support fantasy, to seduce audiences? Alienating the audience would have spelled disaster for her career—and the European and especially French enthusiasm for black performers was a critical, bread-and-butter matter because the reception of black performance at home in the United States paled shamefully by comparison.[52] Surely one can do Baker the service of acknowledging that sometimes (but not always) the performance was "just" an act, and at the same time appreciate her investment in deconstructing stereotypes.

Baker knew when it was expedient—and enjoyable—for her to play seductress,[53] to play to French (male) fantasies. Especially in her early years, Baker was noticed "not because of her dancing . . . but because of her irreverent and comic antics on stage."[54] And besides, *l'art nègre* had immense vogue among Paris's artistic avant-garde[55] just as, more recently, black culture in the United States has been appropriated by performers such as Madonna or Sandra Bernhard, as bell hooks reminds us.[56] And we should add Eminem to the list of those who have drawn from black performers. Even the high point of her career, the Revue Nègre, which drew enthusiastic praise from avant-gardists such as Fernand Léger, Jean Cocteau, Darius Milhaud, and Paul Guillaume, was redesigned specifically for Paris audiences by Rolf de Maré.[57] Her famous *danse sauvage* was conceptualized by another Frenchman, Jacques Charles, with a view to satisfying the audiences at the Moulin Rouge. So much thought was given to tailoring the performance to the wishes of the particular audience. Baker knew from experience if not instinct the importance of seduction, of playing "primitive," naïve, or even childlike roles, not necessarily laden with irony. In sum, Baker's performance was often a combination of what the audience wanted and what she thought was fun, as when she wore the infamous skirt of bananas: "[I]t was not so easy to exploit Josephine; you couldn't make her do anything unless she was convinced the public wanted it. Besides, there was nothing prurient about all those swinging bananas, they were funny."[58]

Two films in which Baker acted offer remarkable insight into the nature of her "performance" of an overdetermined blackness. *Zou Zou* (directed by Marc Allegret, 1934) and *Princess Tam Tam* (directed by Edmond Greville, 1935) are films that, if read in the light of a documentary about her

(*Josephine Baker: Her Story*) and material from some of the biographies, offer a substantial case study. *Zou Zou* is set in Martinique, a former colony of France. Jean and particularly Zou Zou (played by Baker) are twins of different colors—brought up by Père Mélé (the name suggests "mixture," even "melanin"). Zou Zou is the dark twin and socially underdeveloped (she is always clowning around childishly), and even somewhat wild (she bites a stage assistant and is called "cannibal"). She is introduced to the public as a curiosity, a "freak." Her aspiration to normative (white) subjectivity is represented not only by her attempt to lighten her complexion with face powder but also by her adult vocation of laundress. Jean and Zou Zou are "like" brother and sister, and their sibling love is deep. However, when they grow up, she comes to love him as more than even a twin brother—more his "other." The incest taboo is a thematic "problem" here, complicated by the fact that her friend Clare also falls in love with Jean. Jean cannot return Zou Zou's erotic love: His destiny is to give his love to a white woman, and at the end, Zou Zou remains alone. The film can certainly be adduced as testimony to Baker's self-reflexivity about representations of "race," sexuality, infantilism, or pathology. But again, what we see is not so much parody or subversion but (admittedly sentimental) pathos. And it is not as though Baker plays the "primitive" exclusively. Especially as a grown woman in the film, Baker's character dresses either as a working-class woman (a laundress) or as an elegant French woman who projects a powerful sexuality—here, interestingly, the category of "race" is almost subsumed.

I observed earlier that Baker's theatrical performances were managed or conceptualized, and therefore controlled, by white men such as Jacques Charles and Rolf de Maré. Similarly, both *Zou Zou* and *Princess Tam Tam* were the brainchildren of white Frenchmen. Thus, what we are looking at is in large measure a white creation. Baker's performance of course is directed by these men, and it would be unfair to judge her degree of self-reflexivity entirely on the basis of these films. In the films she is represented primarily as an *object* of white male fantasy, rather than a self-determined *subject*. At best the "political" achievement of this film is that it succeeds in presenting to the audience several "problems" of sexuality, race, representation, and white desire. And yet it would be a mistake to suggest that neither the stage nor the film performances allowed Baker any room to inject something of her own into the performance.

Princess Tam Tam (1935) presents another wild child. Baker plays a North African (Tunisian) "savage," Alwina, complete with American-accented French. Alwina becomes the Pygmalion of a French aristocrat whose creative springs have run dry; her primitive and uncivilized freshness rejuvenates him and becomes the germ of a fantasy that he spins out as his new literary creation. Even civilized into Tam Tam, however, the "black princess" cannot escape the realization that the West will never accept her. Her only alternative is to choose "the East," which, confusingly, includes Africa and India, as if nonwhite spaces were an undifferentiated geopolitical and psychic figment of European colonial imaginations. Presumably this is why she is an "Indian" princess. A "maharaja"—who is ironically also romancing the aristocrat's white wife—tells her to return to "her country." Alwina is thus returned once again to her "natural" space—village life with the servant Dar (a European in blackface!). The aristocrat is reconciled with his wife; the "orientals" fulfill their destiny as whetstones to sharpen the sexual appetites of the "normal couple"—a European husband and wife.

Baker's performance here is anything but subversive or parodic. It risks reinforcing stereotypes of the highly cathected representations of the savage, the maharaja, the aristocrat, the vulnerable white woman—except perhaps that the film's self-reflexive deployment of orientalist, racialist, and culturalist geotropism does call attention to representationalist politics. Yet that is not to say it is destitute of an emancipatory subtext. The very names "Tam Tam" and "Zou Zou," with their childlike repetition of almost preverbal lexical elements, seem to index the infantilization of the protagonists.[59] But the narratives are propelled by a drive or logic of *Erziehung*: a development *toward greater self-reflexivity*. Alwina, for instance, finds herself in the slowly dawning recognition that she ultimately cannot belong to this white culture; trying to become a white Frenchwoman is a vain goal. At the end Alwina rejects the white man's culture. A late scene shows her entering the white man's home eating like the savage she "really" is, but then cuts to an idyllic scene with Dar and Alwina seated against an African or eastern landscape, and later still the scene returns to the abandoned mansion she had shared with the aristocrat, now crowded with all kinds of animals. A donkey eats the aristocrat's book, called *Civilization*.

In *Zou Zou* too, the question of Baker's belonging to Europe had been foregrounded at the very outset, when Zou Zou sang of longing for her homeland, Haiti, which she called "*mon désir.*" The film's conclusion reinforces this desire for a "natural home" by staging, as in *Tam Tam*, the heroine's recognition that the black woman has no true place in the West. Again the point is that the recognition is to some degree empowering, as self-reflexive knowledge always is. At the end of Baker's earlier film, Zou Zou performs in her one hundredth stage appearance. On this important occasion, she sings a love song about her unrequitable desire for her true love Jean; what is different is that she is for the first time acknowledging that their love is impossible, and that she is able to live with the cruel truth of its impossibility. In *Tam Tam* there is a similar message: The happiest moment

Alwina has is when she is dancing with her nonwhite peers—"her own people"—in a bar that the aristocrat's wife would describe as "vulgar." Alwina too sings a song that contains lines to the effect that "It's a mistake to dream of happiness in a land that is not your own." There are proper realms for the civilized and the "savage," however noble, even though the "savage" lends significance, meaning, to the civilization of the civilized. These moments dramatize an emergent self-awareness, or dawning of self-reflexivity. West is West and East is East, and never the twain shall meet. The narrative tells of the protagonist's bitter rejection of a culture and a civilization that deny her, the non-European, as an equal or a proper—possible—object of the committed love of a white man. No parody or sub-version here either: This film, like *Zou Zou*, hardly eschews stereotype. A nuanced interpretation of these films would, however, note not only the films' retention of tropes from a racialist and sexist imagery but also that Baker manages to capitalize on a visceral racism *and* the erotic fantasies of contemporary European viewers.[60] She "lends herself" to the fantasies even as she performs the protagonists' dawning recognition that if the West will not welcome the black subject (even though she could only belong there), then the East perhaps is a spiritual home even though it cannot be an actual home.

The mediating term in these narratives of East and West, of the non-West's self-recognition, was the figure of "Africa." It functioned in her performative like a third term. In the Europe Baker knew, "*nègre*" referred more to black Africans and had a different set of valences. Colonial history referenced a specific relationship between Europeans and dark-skinned people different from the case of America's experience of slavery. Yet even for the European avant-garde, the concept of "things '*nègre*'" was "mediated by an imaginary America, a land of noble savages simultaneously standing for the past and future of humanity."[61] As both primitivist fetish and modernist icon, Baker performed "Africanness" not as essence but *as symptom*: She was self-reflexive about its overdetermination. Phyllis Rose points out that Jacques Charles, a producer at the Moulin Rouge in Paris and an "expert in *the fantasy life of Parisian males, invented what he called the 'Danse Sauvage'* . . . [and in] this piece of authenticity . . . Baker and her male partner were dressed in *Charles's notion* of African costume—bare skin and feathers."[62] Feeding such fantasies, Baker *was* guilty of a certain degree of self-orientalization, but that was because she knew the pleasures of performance as well as the pragmatics of performativity. This is testimony to a much more complex range of performance than mere parody of stereotypes, or a predictably "signifyin(g)" deconstruction.

Baker's performance required a measure of intertextuality and intersubjectivity: The meaning of the performance or performative depended on the audience's horizon of expectations. Baker's double or triple conscious-ness also functioned as a model of difference. It not only required her to en-gage the challenge of being black and French; it also required that in performance as well as in her performative she remind Europeans them-selves of the fact of difference, displacing their understanding of the dif-ference that "race" makes.[63] Baker's achievement was to present herself as black, oriental, American—but with a difference that did not yield itself too predictably to the received calculus of race. Baker's performative was a chal-lenge to the pseudocategory of "race," an interrogation of the desire consti-tutive of white subjectivity; however, it was a challenge routed through delicate negotiations or layerings of partial identifications that included an element of capitalizing on and merchandizing of black stereotypes. I have made a case for noticing the broad range for Baker's performance and her performative, and for a certain situational pragmatism.

She was indeed a consummate pragmatist; she understood political con-tingency. She became a French citizen when she sensed that she would not be warmly welcomed back in the United States. (She wrote to her friend Miki Sawada, a Japanese diplomat's wife, "You mentioned . . . you were trying to love America. Darling, forget it.")[64] When she chose, she could cer-tainly make an ideological point, sometimes through parody but at other times through more direct means, as when she wore a Star of David in fel-lowship with victims of anti-semitism and later was decorated as a Résis-tance hero. In 1948, she worked for civil rights in the United States. In May 1931, she was appointed Queen of the Exposition Coloniale Internationale, over objections that she was American and not French: The ideological niceties of the appointment did not deter her. Sometimes, of course, she found herself disastrously on the wrong side of history, as when she pub-licly praised Mussolini.[65] Baker's record of political activism in the United States may not equal Katherine Dunham's or especially Paul Robeson's. Robeson lent his baritone to progressive causes in twenty-five languages round the world and donated considerable sums to support Jewish refugees from Nazi Germany. But when, following World War II, Baker returned to the United States, her renown as a Résistance agent preceded her. She was welcomed by African Americans because she declared her readiness to fight for the Civil Rights Movement and boycotted performances for segregated audiences. In 1951, the National Association for the Advancement of Col-ored People (NAACP) named her Most Outstanding Woman of the Year. In 1963, she participated in the March on Washington and gave a benefit con-cert at Carnegie Hall for the NAACP, the Student Nonviolent Coordinating Committee (SNCC), and the Congress of Racial Equality (CORE).

For all her impassioned ideas about erasing the color line, however, it is division—emotional, spiritual, and social alienation—that rules over

Baker's life. Even though her 1975 funeral at the Madeleine in Paris drew more mourners than ever before in France's history, she died in what was always to her a foreign country. Her legacy may not be that of a profoundly subversive and parodic cultural activist. And in purely aesthetic and technical terms, her performances may not have been as precedent-setting as the performances of Katherine Dunham or Ruth St. Denis or Isadora Duncan. But no one can deny her her immense performative breadth or the role she played in the "blackening" of the European cultural scene. Nor can it be denied that her presence in that scene brought to the fore how intimately "blackness" was sutured to the construction of modern white European subjectivity.

Notes

1. Jean-Claude Baker and Chris Chase, *Josephine: The Hungry Heart* (New York: Random House, 1993), 5.
2. Quoted in Baker and Chase, *Josephine: The Hungry Heart*, 5–6.
3. Judith Butler, *Gender Trouble: Feminism and the Subversion of Identity* (New York: Routledge, 1990).
4. Of course, the conditions of production for the stage and the film performances were different, but because in each case the power and the purse strings were controlled by white men and were intended primarily for white European consumption, the differences do not militate against the kinds of comparison I am offering in this essay.
5. Toni Morrison, *Playing in the Dark: Whiteness and the Literary Imagination* (Cambridge, Mass.: Harvard University Press, 1992), 9–10.
6. See W. E. B. Du Bois, *The Souls of Black Folk* (London: Penguin, 1989 [1903]). Other luminaries one might mention are James Baldwin, Chester Himes, and the whole "Lost Generation."
7. Phyllis Rose, *Jazz Cleopatra: Josephine Baker in Her Time* (New York: Doubleday, 1989), 9–10.
8. Sander Gilman, *Difference and Pathology: Stereotypes of Sexuality, Race, and Madness* (Ithaca, N.Y.: Cornell University Press, 1985), 29.
9. Paul Gilroy, *The Black Atlantic: Modernity and Double Consciousness* (Cambridge, Mass.: Harvard University Press, 1993), 205–16.
10. I use the phrase "Enlightenment modernity" expressly to mark the critique of the traditional Euro- or EuroAmerico-centric assumption that modernity is universally marked as Western. The subaltern studies scholars, many Latin American scholars such as Walter Mignolo, and the critics who are proposing "alternative modernities" all have been making the case that Enlightenment modernity is only a specific case, not to be enforced as the only cultural telos, however "unfinished" or unachieved. Enlightenment implies a specific ideal of reason and a particular kind of emphasis on the individual. It institutes a peculiar vector for "progress." These are not ideals, emphases, or vectors today assumed to be universally accepted in every society or in every locality, no matter how widespread globalization is, and in any case, not the same thing as Enlightenment come to fruition. "Enlightenment" here is an adjective specifying one type of modernity. I thank Heike Raphael-Hernandez for discussions on this issue.
11. This point is also made by others. See Paula Gidding, cited in Yvette Abrahams, "Images of Sara Bartman [*sic*]: Sexuality, Race, and Gender in Early Nineteenth-Century Britain," in *Nation, Empire, Colony: Historicizing Gender and Race*, ed. Ruth Roach Pierson and Nupur Chaudhuri (Bloomington: Indiana University Press, 1998), 223.
12. Gilman, *Difference and Pathology*, 88.
13. James Clifford, *The Predicament of Culture* (Cambridge, Mass.: Harvard University Press, 1991), 145.
14. Nancy Leys Stepan, *Picturing Tropical Nature* (Ithaca, N.Y.: Cornell University Press, 2001), 93, 95; see also Gilman, *Difference and Pathology*, 89.

15. David Farrell Krell, "The Bodies of Black Folk: Kant, Hegel, Du Bois and Baldwin," *Boundary 2* 27, no. 3 (fall 2000), 103–34, esp. 116–17. See also Theodor Adorno and Max Horkheimer, *Dialectic of Enlightenment* (London: Verso, 1979), 186.

16. Stepan, *Picturing Tropical Nature*, 88.

17. Gilman, *Difference and Pathology*, 107.

18. Ibid., 81.

19. Ibid., 120, emphases added.

20. Mary Louise Pratt, *Imperial Eyes: Travel Writing and Transculturation* (London: Routledge, 1992).

21. The presence of the ex-colonized Algerian immigrant is quite different, for many political reasons. So it would be quite incorrect to assume that all nonwhites in France would have generated the same kind of enthusiasm as did the black artists and intellectuals between the world wars. It is important then to historicize the argument about Baker's role in Paris.

22. Paul Colin designed a poster for Baker in which "her face, with its exaggerated lips, barely rises above the stereotypes of Sambo art" (Rose, *Jazz Cleopatra*, 7).

23. Andreas Huyssen, *Twilight Memories: Marking Time in a Culture of Amnesia* (London and New York: Routledge, 1995), 13.

24. Abrahams, "Images of Sara Bartman [*sic*]," 225.

25. Ibid., 227.

26. Benedict Anderson, *Imagined Communities* (London: Verso, 1992).

27. Nicholas Mirzoeff, ed., *Diaspora and Visual Culture: Representing Africans and Jews* (New York: Routledge, 1999), 1.

28. Lauren Berlant, *The Queen of America Goes to Washington City* (Durham, N.C.: Duke University Press, 1997), 27.

29. Stepan, *Picturing Tropical Nature*, 89.

30. Hortense Spillers, " 'Mama's Baby, Papa's Maybe': An American Grammarbook," *Diacritics* 17, no. 2 (1990): 67.

31. Gilman, *Difference and Pathology*, 113.

32. Ibid., 124.

33. Jody Blake, *Le Tumulte Noir: Modernist Art and Popular Entertainment in Jazz-Age Paris, 1900–1930* (University Park: Pennsylvania State University Press, 1999), 28.

34. Jacques Lacan, *The Four Fundamental Concepts of Psycho-Analysis*, ed. Jacques-Alain Miller, trans. Alan Sheridan (New York: Norton, 1977).

35. Baker, *Josephine: The Hungry Heart*, 33. See also Charles Baudelaire, *Les Fleurs du Mal* (Paris: Gallimard, 1994).

36. This division, as the histories of slavery and contemporary ethnic violence in Bosnia, Rwanda, Kashmir, and elsewhere have shown, ought to provoke a recognition of how potentially explosive is the yoking of the discordant impulses of attraction and repulsion when "race" and sex come into play simultaneously in politically fraught contexts.

37. Krell, "The Bodies of Black Folk," 124.

38. Dorothea Fischer-Hornung, for instance, cites copious evidence to demonstrate that "Dunham consciously intended to cross the borders of 'low' and 'high' culture, folk and commercial art, the 'primitive' and the 'civilized,' the sensual and the cerebral, as well as the written and the embodied text" (93) in order to defeat stereotypes about black identity. See Dorothea Fischer-Hornung, "The Body Possessed: Katherine Dunham Dance Technique in *Mambo*," in *EmBODYing Liberation: The Black Body in American Dance*, ed. Dorothea Fischer-Hornung and Alison D. Goeller (Hamburg: LIT Verlag, 2001), 91–111. Similarly, Alison Goeller documents Ailey's self-reflexivity about consistent and calculated deconstruction of essentialisms of black selfhood: "It was as if Ailey were declaring to the dance world: boundaries, labels, mean very little; look what's possible when even the most incongruous elements are joined together" (117). See Alison Goeller, "(Re)Crossing Borders: The Legacy of Alvin Ailey," in Fischer-Hornung and Goeller, *EmBODYing Liberation*, 113–23. Goeller underscores Ailey's "lively hybridity" and antiessentialist philosophy (Ailey quoted in Goeller, 117).

39. See especially Henry Louis Gates Jr., *The Signifying Monkey: A Theory of African-American Literary Criticism* (New York: Oxford University Press, 1988).

40. Quoted in Josephine Baker and Jo Bouillon, *Josephine* (New York: Paragon House Publishers, 1975), 55. See also Michael Borshuk, "An Intelligence of the Body: Disruptive Parody

through Dance in the Early Performances of Josephine Baker," in Fischer-Hornung and Goeller, *EmBODYing Liberation*, 41–57; see especially 43.

41. Borshuk, "An Intelligence of the Body," 41.

42. Ibid., 42–43. Baker did receive considerable criticism for "prostituting of Negro talent" (Will Marion Cook's review of La Revue Nègre quoted in Rose, *Jazz Cleopatra*, 80). But this was also an overdetermined masquerade, made necessary not only by the imperative to meet the horizon of expectations that defined her audience but also by the need for self-preservation as a performer.

43. Homi Bhabha, *The Location of Culture* (London: Routledge, 1994), 67.

44. Butler, *Gender Trouble*, 136, emphasis original.

45. Abrahams, "Images of Sara Bartman [*sic*]," 223.

46. See Kenneth Ballhatchet, *Race, Sex and Class under the Raj: Imperial Attitudes and Policies and Their Critics, 1793–1905* (London: Weidenfeld and Nicolson, 1980). See also Ronald Hyam, *Empire and Sexuality: The British Experience* (Manchester and New York: Manchester University Press, 1991 [1990]) and Vron Ware, *Beyond the Pale: White Women, Racism, and History* (London: Verso, 1992).

47. Thomas Laqueur, *Making Sex: Body and Gender from the Greeks to Freud* (Cambridge, Mass.: Harvard University Press, 1990), 19.

48. Marjorie Garber, *Vested Interests: Cross-Dressing and Cultural Anxiety* (New York: Routledge, 1992), 280.

49. Butler quoted in Borshuk, "An Intelligence of the Body," 50, emphases Butler's.

50. Ibid., 51.

51. Ibid., 43.

52. Glenn Watkins, *Pyramids at the Louvre: Music, Culture, and Collage from Stravinsky to the Postmodernists* (Cambridge, Mass.: Belknap, 1994), 146.

53. Baker and Chase, *Josephine: The Hungry Heart*, 117.

54. Watkins, *Pyramids at the Louvre*, 134.

55. Ibid., 135.

56. bell hooks, *Black Looks: Race and Representation* (Boston: South End Press, 1992), 157. See also Mae Henderson, "Introduction: Borders, Boundaries, and Frame(work)s," in *Borders, Boundaries, and Frames: Cultural Criticism and Cultural Studies, Essays from the English Institute*, ed. Mae Henderson (New York: Routledge, 1995), 1–30.

57. Bernard Gendron, *Between Montmartre and the Mudd Club: Popular Music and the Avant-Garde* (Chicago: University of Chicago Press, 2002), 115.

58. Baker and Chase, *Josephine: The Hungry Heart*, 135, emphasis added.

59. "Tam-tam," of course, is also a reference to an African group dance (Blake, *Le Tumulte Noir*, 23).

60. See Blake, *Le Tumulte Noir*, 99.

61. Clifford, *Predicament*, 198, n. 7.

62. Rose, *Jazz Cleopatra*, 6, emphases added.

63. Rose writes that "European audiences of the 1920s, seeking a renewal that was decidedly racial, focused their fantasies of finding joy, freedom, and energy all the more easily on Baker because she was black" (*Jazz Cleopatra*, x).

64. Quoted in Baker and Chase, *Josephine: The Hungry Heart*, 184. Her rejection by America did hurt her terribly, and she cried, "America will not welcome home her own daughter" (quoted in Baker and Chase, *Josephine: The Hungry Heart*, 191).

65. Ibid., 190.

3
"Jungle in the Spotlight"?
Primitivism and Esteem:
Katherine Dunham's 1954 German Tour

DOROTHEA FISCHER-HORNUNG

Katherine Dunham—dancer, choreographer, instructor, and anthropologist of note—had contributed as a dancer and choreographer in the films *Cabin in the Sky* (1943) and *Stormy Weather* (1943) and had also successfully established the Katherine Dunham School of Dance in New York when she left the United States to tour Europe in 1948. Her first engagement was planned as a three weeks' booking in London but stretched into three months. Over the next fifteen years, the Katherine Dunham Dance Troupe toured more than fifty countries as the largest nonsubsidized, independent U.S. dance troupe of its day.

In 1948, the London newspapers reported that Dunham was sweeping England in a wave of popularity greater than that of Isadora Duncan many years earlier. She even influenced hat styles, the spring collection including the "Dunham line" and "Caribbean Rhapsody," featuring vivid colors, large bows, and flowers.[1] And it was in the following year that Richard Buckle published *Katherine Dunham: Her Dancers, Singers, Musicians,* the first major study (with a bilingual text in English and French and a sizeable collection of outstanding photos taken by Roger Wood) of Dunham's performances in Great Britain. Similarly, she took Paris by storm, second only to Josephine Baker's triumph in the 1920s.

Several years later, in spring of 1954, Dunham embarked on her first tour to (West) Germany and Berlin at a time when the country was beginning to emerge from the bleak period after World War II. The *Stunde Null* (zero hour) had come and gone, and Germany was embarking on what was to become the *Wirtschaftswunder* (economic miracle) of the next decades. Contemporary reviews, personal correspondence, films, and newsreels attest to the effect of Dunham's performances in her highly publicized role as an African American dancer and scholar on a society trying to recover materially and psychologically from the lost war and the deeply racialized crimes of the Holocaust. Dunham toured West Germany at the decisive moment when the uncertainties of the destructive past were still very apparent but hints of a new and better future were emerging.[2] In this liminal moment in German history, Dunham as an African American dancer and intellectual not only left a lasting imprint on the larger world of German dance and performance as reflected in contemporary reviews, but also had a profound impact on individual lives, as reflected in personal correspondence.

In order to gauge the impact of Katherine Dunham in the 1950s, we need to look back to the time preceding her appearance on the German stage. Africans had been a part of European culture since the Middle Ages, and Germany was no different than the major European colonial powers in its strongly racialized thinking about people of color.[3] Stereotypical thinking about blacks, as Sander Gilman has shown, was appropriated by Germans despite the fact that very few blacks were actually present in German society before the twentieth century.[4] For much of the German population, African soldiers, who were part of the French troops stationed as occupation forces after World War I, were the first major encounter with larger numbers of Africans. The occupation not only by fellow Europeans but by colonial troops from Africa as well—often referred to as the "Black Horror on the Rhine"—was later exploited for propaganda purposes by the Nazis, firing the racialized fear of subjection and defeat.[5] Yet, the appearance of African American occupation troops after World War II actually had the opposite effect. Black soldiers did not elicit horror, but, on the contrary, were often preferred to other members of the U.S. occupation forces. Frequently, a kind of solidarity among the downtrodden developed and served to unite the victor and the conquered:

> In Austria as well as Germany, the Afro-Americans quickly became the best-liked members of the US occupation force. "We got along best with the Negroes," was stated in many different oral history interviews. Something like a demonstrative, emotional bond of solidarity was formed in line with the perception that "You're a slave, I'm a slave."[6]

The presence of African American soldiers during the U.S. occupation deeply influenced German society in that its racially homogenous nature was fundamentally changed and German culture was challenged and fundamentally enriched by African American popular culture.[7]

In the Weimar Republic of Germany, the period immediately preceding the Nazi takeover, the world of dance and entertainment had already enjoyed a wide range of African American performance, particularly in Berlin, where a rather large pool of resident African American performers was available. Sam Wooding and his Orchestra with the Chocolate Kiddies performed before enthusiastic audiences throughout the 1920s, consciously forming a bridge to German culture by incorporating a medley of German songs in their performances. Paul Robeson starred in Eugene O'Neill's *The Emperor Jones* in Max Reinhardt's Deutsches Künstlertheater in 1930.[8] Yet, undoubtedly, no single entertainer left a mark as strong and indelible as Josephine Baker. When Baker danced the Charleston on New Year's Eve of 1925/26 at the Nelson Theater in Berlin, the audience stormed the stage. Only one year later, the Charleston was already officially incorporated in the German ballroom dance championships.[9] All this came to an end in the mid-1930s when the Nazis categorized jazz and (African) American culture as *entartet* (degenerated), along with Jewish culture. Adolf Hitler had paved the way by decrying the fact that:

> [i]t was and is the Jews who bring the Negro to the Rhine, always with the same concealed thought and the clear goal of destroying, with the bastardization which would necessarily set in, the white race which they hate, to throw it down from its cultural and political height and in turn to rise personally to the position of master.[10]

It was an irritation to the Nazis that German audiences often considered African American performance a positive alternative cultural link to a better world—"the exotic protagonist of a paradise lost."[11] This was in complete contradiction to the ideals of German nationalism, and the Nazis were appalled that "German youth, who should be the hope and the future of our German fatherland, demands foreign—American—Negro music."[12] The racialized image of African Americans and Jews was melded in the realm of degenerated "non-German" culture; the Left and the avant-garde were equated with Jewishness, as were jazz and African American music. The famous Nazi propaganda poster based on a crude distortion of the poster for Ernst Kranek's opera *Jonny spielt auf*, which was used to advertise the exhibition *Entartete Musik* in 1938, shows a black Sambo-like saxophonist wearing a Star of David in his buttonhole.[13] The National Socialists—in an amazing testament to the power of culture—officially classified jazz as part of the aggressive war strategy of Jews and Americans, and a proclamation prohibiting broadcasts of jazz was issued on the national German radio station in 1935.[14]

During the same period, the Swing Kids developed an oppositional German youth culture. The Swing Kids expressed themselves in a characteristic clothing style, listened to American music, and read foreign newspapers in clear opposition to the ethnic and racial ideas perpetrated by the

Nazis. The Hitler Youth harassed them, and some Swing Kids were arrested by the Gestapo to "protect them," according to official statements, from further degeneration. In isolated cases they were even sent to the front or to concentration camps.[15]

In the realm of dance, the Nazis preferred modern expressive dance (*Ausdruckstanz*), and they rejected not only contemporary African American dance forms but classical ballet as well. Expressive dance events staged by Rudolf von Laban while at the Ministry for People's Education and Propaganda[16] were considered a deep expression of the German soul. Dance festivals were organized to highlight modern expressive dance and gymnastics, incorporating large numbers of lay participants; these staged mass events were considered part of the avant-garde of National Socialist art. The opening of the 1936 Berlin Olympics can, therefore, be seen as the staging of the fusion of dance and sports in the context of a holistic approach to German physical culture—dance and gymnastics hardly separated in the mental construct of the fascist appropriation of *Ausdruckstanz*.[17]

With the particularly racialized context of Germany's past, it cannot be surprising that the discourse of race was an important feature in the rehabilitation of (West) German identity in the 1950s. The collapse of National Socialism, the defeat in the war, the shame and guilt of the Holocaust, the enormous loss of life and property, and the general sense of the loss of national identity and purpose form the backdrop for my exploration of the effect of Katherine Dunham and her African American dance troupe in postwar Germany. Entertainment, and especially dance as an embodied art form, according to Judith Lynn Hanna, "evokes, reinforces, and clarifies desires and fantasies, some of which would otherwise be incoherent. Holding up a mirror, dance says to us: Look at yourself or at how you might be."[18] Katherine Dunham and her dance troupe were precisely such a mirror of not only a better United States of the victors, but a better Germany of the defeated as well.

In Germany, the Katherine Dunham Dance Company, with its exuberance, energy, and outstanding entertainment value, provided a staging of African American and African Caribbean culture that to Germans seemed, on the one hand, foreign or exotic but, on the other hand, was understood to be equally rooted in European culture. Dunham's colorful "Caribbean Rhapsody" revue provided an exciting way to overcome the drab reality of everyday postwar life and fit well into the strong utopian thrust that U.S. culture in general and African American culture in particular had for Germans. A particularly complex discourse on race developed in the reading of the performances of the Dunham dancers in post-Holocaust Germany as simultaneously primitively essentialist and intellectually emancipatory.

African diasporic dance became a mirror or sounding board for German reconstruction, and the black body on the stage became a part of the discourse of race in its larger social context:

> The dancing body is a cultural production, dynamically interacting with the sociocultural matrix of which it is a part, and dances are projected images, not mere mirror reflections of already existing social realities. Dance's capacity to project images of the body's action in the world marks it as powerful means of enculturation.[19]

The positive image of racial mixing presented by the Katherine Dunham Dance Company—Dunham's dancers ranged in appearance from deep black to white—as well as Dunham's very public racially mixed marriage to John Pratt, her set and costume designer, provided a sounding board in the attempt to come to terms with the devastating racial politics of fascism and the subsequent presence of dark-skinned occupation troops. Dunham consciously structured her review to feed into these positive feelings toward the United States and African Americans. Every performance ended with a traditional African American cakewalk, featuring a huge white cake decorated with U.S. and German flags and the orchestra playing rousing renditions of John Philip Sousa's "Stars and Stripes Forever" and "Yankee Doodle":

> Then a big sugarwhite wedding cake is brought on stage, decorated with tiny American and German flags, new hits sound until they wind up in the Yankee Doodle. With every curtain call the beautiful Katherine is in a new dress with her still childlike melancholy smile. Every new dress suits her better than the last one and still the audience wants to see new dresses.[20]

The celebration of unified flag-waving German-American friendship combined with a fashion show in which Dunham had an extravagant six changes of costume tapped into the desire for not only a better America, but also a better Germany. The audience could envision a day when the German flag could stand proud next to that of the victor and German women could again afford such luxuries as fashionable gowns. The victor and the newly rehabilitated vanquished would triumph together in a positive image of reconstruction after defeat. One Berlin reviewer speculates that Dunham "probably feels that her motto 'come and conquer' had now been realized for Berlin, too."[21] Yet she had not only "conquered" Berlin but had already reigned supreme in France and Great Britain, indirectly elevating Germany's position from a defeated nation to one that was honored with a visit by the same star that had graced the victors' capitals.

References to the most famous African American star in Europe, Josephine Baker, "the half-legendary prima ballerina of black dance" abound.[22] Baker is reported to have sat in the front row on four consecutive nights during Dunham's 1948/49 tour in Paris, and "since her [Baker's] own appearance on the Seine in 1924, there has been no comparable excitement associated with a black dance troupe."[23] Dunham and Baker are positioned together as extraordinary entertainers, specifically in the context of the perceived "primitivism" of their performance styles. Yet a significant distinction between the two stars often emerges in that a number of reviewers emphasize the "civilized" performance style of the Dunham dancers in contrast to what was viewed as Baker's "primitivism": "The Dunham dance theater is unprecedented in the history of dance. It is rooted in the originals of primitive peoples, but utilizes the artistic means of expression of the civilized world."[24]

Like Baker, Dunham is not exclusively portrayed as the foreign Other; the German reviews often try to recuperate the European character of her art, viewing her as the "black Mary Wigman,"[25] the leading proponent of *Ausdruckstanz*, German modern expressive dance. Dunham is also compared with Isadora Duncan, whose dance style incorporated Greek and Renaissance themes with natural body movement.[26] The direct comparison with Wigman and Duncan are a gauge of Dunham's stature in the eyes of German critics.

Her "Caribbean Rhapsody" revue fits neatly into the desire for entertainment and glamour that characterized a whole series of German postwar song and dance revue films. *Die Grosse Starparade* (1954) was one such production, in which the Dunham troupe appeared along with such up-and-coming German stars as Peter Alexander, Catarina Valente, and Cornelia Froboess.[27] In addition, the *Deutsche Wochenschau* newsreels of 1954 frequently focused on the popular dance scene in the budding postwar German jazz clubs, with footage of hectic jitterbug competition—one voiceover stating that the jitterbug is "the black man's answer to Europe" and describing the happy winners of the jitterbug contest as "in the jungle for the time being."[28] However, beyond the spread of popular dance culture, various segments of the Deutsche Wochenschau in the course of 1954 position Katherine Dunham in the context of African American stars such as Ella Fitzgerald and Oscar Patterson[29] performing in Hamburg, Marian Anderson shown singing Schubert songs in a girl's dorm in Munich,[30] Louis Armstrong filmed clowning with his trumpet while disembarking from an airplane in Düsseldorf,[31] and Josephine Baker giving a farewell concert in Berlin after serving a meal to one hundred war orphans.[32] The facial close-ups of the audience reflect the deep enthusiasm for and devotion to this alternative African American culture from the United States. This is particularly evident in the performance of a group of Caribbean singers performing for an awestruck group of refugees in a displaced persons camp in Berlin, traces of the deprivation of these refugees still evident in their faces. These were the years that West Germany was opening up to the outside world, and American culture became a model for a new, desirable, and easier way of life.

Two *Deutsche Wochenschau* newsreels screened in movie theaters in 1954 show the Dunham dancers in performance. In the first segment, the troupe is seen performing in Paris with a sound track that consists of a disturbingly asynchronous jazz overlay that almost drowns out the original drumming.[33] The second segment documents the opening of "Caribbean Rhapsody" in Frankfurt. Dunham and her dancers are shown performing "The Woman with a Cigar," one of Dunham's signature numbers. This segment also suffers from two sound tracks imposed one over the other, both the original drumming and some added jazz. Perhaps the jazz sound track in both segments is intended to "familiarize" the German audience with the "primitive" dances. The voiceover notes that these are "full-blooded, colorful dances that are similar to ritualized Negro dances which reveal the strong expressive power of the troupe,"[34] undercutting any naïve claim to authenticity. These newsreel segments taken together add up to a strong indication of the range and power of African American performance in Germany in the early to mid-1950s.

Contemporary newspaper reviews vacillate between awestruck admiration for the well-honed dance technique of the Dunham company—"This alone [five to six barefoot pirouettes] would make our dancers despair, if they were deprived of the help of a ballet shoe"[35]—and the attribution of this excellent technique to the troupe's "natural" talent. Nevertheless, there are voices that clearly state that what the audience sees as "natural" is the product of hard work comparable to other concert dance forms. Thus, the German reviews oscillate between the two poles of unending esteem for the quality of the troupe's well-trained performance and primitivist gaze upon their "natural" talent.

The public construction of her academic and personal integrity, however, precluded the mere reduction of Dunham to the "primitive." Her *Journey to Accompong*, the results of her Jamaican research (1936),[36] had been published by Henry Holt in 1946, and *Las Danzas de Haiti*, the research for her master's thesis, had been published in Mexico in Spanish and English in 1947.[37] In 1949, Buckle had already noted the nature of Dunham's mission based on her role as "explorer, thinker, inventor, organizer and dancer," lauded her achievement, and noted that that she "should have reached so high a place in the estimation of the world has done more than a million pamphlets could for the service of her people."[38] Dunham's own conscious construction in public discourse as an intellectual with sound academic qualifications was assuredly a part of this mission. Performativity characterized Katherine Dunham not only on stage but was also a part of her clever and effective public relations campaign.

In a seemingly unending number of interviews, she carefully molded her dual identities of energized primitive dancer and rational scholar, playing the German press like a finely tuned instrument. Amongst the numerous press clippings in scrapbooks now housed in the archives of the Missouri Historical Society in St. Louis and in the Katherine Dunham Archives of Southern Illinois University, Carbondale, there is no evidence that she tried to clarify that she was not "Frau Doktor," that she had given up her formal academic career shortly before completing her master's degree to pursue her career as a performer. Certainly Dunham must have felt some understandable regrets at having made the choice to give up her academic ambitions for the world of entertainment,[39] and there is no denying her pioneering contributions to dance anthropology. Nevertheless, she was surely aware of the usefulness of an academic persona as a black woman performer in a nation that, after the barbarism of the Holocaust, sought to look at its better self as a nation of artists and philosophers.

The effectiveness of her campaign is reflected in a written request for a copy of her dissertation made by Professor Franz Vilsmeier, secretary of the Bavarian Gymnastics Association.[40] Vilsmeier's letter does not clarify why he was interested in the text, merely stating that they want the document for their archives. The strong association of dance and gymnastics,[41] as well as the amazement over the fact that a black entertainer could be a notable scholar, is a likely motivation for his request.

Dunham's portrayal as the sexy scholar is perhaps best reflected in a cover story in *Der Spiegel*, one of the most influential postwar German weekly newsmagazines. After expressing her dismay about the fact that many people make a sexual issue of her programs,[42] *Der Spiegel* quotes Dunham's deceptively flippant solution: "I simply portrayed myself as an intellectual, you know." Having staked out her intellectual turf, she concludes: "Today I can afford to simply say: 'What's wrong with sex?'"[43] The German magazine even provides a trendy Americanizing touch by leaving Dunham's words in English and providing a suitably colloquial German translation.

In this same *Der Spiegel* feature, Dunham characterizes herself as a "catalyst who wants to bring together contrasting cultures,"[44] making of herself "a floating island of negritude"[45] that "would return [to African Americans] some of that unadulterated race consciousness, to return the strongly rhythmic impulses, which they consciously or unconsciously deny because of their inferiority complex regarding industrially advanced Americans."[46]

The extensive background information on Haitian history and culture provided by *Der Spiegel* enables the melding of the cultural contexts of Germany and the Caribbean, thereby fulfilling Dunham's intention to act as a catalyst in making the African diasporic culture of Haiti accessible not only to African Americans but Germans as well. Dunham is positioned as an important part of an Afro-Caribbean awakening in Haiti, reflected in the cultural center she established at Habitation LeClerc in Port au Prince.[47] Haiti, by implication, is turned into something of a model for postwar (West) German culture, both countries experiencing a potential cultural revival after troubled years.[48]

In their enthusiasm, the reviewers often seem to reflect amazement at the fact that a beautiful, exotic, sexy, dark "primitive" can speak eloquently and think rationally—"an impressive example of the intellectual and artistic potential of the colored race!"[49] Dunham is consistently portrayed as an exceedingly multifaceted star and scholar:

> For four weeks Katherine Dunham has been touring Germany and word has gotten around that this dark-skinned, elegant American, the daughter of a Negro and a Franco-Canadian, is a phenomenal dancer, director, choreographer, impresario all wrapped up in one—very attractive—person. To top it off, she holds a Ph.D., is a professor at Yale University, a writer, renowned ethnologist, honorary member of the Royal Society of Anthropology and a painter.[50]

And if all this is not enough to wow the German audiences sufficiently, Dunham is staged as a glamour star who receives priceless gifts from the likes of Prince Ali Khan.[51] A full two-page photo glamour spread was devoted to the production of the Dino De Lauretiis and Carlo Ponti film *Mambo*, which had been filmed the previous year in Italy. *Mambo* is based loosely on Dunham's career and featured Silvana Mangano, Shelley Winters, Vittorio Gassman, and Michael Rennie.[52] Even Dunham's private life has glamour written all over it—even if the details are often a bit skewed. She is described as married to a "gentlemanly Englishman [he was Canadian], Mr. Pratt, with graying temples who advises her in decorative matters [he was her set and costume designer]. A six-year-old boy [they had adopted a girl Marie Christine, from Martinique in Paris in 1951] is the pride of his parents."[53]

Dunham's public image as the ultracivilized intellectual and the simultaneously naïve primitive also finds its way into the reviews of her and her troupe's performances: "Her dance is in the realm of the emphatically erotic, but is simultaneously the properly restrained expression of pure, naïve love of life."[54]

The reviews of the troupe's dancing reflect a whole array of the most familiar stereotypes. The black bodies of the dancers are, for example, often extremely eroticized: "The 45 dark-skinned dancers in the troupe—graceful, enchantingly proportioned mulatto girls in fantastic costumes and panther-like young men with animalistic, energetic grace—come from the Islands in the Caribbean."[55] Dunham, the scholar and intellectual, is portrayed as the taming force that keeps the troupe from running out of primitivist control: "Again and again, her voice manages to force the natural, exuberant temperament and her dancers' wild urge to move into an ordered form."[56] The sheer physical, animalistic character of the supple and graceful limbs of dancers with gleaming sets of teeth slips into the worst kind of racialized exoticism in the following description:

> In particular among the male dancers, each seems to outdo the other in animalistic suppleness, rhythmic possession, artistic intensity, and dance technique. But also among the graceful female dancers with their slender limbs and gleaming smiles [literally "sets of teeth"] there are extremely skilful, charming, and expressive dancers.[57]

In particular, the sexuality of the male dancers is commented upon repeatedly, often with a distinct homophobic undertone. The emphasis on strong masculinities cannot be too surprising coming from reviewers in a country that had been defeated in the most "manly" of all endeavors—war. The discourse of overdetermined heterosexuality takes on particular importance in the context of the felt need to reestablish traditional gender roles after their disruption during the war:[58]

> The men among the colored dancers do not have anything effeminate, perfumed or even neutral and selfcentered that so often irritates and annoys in the gentleman of the European ballet. Looking at the Negroe [sic] dancers one does not get any misleading ideas. They have such a strong gripping way of looking at their female partners that this already creates the crackling tenseness one misses so often in our duo scenes.[59]

Racist fantasies about black masculinity—of the "power of animalistic movement"[60]—are also clearly at work: "The men in the chocolate-colored dance troupe deserves particular mention: supple, very masculine, well-defined bodies, a symphony of muscles."[61]

The familiarity with modern expressive dance provided a context for the German critics to approach Dunham's intentional mix of dance genres: "They are ancient, mythic ritual dances from the Caribbean; the ceremonial elements are cleverly mixed with elements of classical and modern ballet."[62]

Der Spiegel makes this point even more succinctly: "She fascinates the audience in the western civilized world primarily through the natural power of ancient pagan rituals and folk dances from the Caribbean, which she translates into the stage form of modern ballet."[63] This recognition that

Dunham's choreography is art and not nature fits well into her own conclusion: "Authentic dances are for museums."[64]

It was clear to most German reviewers that the Dunham troupe's performances were based on a sophisticated—certainly not as "arbitrary" as the critic implies—mélange of forms extracted into a unique product and that her dancers achieved excellence like all dancers in the world do: through hard work and dedication. "Dunham's dances are only apparently ecstatic. In almost a pedantic manner, she practices every twitch of the body in tough daily training. Her style is an arbitrary mixture of classical ballet, modern expressive dance, barefoot acrobatics, pantomime, and acting."[65] Wolfgang Schlüter succinctly characterized the creative process that Dunham's art set in motion in the meeting of African American and German culture:

> The fruitful tension that is created when extremely different cultures meet has been reflected in the history of art since antiquity. And which astounding artistic products have resulted from the contact of western high culture with the natural primitivism of foreign peoples and races has only become apparent in Europe since our world has become smaller.[66]

Dunham's influence on both her audience and members of the dance world is revealed in the following reflections on German audiences, which clearly position her as an authority able to judge audiences throughout the world. Her description of the reserved German audiences is in clear contradiction to that of unbounded audience enthusiasm in the reviews. Apparently in a signifying mood, she describes how a tearful German dancer begs her to join her troupe—willing to appear in blackface if that is what it takes:

> I found the German audiences generally more reserved, much more conservative than I had imagined they would be. And then—one isn't, I think, used to me. One has to see me more often. . . . In London there was someone who came to the same show 72 times. And I experienced something similar again in Berlin. There was a young man, a professional dancer, who sat evening for evening in the Titaniapalast. It was only when we were about to leave that he came to me with tears in his eyes—really he had tears in his eyes!—and wanted to come along. "Please make me a part of your ensemble—I will even paint myself really black—you only need to say the word."[67]

Over and above her career as a dancer, Dunham had a deep influence on individuals in Germany that went far beyond that of her performances. I have already noted the request for a copy of her dissertation from the Bavarian Gymnastics Association, which clearly documents her acceptance as an authority on dance and physical education. But perhaps the most moving testament to the depth of her influence is reflected in a letter (19 June 1954) from Elizabeth Willer, a young German mother of two racially mixed Afro-German children (*Mischlingskinder*), whose father was a departed U.S. soldier. She writes to Dunham asking for work because of the difficulties she encounters based on the discrimination she and her dark-skinned children were suffering.

A 1960 study, *Colored Children in Germany* (*Farbige Kinder in Deutschland*), found that in Germany, the situation for children of mixed race background as well as for their mothers was extremely precarious: The belief that racial mixing always manifested itself in the most negative aspects of both "races" was still widely accepted, as well as the belief that Afro-German children had lower intelligence. In other words, they experienced the full range of negative racial stereotypes found in the United States and Europe in general and, in addition, specific discrimination in Germany because they had fraternized with the enemy. Yet despite the fact that they encountered significant prejudice, a vast majority of the mothers of mixed-race children decided to raise them themselves and did not give them up for adoption.[68]

According to this study, prejudice was particularly virulent in Germany because of the still prevalent race theories that had been perpetrated by the Nazis. In the opinion of the authors of this study, this therefore entailed a special obligation on the part of a new and better Germany to their own African American population:

> After the defeat of humanism and sound human judgment while under the sway of racial madness, we cannot allow ourselves and in the face of others, not to act in accordance with our loudly heralded ideals and laws, in that we deny members of our own people to take up their rightful place in our society just because they have different racial characteristics.[69]

In this racialized context, it is significant that photos of Dunham and her adopted daughter Marie-Christine circulated in various personal interest stories were put into a very positive light, nevertheless with a somewhat condescending tone. In one photo, Marie Christine, "the cute little creature," is shown wearing a very German hairstyle "with nice dark circles of braided hair [literally "snail-shaped hair"] over her ears."[70] In addition to her dance and academic qualifications, Dunham is now constructed as the devoted mother: "My daughter should not get carried away by all this to do. But I must have her with me when I am touring—in the intermissions, you know . . ."[71]

Several human interest stories point out that Katherine Dunham and John Pratt were looking for a little boy to adopt while in Germany, and a caption under the photo of Marie-Christine reads: "This is Marie-Christine, a mixed race child that Katherine and her husband got from a French orphanage and adopted. . . . In a German orphanage, Marie-Christine will soon be able to pick out a little brother who has lost his parents."[72]

It seems reasonable to assume that it was an article like this that moved Elizabeth Willer to write to Dunham. Her request—written in imperfect but quite serviceable English, its Germanness reflected in its syntactical structures as well as the capitalization and punctuation—uses the adoption idea as an opener: "Please don't draw this letter away, before Yo have read it. There was a few weeks ago a notice in the news paper, that You are loocking for a little german-colored boy for adoptions."[73] She quickly makes it clear that she does not want to give her children away: "I have twoo little boys (5½ and 3½ jears old),[74] but I don't want to give them away, because I love them much to much." Just how much she loves her boys and how proud she is of them seems to literally radiate from the photograph she enclosed of herself and her boys (Figure 4). Elizabeth Willer makes it clear that all she wants is work in order to survive and maintain her dignity: "I am not a begger, I don't want nothing, but a job."

Many of the problems outlined in *Colored Children in Germany* are reflected in Elizabeth Willer's letter. Like a majority of German mothers of mixed-race children, she does not want to give up her Afro-German children for adoption: "I would gladly work day and night, just to be with my boys." She makes it clear that her situation is extremely difficult because of the reaction of others to her children: "I don't care where it would be, just as long as it is outside of Germany. I have desired already to go out of life with my boys, so I don't have to hear and see no more, how people are looking, laghing and argue at me and my boys." The father of her children had left her three months earlier, "a very long and unhappy story." Her extremely moving and direct plea in her suicidal despair ends: "If You could help me back to happiness, my boys and me would always be thankfull to You a whole long life . . . I do any kind of work and anything."

Clearly, Katherine Dunham had a deep effect on this one woman's life as it did on a small gymnastics club in Bavaria and a lone dancer who was willing to appear in blackface if only he could join her dance company. The fundamental respect that Dunham and the public construction of her life and work in performing African American diasporic dance culture elicited went far beyond the primitive exotic. On the one hand, although contemporary reviews make clear that her physical appearance both on and off the stage are often spontaneously rendered as essentially "primitive" and natural, Dunham's careful construction in the press of her public and private persona also enabled a different reading of what it means to be an (African) American dancer and individual.

Dunham simultaneously embodied and deconstructed the gendered and racialized image of the African American dancer, scholar, and individual, initiating a significant shift in the image of the African American, American, Afro-German, and German in postwar Germany, in the public sphere of performance, but also in the most private sphere of family and

Fig. 4 Elizabeth Willer and her two boys, Ernest and Willy. Photo with permission of Special Collections, Morris Library, Southern Illinois University, Carbondale, Illinois.

personal relations. As Rudolf Riedler put it: "That is the unique thing in Katherine Dunhams [*sic*] art, which stands at the intersection of different traditions and influxes. From the meeting of black and white, Katherine Dunham made the jungle stage ripe. What she shows is Negroe [*sic*] dance seen through the glasses of western civilization."⁷⁵ In Germany, despite the primitivist gaze—"the jungle in the spotlight"⁷⁶—Dunham's performances, life, and career were deeply influential and the source of unending esteem.

I would like to thank Mary Ellen Adams for her help in making this research possible. Her generous provision of housing, transportation, as well as scholarly support in wading through innumerable boxes of archive material over the years has reflected more than friendship. My sincere thanks also go to Ramsay Burt; his work on Katherine Dunham and the scholarly exchange with him are always an inspiration.

Notes

1. "Biography," inventory of the Katherine Mary Dunham Papers 1919–1968 (9 pages, 1970), Special Collections of the Morris Library, Southern Illinois University at Carbondale, 5. Hereafter this source is cited as SCML.
2. Postwar West Germany had passed through the monetary reform (1948) and had survived the Berlin blockade and airlift (1948–49). The early 1950s marked the beginning of budding economic and social recovery, but this was still a very fragile period in German history.
3. See Hans Werner Debrunner, *Presence and Prestige: Africans in Europe: A History of Africans in Europe before 1918* (Basel: Basler Africa Bibliothek, 1979) and Peter Martin, *Schwarze Teufel, edle Mohren: Afrikaner in Geschichte und Bewußtsein der Deutschen* (Marburg: Hamburger Editionen, 2001).
4. Sander L. Gilman, *On Blackness without Blacks: Essays on the Image of the Black in Germany* (Boston: G. K. Hall, 1982).
5. Keith L. Nelson, "The Black Horror on the Rhine: Race as a Factor in Post World War I Diplomacy," *The Journal of Modern History* 42, no. 2 (1970): 618.
6. Ingrid Bauer, "Schwarzer Peter—A Historical Perspective: Henisch and the Postwar Austrian Occupation," http://www.zeitgeschichte.unilinz.ac.at/modern.history.linz/007.prffebr. 2002 (17 October 2002), 3. See also Klaus Eyferth et al., ed., *Farbige Kinder in Deutschland: Die Situation der Mischlingskinder und die Aufgabe ihrer Eingliederung* (München: Juventa Verlag, 1960), 73–74.
7. See Monroe H. Little Jr., "The Black Military Experience in Germany: From the First World War to the Present," in *Crosscurrents: African Americans, Africa, and Germany in the Modern World*, ed. David McBride et al. (Columbia, S.C.: Camden House, 1998), 192.
8. See Christine Naumann, "African American Performers and Culture in Weimar, Germany," in McBride et al., *Crosscurrents*, 100–102.
9. See Ursula Fritsch, *Tanz, Bewegung, Gesellschaft: Verluste und Chancen symbolisch-expressiven Bewegens* (Frankfurt: AFRA Verlag, 1988), 200.
10. Quoted in Little, "The Black Military Experience," 182.
11. Naumann, "African American Performers," 100.
12. Ibid., 100.
13. See Michael Meyer, "Eine musikalische Fassade für das Dritte Reich," in *"Entartete Kunst": Das Schicksal der Avantgarde im Nazi-Deutschland*, ed. Stephanie Barron (München: Hirmer Verlag, 1992), 180–81.
14. See "Die Swing-Kids," http://www.fh-lueneburg.de/u1/gym03/expo/jonatur/geistesw/zwischen/entartet/musik/swingkid.htm (15 October 2002).

15. Ibid. In his autobiography, *Neger, Neger, Schornsteinfeger!*, Hans J. Massaquoi stresses the importance of the Swing Kids in the formation of his own Afro-German identity. See Hans J. Massaquoi, *Neger, Neger, Schornsteinfeger!* (München: Knaur, 1999), 184–89.

16. In "Am Mississippi," a chapter of his memoirs, Laban describes his opinions on African American dance. He felt that blacks were not capable of inventing anything and that black dance was pure imitation because the capability of creativity was the prerogative of other races. Any dances blacks adopted were, therefore, simply grotesque: "I doubt that Negroes can ever create artistic dances. The talent to create dance, just as with the higher level of the other creative arts and sciences, seems to be the prerogative of other races. Negroes adopt our dances just like starched collars and top hats and use them in their changed form and adapted to their own emotional life." Rudolf von Laban, *Ein Leben für den Tanz: Erinnerungen* (Dresden: Carl Reißner Verlag, 1935), 168 (trans. mine). With ideas like these, Laban went from the Berlin State Opera to the Ministry for People's Education and Propaganda, where he had ample opportunity to propagate his opinions to the German people. See Lilian Karina and Marion Kant, *Tanz unter dem Hakenkreuz: Eine Dokumentation* (Berlin: Henschel, 1996), 120.

17. Ibid., 50. Joseph Goebbels exploited Germany's reputation for modern dance, but official "approval" of modern dance declined after 1936, generally preferring light ballet.

18. Judith Lynne Hanna, *Dance, Sex and Gender: Signs of Identity, Dominance, Defiance, and Desire* (Chicago: University of Chicago Press, 1988), xiii.

19. Ellen W. Goellner and Jacqueline Shea Murphy, eds., *Bodies of the Text: Dance as Theory, Literature as Dance* (New York: Rutgers University Press, 1995), 34.

20. Walther Kiaulehn, "The 'Americana' of Katherine Dunham," *Münchner Merkur*, 3 May 1954 (three pages, typed translation of original review), SCML, 1. Very few of the reviews of Katherine Dunham's German tour in 1954 have been translated into English. Occasionally, they were roughly translated for Dunham and are available in her archived scrapbook at the Missouri Historical Society in St. Louis or at Southern Illinois University, Carbondale. When such a translation was available, I have quoted it in its original form, including any irregularities in the English. Unless a translation is specifically credited, the translations are mine.

21. "Der tanzende Urwald," review of Katherine Dunham's "Caribbean Rhapsody," *Telegraf*, 18 May 1954, n.p., clipping, Katherine Dunham Collection, Missouri Historical Society, St. Louis (trans. mine). Hereafter this source is cited as MHS.

22. "Katherine Dunham: Stilisierter Urwald-Rausch," *Der Spiegel* (Berlin edition) 8, no. 21, 10 May 1954, MHS, 25 (trans. mine).

23. Ibid., 25. The date of Baker's debut in *La Revue Nègre* was 1925, not 1924 as indicated.

24. Review of Katherine Dunham's "Caribbean Rhapsody," *Abendzeitung* (no city), 6 May 1954, n.p., clipping, MHS (trans. mine).

25. "Katherine Dunhams Völkerschau," no source [Hamburg?], n.d., n.p., clipping, MHS (trans. mine).

26. Ironically, Isadora Duncan would probably have been appalled at the comparison, clearly separating her style from the "primitivism" of American dance. When writing of the dance of America, she proclaims it "monstrous that anyone should believe that the jazz rhythm expresses America. Jazz rhythm expresses the primitive savage." Furthermore, she describes the Charleston as "tottering ape-like convulsions" and insists that American dance will have nothing in it of the "inane coquetry of the ballet, or the sensual convulsion of the negro [*sic*]. It will be clean." Quoted in Amy Koritz, *Gendering Bodies/Performing Art: Dance and Literature in Early Twentieth-Century British Culture* (Ann Arbor: University of Michigan Press, 1995), 52.

27. *Die Große Star Parade*, film directed by Paul Martin (West Germany: private collection, 1954). The footage shot for this film is documented in detail in the agreements and notes contained in "Conditions for Filming Extracts from 'Tropics,' 'Shoro No. 1,' and 'Shango,'" Munich, 20 June 1954, SCML, and "Decisions about the Movie Discussed at Dinner between Dunham and the Director," Munich, 23 June 1954, SCML. I have been unable to determine the footage actually used in Dunham's uncredited appearance because the film is currently unavailable except in private collections. For general information on this film, see Micaela Jary, *Traumfabriken made in Germany: Die Geschichte des deutschen Nachkriegsfilms 1945–1960* (Berlin: Edition Q, 1993), 131.

28. *Jitterbug Turnier—Negertrommler, Posaune, Jitterbugtänzer auf der Tanzfläche,* Hamburg, 1954, Deutsche Wochenschau GmbH, Filmarchiv Hamburg, film WIB 20/9, 1 min., 40 sec. (trans. mine).
29. *Jazz Konzert. Es singt Ella Fitzgerald, "On the Sunny Side." Am Klavier spielt Oscar Peterson. Am Schlagzeug Gene Krupa,* Hamburg, 1954, Deutsche Wochenschau GmbH, Filmarchiv Hamburg, NDW 162/13, 1 min., 40 sec.
30. *Marian Anderson singt vor Münchner Studenten Schubert Lied,* München, 1954, Deutsche Wochenschau GmbH, Filmarchiv Hamburg, WIF 263/4, 1 min. 10 sec.
31. *Ankunft Louis Armstrong—In Flugzeugtür steht Louis Armstrong mit kleinem Jungen, der Trompete bläst,* Düsseldorf, 1954, Deutsche Wochenschau GmbH, Filmarchiv Hamburg, WIB 16/6, 40 sec.
32. *Adieu Josephine—100 Weisenkinder als Gäste von Josephine Baker,* Hamburg, 1954, Deutsche Wochenschau GmbH, Filmarchiv Hamburg, UFA 68/10, 1 min., 40 sec.
33. *Auftritt von Katherine Dunham mit karibischer Tanzgruppe. Paris: Negertanzgruppe mit Trommlern, Tänzerinnen und Tänzern,* Paris, 1954, Deutsche Wochenschau GmbH, Filmarchiv Hamburg, NDW 49/9, 35 sec. (trans. mine).
34. *Auftritt mit karibischer Tanzgruppe bei Deutschlandtournee,* Frankfurt, 1954, Deutsche Wochenschau GmbH, Filmarchiv Hamburg, NDW 222/9, 1 min., 5 sec.
35. Kiaulehn, "The 'Americana' of Katherine Dunham," 1.
36. For a discussion of the relationship of Dunham and Zora Neale Hurston in the area of Caribbean anthropology, see my "An Island Occupied: The U.S. Marine Occupation of Haiti in Zora Neale Hurston's *Tell My Horse* and Katherine Dunham's *Island Possessed,*" in *Holding Their Own: Perspectives on the Multi-Ethnic Literatures of the United States,* ed. Dorothea Fischer-Hornung and Heike Raphael-Hernandez (Tübingen: Stauffenburg, 2000), 153–68.
37. Dunham's research on Haitian Dance was published as Katherine Dunham, *The Dances of Haiti* (Los Angeles: University of California at Los Angeles Press, 1983), as revisions of "Las Danzas di Haiti," *Acta Anthropologica* 2, no. 4 (no city, Mexico: 1947), and "Les Danses de Haiti" (Paris: Fasquel Press, 1957). She had been studying with Robert Redfield at the University of Chicago for her M.A. and had considered completing her degree with Melville Herskovits at Northwestern University. Herskovits felt that he could not supervise her work unless she transferred to his institution, but Dunham had performance commitments in Chicago. She chose the stage and remained in Chicago rather than move to Northwestern University. He did help her for several months to develop the techniques required for field study on a Rosenwald Foundation grant and was very interested in her work on dance anthropology. See Melville Herskovits, correspondence with Katherine Dunham and Robert Redfield, January–May 1937, The Melville J. Herskovits Files, Deering Library, Northwestern University Archives, Evanston, Illinois. In 1936, Herskovits had provided Dunham with letters of introduction to various persons in Haiti, including Jean Price Mars, the noted Haitian anthropologist. In 1937, however, Dunham was forced to make a choice between her commitment to performance or to academia: "I shall concentrate a while on the dance, hoping for field work in this connection in some way. Frankly, I could be made into a good field worker and shouldn't be forever lost to science." ("Letter to Melville J. Herskovits," 5 May 1937, Melville Herskovits Files.) She chose the stage but continued to publish and lecture throughout her career.
38. Richard Buckle, *Katherine Dunham: Her Dancers, Singers, Musicians* (London: Ballet Publications, 1949), ix–x.
39. See Katherine Dunham, *Island Possessed* [1969] (Chicago: University of Chicago Press, 1994), 239.
40. Franz Vilsmeier, "Letter to Katherine Dunham," 30 April 1954 (1 page), SCML.
41. What here may seem like a racist reduction of Haitian dance to athletics is rather a reflection of the continuing difficulty in academia of categorizing dance into an aesthetic rather than a physical education activity. Ever since the opening of the Bennington School of Dance at Bennington College in 1934, dance has, until recently, often been taught in school as part of gym classes. The text-centered disciplines at universities long viewed dance as "unintellectual, intuitive, and uncritically expressive" (Goellner and Murphy, *Bodies of the Text,* 3).

42. Ramsay Burt points out the difficulties American critics had with Dunham both as an intellectual and a frankly sexual dancer. See Ramsay Burt, "Katherine Dunham's *Rite de Passage*:
Censorship and Sexuality," in *EmBODYing Liberation: The Black Body in American Dance*,
ed. Dorothea Fischer-Hornung and Alison Goeller (Hamburg: LIT Verlag, 2001), 79–89.
43. "Katherine Dunham: Stilisierter Urwald-Rausch," 27 (trans. mine).
44. Ibid., 27 (trans. mine).
45. Veve Clark quoted in Ramsay Burt, "Katherine Dunham's Floating Island of Negritude: The
Katherine Dunham Dance Company in London and Paris in the Late 1940s and Early
1950s," forthcoming.
46. "Katherine Dunham: Stilisierter Urwald-Rausch," 27 (trans. mine).
47. Since Dunham's purchase of Habitation LeClerc in 1949, it has functioned as various times
as a culture center, dance training center, hospital and feeding station, and tourist retreat.
According to Jeanelle Stovall (personal conversation, 12 April 2001), it is still in Dunham's
possession, but it has been taken over by squatters.
48. "Katherine Dunham: Stilisierter Urwald-Rausch," 25–27 (trans. mine).
49. "Menschlich gesehen: Tanzende Professorin," *Bild Zeitung*, 26 May 1954, n.p., clipping, MHS
(trans. mine).
50. "Interview mit Katherine Dunham: Tänzerin und Dr. phil.," *Welt am Sonntag*, 30 May 1954,
clipping, MHS (trans. mine), 5. The Ph.D. idea is still in circulation to date; the confusion
probably results from the fact that she received a Ph.B. from the University of Chicago in
1936. http://www-news.uchicago.edu/resources/alumni/ (15 September 2002). Her "pro-
fessorship at Yale" was described as follows on the dust jacket of *Journey to Accompong*:
"While Katherine Dunham was appearing in 'Cabin in the Sky' she spent a Sunday evening
at the Yale University Graduate School, delivering a lecture and demonstration to the
Anthropology Club." See Katherine Dunham, *Journey to Accompong* (New York: Henry
Holt, 1946), dustjacket. In Great Britain, *The Sphere* (16 October 1948) had published photographs of Dunham lecturing at the Royal Anthropological Institute at University College,
London; see Burt, "Katherine Dunham's Floating Island of Negritude."
51. "Der Urwald tanzt. Katherine Dunham und ihr berühmtes Negerballett," review of Katherine Dunham's "Caribbean Rhapsody," *Der Mittag* (Munich), 13 May 1954, n.p., MHS.
52. "Mambo-Rhythmen am Canal Grande," photo feature on film *Mambo*, source unknown,
n.d., n.p., clipping, MHS. For an extensive study of the film *Mambo*, see my "The Body Possessed: Katherine Dunham Dance Technique in *Mambo*," in Fischer-Hornung and Goeller,
EmBODYing Liberation: The Black Body in American Dance, 91–112.
53. "Menschlich gesehen: Tanzende Professorin," n.p.
54. "Die barfüßigen Wundertänzer: Katherine Dunham im Titania Palast," review of Katherine
Dunham's "Caribbean Rhapsody," *Berliner Zeitung*, 17 May 1954, n.p., clipping, MHS (trans.
mine).
55. "Der Urwald tanzt." The dancers were almost exclusively from the United States, but most
reviews locate them as coming from the Caribbean. This is either intentional to underline
the program's authenticity or it simply reflects sloppy journalism.
56. Dr. B., review of Katherine Dunham's "Caribbean Rhapsody," n.d., n.p., clipping, MHS
(trans. mine).
57. Wolfgang Schlüter, "Großer Rausch aus Tanz und Farbe: Katherine Dunham—Gastspiel im
Theater am Aegi Hannover," *Norddeutsche Zeitung*, 12/13 June 1954, n.p., clipping, MHS
(trans. mine).
58. There was a general concern in postwar Germany about the reconstruction of prewar gender roles and family structures. The war had made broken men of many German males,
and the absence of these men during the war years had forced women to develop a high degree of independence. A return to normalcy meant a return to earlier gender roles; see Alan
Swensen, review of Heide Fehrenbach's *Cinema in Democratizing Germany: Recruiting National Identity After Hitler*, http://www.colgate.edu/scene/nov1995/authors.html (9 September 2002). The military occupation of both countries, West Germany and Haiti, by U.S.
troops can be seen as an additional parallel in the situation of the two countries.
59. Kiaulehn, "The 'Americana' of Katherine Dunham," 1.
60. "Karibische Rhapsodie," review of Katherine Dunham's "Caribbean Rhapsody," [Hamburg?]
n.d., n.p., clipping, MHS (trans. mine).
61. "Die barfüßigen Wundertänzer," n.p.

62. "Der Urwald tanzt," n.p.
63. "Katherine Dunham: Stilisierter Urwald-Rausch," 25.
64. Ibid., 25.
65. Ibid., 27.
66. Schlüter, "Großer Rausch," n.p.
67. "Interview mit Katherine Dunham: Tänzerin und Dr. phil," 5.
68. Eyferth et al., ed., *Farbige Kinder in Deutschland*, 36.
69. Ibid., 109.
70. "Liebe? Kommt nicht in Frage!," *Heim und Welt*, n.d., clipping, MHS (trans. mine), 13.
71. "Interview mit Katherine Dunham: Tänzerin und Dr. phil," 5.
72. "Liebe? Kommt nicht in Frage!," 13.
73. Elizabeth Willer, "Letter to Katherine Dunham," 19 June 1954 (2 pages), SCML. The quotes that follow in the next two paragraphs all refer to this source.
74. This would mean that her first child was born in 1949, several years after the first large wave of births of mixed-race children in 1946. An estimated 1,112 Afro-German children were born in the first year after the war ended, dropping to half that number in the following year. By 1949, the birth rate was estimated at 315. See R. Sieg, "Mischlingskinder in Westdeutschland. Eine anthropologische Studie an farbigen Heimkindern," in *Festschrift für Frédéric Falkenburger*, ed. W. Busanny-Caspari et al. (Baden-Baden: Verlag für Kunst und Wissenschaft, 1955), 19.
75. Rudolf Riedler, "Jungle in the Spotlight: Dr. Dunham Dances Exotically," translation of interview, *Landeszeitung* (Munich) n.p., n.d., SCML.
76. Ibid., n.p.

4
Black Music, White Freedom
Times and Spaces of Jazz Countercultures in the USSR

IRINA NOVIKOVA

"Discussion of jazz must begin, like all historical analyses of society under modern capitalism, with technology and business: in this instance the business of supplying the leisure and entertainment of the increasingly urban masses of the lower and middle classes."[1] Eric Hobsbawm's idea of technology and business, however, does not seem to provide the most promising approach to an historical analysis of jazz under socialism. Yet, what could be a beginning in the discussion of jazz as a historical analysis under socialism? The system celebrated perpetuation of its cultural domain with few elements of technology and no entrepreneurship, leisure and entertainment being provided by state-owned institutions in charge of developing socialist aesthetic tastes among the masses. Jazz, however, was largely subversive with regard to those institutions and advanced to carve out its own countercultural chronotope, with black music becoming an expression of yearnings for white freedom in the USSR and its satellite countries.

The very practices and experiences of jazz in the former USSR as counterculture—a form of musical expression that on many levels created a borderless and nonhierarchical community—were conceptualized as a unifying, inclusive, border- and boundary-dissolving phenomenon, a revolution "of their own," a grassroots revolution in the world of the Cold War. The call-and-response technique of jazz was a revelation to enjoy: Shared improvisations

73

of melodies became shared freedom of bodies. Apart from stylistic influences on different musicians and schools in the USSR, jazz became a distinct countercultural space of resistance and dissent in which the principles of polyrhythm, spontaneity, and improvisation became expressions of political counterpoint and "underground" social geography across constructed political borders and ethnosocial boundaries. The Soviet postwar jazz counterculture enabled people to challenge prevailing cultural and political stereotypes by representing themselves as complex subjects with multiple and contradictory experiences.

Jazz arrived in the Soviet Russia of the 1920s with the first tours of black American jazz bands, such as the Frank Witers Collective in 1926 or Sam Wooding with his Chocolate Kiddies. By the late 1980s, jazz had webbed the whole Soviet cultural territory; jazz had turned into a multirooted and rhizomic process that countered the pressure of power and ideology in the Soviet cultural context.

Jazz came into the Soviet territories in very diverse ways—to Riga and Tallinn—via the Berlin and Paris cultures of cabarets and varieties, and by way of famous orchestras, such as those previously mentioned and Oleg Lundstrem's well-known orchestra. Later, jazz traveled in films that were coming as "trophy" shows that introduced the Soviet public to bands such as Glenn Miller's orchestra. Jazz in the USSR cannot be tracked down to singular genre origins.

These direct influences were interrupted during the Stalinist period when jazz was stigmatized as "music of spiritual poverty" and "music in the service of reactionary forces." In the 1950s, not a single first-rank international jazz star performed in the Soviet Union, and not a single Soviet jazz musician was permitted to travel abroad to hear leading foreign jazzmen. "We didn't even know what jazz musicians looked like," recalled saxophonist Roman Kunsman.[2] Paradoxically, during the same time, there were attempts to apply jazz to the Soviet politics of race and class and to politically instrumentalize jazz as music of the oppressed black race in the American South. Jazz was seen as an explicit example of the authenticity of black self-expression in a capitalist system that discriminated again African Americans. The constraint strategy toward jazz was lifted after Stalin's death.[3]

The development of Soviet jazz toward an expression of counterculture is very much connected to its perceived function of being an African American expression of protest and resistance. Its African American cultural roots have always been acknowledged.[4] Yet, Soviet jazz theorists argued that jazz could only develop in the United States because of specific African American oppression and suffering in U.S. history. Sergei Belichenko, for example, asserted that jazz is alien to African folk music and could be engendered only in the situation of suffering, oppression, and resistance of the black race on the alien continent. Suffering, alienation, and resistance, thus, were singled out of their "racial" context as the universal emotional and psychological continuum of jazz. He writes:

> MY NATIONALITY IS MUSICIAN! Jazz is beyond any nationality, beyond any religiosity and beyond any social belonging! Jazz is beyond race! JAZZ is the music of MEN! Apart from jazz vocal singing, under women's domination, there are very few (in comparison with rock music) sexual minorities. Jazz does not know homosexuals! Jazz was created, organized and promoted by men although it is very feminine as feelings prevail most often in jazz. Particularly you can hear this in the early forms of jazz.[5]

Spontaneity, complexity of rhythmic structures, and corporeality were hardly seen as African traits but most probably as something inherent in humans that was revealed to African Americans under the conditions of repression. Thus, African American jazz expressions became in Soviet perspective expressions of creativity, of access to each other in the "Eden" of jazz, of reclamation of one's body, of purification from "other" unnatural conditions of existence. The Soviet developing jazz community, in proselytizing such jazz moments as improvisation, "zero" standardization, "zero" synchronization, decentralization, open community of music creation in a concert hall, and "zero" commodification, turned jazz into an alternative existential vision of "order born out of chaos." In other words, the perceived shared "musical vernacular" that was allowed to express borderlessness of musical imagination and of feelings in transcending the rigidity of canons and norms in Soviet musical theory and academy became symbols for "tonal resistances."[6] Free expressions in a polyperformance meant freedom from a repressive society. In his online memoirs, Sabidjan Kurmaev describes this special perspective: "Jazz is created by non-conformists as an expression of inadequacy between human inner conditions and what they see around. I thought that jazz is created by special people, for special people. A jazz person is a character living through a constant resistance of the society to his aspirations."[7] And Sergei Belichenko adds up some elements into this portrayal: "The pedestal of a jazz musician is not high. In a common-sense view, he is an absolutely abnormal man, inclined to do weird things, playing a strange music, speaking too much about this music, inclined to sins, very peculiar in communication, sensuous—in short, an ALIEN!"[8]

Thus, a space of pleasure in the world of permission/ban, jazz triumphed as music for intellectuals more than as a music for dancing. Jazz became "social music for many young people" in urban areas and—particularly—for students.[9] What was seen and heard in jazz sessions was the moment of repressed freedom of expression being overcome by music and thereby experiencing multiple and shared routes into a bigger world. Oleg Stepurko remembers: "It was also important because it happened in the horrible years when the communist pressure 'erased' any individuality, when an individual view upon the world was a crime. Jazzmen were a special tribe with its own myths, language and even clothes. . . . Jazz at those times was not a music style, but a way of survival in the Soviet desert."[10] What Burton Peretti points out for jazz culture in general was also very true for the sedimentation of the jazz counterculture in the USSR:

> Jazz—popular thought has it—created both a music and *a culture*, a way of life differing from the root culture and the dominant society that now surrounded it. Thus culture is thought to be the social equivalent of the music, a jiving, swinging, improvisatory mode of existence, as funky in expression as a good horn is in timbre, as collegial as a combo in full cry. After 1940, social scientists and others considered jazz a self-consciously *deviant* subculture, cradling angry young men who wanted to be despised by the squares around them. [11]

Sabidjan Kurmaev, one of the 1960s' Soviet angry young jazzmen, "translated" with a romantic stance Peretti's theoretical approach into Soviet sociopolitical reality by pointing to the controversy between the homogenizing pressures of the system and the uniqueness of a creating personality:

> Impossibility of victory in everyday opposition to "public prescriptions" shifts the way to freedom into the abstract world of sounds. . . . With the progress of jazz, the flight of spirit is more and more liberated—improvisation and the sense of getting liberated from the quanted time—swing. Jazz can be defined not only by privileged personalities, but every jazz person has his own vision of jazz. . . . The more definitions are given, the more motley the mosaic of opinions irreducible to a unifying denominator. In other words, in order to "understand" jazz, one has to live a jazz life.[12]

Aleksei Batashev, a well-known jazz theorist and historian in the USSR, echoes Kurmaev's argument on jazz as an alternative social vision of freedom beyond "translation necessary": "Jazz is a model of the world where everything is based on interaction, where there is space, but not commodity, where a person speaks for himself and is responsible for himself. Free music for free people. Jazz is hated by any enemies of freedom."[13]

The principle of "free music for free people" was a direct challenge to the ideologically groomed principles of classical music, such as division into producers and consumers, standardization (orchestra structure, unified teachable principles, genre hierarchy), commercialized maximalization of performances (stadium shows), centralization of music institutions in Moscow, and so on. All these principles were considered both as specific to the Soviet ideological climate regarding culture, and as symptomatic of a global need and desire for music objectification. Classical music in the Soviet politics of musical tastes called for dictation of boundaries, rules, and canons, imperative for maintaining ideology's social and cultural role "as a mode of dominance in sustaining the structure of the status quo."[14] Resistance to musical "mainstream" principles was a central component of a personal resistance to political and ideological depersonification in the USSR. "When one has to act not in compliance with instructions, but according to his own understanding, jazz is the music of those who are used to thinking and taking decisions by themselves,"[15] writes Batashev. Improvisation and syncopation—which demands from musicians to take patterns that are even and regular and break them up, make them uneven, and put accents in unexpected places—were the formal elements of jazz, counter to the very principles of socialist realism and canons of musical theory. The element of improvisation was particularly unacceptable in the ideologists' circles of Soviet theorists. As Batashev recalls in his *Music of Life*: "I remember the debates of the 1950s among our top composers. 'You say—improvisation? A composer is in the torture of creating music at home, and you mean that it is created directly here, on stage, one-two-three, and it is ready? Isn't it shameful to take your experiments and impromptus into the public arena?'"[16] The official and conservative Union of Soviet Composers began to marginalize composers who became part of the jazz musical world, such as Edison Denisov, Alfred Schnittke, and Sofia Gubaidullina in Leningrad.

This type of music—experimental, improvisational, and audience-involving—was counter to the production of so-called national opera traditions—socialist, even, and regular—in the Soviet politics of music. Musical developments in every single Soviet republic were "packaged" politically as progressive achievements en route from their authentic folk epics to manifestations of their authentic socialist-modernized spirituality in the sublime genre of opera. Socialist operas were ambiguously ideologized from a former mode of elite art production into an art object of mass cultural consumption because now every worker in socialism was able to understand the sublime in this superior art form of communicating emotions.

In its role and meaning of the "free music for free people," jazz gradually became a politically significant component of youth culture and intelligentsia culture that thoroughly enjoyed the shared "musical vernacular." It marked a distinct cultural belonging and self-identification for Soviet intelligentsia and its "underground" or "second life" in jazz, which saw the principles of creative freedom and self-expressionist spontaneity opposed to the determinist spirit that saturated official cultural spaces. Jazz members (jazz fans, jazz composers, jazz critics, and so on) became aware of the power of self-awareness and their own relatively peripheral, but potentially explosive, positions within the Soviet context. In such a context, jazz as one expression of the oppressed black American race became an existential metaphor of the "other," of disparate cultural identity, resistance, protest, diversity, and creative empowerment. Jazz became a key idiom of and a means to freedom. Hobsbawm emphasizes that "the 1960s jazz avant-garde was consciously and politically black, as no previous generation of black jazzmen had been, though 'The Jazz Scene' [had] already noted the links between jazz experimentation and black consciousness. . . . Political consciousness continued to link the avant-garde to the mass of the American black people and its musical traditions, and therefore provided a possible way back to the mainstream of jazz."[17] Historical and contemporary experiences of black people in the United States, like slavery and discrimination, became metaphors for the "oppression" of the free creative spirit by the rigid limits of the Soviet ideology and politics of personality/voice/music. The American Civil Rights Movement was not an unknown process to Soviet people. In this sense, the African American struggle for civil rights received a symbolic meaning in the Soviet jazz world, yet a different one than in the United States—a struggle against borders and constraints rather than one for equal rights.

A political function of Soviet official culture was to regulate and control leisure time, or free time, and private activities of Soviet people in general. In addition to ideological objections against jazz as a musical expression, official governmental politics heavily objected to jazz as a means of cultural rejection of regulation of private life. Nothing was ideologically wrong with lyrics, but what was "wrong" was freedom of leisure time and the growing awareness of privacy and choice. Leisure time became central to the self-identification of a jazz musician, theorist, fan, or collector; belonging to jazz culture meant to recreate his/her cultural identity him/herself, thus challenging the unified political cultural identity of official regulation. In these spaces, leisure time, or in Russian, "free time," was literally becoming a chance for emotional and spiritual freedom and was starting to create for the Soviet jazz communities what Stuart Hall has called "identity-in-becoming."[18] Jazz, as a cultural space of individual leisure time shared with kindred spirits, carried a meaning of stepping into the dissent space of the underground production of carbon copies of jazz music and of secret listening to jazz programs of "Voice of America." A typical social portrayal of such a "leisure time" jazz person would be someone who was an engineer during working time (work was a legally binding obligation of a Soviet citizen; otherwise, s/he became "tuneyadets" like Joseph Brodsky) who turned into a jazz musician or theorist or fan or collector during his or her leisure time. A typical example would be Yuri Vermenich, a professional engineer, who founded the jazz club in the Russian city

Voronezh. He is typical of the idea to found "from below," to found in the spirit of grassroots movements. Sergei Belichenko, who himself turned from a profitable career as a gynecologist to the thorny way of a jazz musician, writes that the first Soviet jazzmen were not professionals, indeed, but young people, students: "Many pioneers of Soviet jazz such as Georgii Garanian and Aleksei Kozlov were students of institutions other than music academies. They were future engineers, scientists, doctors—creative intelligentsia."[19] They constituted the major group in this Soviet countercultural jazz world, calling themselves proudly the "second culture."

In this counterculture or "second culture," all the rules of official cultural regulation were ignored. Alex Kan remembers somewhat nostalgically:

> The "second culture," as we proudly called ourselves in those days, functioned with its own rules and norms and managed even to create an infrastructure of its own, complete with festivals, concerts, theater performances, film screenings, literature, art, film and music journals, *samizdat* and *magizdat*. If *samizdat* stood mostly for banned books, painstakingly multiplied on carbon copies paper with the help of a regular typewriter, *magizdat*—from *magnitofon*, a tape recorder, meant tape copies of subversive protest songs and later rock. Jazz existed somewhere in between—a complete outcast barely two decades earlier, in the minds of many it still indiscriminately bore an image of a liberating spirit, with improvisation—a musical metaphor for freedom—at the heart of it.[20]

Because no tours of major foreign jazz bands were sponsored, technology advanced the opportunities of the talented young people to catch melodies and rhythms from records by memory. Technology became indeed "guilty" for the gradual penetration of jazz into the USSR as Belichenko recalls: "In the USSR the development and penetration of jazz became possible only because of records. Until 1970 there had been no jazz manuals (except for Mehigan), and there were no pedagogical resources. . . . The main manual was a tape recorder."[21]

One can hear again and again these personal stories of individuals like Boris Kuznetsov and their clever attempts to meet jazz through technology:

> At a school dance party I heard an accordion player. He was playing fox-trot, and I recognised the melodies that I had heard in Kharbin. To play like that man, I joined a music school but they did not teach jazz there, so I quit it quickly. By that time my elder brother, a fan of radio technology, had made up his own radio-receiver. So, we spent hours by catching waves, and once heard a very low voice in a foreign language, and a trumpet was playing powerfully. I was enchanted and I decided that I would play a trumpet. That was of course a superb Louis Armstrong![22]

During the whole period of jazz's countercultural development, official cultural attempts to appropriate jazz existed. Yet, these commodification attempts were not a threat to the counterculture of those times. On the contrary, in its countercultural meaning, jazz became a symbol of internal dissent in a sort of a clever and humorous game—one only had to know how to play the rules of socialist realism. For example, during the 'thaw' period of the late 1950s to early 1960s, jazz became available to larger audiences in popular lectures about jazz, but only under the auspices of the political and ideological agenda "Freedom to Africa!" Jazz lectures could take place either at the Institute of World Literature, or they could be hosted for more private audiences, or even at Komsomol meetings as long as they dealt with jazz as an ideological issue or a means ostensibly to support the official agenda. In Riga, for example, every time Leonid Nidbal'skii, a chair of the Riga jazz club, asked Komsomol authorities for financial support, he couched his request in an ideological framework: "Young people will go to our jazz club where they will be introduced to authentic jazz, and this will be the way to real classical music, away from detrimental rock."[23] As Kurmaev recalls, in the 1970s, the ideological argument had financial "stuffing." Komsomol committees obtained a right to "allocated means"; thus, they could sell their tickets for a concert or a series of concerts.[24] Soviet officialdom wanted to attract young people into its cultural domain, and state concert-tour organizations even financially profited from these attempts. Thus, it became possible for the jazz "diaspora" to reappropriate cultural hegemonic space by playing in small clubs, at private parties, at schools, in Komsomol clubs, and even at army bases—all over the USSR.

Many government-organized events took this turn of official jazz appropriation turned upside down as it was the case with the Sixth World Youth Festival in Moscow in July 1957, which hosted jazz musicians from both sides of the Iron Curtain. The festival—as a sign of political "thaw"— had to demonstrate the openness of the USSR and, at the same time, the principles of Soviet cultural superiority, including the sphere of music. However, thousands of Soviet young people participating in the festival reacted to the immediacy of time and pleasure. Both moments—immediacy and pleasure—"detracted" younger generations, in the official views, from the "pleasure" of being instrumental and being permitted to take on the identity of a builder of the happy new world. The festival's impact was seminal in carving out jazz spaces for youth and intellectual cultures to articulate a newly assertive stance of freedom and openness as well as a means of individual identification.

Only because of this official governmental appropriation "turned upside down"—official jazz appropriation reclaimed by countercultural reappropriation as a clever, but hidden game—was it possible that jazz culture could even be found in socialist cultural institutions. For example, in the 1970s and 1980s, many jazz festivals, concerts, and sessions usually took place in so-called Houses of Culture, which were regional district

Houses of Culture for specific professions, such as teachers or medical workers or the militia or even the KGB. Or, as another example shows, an official publishing agency, Muzgiz, published books on jazz history and jazz theory. In addition, official conferences on jazz, for example the Novosibirsk symposium on improvisation, took place and contributed to a proliferation of jazz studies and jazz studios. Jazz fans translated texts of jazz theory and studies into Russian, thus showing a special meaning of jazz in the USSR, in one of the first books, *Black Music, White Freedom* by Efim Barban in 1977.[25]

As I have already demonstrated, official classical demands of music stood in contrast to jazz's idea of individualism and freedom of choice. Hobsbawm characterized jazz as a folk art of the people and counterposed it to the elite art of bourgeoisie. For Soviet officially enforced and regulated cultural politics, the "ethnic" dimension had indeed been discovered for ideological purposes: Folk art of the different peoples of the USSR was portrayed as the "art from below" being in harmony with the "art from above," thus sanctifying official cultural politics. Jazz's idea of individual choice of representation was not an option for the officially described "ethnic inclusion." A Kazakh man could not have been imagined without his "authentic" string instrument, or a Latvian woman could not have been imagined without hers. During official pompous concerts or big festival events, ideological commodification of folkness in which one could a priori expect what an Ukrainian ensemble would dance on stage or what a Georgian singing group would sing became performances of representation of the Soviet nation, with its hierarchies of ethnicity and race. Folk dance ensembles, folk song groups, and so on, were an ideological means of social control of nations in the development of their "authentic" folk traditions. As one can easily understand, required politically correct integration of "ethnicity" into jazz compositions and performances was met with resistance, and jazz's individualism turned to the "ethnic dimension" in a rather politically incorrect way. For example, jazz experimentation with ethnic melodies and even with the "revival" of alternative and "authentic ethnicity" (such as Andrei Tovmasyan's "Mister Great Novgorod," the title referring to authentic, pure roots of Russia in Novgorod medieval society, lost historically to the Moscow/St. Petersburg rule) curiously exposed the ambivalence of resistance. And jazz composers and performers from Trans-Caucasian and Asian Soviet republics produced compositions that integrated ethnic themes and melodies in their arrangements without making them sound folkloric. In retrospect, I would claim that this celebration of "alternative essence" in the world of jazz musicians in different Soviet republics, seen as "ethnic threatening" by official policy, became a constitutive element of cultural legitimation in postsocialist political hierarchies and national independence desires.

By deconstructing the dominant Soviet political discourse of "center/margin," jazz, in its multiple sedimentations of "countercultural diaspora" countered—not unsuccessfully—any official attempts to collude with the process of political commodification of art and music. This "center/margin" deconstruction also became important for another geographical hierarchy. Official Soviet ideology saw the USSR as occupying a very hegemonic stance in political and cultural affairs; therefore, it served as the "donor" to its brother countries. However, in the jazz counterculture movement, the "recipient" status was turned around or "equalized," thus ironically executing in reality the otherwise just rhetorical and theoretical principles of socialist art. In its "musical vernacular," jazz created the geography of a countercultural "diaspora" in which the dominant Soviet political discourse of "center-margin" was deconstructed by proclaiming itself as an "equal-rights" jazz nation across Eastern European borders. Thus, member countries in the socialist "camp," such as Poland, Czechoslovakia, East Germany, or Hungary, provided themselves significant cultural "donations." Alex Kan recalls that "it was exactly through the Czechoslovakian pop and jazz magazine *Melodie* that I first learned about the existence of Kvadrat Jazz Club in Leningrad and a certain saxophonist Anatoly Vapirov who, according to *Melodie*, played ambitious new music."[26]

But even inside the USSR, the hegemonic "center/margin" claim was turned around by countercultural jazz. Soviet jazz cultures saw themselves as cultures of a "jazz nation," overcoming hegemonic "Moscow" and creating its diasporic centers, such as Khabarovsk, Tallinn, Riga, Vilnius, Yerevan, Donetsk, Leningrad, Arkhangelsk, or Novosibirsk, in the middle of Siberia, which "might seem a weird geographic location for decadent Western music, but with Akademgorodok—its academic and intellectual suburb—a remote Siberian city boasted intellectual, political and cultural intensity as strong as anywhere in the country. It was in Novosibirsk in the spring of 1978 that the first New Jazz Symposium was organized by Sergei Belichenko."[27] In this turned-around geography of jazz counterculture, the Baltic jazz developments, for example, present a specific case of political-cultural dissent. In the Baltic republics, the continuity of jazz cultures had not been dramatically disrupted by the events of World War II. In addition, the Baltics, and in particular, Estonia, saw themselves and were glad to be seen by others in the USSR as the "West" with a half-open window to Europe. In Estonia, jazz developed into a "highly intellectualised"[28] form and attracted elite musicians and composers such as Aarvo Part and others. Moscow jazz people were amazed at the Riga musician Vadim Vyadro's experiments with twelve-tone jazz. Jazz culture in the Baltics did not fall victim to official bans of jazz to the extent of Moscow and Leningrad "in the years when saxophonists were having their instruments taken from them,"[29] and this might also explain why later, in Riga, "as elsewhere in the Baltics, the distinctions between styles were more fluid, less militant, than in Moscow."[30]

As I have argued, jazz in the USSR was perceived as a cultural coup. Jazz as an alternative idiom of countercultural expansionism—expansionism of freedom, individuality, and creativity—was rewritten into a metaphor of an alternative dream of freedom. Therefore, jazz in the USSR can be viewed as one form of civil disobedience. However, it is hard to disagree with Kurmaev's argument that, without its countercultural stance, the post-Soviet jazz scene is languishing today:

> With a collapse of the USSR, a jazz movement was over as the necessity to struggle and overcome ideological constraints—an important part of the Soviet cultural life—dissolved. No Comsomol that could order rooms allocated for jazz musicians in hotels, or give them concert halls during tours for free. . . . Opportunities to enjoy one's favourite music has increased, but there is a considerable financial limit. Jazz audience is still here, but its number has significantly decreased—some have turned into professionals, some are unable either to buy a ticket for a concert or to go to a festival in another city.[31]

How jazz began to survive in a society under late modern capitalism—now "with technology" available, but with the "business of supplying the leisure and entertainment of the increasingly urban masses of the lower and middle classes,"[32] as Hobsbawn's idea at the beginning of my essay calls for—is already another story.

Notes

1. Eric Hobsbawm, *Uncommon People: Resistance, Rebellion, Jazz* (London, New York: Weidenfeld & Nicolson/New Press, 1998), 265.
2. Frederick S. Starr, *Red and Hot: The Fate of Jazz in the Soviet Union 1917–1980* (New York: Oxford University Press, 1983), 259.
3. See the detailed account of the post-Stalin jazz history in Starr, *Red and Hot*.
4. See, for example, Efim Barban, www.downbeat.ru/opinion/opinion02120401.asp (24 January 2003).
5. Sergei Belichenko, "A True History of Jazz in Russia Has Not Been Written Yet!," www.lebed.com/art2046.htm (23 January 2003). Translation mine.
6. Oleg Stepurko, "Jazz Sketches," www.jazz.ru/books/stories/9.htm (23 January 2003). Translation mine.
7. Sabidjan Kurmaev, "Jazz—Music of the Twentieth Century," www.lebed.com/art2392.htm (23 January 2003). Translation mine.
8. Belichenko, "True Story," translation mine.
9. Starr, *Red and Hot*, 268.
10. Stepurko, "Jazz Sketches," translation mine.
11. Burton W. Peretti, *Creation of Jazz Music, Race and Culture in Urban America* (Urbana: University of Illinois Press, 1992), 120.

12. Kurmaev, "Jazz," translation mine.
13. Aleksei Batashev, "Music of Life," balkaria.narod.ru/people/alexeybatashev/music.htm (24 January 2003). Translation mine.
14. Edward W. Said, *Musical Elaborations* (New York: Columbia University Press, 1991), 57.
15. Batashev, "Music of Life," translation mine.
16. Ibid, translation mine.
17. Hobsbawm, *Uncommon People*, 286.
18. Stuart Hall, "Cultural Identity and Cinematic Representation," in *Black British Cultural Studies: A Reader*, ed. Houston Baker Jr., Manthia Diawara, and Ruth Lindeborg (Chicago: University of Chicago Press, 1996), 213.
19. Belichenko, "True History," translation mine.
20. Alex Kan, "Golden Years of Soviet Jazz: A Brief History of New Improvised Music in Russia," www.jazz.ru/books/default.htm (23 January 2003).
21. Belichenko, "True Story," translation mine.
22. Boris Kuznetsov, "From Fox-trot and Harmonica to Drumming," www.jazz.ru/books/stories/5.htm (23 January 2003). Translation mine.
23. Kurmaev, "Jazz," translation mine.
24. Ibid., translation mine.
25. Efim Barban, *Black Music, White Freedom: Music and Perceptions of New Jazz* (Leningrad: samizdat, 1977). *samizdat* stood mostly for banned books, painstakingly multiplied on carbon copies paper with the help of a regular typewriter.
26. Kan, "Golden Years."
27. Ibid.
28. Starr, *Red and Hot*, 256.
29. Ibid., 230.
30. Ibid., 256.
31. Kurmaev, "Jazz," translation mine.
32. Hobsbawm, *Uncommon People*, 265.

PART II

Accompanying Europe into the Twenty-first Century

5

Monuments of the Black Atlantic

*Slavery Memorials in the United States
and the Netherlands*

JOHANNA C. KARDUX

In a 1994 interview, Toni Morrison pointed out that the Middle Passage is "violently 'disremembered,' " "a silence within the race": "Millions of people disappeared without a trace, and there is not one monument anywhere to pay homage to them, because they never arrived safely on shore. So it's like a whole nation that is under the sea. A nameless, violent extermination."[1] Morrison's 1987 novel *Beloved*, which is dedicated to the "Sixty million and more" victims of the transatlantic slave trade, and numerous other literary works in which writers in the African diaspora have borne witness to the slavery past, provide a site of mourning and memory for what has controversially been called the "Black Holocaust." Together with a number of related public events—including President Bill Clinton's 1998 visit and apology to Africa, the French parliament's denunciation of the slave trade and slavery as crimes against humanity, and the United Nations conference against racism in Durban in 2001—these paper monuments gave rise to local, national, and transnational movements whose goal has been the construction of slavery memorials of a more material kind, made of stone, granite, or bronze. Two of the memorial projects that came out of the new public awareness of a shared history of slavery, which spread from African America to diasporic communities throughout the Atlantic world, are the Middle Passage Monument of the U.S.-based Homeward Bound

Foundation and the National Monument for the Remembrance of the Slavery Past in the Netherlands.

These two memorial projects exemplify a turn toward memorialization in the late twentieth century that, according to French historian Pierre Nora, is produced by the collapse of a living, collective memory that in earlier times bound diverse individuals and social groups and their competing ideologies together as a nation. "We speak so much of memory because there is so little of it left," Nora writes in his seminal essay, "Between Memory and History" (1989). "The less memory is experienced from the inside," Nora argues, "the more it exists only through its exterior scaffolding and outward signs," such as archives, museums, and monuments.[2] Intended to introduce the theoretical concept of "memory sites" to an international audience, Nora's essay is an adaptation of his introduction to *Les lieux de mémoire*, a multivolume, collaborative history of national memory in France. The nostalgic longing for a more cohesive national past that haunts Nora's essay and the larger historical project of which it is part is not politically innocent. It is precisely in the decade in which the seven volumes of *Les lieux de mémoire* were published—1981 to 1992—that the twin forces of European unification and postcolonial immigration increasingly challenged traditional constructions of national unity, history, and identity in France as well as in other Western European countries.

That Nora's revisionist historical project was partly a response to the transformation of France brought about by postcolonial immigration is suggested only indirectly by two brief references to ethnic minorities in his 1989 essay: Describing decolonization in quasi-Hegelian terms as an unfortunate fall from memory into history,[3] Nora suggests that ethnic minorities formed the vanguard of the modern historical culture he deplores. Having lost access to a repository of shared memory and marginalized in traditional history, these postcolonial subjects were the first to reclaim their buried pasts in search of "roots," soon to be followed by other groups and individuals.[4] Not only does Nora fail to recognize that his notion of collective memory is a romantic construct, but also that it is linked with a concept of national unity that by 1989 had already become obsolete in modern France and other European societies, which increasingly resemble the multiethnic United States. Rather than representing, as Nora would have it, superficial and artificial attempts to recover a lost past, the two memorial projects I will discuss are vital, if conflicted, attempts to redefine and renegotiate national and cultural identities. Rather than reclaiming a lost sense of national unity, these two modern sites of memory reflect a desire to imagine (trans)national and multicultural communities that are more attuned to the exigencies of our postcolonial age.

The Dutch memorial project, which will be my main focus, was partly inspired by a similar initiative undertaken by African American fashion designer Wayne James. Both projects emerged as slave descendants throughout the Atlantic world were preparing for the 1998 celebration of important anniversaries of the abolition of slavery. Claiming to have been inspired by an ancestral presence in a dream, James conceived of the idea to construct a monument to pay tribute to the millions of Africans who died en route to or in slavery. With this purpose in mind, he founded the Homeward Bound Foundation in 1998 on the occasion of the 150th anniversary of the abolition of slavery (3 July 1848), in what are now the U.S. Virgin Islands, of which James is a native.[5] With the endorsement of United Nations Secretary General Kofi Annan, the Congressional Black Caucus, and Louis Farrakhan, among others, James was successful in raising grassroots support and funds, and within a year the Middle Passage Monument was realized. Designed by a collective of seven metal artists from James's native island of St. Croix, the monument is shaped as a seventeen-foot-wide, twelve-foot high brushed aluminum arch, composed of two halves that symbolize "the need for the past, present, and future to converge in order for cultural identity and pride to be realized."[6] On 3 July 1999, the monument was dedicated during a daylong ceremony in New York City's Riverbank State Park, attended by more than five hundred people. After the monument was blessed, it was placed aboard a replica of a slave vessel and taken to its final destination, 427 kilometers off New York harbor, where it was lowered to the bottom of the ocean. There it is to remain to the end of time, serving "as a grave marker on the world's largest, yet unmarked graveyard, the Atlantic Ocean's infamous Middle Passage" and providing "an opportunity for Black people to collectively begin healing from the atrocities of slavery."[7]

The meaning of the Middle Passage Monument project transcends its commemorative function. Representing a way of imagining a transnational community and a diasporic identity, it can be seen as a postcolonial alternative to the unified nation-state and the traditional concept of national identity whose passing Pierre Nora regrets. Taking the Internet as its main venue of publishing and realizing its goals, the U.S.-based Homeward Bound Foundation successfully called for people from across the African diaspora to support the Middle Passage Monument. The e-mail messages posted on the foundation's website, which were sent by people of African descent throughout the Atlantic world, confirm James's claim in the Homeward Bound Foundation's newsletter that "We have done an excellent job at spreading the word throughout our internet/e-mail communities."[8] The proclaimed long-term purpose of the Homeward Bound

Foundation is "to encourage Black people around the world in taking a more active interest in each other culturally, economically, politically, and socially."[9] In more than one way a kind of latter-day Marcus Garvey, James locates the basis for this sense of community not only in a shared history of slavery and black achievement, but also in a vision of Africa as a homeland. As James explains, "The Homeward Bound Foundation was given its name because of its founding members' desire for Black people to see Africa as home."[10]

The romantic idea of Africa as home central to James's vision of a Black Atlantic community inspired the foundation's next project, the plan to create six identical, on-land Middle Passage memorials. The original design of the on-land memorials consisted of a replica of the arch, to which were to be added statues of an African family in chains and a one hundred-foot granite walkway engraved with African symbols leading from the arch to a female statue, standing with her arms open to welcome her children. The Middle Passage Monument, particularly its sea burial, challenges us to produce our own meanings and to some extent resists being put into narrative, whereas the figurative design of the on-land memorials imposes a narrative, constructing a Black Atlantic identity without leaving space for the viewers to imagine one themselves. Possibly in response to criticism of this kind, the design for the on-land memorials was altered, a slave ship replacing the statues of the slaves and Mother Africa in the initial design. In the new design, the meaning shifts from a homecoming to a symbolic rendering of the history of Africa as well as a therapeutic reliving of the Middle Passage: Visitors entering the memorial are to walk in the footprints of victims of the transatlantic slave trade imprinted on the walkway and thus embark on "a cathartic and cleansing journey."[11]

In accordance with his vision of a transnational black community, James planned to have replicas of this on-land memorial placed in each of the six regions involved in the transatlantic slave trade—Africa, the Caribbean, Central America, Europe, North America, and South, America—between 2000 and 2005. Among the potential sites for an on-land memorial James visited were the Dutch Antillean island Curaçao and the Netherlands, and in June 2000 a bill was introduced in the U.S. House of Representatives for a land grant for an on-land memorial in Washington, D.C.[12] However, none of these efforts have so far come to fruition, suggesting that one reason the Middle Passage Monument could be realized so quickly was that it was lowered to the bottom of the ocean in international waters. As might have been expected, to secure land grants in various parts of the world was a different matter altogether, requiring institutional support. After the sea burial of the Middle Passage Monument, the main purpose of the Homeward Bound Foundation seemed fulfilled, and the initiative for constructing slavery memorials was passed on to local and national movements elsewhere in the Atlantic world, which James and his foundation helped inspire.

When Wayne James visited The Hague in December 1999 to discuss the possibility of having a Middle Passage Monument replica placed in the Netherlands, the long overdue confrontation with the Dutch colonial slavery past had only just begun. The Dutch example suggests that the sense of national unity and identity Nora laments as now being lost may have been based not so much on collective memory as on collective forgetfulness. Taking great pride in their "Golden Age," when Holland ruled the waves, the Dutch partly derive their national identity from the collective memory of imperial greatness in the seventeenth century. What has been virtually erased from Dutch public memory, however, precisely because it clashes with the cherished national self-image of tolerance and freedom, is the fact that, from the early seventeenth century on, Dutch slave traders transported about half a million Africans to the Americas, three hundred thousand of whom were taken to the Dutch Caribbean colonies Curaçao and Surinam.[13] A brief survey of six of the history textbook series most frequently used in Dutch schools in the 1990s concluded that only half of them discussed this chapter in Dutch national history in some depth, and two did not mention it at all.[14] Even today, Dutch students are more likely to know something about slavery in the United States than in their own nation's former colonies. This historical amnesia ironically persisted long after the return of the repressed past in the form of a mass migration of eventually four hundred thousand people from Surinam, the Dutch Antilles, and Aruba to the Netherlands, more than half of whom are descendants of slaves.[15] Starting in the mid-1970s, when Surinam became independent, this postcolonial migration continued throughout the 1980s and 1990s as the economic situation in the Dutch Caribbean deteriorated.

Although slavery had also long been, in Morrison's words, "a silence within the race," it began to enter and even dominate public debates about culture and identity in the Dutch black communities in the late 1980s. That this transformation of the slavery past from a source of shame into a source of positive cultural identity was inspired by African America is suggested by the fact that some people of African descent in Surinam and the Netherlands began to adopt the hyphenate ethnic labels *Afro-Surinaams* and *Afro-Nederlands* (Afro-Surinamese and Afro-Dutch).[16] The erasure of slavery from Dutch public memory became the source of frustration and resentment among many members of the Afro-Dutch minority. In order to raise public awareness of the slavery past, in 1993 a group of Afro-Surinamese people in Amsterdam founded the June 30/July 1 Committee. On the occasion of the 130th anniversary of the emancipation of the slaves in the Dutch West Indies on 1 July 1863, the committee proclaimed June 30 as an annual day of reflection and July 1 as a day to celebrate *Keti Koti,* "Day of Broken Chains," as Emancipation Day is called in Surinam, where July 1 is a national holiday. The organization's chosen name, the June 30/July 1 Committee, left no doubt about its political agenda and was deliberately confrontational: The two dates were obviously meant to call to mind the annual national commemoration of the Jewish and other Dutch victims of World War II on May 4 and the celebration of the nation's liberation from Nazi occupation on May 5. Every year since 1993, the committee has organized a commemorative gathering in Surinam Square in Amsterdam on June 30, and another local Afro-Dutch organization annually organizes a parade in Rotterdam on July 1. Although in the last few years the parade has been a short news item on Dutch national television, it is presented as a (multi)cultural rather than memorial event, and the commemorative gatherings in Surinam Square are reported only in the local and Afro-Dutch media.

The black community's growing interest in the slavery past led to the call for a monument for its remembrance. The June 30/July 1 Committee successfully lobbied with the city council of Amsterdam for a slavery memorial: On 30 June 1999, a small plaque was unveiled in Surinam Square in Amsterdam. The text on the plaque records the city's commitment to placing a more substantial monument there at a later date with the aim of promoting "the emancipation of descendants of the victims of Dutch slavery." This local initiative helped give rise to a plan for a national slavery monument. In the spring of 1998, just as James started his Middle Passage Monument project, the call for a slavery memorial at last entered the national public discourse. In March, Antillean writer Frank Martinus Arion published an article in an influential Dutch opinion magazine in which he proposed that the Dutch government erect a slavery monument as "*un beau geste*" (a gesture of goodwill) to the descendants of slaves.[17] In July, representatives of the Afro-European women's organization Sophiedela offered a petition to the Dutch parliament, requesting the government's acknowledgment of the slavery past and active involvement in efforts to commemorate it. This shrewdly timed grassroots effort succeeded in finally putting the Dutch slavery past on the national political agenda. In the same year that President Clinton offered an apology for slavery to Africa and a bill was proposed in the French legislature declaring the slave trade and slavery a crime against humanity,[18] the Dutch political climate, too, was finally ripe for a formal confrontation with the nation's slavery past. The idea of a national slavery monument was discussed in the Dutch parliament in the fall of 1998, where it met with approbation.[19]

The plan was eagerly taken up by the newly appointed minister of integration and urban policy, Roger van Boxtel, and a two-pronged effort was immediately launched to mobilize public support for a national monument both within the black communities and in Dutch society at large. Wishing to negotiate with one representative body, the minister asked Sophiedela to form a committee of representatives from the various organizations of slave descendants. Nine (eventually eleven) Surinamese, Antillean, and African organizations in the Netherlands agreed to be represented in this national committee, named *Landelijk Platform Slavernijverleden* (National Platform for the Remembrance of the Slavery Past, hereafter National Platform). The National Platform developed a plan of action. The national slavery memorial was to consist of both a "static" and a "dynamic" element: a monument and an institute dedicated to the study, documentation, and public education of the history of Dutch slavery, modeled on the Schomburg Center for Research in Black Cultures in New York.[20] In the meantime, as articles in support of the monument began to appear in the newspapers, Dutch Caribbean scholar Gert Oostindie compiled a collection of short essays by national and international scholars, writers, and public figures, titled *Het verleden onder ogen* (*Facing up to the Past*), which made a collective plea for a national monument in commemoration of slavery.[21] During the widely publicized presentation of this book on 30 June 1999, Minister van Boxtel formally endorsed the plan. The purpose of a slavery monument, he said in his endorsement speech, is to restore the slavery past to its rightful place in Dutch history and to make sure that it is not forgotten. The endorsement speech had great symbolic significance: For the first time, the Dutch government publicly acknowledged responsibility for its slavery past, thus declaring what Nora calls its "will to remember."[22] Minister van Boxtel appointed a Committee of Recommendation, whose task it was to advise the government, seek popular and institutional support for the monument, and raise public consciousness about the nation's history of slavery. Minister van Boxtel and Deputy Minister of Cultural Affairs Rick van der Ploeg became closely involved with the national monument project, lending it prestige as well as financial support.

It is this institutional support that marks the Dutch memorial's fundamental difference from James's Middle Passage Monument project. Both projects started as black grassroots movements, but whereas James's project was entirely privately funded, seems to have received (and sought) little attention and support outside the black communities, and had transnational rather than national aspirations, the government's support nationalized and politicized the Dutch memorial movement. The National Platform's decision to have the monument funded by the government as a form of reparation meant that the Platform was no longer fully in control of the project and to some extent became dependent on the government. Although the government's entry into the project gave it momentum, it also was the source of conflicts, leading, for instance, to questions about the representative nature of the National Platform and the position of the Committee of Recommendation.[23] At the same time, it sparked a lively and at times heated public debate about the meaning of the slavery monument, exposing divisions within and among the various groups and institutions involved in the project. Intended to commemorate a shared past in the spirit of reconciliation, the Dutch national slavery memorial project became a site of contestation, an arena for the politics of memory and identity.

Constituting itself a discursive monument to the Dutch slavery past, the public debate about the national slavery monument was conducted in numerous meetings and symposia, as well as in the more than two hundred articles on or related to the monument that appeared in Dutch newspapers, opinion weeklies, and magazines between the spring of 1999 and the late summer of 2002. Among them were a few dozen substantial articles, including cover and front-page stories, editorials, and op-eds. Moreover, the slavery memorial project inspired the editorial boards of the three most widely read Dutch history journals, including that of the national organization of history teachers, to devote a special issue entirely to the history of Dutch colonial slavery, which is bound to have an impact on the way this history will be taught in Dutch schools.[24] Finally, in anticipation of the national slavery institute, as the "dynamic" element of the memorial is generally called, an official Internet site was set up as a source of information about slavery and as a forum of public debate.[25]

Although the idea of a national slavery monument was generally well received, from the beginning there was some opposition to the monument among representatives of both the majority population and slave descendants. In an early opinion article in the center-left newspaper *de Volkskrant*, journalist Jeroen Trommelen called the initiative an "empty and meaningless gesture," claiming it would neither raise historical consciousness nor contribute to an understanding of the historical reality of slavery, a view that was shared by some black intellectuals.[26] Both inside and outside the Afro-Dutch community, there were many voices that said the past should be left behind. Others feared that the monument would allow people of African descent to adopt or be pushed into the role of victims, and whites into that of victimizers. Some argued, for instance, that the view of blacks as victims of historical trauma conflicted with the project's avowed goal of furthering black emancipation.[27]

Among the Afro-Dutch opponents to the national monument was, notably, the June 30/July 1 Committee. Protesting against the government's "takeover" of the memorial project, the Amsterdam-based committee refused to join the National Platform. The National Platform and the government were committed to a speedy realization of the national slavery monument, but a spokesman for the committee complained that things were going too fast: As long as most Dutch people were unaware of their nation's colonial past, a national monument was "untimely" and the government's efforts little more than a "political show."[28] At stake was more than the slavery past, the committee's chairman Winston Kout explained: In acknowledgment of the indissoluble ties between Surinam and the Netherlands, the Dutch government owed an apology and possibly reparation payments to its former colony and the descendants of slaves.[29] Kout's critique of the national memorial project set the tone for the ensuing debate. At various stages in the development of the memorial project—the selection of location, artists, and designs—conflicts erupted, revealing fundamental differences of opinion about the symbolic meaning of the monument.

During a commemorative gathering on 1 July 2000, Minister van Boxtel announced that the "static" monument was to be located in Oosterpark in Amsterdam, a park adjacent to the Royal Tropical Institute. The heated debates that preceded and followed this decision showed that the choice of location had important symbolic implications. Among the contenders for the monument were the city of Middelburg, formerly the Netherlands' main slave trading port, and Amsterdam, in the seventeenth century co-owner of Surinam and now the city with the largest Afro-Dutch population. Although the selection of Middelburg would have made it a Middle Passage monument, the choice of Amsterdam emphasized the symbolic link of the colonial and slavery past with the postcolonial present. The choice of the national capital met with general approval, but many felt that Oosterpark was a second-class location. Apart from the vicinity of the Royal Tropical Institute, the park has no link with the slavery past or the Afro-Dutch community and is not centrally located. Most Afro-Dutch people preferred Dam Square, the site of the National War Monument, where the national commemoration of World War II takes place annually on May 4. A placard carried in the parade that preceded the unveiling ceremony of the national slavery monument captured the general sentiment:

5 years of [Nazi] occupation:
monument on Dam Square!!!
400 years of slavery:
monument in Oosterpark???!!![30]

To many in the Afro-Dutch community, the choice of Oosterpark as the location for the slavery monument was a sign that the government did not take the memorial seriously.

Nine artists from Surinam, the Dutch Antilles and Aruba, West Africa, and the Netherlands were invited to submit designs for the monument. In the spring of 2001, the competing designs were exhibited in the city hall of Amsterdam, and the public were invited to vote on the designs. The

National Platform and about half of the five thousand people who sent in a vote by ballot or e-mail voted for the design by Erwin de Vries, *éminence grise* among Surinam's artists. A committee of art experts appointed by Minister van Boxtel judged none of the designs satisfactory, however, concluding that it was impossible to make a choice. The Committee of Recommendation expressed appreciation for de Vries's design, but preferred the more abstract design of Curaçao artist Nelson Carrilho. Faced with conflicting advice, the minister in effect allowed the public vote to be decisive, motivating his choice for de Vries's design by praising its accessibility to a broad audience.[31]

According to the exhibition brochure for the competing designs, the slavery monument had to "make visible the Dutch slavery past and its continuing impact on the present and future in our multicultural society, and that it represent the struggle for freedom and emancipation of the slaves' descendants." Of the nine competing artists, de Vries, who calls himself a neoexpressionist, took this assignment most literally. The monument he created, which is four meters high and twelve meters long, comprises three parts and combines figurative and abstract elements. The first part, a group of chained slaves, dramatizes the yoke of servitude; the middle part shows the human individual passing under an arch, symbolizing the strength that allows him to cast off his chains and enter into the present; and the third part, an abstract representation of a female figure with spread-out arms, symbolizes the irrepressible urge for liberty and a better future shared by all individuals, or, as de Vries put it, "total freedom" (Figure 5).[32] The middle part may well have been influenced by the arch-shaped Middle Passage Monument, and the Dutch monument's tripartite structure recalls the original design of James's proposed on-land memorials, the allegorical statue of liberty replacing that of Mother Africa.

Journalist Mark Duursma called all nine designs for the national monument pompous and old-fashioned, asserting they did not leave space for the viewer's own imagination.[33] Though a few individuals in the general public expressed similar complaints about de Vries's design, most viewers who commented on their choice of de Vries's design praised it precisely because its message was immediately clear. "It speaks to me," several wrote on the slavery monument website. At issue was more than aesthetics. Memorial art always has a story to tell, but the divergent views of the memorial designs indicate that the various groups involved or interested in the memorial project had different narrative and ideological agendas. Emphasizing the story of oppression, resistance, and emancipation, the grassroots Afro-Dutch groups demanded recognition, respect, and increasingly reparation for what many claim was a "Black Holocaust."[34] Aiming to take public responsibility for a shameful past, the government admitted that slavery was a "black page" in Dutch history, but rejected the notion of a black

Fig. 1 The Netherlands Monument for the Remembrance of Slavery, Amsterdam. Photograph: Eduard van de Bilt.

genocide. Insisting that the monument was to have not only a commemorative function, but also had to have meaning for the nation's present and future, the government gradually shifted its memorial agenda to the ideal of a multicultural society, which is perhaps more difficult to represent in visual narrative.

The Dutch slavery monument project thus came to represent conflicting ideas about collective memory and identity. Keeping in close touch with relatives and developments in Surinam or the Antilles, Dutch citizens of African descent, like most postcolonial and economic migrants, almost by definition belong to transnational communities, which partly overlap with the local and national Dutch communities to which they also claim allegiance. For some Afro-Dutch groups, however, the national memorial movement became an occasion to imagine an expanded transnational racial and cultural identity, linking them with other peoples in the African diaspora, living and dead. One of the tasks the National Platform envisions for the national slavery institute, for instance, is that it strengthen an Afro-cultural identity by fostering a sense of connectedness among peoples in the African diaspora.[35] The importance attached to a Black Atlantic identity is further suggested by the participation of a network organization of Ghanese and other Africans living in the Netherlands in the National Platform, as well as in the National Platform's contacts with Wayne James and his Homeward Bound Foundation. Like James, many Dutch slave descendants regard Africa as home: "When I look into the mirror I see Africa," Platform chair Barryl Biekman said in an interview about the slavery monument, naming Marcus Garvey, Malcolm X, and the black emancipation movement in the United States as her sources of inspiration.[36] That a Black Atlantic identity is imagined across time as well as space is indicated by the Dutch slave descendants' frequent invocation of their slave ancestors and by their use of the word *nazaten* (Dutch for "descendants") as an almost sacral term to refer to themselves.[37] Their use of the word *nazaten*, often coupled with a discourse of trauma, indicates that Dutch people of African descent tend to identify with the victims of slavery, whereas slave descendants in the Antilles and Surinam are more inclined to identify with the slave heroes.[38]

At the same time, the slavery memorial project became enmeshed in a political and cultural debate about Dutch national identity. Responsible for developing policy for the integration of ethnic minorities, Minister Roger van Boxtel used the monument to promote the idea that the Netherlands is a multicultural society, perhaps even an immigration nation—a national self-image that is far more contested in Europe than in the United States, as the French and Dutch national elections of 2002 have shown. This idea is symbolized by the memorial project's official motto, *verbonden door vrijheid*—"joined by freedom." Expanding the monument's meaning by including ethnic minorities who do not share the nation's slavery history, the motto represents a multicultural vision that stresses integration rather than diversity.[39] As the project's website explains, the monument's main purpose is "to ensure that all citizens know that in our society they are joined by freedom. The realization that our past has a continuing impact on today's multicultural society is essential for this sense of connectedness and cooperative shaping of our culture." To be joined by freedom demands "more than equality, tolerance, or respect. It demands that we show interest [in each other's culture and past]."[40] Representing the government's agenda, the motto was controversial among members of the National Platform because it was felt to deflect attention away from the monument's commemorative function.[41] The official poster that announced the unveiling of the monument powerfully reproduced its dual (and conflicted) purpose by juxtaposing a photographic detail of the monument, featuring slaves linked by ropes, with the memorial project's "joined by freedom" vignette: a colorful row of seven human figures, joined at hands and feet like a chain of paper dolls. Although we are obviously invited to make an imaginative leap from the past bonds of slavery to the wished-for bonds of intercultural solidarity, the tumultuous unveiling ceremony suggests that this leap may have been a bridge too far.

The symbolic importance of the national slavery monument was indicated by the attendance of Queen Beatrix, Prime Minister Wim Kok, and other members of the Dutch cabinet at its unveiling, but the security measures their presence required unexpectedly brought the Dutch monument project to a dramatic closure. On the rainy afternoon of 1 July 2002, an estimated seven or eight hundred Afro-Dutch people of all ages, many dressed festively in colorful traditional Surinamese costume, and a much smaller group of white men and women, mostly middle-aged and older, came to the unveiling ceremony of the slavery monument in Amsterdam. Only upon arrival in the park where the monument would be unveiled did the crowd learn that they would not be able to attend the inauguration, but could follow it only on a large video screen that was put up in another section of the park. The secluded memorial site was kept from the public view by means of high fences covered with black plastic and guarded by mounted police and security personnel. Angry but unresisting, most people gathered in groups around the video screen in the drizzling rain. A small group of perhaps two or three dozen people (mostly black women) assembled at the guarded entrance to the memorial site, however, vocally demanding admission to the unveiling ceremony. Although the ceremony proceeded without interruption, speeches alternating with musical performances and libation rituals, neither the invited guests nor the people gathered around the video screen could miss the clamor of protest. While the crowd watching the video screen spontaneously applauded when they heard Minister van Boxtel offer a formal apology for slavery,[42] the more militant people at the entrance shouted their outrage. Intended as a symbolic gesture of inclusion, the inauguration of the national slavery monument was experienced by many in the Afro-Dutch community as a sign of continued exclusion.

When immediately after the unveiling of the monument and the departure of the invited guests the public was allowed to enter the memorial site, the event took the form of a reappropriation ritual. Many people, often in tears, stroked the heads or held the hands of the slave figures in the monument, as if greeting their slave ancestors. After the first emotional encounter with the monument, which was soon covered with flowers, the crowd burst out in song and dance, waving the Surinamese flag and chanting the Surinamese national anthem. The joint singing of the American civil rights movement's freedom song "We Shall Overcome" indicated that the commemoration had assumed the character of a nonviolent protest meeting. Six weeks later, on August 13, a group of about one hundred Afro-Surinamese women from Amsterdam held a silent march to the monument, symbolically taking repossession of the memorial with a quiet dedication ceremony.

The unveiling ceremony, which received extensive news coverage, deepened splits among the various groups involved in the memorial project, leading to mutual accusations and nonconclusive official reports about who was responsible for failing to inform the public in advance about the security measures. If the monument's dramatic inauguration and the debates that preceded and followed it prove anything, however, it is the vitality of the Dutch slavery memorial project, thus refuting Pierre Nora's representation of modern memorial culture as artificial and "dead," as opposed to the putatively "living" national memory of the past. As Alex van Stipriaan argues, the commotion surrounding the unveiling is a sign that the Dutch memorial project has served its function of putting in motion the painful process of working through the legacy of a traumatic past, whose wounds have not yet healed.[43] Moreover, for the white participants, the public debate about the slavery memorial derives much of its emotional intensity or moral urgency from its being linked with the very much living and conflicted memory of World War II. The strategic use of phrases such as "black Holocaust," *Wiedergutmachung*, and "never again" by some black participants in the memorial debate was vehemently contested partly because it undermined another cherished national self-image, that of the nation's united resistance to Nazi occupation. This self-image became tarnished in the 1990s as the Netherlands was beginning to come to terms with a silenced chapter of its more recent history: the widespread passivity and indifference that, besides active collaboration, made possible the deportation of more than a hundred thousand Jews from the Netherlands to Nazi Germany. Among the mixed motives for white public and institutional support for the slavery monument may well have been the desire vicariously to do penance for the failure to prevent the deportation of Dutch Jews—or more recently, for the Dutch U.N. troops' failure to prevent the deportation and massacre of thousands of Bosnian Muslim men during the fall of Srebrenica in July 1995. Nevertheless, the suggestion that slave descendants might be just as entitled to financial reparation as Dutch Jews was unacceptable to the Dutch government as well as to most white contributors to the debate.

At the same time, the Dutch slavery debate coincided and became linked with an equally urgent and contentious debate about multiculturalism. The multicultural debate started early in 2000 with the publication of a polemical essay by Paul Scheffer, in which the author argued that the government's social integration policy for ethnic minorities had failed, resulting in the presence of an immigrant underclass in Dutch society and the emergence in the large cities of "black" schools, in which the majority of children belong to ethnic minorities.[44] While the professedly liberal Scheffer called the government's ideal of a multicultural society an illusion, voices on the conservative side of the debate rejected the idea of a multicultural society altogether. The multicultural debate came to a climax in the fall of 2001 with the meteoric rise of the populist political leader Pim Fortuyn. Fortuyn's anti-immigration platform made immigration, coupled with security, the main issue in the national election campaign of 2002. In his campaign book, Fortuyn ridiculed the idea of reparation for slavery, writing that "those who still suffer from their ancestors' enslavement" should seek psychiatric treatment rather than financial compensation.[45] In the context of these political developments in the first two years of the new millennium, the national slavery monument project became an important platform for the Dutch government to communicate and defend its increasingly beleaguered multicultural vision. The brutal murder of Fortuyn nine days before the May 2002 national elections, the first political assassination in the Netherlands since 1672, sent shock waves through Dutch society, leading to a political revolution. All three political parties that had been in the government coalition since the memorial project's inception lost dramatically during the 2002 elections, and Fortuyn's three-month-old party (Lijst Pim Fortuyn) became the second largest party in the country, receiving 17 percent of the vote. The new conservative government—a coalition of Christian Democrats, Fortuyn's party, and Conservative Democrats—fell less than three months after its installation. However, the fact that almost all Dutch political parties have now taken over Fortuyn's anti-immigration agenda and repressive integration policy bodes ill for the future of the multicultural ideal that was a central impulse behind the conception of the Dutch national slavery memorial.

Nevertheless, the slavery memorial project has put an end to what Alex van Stipriaan has called the "crashing silence" over the Dutch slavery past.[46] That the sometimes acrimonious public debates about the monument tended to turn on the politics of racial and national identity and memory was, I would argue, an inevitable stage in the process of reconciliation with a painful and shameful past that had too long been repressed. In fact, these debates in the media, in forum discussions, and on Internet discussion boards have themselves been a form of modern memorial activism. In the end, the best memorial to Dutch slavery may not be the Dutch national slavery monument and institute themselves, but, to borrow James Young's words, "the never-to-be-resolved debate over which kind of memory to preserve, how to do it, in whose name, and to what end" to which they gave rise. Breaking down the concept of collective memory in which Nora grounds a sense of national unity, this dialectical model for modern memory work proposes the alternative concept of what Young calls "collected memory,"[47] a concept that more adequately accommodates the diversity of today's postcolonial and multiethnic societies without re-linquishing the ideal of social integration, based on equal rights, that is perhaps the American civil rights movement's most important legacy to the modern world. Thus, the Netherlands' national slavery monument and institute may serve as a site where ethnically and culturally diverse groups and individuals can gather to collect their memories of the past and reflect on their connections to both the national and transnational communities to which they belong.

Resting on the ocean floor, the Middle Passage Monument obviously cannot serve as a place where people can gather. In this respect, it resem-bles some of the German countermonuments Young describes in his study of Holocaust memorials. Like Jochen and Esther Gerz's *Monument against Fascism*, which was designed to sink gradually into the ground after its dedication in 1986, the Middle Passage Monument, once vanished into the sea, "leaves behind only the rememberer and the memory of a memor-ial."[48] The burden of what Young calls the "memory-work"—recalling the victims of the Middle Passage—is turned over not only to the relatively few who witnessed the dedication or lowering of the monument, but also to those who have read or heard about the monument. Monuments of the Black Atlantic, both the Middle Passage Monument and the National Monument for the Remembrance of Slavery in Amsterdam, provoke us ac-tively to engage with the slavery past and explore its meaning for the pres-ent and the future.

I wish to thank Gert Oostindie for generously sharing sources and ideas; Frank Dragtenstein, Rosemarijn Hoefte, and Alex van Stipriaan for pro-viding helpful comments; and Joanne Braxton for permission to borrow the title of her conference, "Monuments of the Black Atlantic" at the Col-lege of William and Mary in May 2000, where I presented an early version of this essay.

Notes

1. Angels Carabi, "Conversation with Toni Morrison," *Belles Lettres* 9, no. 3 (1994): 38.
2. Pierre Nora, "Between Memory and History: *Les Lieux de Mémoire*," trans. Marc Roude-bush, *Representations* 26 (1989): 7, 13.
3. At the outset of his essay, Nora writes, "Among new nations, independence has swept into history societies newly awakened from their ethnological slumbers by colonial violation. Similarly, a process of interior decolonisation has affected ethnic minorities, families, and groups that until now have possessed reserves of memory but little or no historical capital" (7). For this insight into Nora's Eurocentrism, I am indebted to Hue-Tam Ho Tai's review, "Remembered Realms: Pierre Nora and French National Memory," *American Historical Re-view* 106 (2001): 915.
4. Nora, "Between Memory and History," 7, 15.

5. James discussed his calling in an interview with Clarence Williams, "Sea Monument for Forgotten Slaves," *Washington Times*, 24 June 1999, C8. All other information about and quotes related to the Middle Passage Monument are taken from the Homeward Bound Foundation's website: http://middlepassage.org (last updated October 2002). I last retrieved the website on 20 December 2002. Since then it has been removed and the domain name *middlepassage.org* is offered for sale.

6. Homeward Bound Foundation, middlepassage.org/monument.htm (20 December 2002).

7. Homeward Bound Foundation, middlepassage.org/middlepassage.htm (20 December 2002). On this webpage James also explains that the number of kilometers was chosen to honor the 427 human remains that were unearthed in 1991 in New York City at a site where throughout the seventeenth and eighteenth centuries African Americans were buried.

8. Homeward Bound Foundation, middlepassage.org/rites1–72199.htm (20 December 2002).

9. Homeward Bound Foundation, middlepassage.org/foundation.htm (20 December 2002).

10. Homeward Bound Foundation, middlepassage.org/rites31099.htm (20 December 2002).

11. I found the description of the original design of the on-land monuments on the Homeward Bound Foundation's website when I started my research for this article in spring 2000. It was later replaced by a drawing and description of the new design: middlepassage.org/landmonuments.htm (20 December 2002).

12. Homeward Bound Foundation, middlepassage.org/update.htm (20 December 2002). For newspaper reports of James's visit to Curaçao and the Netherlands, see *Amigoe*, 12 October 1999, 4, and *Financieel Dagblad*, 24 December 1999, n.p. respectively.

13. The Dutch were responsible for about 5 percent of the total slave trade. P. C. Emmer, *De Nederlandse slavenhandel, 1500–1850* (Amsterdam: Arbeiderspers, 2000), 229. See also Johannes M. Postma, *The Dutch in the Atlantic Slave Trade, 1600–1815* (Cambridge, Mass.: Cambridge University Press, 1990).

14. Alex van Stipriaan, *1 Juli: Tussen symbool en actualiteit* (Rotterdam: Landelijk Bureau ter Bestrijding van Rassendiscriminatie, 1999), 11–12.

15. Gert Oostindie, ed., *Het verleden onder ogen: Herdenking van de slavernij* (The Hague: Arena/Prins Claus Fonds, 1999), 11.

16. See Humphrey E. Lamur, "The Evolution of Afro-Surinamese National Movements," *Transforming Anthropology* 10 (2001): 18, 21. Only slightly more than a third of Surinam's multiethnic population consists of slave descendants, including Maroons, descendants of slaves who escaped during slavery and settled in the interior. With the Hindoestani and Javanese, descendants of indentured laborers from India and Indonesia who constitute about 30 and 25 percent of the population, respectively, the Afro-Surinamese form the three largest ethnic groups in Surinam (18).

17. Frank Martinus Arion, "Een 'beau geste,'" *De Groene Amsterdammer*, 11 March 1998. Reported in Oostindie, ed., *Verleden*, 19–23.

18. Proposed by Christiane Taubira, a black representative from French Guiana, in December 1998, this bill was enacted in 2001. See Louis Sala-Molins, "Devoir de réparation? La France ne veut rien savoir" in a special issue on "L'Esclavage: Un tabou français enfin levé," *Historia Thématique* 80 (November–December 2002): 68–74.

19. Wouter Gortzak, "Bij de herdenking van het slavernijverleden," *Socialisme en Democratie* 9 (2000): 413–14.

20. *Van monument tot instituut: Een schets op hoofdlijnen*, unpublished report presented to Minister van Boxtel by the National Platform for the Remembrance of the Slavery Past, August 1999, 14–16.

21. In 2001, a revised edition of the book was published in English translation: *Facing up to the Past: Perspectives on the Commemoration of Slavery from Africa, the Americas and Europe*, comp. and ed. Gert Oostindie (Kingston, Jamaica: Ian Randle, 2001).

22. Nora, "Between Memory and History," 19.

23. Alex van Stipriaan, a white historian and independent member of the National Platform, has argued that the Committee of Recommendation increasingly became a buffer between the government and the Platform. Attempting to contain the more radical forces in the organizations of slave descendants, the multicolored committee may have contributed to a "whitening" of the memorial project. Van Stipriaan, "The Long Road to a Monument," in Oostindie, *Facing up to the Past*, 120–21.

24. *Spiegel Historiael*, June 2000; *Kleio*, June/August 2001; and *Historisch Nieuwsblad*, June 2002. Among other educational projects that have been set up are a series of exhibits on the slave trade in the Amsterdam Maritime Museum and a documentary series on slavery for Dutch school children scheduled to be televised in 2003.

25. The official website's URL is www.slavernijmonument.nl. The National Platform set up its own website: www.platformslavernij.nl.

26. Jeroen Trommelen, "Slavernijmonument leeg en zinloos initiatief," *Volkskrant*, 13 July 1999, 9.

27. See Guno Jones, "Het belang van een gedenkteken," *Kleio* 42, no. 5 (2001), 7:12.

28. Janna van Veen, "De tijd is nog niet rijp," *Contrast*, 27 January 2000, 4.

29. Mark Duursma, "De discussie over het Nederlands slavernijmonument," *NRC Handelsblad*, 28 July 2000, 19. The call for reparation payments was also heard within the National Platform: One of the Platform's member organizations, the Stichting Eer en Herstel Betalingen, was even founded with this goal in mind, calling for a Marshall plan for Surinam (*Van monument tot instituut*, 21). This position seems close to that of the Surinamese government: Speaking as the official representative of the Surinamese government during the inauguration of the national slavery monument, Minister Romeo van Russel asked the Dutch government to give more money for the economic development of his country, suggesting that a monument offered inadequate compensation. This speech was reported and endorsed in an editorial in the Surinamese newspaper *De Ware Tijd*, 2 July 2002.

30. My translation. A photograph of the placard, made by Irene Rolfes, can be found among a small collection of photographs of the unveiling ceremony at the Royal Institute of Linguistics and Anthropology in Leiden.

31. www.slavernijmonument.nl/SA105002.htm (15 August 2002). My account of the selection proceedings is based on personal communication with Gert Oostindie, who has been actively involved in the monument project as a member of the Committee of Recommendation.

32. The interpretation of the monument is de Vries's own, summarized by me from his comments in interviews (*Trouw*, 20 June 2002, 2, and *Contrast*, 27 June 2002, 18–19) and in the television documentary *Totale Vrijheid*, directed by Annemarie van Zweeden and Liesbeth Babel (IKON, 2002).

33. Mark Duursma, "De ontwerpen voor het slavernijmonument: Negen keer lelijk," *NRC Handelsblad*, 29 June 2001, 24.

34. "Our holocaust lasted 350 years," said National Platform Chair Barryl Biekman, for instance, in an interview on the eve of the unveiling of the monument (*NRC Handelsblad*, 11 June 2002, 7). Until recently, an inscription on a memorial stone in the slavery museum Kura Hulanda in Curaçao quoted Martin Luther King Jr. as having called the "genocide of 50–100 million African[s]" the "Black Holocaust." This may explain why in Dutch publications the term "Black Holocaust" is frequently attributed to Dr. King. Although King used the term "holocaust" a few times with reference to the economic condition of African Americans in the 1960s, I have been unable to find any evidence in King's papers that he compared the slave trade and slavery with a "Black Holocaust."

35. *Van monument tot instituut*, 14.

36. Duursma, "Discussie," 19.

37. *Nazaten* is a somewhat archaic Dutch word for "descendants," which is now almost exclusively used for (and by) descendants of slaves, the more common words being *afstammelingen* or *nakomelingen*.

38. The slavery memorial *Desenkadena* that was erected in Curaçao in 1998, for instance, commemorates the 1795 slave revolt rather than the slaves' suffering or emancipation.

39. The emphasis on integration is, for instance, clear in an early speech by Minister van Boxtel: "The denial of historical injustice makes those who identify with the victims of slavery feel excluded from, and therefore unsafe in, society; as a token of recognition, the slavery monument aims to give them a sense of belonging to Dutch society" (speech delivered on 14 December 1999; copy in my possession; my translation). In the minister's later speeches, the monument's integration symbolism is extended to other ethnic groups, reflecting a shift in the Dutch multiculturalism debate toward the integration of Islamic minorities, a topic that gained in importance after the terrorist attacks of 11 September 2001.

40. "Thema: Verbonden door Vrijheid," www.slavernijmonument.nl/SA3050000.htm (26 June 2002).

41. Gert Oostindie, "Slavernijmonument ontbeert brede discussie," *Contrast*, 27 June 2002, 17.
42. In September 2001, Minister van Boxtel had already publicly expressed the Dutch government's "deep remorse" over slavery, first during the U.N. conference against racism in Durban and a week later during a visit to Surinam. In April 2002, a few weeks before the unveiling of the slavery monument, Queen Beatrix's eldest son, Willem Alexander, also briefly expressed remorse about the slave trade during a formal visit to the former Dutch slave fortress Elmina in Ghana. Mark Duursma, "Wroeging in een oud Ghanees fort," *NRC Handelsblad*, 16 April 2002, 2.
43. Alex van Stipriaan, "Erfenissen van het slavernijverleden," *Allochtonenkrant*, 17 June 2002, 4.
44. Paul Scheffer, "Het multiculturele drama," *NRC Handelsblad*, 29 January 2000, 6.
45. Pim Fortuyn, *De Puinhopen van acht jaar Paars* (Uithoorn: Karakter, 2002), 158.
46. Alex van Stipriaan, "Hunne vrijmaking zou zoo veel geld kosten," *Trouw*, 31 March 2001, 49–50.
47. James E. Young, *The Texture of Memory: Holocaust Memorials and Meaning* (New Haven: Yale University Press, 1993), 81, xi.
48. Ibid., 30–31.

6

Dancing Away toward Home
An Interview with Bill T. Jones about Dancing in Contemporary Europe

P. A. SKANTZE

On a dais sit several white, male, European scholars of a certain age. All morning the discussion has been of the influence of "La Cultura Latina" on the European world, on the modern world. One scholar sincerely and passionately argues for the return to Latin as the single language with which to communicate. It is time for the last speaker. He begins, his voice booms out over the room, rich and shocking because he is singing: "Don't you want to have your freedom, don't you want to have your freedom, don't you want to have your freedom, children of the Lord." The voice is that of dancer/choreographer Bill T. Jones, the song, a "negro" spiritual, the rupture his voice makes both upends the scholarly tone of the conference and reasserts the presence of the "new world" into the largely European audience.[1]

BTJ: One of the strongest things I have been able to do in Europe since I have worked here is just to be myself and to try to talk as if we all have the same values. I don't know how to say that other than, when you sing like that in an intellectual forum, it can make some people uncomfortable. They will say this is exactly what you don't want; it's too soft, it's not precise enough; it's playing to an aspect of human experience that will always get us in trouble; it's only about the emotional stage, which is what we love romantically in these people; this is not the hard-edged tradition of Western thought, this is not analysis. So it's a vulnerable stand . . . once you do it. They have to deal with it; they also have their emotional responses, and they are going to find a way to express those responses from a distanced and objective point of view.

It would be a mistake to assume that Bill T. Jones' voice—by this I mean all his work, with his own body and those of his dancers—shocks because it is foreign, other, exotic. In Bologna in 2000, as well as all over Europe, Bill T. Jones's work has already inspired a generation of choreographers.

In 1998, when the Committee for Bologna Cultural Capital 2000 commissioned a work by Bill T. Jones whose subject was "La Cultura Latina," the committee created an opportunity for this artist, whose influence can be seen throughout European dance in the late twentieth century, to address directly the heritage of European culture for an African American artist. Jones writes that he thinks of "Latin culture" as something that *is and is not* his: "The thing that intrigued me was to reunite various protagonists [in the history of Latin culture] in my own analysis of the events of the last 500 years [and] in my conception of art which has sprung from and continues to spring from this same heritage."[2]

PAS: I had gone to Bologna for the conference on "La Cultura Latina." Before you came on Saturday, it was deadly. People talking about what it means to have one culture and how one culture unites people. . . .

BTJ: Language based.

PAS: I would also say "education based,"[3] not that those two—language and education—are necessarily separate. Before you sang and spoke, someone was arguing quite sincerely about going back to Latin, and I sat there thinking about your work and thinking this is just too surreal. . . . So when you began by singing . . . there were many, many young people in the audience who were visibly grateful and stimulated and moved, but I could also see the feathers ruffle. Yet, in the best sense, in that sense of "Let's think about this again, what does this mean?" So my question to you is, when they came to you to commission that piece . . .

BTJ: What? [laughing]

PAS: What? [laughing]

BTJ: I was thinking at that time that I am not really interested in doing anything that is "topic-driven" or programmatic. . . . I think at that time I felt that I needed to distance myself from things that allowed people to call me an

*angry black man and a homosexual, dismissed me as being more about social
work than about art. People would say that I didn't have the chops to really
create art that was independent of my personality and its charm. . . . As a result, maybe I needed to be more clear, more formal. And here the Italians come
along and want me to make a piece that deals with the impact of Latin culture
in the world. Yes, it is true I think it was a good reason to keep my company together—we were at a point where we needed a project we would be paid for.
I was not being cynical in that, but I also thought, How is it possible to make a
work that talks about polemical and historical information, and still be at
once a visual experience that escapes an easy narrative, that talks about ambi-
guity in terms of its subject matter in what you see, what you hear, how we
move? . . . I thought that would be a good messy exercise for us. So that's why
I took it. I knew it was going to be a problem. I thought, okay, it will be neither
fish nor fowl: Make a statement about the blood and gold that motivated the
great age of exploration, and now talk about what it means to be an artist who
relies on European forms, whose hero is Proust. I have my mother's African
American prayers and songs on the tip of my tongue and in my blood . . . How
do you talk about all those things that you are? That is what* You Walk? *was
going to be. And that's why it turned out the way it did. Many people enjoyed
it; others said it was totally misguided, it was betraying what I do best, which
is the presentation of a multitude of human bodies in this joyous union, working out problems. That was more than what your question was . . .*

What my questions were in the interview with Bill T. Jones began with
the "is and is not" of cultural identification, about cultural inheritance in
the work of Bill T. Jones and the reception in Europe of Jones's work.[4]
Jones's increasing presence as a choreographer working in Europe, with its
mix of inheritance, and how he embodies that inheritance in his choreography influences the way new choreographers conceive of the roots and
springs of contemporary dance (Jones now performs every season at Mai-
son de la Danse in Lyon). His company, Bill T. Jones/Arnie Zane Dance
Company, began touring in Europe in the 1980s. As Jones's work became
more widely known, these tours would include opportunities for student
choreographers and dancers to attend workshops or master classes with
the company. By the early 1990s, the most controversial pieces by the company—*Last Supper at Uncle Tom's Cabin* (Spoleto 1992), *Still/Here* (Lyon
1994)—had been danced all over Europe, where young choreographers
and dancers saw and adapted Jones's style.

The commission of *You Walk?* made manifest Jones's position not solely
as an African American choreographer being asked to commemorate an
occasion, but also as a choreographer whose presence has changed European dance. The commission also exposed the intersection of questions

about race, about colonization, and about traditional stories of European history and culture. Certainly the committee would not have commissioned a work from Jones had they not wanted a piece that would reflect on "La Cultura Latina" from the perspective of its oppressions as well as its riches.

The dance consisted of nine vignettes with titles ("We Wore Time Shamelessly," "Spent Days out Yonder," "Choosing Free Fall," and so on), a "lost" opera by Domenico di Zipoli from the Amazon, and African, Brazilian, and Spanish music. Mozart was played on a boombox in one segment, and in "Choosing Free Fall," Jones used a recording of John Cage's 1978 performance of "Empty Words" in Milan, in which the audience becomes angrier and angrier at Cage's attempt, in Jones's words, "to redefine our capacity to comprehend language and music and its execution." Jones takes his title out of the mouth of Achilles in Derek Walcott's *Omeros*—itself a deliberate yoking together of the Western tradition represented by Homer and African/Jamaican adaptations of and interventions in that tradition.

PAS: It was an exquisite evening, and this question has two parts. I wonder if the ampleness of the piece, because it was ample and generous . . .

BTJ: Way ample [laughing].

PAS: [Laughing] It was ample for the watcher, maybe "way ample" for the person making it . . . it seems to me there is a certain permission for ampleness in Europe. There's that question I have. The other is, there seems not to be as strict a division between the political and artistic in Europe. People will not always ask, as you are asked in every interview, "Is it politics or is it art?" They might say something is too political or too polemical . . . but artists have been making that kind of political dance for a long time. Forms of art are expected to be related to people's lives.⁵

BTJ: Thank you for putting it in those terms. In other words, when they are asking me "What does the work aspire to do?", they are asking "What relationship does this work have to the lives of people?" and "Because of your [Bill's] definition, in our eyes as a black person or a traditional victim of racism, of colonialism, what are you trying to say to us?" Now, the belligerent maverick in me never wants anyone to have me so easily understood. . . . I must stand for something other than myself in the eyes of certain people and therefore in my work. People in Europe, they still are idealistic enough to want moral authority in their artists, and that moral authority is doubled when the artist from the United States is viewed as a member of a downtrodden minority. . . . They [audiences and critics] applaud this artist's brave attempt to talk about hypocrisy, and they can feel they themselves are involved in the same fight against the darkness in the world. Well, that's kind of heavy and a little boring for artists. So I am saying that even with the best intentions, sometimes I find it oppressive. Now I know—I don't want to bite the hand that feeds me—people have been very warm and open and accepting. But I realize that when I step away from something that they expect me to do, then they are kind of lost. They distrust. Whereas their own artists—"their own artists"— in our discussion there is an unacknowledged racial point of view.

PAS: Absolutely.

It is my contention that over the last two decades the work of U.S. artists, particularly African Americans, has been imported as a language with which to speak about the issue of immigration in Europe. The history of American modern dance included considerations of the racial injustices at work in the United States; this danced discussion continues through the work of contemporary choreographers, particularly in the work of Bill T. Jones. In the aftermath of the unification of the European Union (EU) and political conversations about nationalism and open borders for immigrants, artists working in Europe adapt the social struggle of the civil rights era as well as the contemporary arguments about identity from the work of U.S. writers, musicians, and choreographers to apply to European tensions of race and place.

BTJ: Well, the way I see it, the Europeans are caught in a real moral quandary. They would like to stand for openness and clarity and life and liberty and equality. Yet they have big problems around immigration. I don't need to tell you; you know that. You know that they would like to feel a moral superiority to the U.S., but then . . . the pie is only so big. And if you have dreams to share, if the door is truly open, then what is European culture, and is it changing? Therefore, I think that they—I don't know who the "they" is—they do want to feel the art is relevant to this great project of theirs. And relevance, what does it mean? It means to be addressing issues. I do think they have traditionally depended on outsiders to do that. I see where your title is coming from, Blackening Europe.

PAS: In Bologna (2000) and in RomaEuropa (1999), there were three pieces: You Walk?, Le Costume by Peter Brook [the piece Peter Brook brought to Bologna based on a short story by South African writer Can Themba in the same season as You Walk?], and Peter Sellars's The Story of a Soldier by Stravinsky set in East Los Angeles with a new libretto by Chicana poet Gloria Enedina Alvarez. Through these importations, Europeans seem to be borrowing the language of American race relations and South African race relations in order to articulate their own immigration issues.

BTJ: Hmmm. They were lost with Uncle Tom's Cabin.

One of the many intersections of European cultural heritage in this extra-ordinary dance about slavery was the setting of Leonardo DaVinci's *Last Supper*, which formed and reformed with different members (in one in-stance an older woman) of the cast in the position of Christ and of Judas. The spectator needed to be familiar with the painting to get both the refer-ences and the readjustments Jones was suggesting through the visual lan-guage of our memory of "great art." Critical responses to *Last Supper* tended to enforce the sense of the exotic rather than seeing the ways in which Jones's choreography performed a mix of the European and the African American. "The most eagerly awaited dance company at Spoleto, and one of the most interesting companies from the U.S., is Bill T. Jones/ Arnie Zane and Co., under the direction of choreographer and dancer Bill T. Jones. They will present a dance called *Last Supper at Uncle Tom's Cabin [in] the Promised Land* dedicated to the man with whom Jones shared his life and the stage, Arnie Zane, who died from AIDS. The dancers dance nude; the dance is inspired by *Uncle Tom's Cabin*, the novel by Beecher Stowe. The dance is about racism in its diverse forms, skin color and homo-sexuality."6 While the critic from *La Stampa* prepared an audience to receive the work in terms of racial coding and sexuality, Dominique Fretard's review encouraged a European audience to see beyond the exotic difference: Bill T. Jones's "love of bodies and the nudity frank and provoking at once: dozens of dancers, male and female, actors and players of all ages, all forms and all colors. The superabundance of chairs finished by revoking the pos-sibility of forming a unique body, a body innocent, unaware of what will become of it, because of difference, illness or decomposition."7 Whose table do we pull our chairs up to? Whose table do we leave? Whose table to we turn over and whose do we reinvent?

PAS: That doesn't surprise me. . . . I think it has changed even in the short time since Uncle Tom's Cabin *toured. The EU had just come into being as a political entity, the monetary union had yet to be forged. There was far less political attention to difference, to immigration, and the calculated incite-ment of the public's fear of open borders had not yet begun. For example, Paris in the last ten years has become a European capital that is integrated in ways that are astonishing, even with the tensions and the injustices inherent in a racist/classicist system . . . so it is complicated, it changes, and national stereo-types don't work. You end up saying "they" and you can't say "they." I think in each of those works [Jones, Sellars, Brook] the endless exoticism of the other continues to play its age-old part. But this is not the person who is at the door waiting to get into your country, this is the person on the stage.*

Although his is an aesthetic that works in close partnership with his reve-
lations about the social and political world, it is important to remember that
Jones has had an enormous influence on the aesthetic of contemporary
dance. When he came to the Spoleto with his company, Jones was indeed one
of the most awaited of contemporary choreographers. Young dancers, young
choreographers in Italy, in France, in England, in Germany, would hear
about his work through the press or word of mouth. Then they would see it:
Often in this period his was one of the few companies with bodies that varied
in style, in color, in form, and in age. His particular use of bodies in groups
on the stage, of a choreography at once graceful and athletic, the tenderness
characterized by his solos and duets, now informs contemporary German,
Italian, French, European dance. In fact, recently at a conference on "new circus"—a hot new genre of dance/circus in Europe—one critic suggested that
new circus had been most influenced by the choreography of Bill T. Jones
and his use of bodies in space. When we met to speak in Lyon, Jones was in
the midst of filming *Black-Eyed Susan* for ARTE, the television company run
by French and German television. Jones was the U.S. artist whose company
joined a list of accomplished companies from all over the world in successive
evenings of dance performances.

BTJ: *[The stage] has traditionally always been the first place that you [a
person of color, an immigrant] are allowed in. At least in French and U.S.
relation . . . let's think about the Montalvo for a moment . . .*

Montalvo-Herlieu was one of the companies doing a performance for
ARTE. Bill T. Jones and I talk quite a bit about their work in the section of the
interview that follows. I had just seen *Babelle Heureuse* at the RomaEuropa
Festival a few days before. The company was made up of eighteen dancers
whose ethnic backgrounds included African, Iranian, Algerian, French, and
German. Live music was performed by two Iranian men with drums and
Iranian instruments, themselves a product of the immigrant culture in the
south of Iran.

BTJ: *There is a strange silence around them. They came to the States twice, and
I thought both shows were fantastic. I was concerned where he was going to go
. . . the proposition is an audacious one. Bring in all of these opposing—these
particular traditions—and we will make, in my parlance, a microcosm of a
world community that he envisions. Now aesthetically, artistically, formally,
the next phase is, can they all stay so distinct? The expectation of my training is
that the artist's voice must take all of this and synthesize it into something
which is "greater than its parts," that is "successful." That's what many people
in the States want instead of "it doesn't really hold together as a work."*

PAS: If I read "hold together" one more time . . .

BTJ: You know what I am talking about.

PAS: I know exactly what you are talking about . . . What are these people thinking?

BTJ: They are addressing some sort of aesthetic tradition, intellectual tradition, which is not an "ism." Picasso saw something in the Iberian sculptures, in the Sephardic, in the African, and in his great genius he pooled all of it and made something we call art . . .

PAS: But contemporary critics of Picasso said, "It doesn't hold together."

BTJ: Is that what they said?

PAS: In another parlance. The first people who were shocked by it said, "What is this, this isn't a painting, it's a . . ."

BTJ: A pastiche.

PAS: A pastiche. The desire in the critical moment is to suddenly create a fiat: "Okay, this is what it meant." When in fact, temporally, we cannot say to time—though perhaps we are trying to—"Stand still because you are not holding it together." In a sense, it sometimes seems to me the language of criticism has no way to encompass the possibility that organic is not static, organic is not summed up. Watching a dance that changes as it moves requires a moving critical sensibility unlike that of those who wanted You Walk? *to tell a story. While watching* You Walk? *I thought a lot about the peregrinations of culture.*

BTJ: That is what I was striving to suggest without actually . . . I didn't know how to do it anyway but to be suggestive.

Multicultural, mixed race, multiple identities, hybridity, myriad minded—to expand the narrative of the "European" worldview is to encounter the unmanageable, that which will avoid the tidy avenues of category, slipping from one to another. Many critics in reviewing Jones's work write of the mix, the multiple, of the "mix [of] the colors, the weight, the sizes, the beliefs. [*You Walk?*] is guided by the Jesuit musician Domenico Zipoli who, in ancient Paraguay, composed baroque music . . . and who to the indigenous population, through his teaching the art of singing, became known as the Orpheus of the Indians. Across this work at the heart of it is the musical choice for each tableau that mixes genres and epochs: medieval Spanish dances, traditional Yanomami Indian music from Brazil, contemporary Brazilian songs, fados, Gregorian chant, Mozart, and, most surprising, John Cage."[8] How can such a list be static when those different forms of music not only sound one after another, but when they borrow and lift and give back one from another?

When I write "critic" in an academic context, it generally means she or he who ponders material and creates long essays or books. In performance studies, "critic" crosses the divide; he or she can be both the academic ponderer and the journalist who must review a performance within hours (if fortunate, within days) of seeing it. For years the responsibility of the relation between artists and critic has always seemed to fall on the artist. Make something we can write about, fulfill an expectation, surprise without being inconsistent. Academic critics often work on artists who have died, their work now available for scrutiny only in reports of the performances or photographs or distant memory. Yet if critics look to artists of color, as Bill T. Jones suggests, as representatives of an influence on—a blackening of—European culture, where does the critic's responsibility lie in not reproducing the reductive categories of racism, of sexism, of stereotype in his/her reports, analyses, and appreciations?

PAS: The point is, it is inevitable, that loss is inevitable. We were talking about Montalvo-Herlieu together with your work. One of the things they don't challenge in that piece—which is fine, because it is not what they are doing—they don't challenge the temporary exclusion that most people feel.

BTJ: Temporary exclusion?

PAS: In the sense that you can be a part of the community, you can be a part of many communities and all of a sudden you can feel not part of them. You can feel that way because your artistic values have changed. . . . For example, in my work in theater I don't want to abandon text. I love Shakespeare; at any moment I would abandon everything and direct anything. But I also love Eugenio Barba's work with Odin Teatret. Why not be richer instead of poorer?

BTJ: But can we do everything?

PAS: No, no, and I think again it comes back to this business of how it feels to see your influence: the letting go in the process of seeing your ideas, moves, forms mutate in the work of others. For example, one way the dances of Montalvo-Herlieu differ from your work is that your work, and I am happy to be corrected here, asks this question about the artist in the world. . . . It seems to me that that is one of these things about your work . . . there is always this moment—well, there are often several moments—in which someone walks out of the community.

BTJ: Well, it's my journey, which I always took to be the modernist journey. I always thought that that was what I was doing. What did someone say, it might have been Miss Croce⁹ when she said she feels that dance is always about the relationship of the individual to the group. And I thought that was a provocative thing to say, but I daresay, to be reflective or self-reflective, don't we have to separate ourselves—the figure from the ground—and in some way examine it? That is why people say the artist is mad or the path of the artist is mad because that is an artificial separation—you pull yourself away and you become obsessive, looking at this thing that is existentially floating.

"Jones's audience has had to question its presumptions about black men dancing in order to appreciate his fierce, formal, and passionate post-modern inventions," Carol Martin writes in her consideration of the defi-nition of classical in the dance of Isadora Duncan and Bill T. Jones.¹⁰ Even the word *classical*, it should be noted, takes most of us back to classics (as it did for Duncan and her desire to reinvent Greek dancing). So if Jones pur-sues fierce form in his dancing, his creations move transhistorically and transcontinentally as surely as his dancers' bodies fly from the United States to Europe. Because for him to meditate on working out the figure from the ground, the traditional "modern" and "modern-European" cate-gories of figure and ground must expand. Jones's figure is a solo body, a choreographing body in a modernist dilemma, and it is a black body, a body against a ground not simply carpeted with the history of white modern dance, but a ground made more diverse by the history of his own interventions in dance over the last thirty years.

BTJ: That is why art is not life. Okay, I accept it, and I find with my Christian, African American heritage, I am thinking always of the mystic in the desert, to find transcendence in this painful way. It hurts because you are trying to break through an invisible skin. I don't think I have ever thought about it as I am doing it. . . . You realize the 1950s weren't that long ago, and to be in a migrant worker family [as Bill T. Jones was] in which the mother and father moved from the South to the North in this age-old desire for upward mobility, you end up speaking a language that you don't have. There is all of this sense of abandonment and betrayal that comes with just self-realization. That is in my work; I think that is what you see traces of all the time. Not nostalgia, but rather a bedrock surety that my mother had of the universe philosophically.

And then wanting to participate in the world of ideas, ideas about what the place of the artist is in society, what morality means, what responsibility means. Our politics and thought sometimes come together to make horrible things happen . . . we cannot live in a world free of striving for ideals, and yet we cannot live in a world without politics. So the artist wants to be free. Another thing about Montalvo, I love him, but I think sometimes there is something drawn from French mentality. Whenever I see works in France, they are usually very well made, but they are superconscious of style. Not just break dancing, but the best example of break dancing . . . in another word, it is never going to be gauche. And I wonder sometimes if he [Jose Montalvo] needs a more challenging crucible, like the United States, that wouldn't just tolerate him as an artist.

Jones's assumption that Jose Montalvo and Dominique Herlieu might benefit from the "crucible" of working in the United States tells us much about the difference between performing "at home" and "abroad." Jones implies that through the well-executed craft of Montalvo-Herlieu's productions, they escape certain scrutiny. Or, to put it more justly, when an African American creates a work to be seen by an audience that includes people of color who live and work in the arts in the United States, then the challenge might include questions of authenticity—as vexed and shifting as that term might be—as well as aesthetics. When Jones's work is performed in Europe, there is an authenticity often too easily granted simply by distance. It is labeled "African American" dance because it is made by one and danced by others. Yet over time, the history of the production of Jones's pieces has indeed shifted from the one-time, once-a-year festival performance to more frequent presentations whose influence extends beyond the exotic racial to the danced questions of autonomy and integration, to the challenges made by dancers and choreographer.

PAS: To even be speaking this way is to remind me that it is inescapable—well not inescapable, but it is very hard at the moment to escape these national stereotypes.

In my work on theater, dance, and performance in the European Union, I have yet to encounter one conference, one interview, one chance meeting during which inevitably I or someone else doesn't say "they," even those who know full well the pronoun cannot hold the weight of the difference in the society, the nation, the class group, the ethnic community being collected under the "they." Where can we go from "they," with "they,"—can we go beyond "they"? Artists' work is still very much received under the banner of nation, as demonstrated by Bill T. Jones's response about French dance and my assumptions about the differences in audience and reception in Europe, specifically Italy, and the United States. Questions of culture, of access to art and learning, recur as well in the context of Western, European culture; even the name *Proust* has the power to signify in our discussion a wealth of history about culture, education, and privilege.

Almost all moments of performance, influence, and importation play across a set of assumptions. What happens to our reception when we expect an African American response to the history of slavery and to the history of colonization to have only one register: that of outrage? As is clear from his discussion of the creation of *You Walk?*, Jones created a work that danced the shock of the rape of the land, of indigenous cultures undone by the imposition of the culture of the colonizer. And yet, the register allows for longing too, for the recognition of the beautiful left behind, rediscovered by an opportunist who no doubt saw the potential in a piece of music that could be accounted ethnic or "world" music *and* European. One might say that the cross-influence of European art on Jones and his on European dance suggests the "blackening" of Europe like "La Cultura Latina" depends upon the "is and is not" of cultural identification.

BTJ: And there we have the enigma of culture . . . that was what I was trying forgive. I don't know whether it is the truth . . . and yet this is a palpable lesson in how art transcends the bloodiness of history. How cultures coming together can produce something that sheds a new light on the political, the economic aspects. Even as it was trying to talk about what was missing.

PAS: One of the things that happens now in this "transnational" performance culture is that you often have people who speak, then there is a pause, and someone translates to the audience. It seems to me in Europe there are these possibilities: thinking in terms of the double feeling one has of both understanding the kind of transcendent joy an art form can give and at the same time understanding there will always be people who say the cost is too high, no art is worth that cost. That tension has always been part of the history of culture, but Europe is now facing a similar transition, though the "blood" maybe not be shed literally. In the expansion of the European Union with Eastern countries, I think what is going to happen will be this influence of the Slavic and also the Muslim Turkish on Europe. When they open the borders—if they do—this will be an experience in which many people who have had nothing will be able to come to places where people have had something for a very long time, and I think the clash will be very powerful. So it is a distinct time . . . Thus, asking you, with the history of your company, to think about Latin culture suggested a manner in which Bologna seemed to acknowledge where a lot of its artistic energy is coming from—wanting, in a sense, to turn away from the very thing that happened at that conference, an attitude of condescension: We've had it, we've always had it, you can come drink at our font from time to time. That was really broken by your presence at the end of the conference.

BTJ: Maybe that is one reason why I have taken refuge in striving for precision and form. . . .¹¹ [One night in a performance of] You Walk? I decided I would put myself in it. I had different ways, sometimes I would dance in, at the end when people pile up—which was a reference to Living Theatre, incidentally, people piling up—I would sit there so they piled up on me. I wanted to talk, I felt, I wanted to say it's not somebody else's village you have burned, it's my village.

In the late 1990s, having been made the poster boy for all that was wrong, I was just coming out of this pain. I was saying, I have many young people who look to me as an example of a person who made angry work, decrying what they did not like. But now I say, okay, I know what you don't like, but now can you show me what you like? Maybe this is a question that faces us all, where we meet in this discourse, this sociopolitical, socioeconomic discourse. This analysis of where we are going is going to become very important. Am I saying artists should be more . . . well, what do you love? I know genocide is wrong, the raping of the planet is wrong, the oppression, the exploitation of people is wrong. Read the papers everyday—there are brilliant minds telling us about it everyday. What is it for you that is life giving, moving forward, what is beautiful to you? Do you have anything in your life? Supposedly, as human beings, one of the things that defines us is that we have an aesthetic response to the continuum of our existence. Now this is maybe nothing more than an exercise for the artist to see the positive . . . but I have to say . . . where is the passion?

" . . . Jones repudiates the centrality of whiteness as he dances on the international touring circuit," Carol Martin argues, and by using dancers of many colors, forms, and ages, "he seems to be saying we have a commonality that is indisputable."¹² Pushing us to understand how Jones's work readjusts our notion of "universality," Martin suggests that the "many stereotypes" Jones has had to confront about gayness, about blackness, about masculinity "have made him propose that the only thing that is really universal is difference."¹³ One senses that the influence of Jones's presence as choreographer, dancer, and artist in Europe has encouraged dancers and choreographers to stage a "universal" difference too long suppressed in the adjective European.

Notes

1. From the vista of the United States, Latin culture generally means Puerto Rican, Dominican, Honduran, and so on.
2. Note to *You Walk?* Translation from the Italian mine.

3. One enormous difference between a U.S. education and a European one is that many Europeans of Jones's generation took years of Latin in school. Thus the story of culture sprung from Latin, the language of empire, is inseparable from the evolution of modern culture. For the U.S. student, Latin is assumed to be the language of priests and scholars; it serves a linguistic purpose in suggesting root words, but it remains the domain of the elite.
4. I want to thank Bill T. Jones for making it possible for me to interview him after many changes of schedule, planned and unplanned. And I want to thank Bjorn Amelan for his inexhaustible willingness to find a time somewhere in Europe when Bill T. Jones and I might meet. The interview took place in Lyon, France, in November 2002.
5. "Why is it now, in so-called liberalised times, that so few films have an atom of political awareness? Is it that no one in America acknowledges politics as a living reality—as opposed to the spin that keeps the hollow immediacy of talk shows going? Is it that so few filmmakers have ever had to accumulate life experience or can recognise no cause to compete with their savage ambition? Whatever the answer, we are closer to tyranny if so many aspects of critical thinking and vigorous speech once taken for granted in America are now defunct." David Thomson, "Lights, Camera, Inaction," *The Guardian*, 3 December 2002, n.p.
6. *La Stampa*, 26 February 1992, 22. Translation mine.
7. Dominique Fretard, *Le Monde*, 17 July 1991, n.p. Translation mine.
8. Marie-Christine Vernay, *Liberation*, 17 November 2000, 41. Translation mine.
9. Arlene Croce wrote a 1995 article in *The New Yorker* in which she refused to review the 1994 New York performance of *Still/Here*. She suggested that using people with terminal illnesses as part of the dance made Bill T. Jones a choreographer of "victim art." The debate continued for many years, taken up by academic scholars, dancers, choreographers, and critics.
10. Carol Martin, "Classical in Difference: Isadora Duncan and Bill T. Jones," in *Gender: Nonconformity, Race, and Sexuality*, ed. Toni Lester (Madison: University of Wisconsin Press, 2002), 127–40.
11. "Our most tolerant radical is part of the canon, and it's encouraging to know he encompasses a love of movement that includes gestures and phrases from every conceivable field, as the Jones/Zane dancers' backgrounds (jazz, ballet, Tharp, Graham, Chinese folk) attest. What does it mean that a choreographer who can pack Alice Tully Hall can segue from a grand jeté to pop-locking, and no one bats an eye? It means not only are Jones and his dancers talented but also that our eyes have, with no fanfare, become acclimated to multiculturalism." Albert Lee, review, *Dance Magazine* (June 2002), n.p.
12. Martin, "Classical in Difference," 139.
13. Ibid., 139.

7

The Melancholic Influence of the Postcolonial Spectral

Vera Mantero Summoning Josephine Baker

ANDRÉ LEPECKI

An intolerance
A non-vision
An inability
A desire
An emptiness
An emptiness
An emptiness
An emptiness
A tenderness
A fall
An abyss
A joy.
—Vera Mantero

Indeed, racial melancholia . . . has always existed for raced subjects both as a sign of rejection and as a psychic strategy *in response to that rejection.*
—Anne Anlin Cheng

Where does history rest, if at all? And how is history reawakened and put into motion? How is it that it finds its grounding, its pacing, its anatomy? These questions are the starting points for a consideration of the critical, artistic, and political effects brought by a recent historical invocation: the choreographic resurfacing of a particularly haunting, particularly iconic image that once filled the European imagination regarding African Americans, dance, and black femininity. Indeed, from the early 1920s to the mid-1930s, the dancing image of a certain African American woman vividly illustrated and troubled the complicated dynamics of what Brett Berliner has called twentieth-century colonialist melancholia: that ambivalent sentiment in the colonizer to both sensually own and to methodically brutalize the colonial and racial other.[1] As indicated in the title of this essay, the iconic, troubling, ghostly image in question, the figure and the voice that I am casting as denouncers of European colonialist and postcolonialist melancholia, belong to Josephine Baker.

To summon the ghostly in Josephine Baker is to reclaim Baker as a contemporary critical voice, one that remains posthumously active and resistant. It is to acknowledge that Baker's force still moves about, that to invoke her presence is to perform a specific political calling. To accept the possibility of Baker's agency today is to acknowledge her participation in the cohort of what Avery Gordon identified as "improperly buried bodies" of history: bodies abjected even in death, denied ground, place, and peace by history's hegemonic narratives and forces.[2] For Gordon, those improperly buried bodies, once racialized, congregate in so many shadowy communities, condemned to a double invisibility under the authority of meticulously enforced violence: the invisibility of the spectral, and the invisibility at the heart of racialization. Writing on the links between scopic racial regimes and the affective regimes of racialization, Anne Anlin Cheng suggests—in *The Melancholy of Race*—that "the racial moment" happens precisely within a social field of "mutual invisibility"[3] between white and colored subjects. But, as Cheng also points out while analyzing Ralph Ellison's *Invisible Man*, racial invisibility does not mean lack of materiality. It is precisely this paradoxical condition of being a material body that nevertheless remains to be seen that initiates the history of violent collisions, clashes, and missed encounters between racialized subjects.

Avery Gordon follows the signs, scars, and markings grafted by history's collisions onto the bodies of those subjects inhabiting the racial field of invisibility to suggest that forces of racial exclusion do leave material traces on those they enforce their violence upon. In a move reminiscent of Michel Foucault, Gordon proposes that history's inscription onto marginalized bodies as the marking of "the violence of the force that made them"[4] generates counteractions of resistance. For Gordon, those acts of resistance constitute precisely the spectral's force across time—performances as well as "stories concerning exclusions and invisibilities"[5] in which the ghost emerges as a "crucible for political mediation and historical memory."[6]

In this essay, I analyze a contemporary choreographic reflection by Portuguese choreographer Vera Mantero on current European racism and European forgetting of its quite recent colonialist history. This reflection happens precisely by Mantero's staging a linguistic and scopic field of invisibility while choreographing the effects of this field on a hyperbolically racialized body. Moreover, Mantero's choreographic reflection came into being and was performed with the help of the haunting figure of Josephine Baker. I will read Mantero's 1996 piece *uma misteriosa Coisa disse e.e. cummings* (*a mysterious Thing, said e.e. cummings*), based on the figure of the African American performer, as informed by, and as proposing a powerful political counterperformance against, racism and colonialism. Mantero achieves this by means of what can be seen as a strategic use of melancholia against racial and colonialist abjection. I will situate Mantero's solo piece as a choreopoetic proposal for a political meditation on European historical amnesias regarding its colonialist brutality and will show how it is through Mantero's uncanny evocation of Josephine Baker's ghostly force that such political proposal can be successfully made. This means that in Mantero's piece, as well as throughout this essay, Baker's figure emerges as the teetering bridge between European melancholia (as a mode of subjectivity structured around oscillating feelings of loss and anger, as suggested by Cheng and Judith Butler[7]) and the historical cohort of living and dead colored, colonized peoples, condemned by colonialism's melancholic imbalance to a subjectivity in which deep grief must always be transformed into a moving spectacle for the colonizer.

Movement takes an important place in my reflections on the spectral, the melancholic, and the (post)colonialist. Indeed, if some recent critical theory and political thought, mostly after Jacques Derrida's *Specters of Marx*, has legitimated the spectral as critical concept, the term has recently emerged as instrumental for race studies as well, particularly through the works of Avery Gordon and Anne Anlin Cheng. Critical considerations of the spectral, the invisible, the absent-present, and the disappeared have also allowed for important developments in critical, political, and philosophical readings of performances, most notably with Peggy Phelan, Diana Taylor, and José Muñoz.[8] However, the spectral's other face in the constitution of its uncanny appearing (of its appearing as the uncanny)—that is, movement—still has to find its place as fundamental critical fact and tool in race, performance, and critical studies.

Randy Martin's *Critical Moves* has offered a sophisticated and engaged Marxist reading of both theatrical and vernacular North American dance.[9] Through the notion of "mobilization," Martin has clearly articulated the added value to performance and social theory of considering movement critically, epistemologically, and politically. What I am attempting here is to take Martin's proposals seriously on the political centrality of movement, but to consider it under a different scale. I am attending to a movement less concerned with mass social mobilization than with the creation of micro countermemories and small counteractions happening at the threshold of the significantly apparent—that is, precisely within the haunted territories of Europe's racist and colonialist melancholia and disavowal. This attending to the small perception responds not only to the challenges of a micropolitics and a choreography of small gestures embedded in Mantero's piece, but also to the phenomenological capacity for "melancholia [to be] kept from view; it is an absorption by something that cannot be accommodated by vision, that resists being brought into the open, neither seen nor declared."[10]

Finally, and to conclude this introduction in method, I would like to add that to theoretically invoke haunting means paying particular attention to the role of the uncanny in the construction of colonialist and countercolonialist narratives and performances.

Sigmund Freud, in his 1919 essay on the uncanny, addressed the spectral in its aesthetic impact as one of the two major characteristics of any uncanny experience. But it is the other major, defining element in the Freudian uncanny that becomes of particular relevance for my argument: unexpected, uncontrolled, unruly forms of motion. Indeed, to attend to actions and words taking place within haunted territories is to pursue the theoretical implications for dance, performance, and race studies of what Freud deemed to be one of the uncanny's most explicit signatures: motion happening where it should not happen, motion occupying a body that should be still, motion occurring at an improper time, with an improper tempo, and in skewed intensities. Indeed, it is striking how Freud's essay is filled with examples of the uncanny as motion misbehaving, motion improperly disturbing the homely sense of a body's "normal" stance or normative behavior.[11] This means that the uncanny would be but motion unexpectedly defying the laws of the home. Moreover, the uncanny is a movement whose source and agency cannot be accounted for visually or scientifically: The motions of the uncanny resist documentation, certification, and economy. What is uncanny in movement then, what turns any moment uncanny, is its apparent lack of purpose, efficiency, and function. Instead, in the uncanny, movement always happens for the sake of movement.

Here, we turn to the ontological problem of Western dancing, as fantastically conceived—at least since the beginning of the nineteenth century with Heinrich von Kleist, but already in the sixteenth century with Thoinot Arbeau—as that mysterious animation of a body otherwise defunct or apathetic. In this European fantasy equating dance to life, or dance to soul, we see the eruption of a familiar theme in racial studies: that of the animation of whiteness's melancholic nature (whiteness's gloom, as painstakingly diagnosed since Robert Burton's famous 1658 treaty *The Anatomy of Melancholy*,[12] and as theorized more recently by Giorgio Agamben[13] and Harvie Ferguson[14] as the mark of European modern subjectivity) by energizing, contagious, black "soul power." The animation of whiteness by black soul and black motions participates entirely and symmetrically of narratives that equate dance with the uncanny infusion of life in the corpse. This "soul power," this surge of motion in the apathetic European body that infects and suspends the endemic melancholia of whiteness every time it witnesses the spectacle of uncanny motions—whether marveling in the colonial plantation at slave dances or seeking in the postcolonial dance halls some groove—this contagious movement bringing whiteness back to life reintroduces in the aesthetic domain the primal fantasy underlying the mode of colonialist exploitation.[15]

Treating the uncanny epistemologically means to first project and then find meaning where there should be but the careless motions of chance.[16] In other words, it means to theoretically foreground the coincidental. To treat coincidences epistemologically is to set the ground for a thicker historical analysis, one that allows for improbable readings, particularly for readings colonialist narratives have foreclosed, prohibited, and censured. It is to treat the geographical distribution and temporal-coincidental collisions of facts, names, and events as designing improbable yet thoroughly historically significant choreographies of encounters and missed encounters. If the history of the colonialist European project has always been one of discursive as well as of adventurous fantasies, of producing teleologically exculpatory narratives for the occupation of lands always depicted as empty (despite the presence of "natives"), and of generating stories for justifying the erasure of others, to invoke improbable histories is to dismantle such a colonialist narrative-machine. It is to identify alternative patterns informing alternative through-lines, a movement Paul Carter sees as the ethical precondition for any project of historicizing, performing, and creating in a colonial (or postcolonial) context.[17] Carter's essays on colonialism are influential at yet another level. Following Derrida,[18] Carter sees no distinction between a postcolonial and a colonial moment, except as a linguistic detour, a flimsy camouflage for the perpetuation of atrocious racist subjection and geopolitical exploitation essentially in place since the colonial period, despite official independence of former colonies. I abide to Carter's and Derrida's position, which is why throughout this essay, although I use "colonial" and "postcolonial" to chronologically demarcate

Portugal before and after the independence of its colonies, I believe both terms must synonymically conflate once they are used to describe contemporary Western hegemonic political and cultural attitudes in regard to the third world. This is also why I have modified the terms "colonial" and "postcolonial" to the harsher "colonialist" and "postcolonialist" so that the record remains straight about the purpose and the nature of the ongoing colonial endeavor.

What are the uncanny historical coincidences surrounding Josephine Baker and the fate of Europe's colonialist projects and fantasies? One could start with the haphazard drawing of a parallel between Baker's ascendancy on the European stage and the beginning of the decline of European colonialist control in Africa. Indeed, the African American singer, dancer, and performer saw the peak of her notoriety in France and in Europe coincide with the beginning of the end of Europe's explicit, political self-definition as a colonialist continent, right before the beginning of World War II—a decline that would only accelerate after the end of the war. One could add that Baker's death in 1975 at the Hôpital de la Salpetriere in Paris coincided with the independence of the last four European colonies in the African continent: Angola, Cape-Verde, Guinea-Bissau, and Mozambique. These were all former Portuguese colonies whose independence was preceded by a military coup in Portugal in 1974 (against the fascist regime in place since 1928) and by thirteen years of bloody colonial wars (in Angola, Mozambique, and Guinea-Bissau, between 1961 and 1974). Perhaps these are not too impressive coincidences; perhaps I am indeed pushing the uncanny unfolding of parallels too hard here. But perhaps the haphazard parallel between Baker's death and the European colonial collapse may become historically and theoretically thicker once I foreground how they delineate an uncanny design—one allowing for the possibility of an unsuspected mobilization in critical race and dance studies.

Motion happening right where there should be stillness announces the spectral creeping in, with the force of an uncontainable agency, exercising its call and its force upon the fields of visibility, movement, and historical awareness. This is the moment when we must consider the fact that it was indeed in Lisbon, in 1996, twenty-one years after Josephine Baker's death and twenty-one years after the debacle of the Portuguese colonial empire, that Baker's figure was posthumously summoned back to stage in order to dance once more for a fascinated, cosmopolitan, mostly white European audience. Baker was back to Lisbon (where she had performed in the 1950s during the fascist regime), answering to a call placed by the National Bank of the last colonialist capital of that not-too-distant colonialist European continent.

Such an eccentric resurfacing of Baker's dancing body resulted from an invitation/invocation made by António Pinto Ribeiro, curator and director of programming for the cultural services of Portugal's National Bank (Caixa Geral de Depósitos). Ribeiro asked three choreographers to create each a twenty-minute solo "inspired" by Josephine Baker. The three choreographers were the North American (but based in Paris) Mark Tompkins, the African American Blondell Cummins, and the Portuguese Vera Mantero. Although all three solos presented by these important contemporary choreographers were extraordinary, I will address exclusively the solo created by Vera Mantero, titled *uma misteriosa Coisa, disse e.e. cummings* (*a mysterious Thing, said e.e. cummings*). I am interested in the ways Mantero's piece provides indications for an understanding of how an African American woman's dancing presence—moreover, her spectral presence—disturbs and subverts current European historical narratives and silences regarding its quite recent, quite brutal, colonialist past. I am also interested in how Mantero's piece may point to Europe's political self-denial regarding its current racist present.

Mantero's task as a performer and as a choreographer was not an easy one. She had to overcome a series of ethical obstacles to create her dance: How does a white European woman, coming from a country that until 1974 saw as its essence and its mission that "of colonizing peoples and lands," portray, invoke, reclaim, and dance in the name, and in the body, of an African American dead dancer?[19]

I am arguing that the way Mantero's European, female, white body chose to address (the ghost of) Josephine Baker as precisely a haunting subjectivity and a haunted body thickens the streams of European colonialist histories and memories, of current European racial fantasies and current colonialist amnesia, by offering an uncanny presentation of a challenging, improbable image of a woman, of a dancer, and of a subjectivity. I will also argue that, from a European audience's perspective, the presence of Baker's resurfacing through Mantero's body proposes an even more complicated affective-mnemonic dynamic—that of what can be called (expanding Berliner's concept) postcolonialist melancholia. In this particular case, in which melancholia mixes itself up with processes of racialization and brutalized exploitation, what informs the dynamic of postcolonialist fantasies is not only the ambivalent desire for absolute sensual possession of the other along with the other's absolute, violent abjection, but also ambivalence's particular psychic mechanism—the mechanism Butler has depicted as leaving the melancholic subject always lingering in between loss and rage.[20] Relevant in Butler's analysis is her emphasis (following Walter Benjamin) on a "topography of melancholia."[21] Such a topography is important not only in addressing European postcolonialist fantasies regarding the "proper" place of and for African Americans within the racial mapping of

European subjectivity, but also for the question of where and when may "improper," uncanny, unruly movements of colored bodies find their place and timing for (re)action.

The topographic clarifies yet another important element in what I am calling postcolonialist melancholia. Freud notes that one may mourn not only "the loss of a loved person" but significantly also "the loss of some abstraction which has taken the place of [a loved person], such as fatherland, liberty, an ideal, and so on."[22] Such mourning of an ideal, or of a lost land, may very well develop into the "morbid pathological condition"[23] of melancholia. This is a point I would like to press and keep in mind throughout this essay: that the feeling of "loss" of Europe's "beloved colonies" creates a morbid melancholic subjectivity that gets energized as rage in contemporary European racism. Melancholia—that incapacity for the subject to let go of the lost object and to accept loss—establishes an odd and perverse symmetry in postcolonialist European affection and racism. In this skewed symmetry, the plaint of the colonized is misheard as voicing the colonizer's own loss. The European's incapacity to overcome colonial loss spatializes Europe as a place where specific kinds of (non)encountering takes place. The lament of the colonized singing, dancing, or performing the loss of her homeland finds an odd, affective, unexpected reverberation in the colonizer's own (antithetical, racist, angry) sense of loss. This explains the type of European fascination with Josephine Baker's body and voice, as I will discuss. It clarifies also Mantero's use of her own voice while choreographing Baker's invocation.

Why is Vera Mantero's piece—which first took place in a peripheral European country and whose spectatorship will be always limited to the few attending European international dance festivals—relevant for a discussion of how Europe blackens itself up in its twentieth-century minstrel fascination with African Americans? And how can we start reconsidering contemporary European fantasies regarding movement, the animation of bodies, and black femininity along with Europe's old fascination with black North Americans dancing in its colonial metropolises? This point is relevant historically and ontologically. Historically, Berliner documents, in his book on European desire toward the black other from the 1910s to the 1930s, how African American dance and music started to circulate in France as "civilized" alternatives to images and sonorities produced by colonized black Africans, who were perceived by the European audience as being more "savage" (and therefore unredeemably inferior) than their North American brothers. Berliner distinguishes between the ways *sauvage* and *primitif* were used in French vernacular as well as in ethnographic texts from the first few decades of the twentieth century. *Sauvage* was reserved mostly for black Africans and for their descendents in the French colonies, but the term *primitif . . .* referred to someone who lacked civilization—but who possessed some morality and capacity for civilization. The primitive, more so than the savage, was often exalted in the 1920s and was the object of many exotic fantasies and quests.[24]

Those exotic (and erotic) fantasies fomented by "the primitive," whose main symbol was the African American performer (dancer, singer, musician), produced in the European an incontrollable kinesthetic response: an impetus to wander, to move about, to get lost, to get off. Movement as quest, as voyage, as dissolution of the self is but movement for the sake of movement, which is exactly modernism's new understanding of movement, as famously announced by John Martin, when in 1933 he wrote about how modern dance made its historical break with the entire Western dance tradition by finally discovering that dance's essence is indeed movement.[25] Modernism's "discovery" of movement for movement's sake is contemporary to the vernacular discovery made by the average European dancing in "Negro" clubs, a place where white bodies are inflamed to move by the sheer contaminating presence of African American "primitive" sounds and dances. I would like to press this point, this fibrillating alliance of erotic/exotic fantasies, African American dances and sounds, and the instigation in the white European of the desire to start moving for the adventurous sake of movement, for this alliance cuts right across ontological (and historical) master narratives of Western theatrical dance—narratives that refuse to see in Western dance's very foundation projects of embodiment and discipline not only profoundly racialized, but also profoundly embedded in a colonialist "exotic fantasy and quest." It is this movement at the core of Western dance, this move toward a complicated desire that necessitates a reinvention of the white body's ability, to move before the mirror of racial colonial alterity, that I am addressing as European dance's melancholic and colonialist ground.

How did Mantero inhabit this troubled, troubling ground when she was asked to invoke the ghost of Josephine Baker in the main theater of the National Bank, twenty-one years after the Portuguese colonial empire collapsed with a whisper so significant in its historical, political, and moral disavowal that it led Portuguese philosopher Eduardo Lourenço to wonder how it was possible that

an event as spectacular as the downfall of a five-hundred-year-old "empire"— whose possession seemed so essential for holding our own historical reality and, even more, for holding our own *corporeal, ethical, and metaphysical image as Portuguese*—ends without drama[?][26]

This is how Mantero laid the ground for her choreographic reflection on the haunting presence of African Americans in the midst of Portuguese (and European) colonialist amnesia.

The stage is dark as the audience enters the theater. Lights go down, and darkness becomes complete. Time passes, and we hear some hesitant knocking sounds on the wood floor. The knocking is uncertain, and it moves about the stage. It soon stops close to us, center stage. Slowly, a faint trace of light, a very narrowly focused spot, reveals a wide, very white woman's face, with very red lipstick on her lips, and very long eyelashes and sparkling blue shadow on her eyelids. This is a hyperbolically staged face, a mask, a mask of a white woman performing a clichéd image of certain vaudevillian seduction. The face, however, does not smile, nor seduce. It is calm, alert. Under the faint spotlight, the face seems to hover, bodiless. After a moment, the very red mouth opens, and endlessly, calmly, quietly, starts to recite, with some accelerations and interruptions, a litany. She begins, in Portuguese: "*uma tristeza, um abismo, uma não-vontade, uma cegueira . . . atrozes. atrozes.*" (A sadness, an abyss, a nonwillingness, a blindness . . . Atrocious. Atrocious.) As time passes, the spotlight gradually widens its field of action, and Mantero's body becomes increasingly more visible. As the very white face gains a body, we realize that hers is a racialized body, the naked body of a white woman who decided to cover most of herself with brown makeup in order to recreate the illusion of blackness. It is a self-conscious illusion, this one, not only because Mantero's face remains white (and, as I have noted, hyperbolically so, as if marking that whiteness already participates in a theater of race, race's masquerade), but her hands also remain uncovered by the brown powder. Both hands and neck become separated from the rest of the body by straight lines of paint. Thus, the brown makeup works not as a minstrelsy device, in the sense that minstrelsy "caricatured blacks for sport and profit,"[27] but rather as a gestic marker of an hyperbolically, artificially constructed racialized body: part brown, part white, both parts emphatically made up.

What we have with Mantero's use of makeup in her blackening of her body is precisely the marking of both whiteness and blackness as forces of tension within the construction of white women's identity, and particularly of white women's sexuality. Once we add the third element in Mantero's "costuming" of her body in *uma misteriosa Coisa . . .*, we have an even more complex figure, disturbing the binary opposition of whiteness and blackness. This third element appears first in the piece aurally, with the knocking sounds about the stage; it is then visually indexed and supplemented by Mantero's constant lack of balance (while the light is still too dim to disclose her body fully), and, once her body is finally fully revealed, it becomes the visual punch line of the dance: Mantero is standing, precariously, strenuously, on goat's hooves. The doubly racialized woman uncovers yet another trap of colonialist, patriarchal, and choreographic subjectivities—her body is also bestial. The beast is the lurking danger of woman's genitalia, it is the "savage" animalization of the body in the racist view of blackness, and it is the savage image Mantero chooses to use in her explicit body in performance. The resulting image of the animal she chose to incorporate prosthetically with her nakedness has a very specific connotation in Portuguese—a connotation that ultimately makes this solo bend over itself in its stream of signification as it gets layered on Mantero's composite figure and this figure's imbrications with Portuguese colonial history, and with Portuguese current efforts of forgetting that history as the country lurks after "Europeanness." The she-goat is, in Portuguese, "cabra," the coarse synonym for whore.[28] Here, signifiers loop around the feminine force field in the ideological terrain of modernity as a project always already engendering, racializing, and colonizing as it "others."

By replacing the ballerina's point shoes with animalesque hooves, Mantero stages two powerful visual statements. Choreographically, she proposes for Josephine Baker a dance of unbalance and pain (she has to stand for more than twenty-five minutes on demi-point, thus foregrounding dance as strenuous labor). Semantically, she brings us back to the figure of the whore. A third element must be added to the composition of this particular plaint: Mantero's litany, almost repeating itself endlessly, calmly, matter of factly, insistently, hovering between factual statement, minimal poetry, and blunt accusation. She starts her recitation:

a sorrow
an impossibility
atrocious, atrocious

an impossibility
a sorrow
atrocious, atrocious

a sorrow
a sadness
an impossibility
atrocious, atrocious

a bad-will
an impossibility
a sorrow
atrocious, atrocious

. . .

a fall
an impossibility
an absence
atrocious, atrocious

a fall
an impossibility
a sorrow
a sadness
atrocious, atrocious

a fall
an absence
a sadness
an impossibility
atrocious, atrocious
. . .

This solo is no happy "tribute" to Josephine Baker. Mantero, while never losing her focus from the figure of the African American dancer, does not attempt to re/present Baker. Rather, she carefully constructs a figure in which she animates not a historical Baker, but Baker's resonating absence as central in the collusion of dance, colonialism, race, and melancholia in the body of women. Mantero cannot just embody the semblance of Baker, not with all the history of minstrelsy, of appropriation of the black woman's body by white women, not with the recent Portuguese colonial past. Mantero takes pain to undo the mimetic machine of racism and minstrelsy—but she does so by indicating precisely the mechanism by which mimicry does bodies.

Homi Bhabha has shown how mimicry plays a central role in the construction of colonial discourses and policies, "as one of the most elusive and effective strategies of colonial power and knowledge."[29] Such a strategy, for Bhabha, operates at the level of a methodical destruction of "body and book," the anatomical and the verbal, running across colonialism's project.[30] What is striking in Bhabha's understanding of colonial mimicry and what I find particularly relevant for an understanding of Mantero's piece as both spectral and melancholic is that Bhabha sees colonial mimicry as fundamentally ambivalent: Mimicry must remain an incomplete project so that the other remains familiar "but not quite" and menacing but not quite.[31] For Bhabha, "the ambivalence of colonial authority repeatedly turns from mimicry—a difference that is almost nothing but not quite—to menace—a difference that is almost total but not quite."[32] This ambivalence toward the methodical discursive creation of a disturbingly unfamiliar familiarity immediately positions the question of colonial mimicry within the operational field of the Freudian uncanny. Moreover, as discussed above, the ambivalence of colonial mimicry has striking similarities to the one Berliner identified in colonial melancholia, and to Butler's understanding of melancholia's operation at the level of subject for-mation. Here, it is not surprising to find that, according to Bhabha, colo-nialism's grounding on ambivalence generates the colonized, racialized other as a spectral, uncanny subjectivity. Indeed, Bhabha offers, "the am-bivalence of colonial mimicry . . . fixes the colonial subject as *partial pres-ence* . . . both 'incomplete' and 'virtual.'"[33] It is at this juncture of a colonialist fixation of the racialized other as an incomplete, not-quite pres-ent, menacingly almost-familiar presence that we can paradoxically start to witness the resistant surfacing of the spectral and racial uncanny as un-ruly motions in the almost familiar—that is, as the colonized's strategically melancholic performance of plaint. How is it that the colonized, abjected, racialized other can generate and sustain counteridentities and counter-movements of resistance once they have been condemned to move and to exist as a half-presence within the field of racial invisibility? This is pre-cisely the choreographic question (how to appear in a body moving the necessary steps) recent race theory has probed through the psychoanalytic concept of melancholia; this is where Mantero's fantastical body and po-etic plaint occupies and resubverts colonialist and postcolonialist repre-sentational strategies.

Muñoz, in his book *Disidentifications*, has mobilized a critical rethinking of both staged and vernacular performance practices that directly address what he calls resistant "disidentificatory acts" within hegemonic regimes of identity formation. Not surprisingly, Muñoz's notion of disidentification engages also the psychoanalytic concept of melancholia. Muñoz aims to promote practices of performance and theoretical practices that lead to fruitful, social, and critical mobilization. Thus, he sees an ethical imperative in reframing melancholia from "a pathology or . . . self-absorbed mood that inhibits activism" to consider it instead as "a mechanism that helps us (re)construct identity."[34] More recently, David L. Eng and Shinhee Han have taken Muñoz's argument further to investigate how "melancholia might be thought of as underpinning our everyday conflicts and struggles with experiences of immigration, assimilation, and racialization."[35] What is critical in Muñoz's project is that his reframing of melancholia as mecha-nism of disidentification can only happen through the invocation and mo-bilization of the spectral within the fields of political critique, social mobilization, and subject formation. As Muñoz puts it, under this new light, melancholia allows us to "take our dead with us to the various battles we must wage in their names—and in our names."[36]

Dancing in the name of Josephine Baker in the former capital of the last European colonial empire, a hyperbolically (not)naked woman performs a series of half-presences before us. Sweating, made up, she proposes an image that refuses to ground itself within a set of fixed identities, within representation. She is, as Bhabha described, fully inhabiting those partial presences colonialism has to offer its racialized others. Within the blind field of mutual racial invisibility, her body anatomically reveals the signs and marks of unsuspected collisions: She is partly whore, partly enchantress, partly accuser; she might be in pain, she may be a monster, she is perhaps beautiful, but she definitely and defiantly teeters at the threshold of what may perhaps still be dance. She attempts to stand, but that is the most excruciating physical task. She methodically and insistently tells us of an atrociously pervasive field of blindness while staring right into our eyes. We can no longer rest neutrally in our places. Her pain and her repetitive recitation summon us into the timing of the piece she carefully weaves. This timing, her time, the time of the specter, of the plaint, secretes a space that becomes metonymic to her body. This is the moment when voice and body, motion and skins generate a topography of (racialized) melancholia. Mantero's wobbling feet, her unbalance, metonymically reveal otherwise invisible cracks in the terrain, denouncing the stage as hollow ground, as gathering place for those bodies atrociously improperly buried by hands of colonialism. Importantly, this ground (Mantero's, Baker's, the mysterious Thing's) is contiguous to where the audience stands.

So, gradually, the invisibility field of racism starts to fill up with presences, voices, and lands. And we cannot avert our eyes from that body under strain, trapped within itself, trapped under its many layers of skin, each skin as historically overdetermined as the other. In her simultaneous exacerbation and deferral of full presence, Mantero's partial stillness functions as a sort of visual reiteration of the poetic repetition of the word "atrocious" throughout her speech. Atrocious blindness, atrocious pain, atrocious silence, atrocious lack of will, atrocious impossibilities, atrocious sadness—at least for the duration of Mantero's summoning of Baker, of her plaint of the beast, of her appearing in the half-presence, half-shadows of a racialized, mysterious Thing, the audience can not escape the position of being utterly contemporary to that lamenting body. Cheng notes:

> When we turn to the long history of grief and the equally protracted history of physically and emotionally managing that grief on the part of the marginalized, racialized people, we see that there has always been an interaction between melancholy in the vernacular sense of affect, as "sadness" or the "blues," and melancholia in the sense of a structural, identificatory formation predicated on—while being an active negotiation of—the loss of self as legitimacy.[37]

Pain happens as a result of Mantero's insistence in trying to stand on her improbable goat feet and by her choreographic decision to stay in one place—that is, by her decision to not move as one expects dancers to move. As Mantero tries to find balance in her grotesque, bestial hooves, thus expanding and exploding with definitions and expectations of what is "dance," she deactivates yet another register in the field of colonial mimicry and representation. As she strains, as she recites, as she stays put under the spotlight, streams of sweat quietly streak down her body. If aurally she provokes with her hyperbolically sad recitation, visually she disturbs the field of dance by making sweat and tremor into explicit agents of meaning. Sweat signifies Mantero's labor when apparently there is none (she seems not to be giving her audience its money's worth). As her physical strain increases, sweat also subtly removes the dark paint from her skin, opening white scars in her body, showing it is all fiction, an image, an image of women-whores condemned to dance to tunes whistled by someone else's lips.

Indeed, through Baker's haunting, the naked body of a contemporary Portuguese female dancer becomes neither excuse nor proxy for voyeuristic jubilation of European fetishism toward African Americans. Nor does it become a vehicle for the reiteration of racial harmonies, but rather it functions as the powerful trigger of an uncanny nausea drawn by the sudden revelation: In its unveiled presence, that woman-whore-beast body is crying out a history of blindness and missencountering, a history of untold violence and labor, a history of meticulous destruction of bodies that remain to be properly seen and buried.

This is when Mantero's composite body reshuffles the ground upon which spectatorship and dance stand. We are not seeing Josephine, despite being there. We are not seeing Vera, despite her exposure. Mantero's naked body transpires opaqueness, literally, as her dark coloration becomes sweat, streaming down her skin and revealing a white body under the overdetermined body of the dancer-whore. Ultimately, presence is deferred: The spotlight that first illuminated only her face and then, in a twenty-minute fade-in, gradually reveals the rest of her body, operates a reverse effect of illumination. For the more light is shed onto Mantero's body, the less we are able to see her, the less we see Josephine Baker, the less we see the she-goat. Instead, what fills up our sensory is sweat, tremor, and mostly her voice. What is left of Mantero's dance is an acoustic image. It is as if the field of light defined on the stage defines also the field of racial blindness, of mutual racial blindness, a field only the aural could break—as in the uncanny tappings of ghosts on furniture, as in the knocking sounds on the stage preceding the piece. In Lisbon, when I saw the piece in 1996, Mantero's recitation provoked an increased and quite raucous amount of discomfort in the audience. Her words became sources for agitation and unrest. The plural form of "atrocious," the word that adjectifies every other one in the piece, is in Portuguese, "atrozes." As Mantero stood on the spot trying to balance herself, telling us of the abyss, the blindness, the bad-faith, one member of the audience, a middle-aged white woman, talked back to Vera, loud, disapprovingly—"Artrose! Artrose!" (Arthritis! Arthritis!).

In the verbal exchange between Mantero and the anonymous Portuguese woman that took place in that odd choreographic séance in postcolonial Portugal, we see how the field of racial invisibility unfolds across the stage. As one plaints, tells of a history of hurt, the other mocks, accusing the suffering body to be, indeed, diseased. This is where European fantasies of dance once again match the colonial project: The body of the dancer, just like that of the slave, is only relevant, productive, meaningful, and valuable as long as it produces properly contained and efficient movement. The slave's biggest crime is to have a body in pain and to voice that pain in direct, noncamouflaged, nonspectacular, uncanny ways. However, despite the slave's condemnation to a half-presence, despite the field of invisibility covering the bodies of colored peoples, despite the current disavowal of European colonialist past and current endemic racism, the ghostly knockings and plaints are always heard by white colonists within the walls of properly guarded homes. The spectral lament always hits its mark, this initiating white melancholia: that ambivalent subjectivity hovering between loss and rage.

One question remains to be answered. Why Josephine Baker? Why was her call heard by the Portuguese postcolonialist cultural programmer, and why was the programmer's call for Mantero to perform Baker answered at all? If we consider that Baker is one of the few African American women that stood out significantly within the field of visibility, representation, and recognition in twentieth-century European imagination, then we apparently arrive at a paradox. How can we talk of Baker's force in terms of a colonized half-presence if she seems so inescapable? Or how can we discuss her performances in terms of a practice of complicity with counteracts of resistance performed by less visible bodies of colonized Africans? How can we talk about Baker's use of uncannily resistant movements of the melancholic spectral, if she had been so successful, so present, so forcibly *all over*? These questions are further complicated once one takes into account that Baker's characters in three of her four French films—*La Sirene des Tropiques* (1927), *Zou Zou* (1934), and *Princess Tam Tam* (1935)—appear as proxies for otherwise unseen, unrepresentable, less noble, indeed (for the European colonizer) "savage" colonized African bodies. In these three films, Baker does not play an African American. She plays a Martinican, a black French (from the Antilles), or an "African." Baker's African American body stands in for those other colored bodies that seem to cause so much discomfort to the European proper, neat, regulated, colonialist home. As a proxy for the colonized African and Martinican, Baker emerges as a complicated half-presence in the general field of racial invisibility because it was as an African American that she could be cast as a colonized African.

But a paradox does not necessarily mean an impasse, neither a giving in. Baker's uncanny agency relies precisely in her quiet understanding of what was at stake in her success in Europe. This awareness can be read everywhere in her autobiography. And it can be seen best in the ways that Baker, throughout her career, voiced and channeled a plaint that markedly situated her right along with the plaint of the colonized—directly within the influence of the colonized's melancholic counteracts of resistance. In all her movies, Baker's characters always appear as hovering between wild spontaneity and deep melancholia. This ambivalence in her character's behavior was certainly a part given to her by her French directors, scriptwriters, and collaborators. But if it was given to her, she took it—and it is no less certain that she fully embodied those parts with an uncanny and reciprocal ambivalence and wisdom. What is truly stunning in Baker's performances for film is that despite the proximity of the camera, despite the filmic structure of command, despite editing and the rudimentary special effects, her dancing remains to be captured—and therefore to be both properly placed and properly seen. A case can be made that Baker's dances for film perform a refusal to enter into the field of the visible. It is almost as if the camera could find neither its proper place nor Baker's placement in space. It is as if Baker's movements could not be properly pinned down, captured, entrapped by the machinic gaze. What we witness mostly while watching Princess Tam Tam's final, "wild" dancing in a Parisian cabaret, or Zou Zou's skits in the vaudeville stage, is the prevalence of a blurred absence made out of quick cuts, strange edits, and odd camera moves. And what glides across this ongoing visual disruption, what moves along Baker's filmic half-presence, is a partly disembodied voice, longing for Martinique, Africa, or freedom. The French loved that noble display of grief by an African American portraying what they thought would represent proper African and Caribbean nostalgia. But the problem she poses to this enchanted European audience, or the uncanny shadow her movements cast in all her movies, is the fact that neither the colonized African nor Baker were ever quite *there.* Baker knew quite well what she was doing in the moving field of colonial mimicry, half-presences, colonialism, and spectral melancholia. She choreographed and danced not for the eye to capture, but for other senses, those activated in the improper field of melancholic subjectivity: senses attuned to all that "cannot be accommodated by vision, that resists being brought to the open, neither seen nor declared," to repeat Butler's formulation on the particular phenomenology of melancholy.[38]

Michael Taussig writes on Josephine Baker's dance as "disorganizing the mimesis of mimesis."[39] For Taussig, Baker fully understands what is at stake for the colonizer in colonial mimicry: basically, the colonizer's integrity as both body and subject whose very being is predicated upon the blunt appropriation and absolute erasure of any independent, autonomous voice and full presence of the colonized, racialized body. Baker's way to escape the colonialist drive informing her European admirers is precisely by eluding the possibility of Europeans replicating, repeating, and reproducing her movements. When Baker attended a soiree at Count Harry Kessler's in Berlin in 1926, the white guests "implored" her to dance. As the count remembers the episode, his guests soon started imitating Baker's movements, "Now and again, Luli Meiern also improvised a few movements, very delightful and harmonious; but one twist of the arm by Josephine Baker and their grace was extinguished, dissolved into thin air like mountain mist."[40]

This understanding of dance as an improper practice, a practice that presents itself as essentially antirepertoire, a practice impossible for a certain subjectivity and body to grasp, to retain; this understanding of dance's potential for the uncanny; this claiming of a movement that is not for the eye to behold; this strategic choreography of the colonized plaint as partly never present; this enactment of the dancer's half-presence within the field of invisibilities that racialization and colonialism inaugurate; this understanding of race as an ontological and epistemological invocation of ghosts, all coalesce in Baker's project of direct destruction of dance's own colonialist premises. This destruction is what turns Mantero and Baker into accomplices and partners in each other's struggles—each an uncanny, unruly half-presence of the other in the melancholic field of the European postcolonial.

Notes

1. Brett Berliner, *Ambivalent Desire: The Exotic Black Other in Jazz-Age France* (Amherst and Boston: University of Massachusetts Press, 2002), 200.
2. Avery Gordon, *Ghostly Matters: Haunting and the Sociological Imagination* (Minneapolis and London: Minnesota University Press, 1997), 16.
3. Anne Anlin Cheng, *The Melancholia of Race: Psychoanalysis, Assimilation and Hidden Grief* (Oxford and New York: Oxford University Press, 2001), 16.
4. Gordon, *Ghostly Matters*, 22.
5. Ibid., 17.
6. Ibid., 18.
7. Judith Butler, *The Psychic Life of Power* (Stanford, Calif.: Stanford University Press, 1997).
8. Peggy Phelan, *Unmarked: The Politics of Performance* (New York and London: Routledge, 1993); Peggy Phelan, *Mourning Sex: Performing Public Memories* (New York and London: Routledge, 1997); Diana Taylor, *Disappearing Acts: Spectacles of Gender and Nationalism in Argentina's "Dirty War"* (Durham, N.C.: Duke University Press, 1997); José Esteban Muñoz, *Disidentifications: Queers of Color and the Performance of Politics* (Minneapolis: University of Minnesota Press, 1999).
9. Randy Martin, *Critical Moves: Dance Studies in Theory and Politics* (Durham and London: Duke University Press, 1998).
10. Butler, *The Psychic Life of Power*, 186.
11. I am not only referring here to the famous outlining of "the repetition-compulsion" Freud discusses in the final pages of his essay, prefacing his musings on the death drive in *Beyond the Pleasure Principle*, but also to Freud's description of his perambulations on the "deserted streets of of a provincial town in Italy" as awakening in him an uncanny feeling

(143); "the uncanny effect of epilepsy" that is due to its uncontrolled convulsions (151); the motions "of animated dolls, and automatons" (132); and, naturally, "Feet which dance by themselves" (151). All are famously portrayed by Freud as symbolic displacements of the appearance and agency in the scopic field of that which should be forever hidden and stilled: the mother's genitals. Sigmund Freud "The Uncanny," in *On Creativity and the Unconscious*, ed. Benjamin Nelson (New York: Harper and Row, 1958).

12. Robert Burton, *The Anatomy of Melancholy* (New York: New York Review of Books, 2001).
13. Giorgio Agamben, *Stanzas: Word and Phantasm in Western Culture*, trans. Ronald L. Martinez (Minneapolis: University of Minnesota Press, 1993).
14. Harvie Ferguson, *Modernity and Subjectivity: Body, Soul, Spirit* (Charlottesville and London: The University Press of Virginia, 2000).
15. For a discussion of blackness as contagion, see Barbara Browning, *Infectious Rhythm: Metaphors of Contagion and the Spread of African Culture* (New York: Routledge, 1998).
16. The "uncanny atmosphere" brought about by repetition "forces upon us the idea of something fateful and unescapable where otherwise we should have spoken of 'chance' only." Freud, "The Uncanny," 144.
17. Paul Carter, *The Lie of the Land* (London and Boston: Faber and Faber, 1996).
18. Paul Patton, "A Discussion with Jacques Derrida," *Theory & Event* 5, no. 1 (2001) muse.jhu.edu/journals/theory_and_event/v005/5.1derrida.html.
19. Article 2 of the Portuguese Colonial Act of 1930, the legislative document regulating the "Empire," reads: "It is the *organic essence* of the Portuguese Nation to fulfill the historical mission of possessing and colonizing overseas domains and to civilize the indigenous populations." Fernando Rosas and J. M. Brandão de Brito, *Dicionário de História do Estado Novo* (Lisbon: Bertrand Editora, 1996), 21. Translation mine, emphasis added.
20. Butler, *The Psychic Life of Power*, 167–98.
21. Ibid., 174.
22. Sigmund Freud, "Mourning and Melancholia," in *General Psychological Theory*, ed. Philip Rieff (New York: Simon and Schuster, 1991), 164.
23. Ibid., 164.
24. Berliner, *Ambivalent Desire*, 7.
25. Martin proposes that it is only with the advent of modern dance (particularly with Martha Graham, Doris Humphrey, Mary Wigman, and Rudolf von Laban) that dance "discovers the actual substance of the dance: movement." John Martin, *The Modern Dance* (Brooklyn, N.Y.: Dance Horizons, 1972), 6. For a discussion of the social and historical implications of such ontological "discovery," see Hillel Schwarz, "Torque: The New Kinaesthetics," in *Incorporations*, ed. Jonathan Crary and Sanford Kwinter (New York: ZONE Books, 1992), 71–126.
26. Eduardo Lourenço, *O Labirinto da Saudade: Psicanálise Mítica do Destino Português* (Lisbon: Publicações Dom Quixote, 1991), 43. Translation mine.
27. Eric Lott, *Love and Theft: Blackface Minstrelsy and the American Working Class* (New York and Oxford: Oxford University Press, 1993), 3.
28. Hers is also a mythic figure in Portuguese folklore. The *Dama dos Pés de Cabra* (*The Lady with Goat's Hooves*) is an enchanted seductress already marked as other—for this lady is also a Moorish woman.
29. Homi Bhabha, "Of Mimicry and Man: The Ambivalence of Colonial Discourse," in *Race Critical Theory*, ed. Phelomena Essed and David Theo Goldberg (Malden, Mass.: Blackwell, 2002), 114.
30. Ibid., 121.
31. Ibid., 114–15.
32. Ibid., 121.
33. Ibid., 115, emphasis mine.
34. Muñoz, *Disidentifications*, 74.
35. David L. Eng and Shinhee Han, "A Dialogue on Racial Melancholia," in *Loss*, ed. David L. Eng and David Kazanjian (Berkeley and London: University of California Press, 2003), 344.
36. Muñoz, *Disidentifications*, 74.
37. Cheng, *The Melancholy of Race*, 20.
38. Butler, *The Psychic Life of Power*, 186.
39. Michael Taussig, *Mimesis and Alterity: A Particular History of the Senses* (New York and London: Routledge, 1993), 68.
40. Quoted in Taussig, *Mimesis and Alterity*, 69.

8

Nights of Flamenco and Blues in Spain

From Sorrow Songs to Soleá and Back

MARÍA FRÍAS

Flamenco is similar to the blues. It has a tinge of sadness, an element of fight and rebellion.
It is pain and suffering with explosions of great happiness.
—Paco Peña

Blues is poetry. Love, pain, flamenco.
—Eric Burdon

The soleá *is a song of longing or lament, like the Afro-American blues.*
—Gilbert Chase

Historically, the blackening of Spain started in the eighth century when the Moors invaded the Andalusian region in the south. When this first period of black influence in Spain ended with the Moors being expelled by force at the end of the fifteenth century, the Moorish influence could be felt almost all over the country. As a result of their superior culture, they had left behind many architectonic treasures, a sophisticated social and political organization, and some of the most astonishing developments in mathematics, music, and philosophy. Soon Spain experienced a completely different kind of blackening: On the other side of the Atlantic—and together with other European imperial powers—Spain participated in the colonial expansion and became involved in the slave trade from the sixteenth to the nineteenth century, and, as a consequence, people of African descent

141

populated the Spanish landscape once more. However, these were relations based on power and supremacy, and there was little respect for black culture. The twentieth century opened a new chapter for black influences in Spain. Surely one of the most important blackening influences is twentieth-century postcolonial migration to contemporary Spain, but this essay will concentrate on the African American impact on Spanish culture.

During the Spanish Civil War (1936–1939), many African Americans fought as volunteers on the Republican side in the International Lincoln Battalion, whereas others worked as war correspondents.[1] Yet, it is definitely through music—blues, jazz, and rap—that African Americans have had an impact on contemporary Spanish culture. One can recently observe a tremendous increase in the number of Spanish rap groups who very closely follow African American lyrics, attitudes, and fashion, but I want to focus in my essay on the blackening of the art form that is specifically Spanish—flamenco. Twentieth-century flamenco, I will argue, has been influenced by African American music to such an extent that contemporary musicologists talk about flamenco blues or new flamenco to refer to this fusion/blending.[2] Therefore, the aim of this essay is to focus on the two-way musical path followed by some African American and Spanish musicians and writers to prove that although the African presence had never totally left the Spanish culture, it is now returning with renewed impetus, vividly and profoundly enriched by African American rhythm and blues.

This musical fusion started in the 1960s with Miles Davis's *Sketches of Spain*, followed by Pedro Iturralde (in the 1960s and 1970s) with his *Flamenco Jazz*, and has continued well into the 1980s and 1990s when we see the so-called new flamenco develop as a combination or creolization of blues, jazz, and flamenco. Musicians such as José Mercé, Enrique Morente, or Tomate, to name just a few, have experimented with and incorporated blues and jazz into their flamenco songs and compositions. Undoubtedly, special attention should be devoted to the collaboration between B. B. King and Raimundo Amador. In view of the increasing fusion of African American rhythms and Spanish flamenco music, the purpose of this essay is to present some of the most outstanding influences, collaborations, and exchanges between blues/jazz and flamenco musicians and writers. As I will show with my discussion of Federico Garcia Lorca and Langston Hughes, one can indeed claim that African American and gypsy[3] culture have so much in common that it is possible for blues and jazz to have an impact on flamenco to such an extent that contemporary musicologists talk about flamenco blues or new flamenco when they wish to denote the blackening of traditional flamenco.

Both Lorca and Hughes already highlighted gypsies' and African Americans' devotion to so-called soul music: blues, in the case of blacks; flamenco,[4] in the case of gypsies. But, what exactly do African Americans and gypsies and their music have in common? Tracing the origins of blues or flamenco in the formative years is not an easy task.[5] African Americans and gypsies are displaced human beings who were forced to live on a distant continent. Blacks were taken by force and brought from Africa to America to work as slaves. Gypsies were either pushed or chose to leave their Eastern communities because of social pressure and/or government persecution. According to Henry Kamen, the gypsies first entered Spain in the early fifteenth century, and in 1499 they began to suffer from official repression. As Kamen adds, "the gypsy question in Spain . . . had always been approached through punitive legislation."[6] It was precisely in 1619—the year that the first cargo of African slaves arrived in Charleston, South Carolina—that an order was passed to expel gypsies from Castille. As with the gypsies, the black question in the United States has also been approached through punitive legislation. African Americans could not legally vote until the 1960s, and discrimination and police brutality is still part of African American life in the 1990s. In Spain, gypsies still suffer from social and political segregation.[7] Blues and flamenco songs are representative of a rich folkloric tradition, and both were transmitted orally from one generation to the next. Blues and flamenco songs were laboriously committed to memory and meticulously transferred to the following generation with the same tinge of sadness and joy. Memorization, repetition, variation, and improvisation characterize the history of blues and flamenco. Both flamenco and blues found their original inspiration in their people's way of life, in their poverty and in the long-lived history of political discrimination and social oppression, but also in their need to find an outlet for their frustrations. That profound sadness explains the *holler* songs in blues or the *quejío* in flamenco's *soleá* and *siguiriya*. Blues singer Booker White asserts, "You want to know where did the blues come from. The blues come behind the mule . . . walking behind the mules way back in slavery time."[8] Interestingly enough, and reminiscent of Hughes's singing-to-keep-from-crying attitude, Lorca accurately captures blacks and gypsies' philosophy of life when he writes, "Two races who feel the same pain singing behind a broad smile."[9] In the same thread of thought, when somebody asked *cantaor* Manolito el de María why he sang, he answered, "Because I remember what I have been through."[10]

As for where and when blues and flamenco were born, there is much controversy.[11] The first blues songs can be traced to the Deep South, to New Orleans, Memphis, and the Mississippi Delta of the nineteenth century. With its mixture of Indian, Arab, Jewish, and vernacular roots, the first flamenco songs spread throughout Andalusia in the eighteenth century. Blues songs were almost exclusively sung first in the jukeboxes, local clubs, and bordellos of the Deep South, and flamenco bars and *tablaos* opened first in Seville and then in Cadiz. Both blues and flamenco developed and quickly spread throughout the respective countries thanks to the mobility of bluesmen and -women, and of *cantaores* and *cantaoras*, and to the proximity of two major navigable rivers: the Mississippi in the United States and the Guadalquivir in Spain. In terms of their form and style, they differ, but both blues and flamenco can be traced from African roots, and they employ the *call and response* pattern of African tradition. The blues audience will freely and loudly interrupt and/or accompany the singer's voice whenever the spirit guides them with a passionate "Oh, play it!," "Yes, mamma!," "Oh, Lordy!," "Preach it, baby!", the flamenco audience will in turn respond with spontaneous "¡Olé!," "¡Arsa!," "¡Ole ese cante!" Both blues and flamenco are intimate, soulful, and stirring types of music that speak about daily trials and troubles, about love and careless love. That intimate connection is reflected in the so-called flamenco's *duende*[12] and the blues' *feeling*. Flamenco and blues have evolved from unconventional, outlawed, and marginal locations such as back doors, taverns, local bars and juke joints, back porches, bordellos, and dance halls. Blues and flamenco artists have finally gained enthusiastic public and worldwide recognition from the White House in Washington to the Palacio de la Ópera in Madrid.[13]

Throughout the twentieth century, a relevant number of Spanish and African American writers and musicians have been in close, direct contact and mutually creative dialogue. This is the case with writers Langston Hughes and Federico García Lorca, and with musicians Miles Davis and Pedro Iturralde, and B. B. King and Raimundo Amador, to name just a few.

Lorca (1898–1936) first traveled to New York in 1929, in time to witness, in shock, the visionary images of an "extra-human architecture"[14] and the financial crash of Wall Street, but also to eagerly enjoy the cultural nightlife of Harlem. Hectic New York—so vividly reflected in his collection of poems *A Poet in New York* (1940)—almost caused the poet to have a nervous breakdown. It was only when visiting Harlem and discovering black culture that he found some spiritual relief and peace of mind.[15] It is little wonder that Lorca, a poet, but also a talented and sensitive pianist and musician who had written about gypsies, flamenco songs, and Spanish folk tradition, could perceive some kind of artistic and creative brotherhood between the blacks of Harlem and the gypsies of Andalusia. Besides, Lorca's genuine interest both in the history of gypsies in Spain and in flamenco led him to conduct years of field research to legitimize an artistic folklore that had been adulterated or devalued.

Lorca's investigations represented more than just an academic purpose.[16] Immersing himself in the oral tradition, and using his own words, Lorca looked at flamenco not only as an aficionado but also as someone with the "soul of a poet."[17] His collections of poems, *Romancero Gitano* [*Gypsy Ballads*] (1928) and *Poemas del Cante Jondo* [*Deep Songs Poems*] (1921), speak for Lorca's celebration of a vernacular people and culture. Furthermore, Lorca's prose and poetry on the subject prove that he could see beauty where others simply saw primitive, banal, and artless folklore associated with low culture that was bordering on bad taste. His lectures, in which Lorca explains the reasons behind his obsession and defends the richness of a valuable folk tradition, only served to emphasize the writer's poetic perception of an ill-treated culture and people. "I think," Lorca states, "that the fact that I was born in Granada pushed me to genuinely understand those who have suffered from persecution. Like the gypsy, the black . . . we all carry deep inside."[18] Once in Harlem, it is no wonder that Lorca could so smoothly associate *cante jondo* [*deep songs*] with black music: He instinctively captured a potential parallel between the gypsies' long-lived oppression, persecution, and poverty, and African American historical segregation and discrimination. In several interviews and lectures, Lorca argues that only the presence of the *duende*—comparable to *feeling* or *soul* in black music—makes the flamenco singer (*cantaor*) create a vibrating and vivid song. To the *aficionado* of Lorca's work, the writer's personal interest in and appreciation of African American and gypsy culture does not come as a surprise: Lorca repeatedly argued that the roots of flamenco songs, or "transplanted songs"[19] as he called them, could be traced back to the presence of Africans in Spain, so Harlem's sensual songs resonated with a language that he could easily understand. He frequently paraded the streets of Harlem "to see blacks dancing, and to learn about what their thoughts were, because dancing is the only way to express their pain and the deepest way to express their feelings."[20] But Lorca does not trivialize African American culture. Deep inside, and behind their laughing masks, the writer perceives the many abuses inflicted on blacks, the historical subjugation and the daily discrimination: "I wanted to write a poem about the black race in the United States and highlight the pain blacks suffer for being blacks in a hostile world, enslaved to all the inventions of the white man, to all his machines."[21] A sensitive soul himself, Lorca denounces social injustice: "I complained every day. I complained about seeing young black men beheaded by hard collars, wearing violent suits and boots, cleaning the spittoons of cold men who spoke like ducks."[22] Undoubtedly, Lorca could both capture the pornography of a racist America and the powerful passion inherent to black culture because he was privileged with a firsthand experience of the black world. Having been invited to a party at Nella Larsen's home, and after listening to some secular and sacred songs there, Lorca writes home: ". . . what a wonderful singing! Their songs are only comparable to *cante jondo* [deep songs]."[23] Until his end, Lorca stayed fascinated by the painstaking power and inner emotion that run parallel through the veins of *cante jondo* and black music.

Only a year after Lorca's assassination, Langston Hughes traveled to Spain in 1937, where he spent three months in besieged Madrid as a war correspondent for black magazines and newspapers. Most interestingly, Hughes found Lorca's works so powerful and moving that he thought of translating him.[24] Hughes associated his personal fight against racial discrimination in the United States—a kind of fascism in Hughes's own words—with Spain's fight. His main goal was to send dispatches about the African Americans who had joined the Republican side. To Hughes's surprise, he discovered that Franco had enlisted Moroccan soldiers on the Nationalist side and that—to Hughes's further shock—these troops were discriminated against and segregated within the military ranks:

> We captured a wounded Moor today
> He was just as dark as me.
> I said, Boy, what you been doin' here
> Fightin' against the free?[25]

But, like Lorca's fascination with black music and black dance in Harlem, the cultural aspect that most struck Hughes in Spain was flamenco because it reminded him of the mournful touch, the sensual force, and the vibrant rhythm of the blues. As a war correspondent in Madrid, Hughes worked frantically by day, often putting his own life at risk. By night, though, Hughes ritually went for a drink to the few and deteriorated *tablaos*—or flamenco bars—which remained open. Only while sitting in those *tablaos*, similar to Lorca's enraptured nightly visits to the *Small Paradise* in Harlem, could Hughes feel that the African musicality of slavery times was still alive in Spanish flamenco songs. Furthermore, Hughes could capture the striking similarities between blues and flamenco when he listened to La Niña de los Peines's *deep songs* or *cante jondo*.[26] Langston Hughes—who saw beauty in the African American folklore tradition, who had a sensitive ear for black speech and idiom, and whose poems reflected the rhythmic musicality and the aching sensuality of the blues songs, and the impromptu and recreation of the jazz music—could not but feel seized by the *duende* of the Spanish *soleá* (from Spanish *solitude* or *loneliness*). For Hughes, the Spanish *soleá* reverberated with the sound of the *sorrow songs*—following Ralph Ellison's definition of the spirituals. Hughes felt as haunted by flamenco in the *tablaos* as Lorca had felt by black music in the night clubs of Harlem:

> The guitars played behind her [Pastora Pavón, *La Niña de los Peines*], but you forgot the guitars and heard only her voice raising hard and harsh, wild, lonely

and bitter-sweet from the bare stage of the theater with the unshaded house lights on full. This plain old woman could make the hair rise on your head, could do to your insides what the moan of an air-raid siren did, could rip your soul-case with her voice. I went to see her many times. I found the strange, high, wild crying of her flamenco in some ways much like the primitive Negro blues of the deep South.[27]

No wonder Hughes could hear echoes of the blues in Pastora's *cante*. In the same thread of thought, American flamencologist Donn Pohren, who firmly believes that "the art of Pastora is inimitable," perceives the connection between blues and flamenco: "Jazz fans will note a remarkable similarity between Pastora and such early blues singers as Ma Rainey or Bessie Smith, particularly, in their earthy approach, rough, untrained voices, and profound . . . emotion."[28]

Lorca disembarked in New York when *the Negro was in vogue*,[29] when the Harlem Renaissance was displaying blacks' superb artistic skills, and when the nights of Harlem were in full bloom. Hughes reached Madrid when a fratricidal civil war was going on. The unrivaled popularity that the *Weary Blues* (1926), with its skillful use of the black vernacular, and the *Romancero Gitano* (1928) brought Hughes and Lorca respectively, weighed heavily on both writers. However, neither Lorca nor Hughes could remain indifferent to each other's use of rich folkloric manifestations, blues and flamenco, as veiled forms of resistance.[30] Neither of them could have survived in a foreign country far from home without the consolation of soulful music.

Yet, jazz and flamenco have inspired not only writers but also African American and Spanish musicians alike. For example, looking for new avenues of self-expression and having been captivated by a flamenco singing and dancing show in New York, Miles Davis (1926–1991) produced *Sketches of Spain* (1960)[31] in collaboration with piano player Gil Evans. Partially based on Maestro Joaquín Rodrigo's *Concierto de Aranjuez* for guitar and orchestra, Davis's trumpet revision was considered by some critics to be one of the most successful and astonishing blends of jazz and classical music ever. *Sketches of Spain* helped Davis to push the boundaries of jazz toward a softer sound. It came about as the result of Davis's own fascination with Spanish flamenco, Spanish dancing, and Spanish guitar, plus his determination to prove to himself how "melodically inventive" he could be. In his review of *Sketches of Spain*, Nat Hentoff wrote, "It is as if Miles had been born of Andalusian gypsies but, instead of picking up the guitar, had decided to make a trumpet the expression of his *cante hondo* ("deep song")." On "Flamenco Sketches," Hentoff adds that Davis "shows a basic affinity with the Spanish musical temperament and sinuous rhythms."[32] Whereas Miles Davis was one of the first African American jazz players to incorporate a Spanish classic, a masterly and most sensitively performed flamenco *soleá* and a *saeta*[33] within his repertoire, Pedro Iturralde, a Spanish saxophone jazz player, got into jazz and flamenco only by accident but ended up producing three albums in the 1960s, a short time after Miles Davis's *Sketches*. It all started at the Jazz Festival in Berlin (1967), where Iturralde accepted an invitation to play jazz while accompanied by flamenco guitarist Paco de Lucía. The combination of the jazz sound of the sax and the flamenco sound of the guitar could not have worked better. Together with the mastery of both players, the themes chosen fit both Iturralde and de Lucía wonderfully.[34]

If, in the 1930s, Hughes's and Lorca's warmth of feeling for blues and flamenco was authentic, and in the 1960s Davis and Iturralde actually worked on the fusion of flamenco and jazz, it is only in the 1980s that we perceived an interest in and a preoccupation with stretching the boundaries of pure flamenco in an attempt to enrich it by incorporating the rhythm of the electric guitar and by combining the feeling of blues lyrics with the *cante jondo*. Nevertheless, this trend has met some detractors among musicians, critics, and the public at large. Although the exhilarating collaboration between Raimundo Amador and B. B. King ignited the fire, other traditional *cantaores* and *cantaoras* have recently contributed to pushing the boundaries of new flamenco. For example, and to name just a few, at the Bienal de Flamenco in Seville in 1992, *cantaor* Enrique Morente sang—accompanied by fourteen young African guitarists—while African American percussionist Max Roach played with Morente and twelve of the players from Roach's band M'Boom. When asked about his recent fusion of flamenco and blues, *cantaor* José Mercé answered that as long as one preserves the very roots of both flamenco and the blues, the fusion will work for him.[35] Another traditional *cantaor*, José Soto (Sorderita) stresses that African American music is the closest thing to flamenco.[36] *Cantaora* Esperanza Fernández, who has participated in flamenco/jazz jam sessions, believes that she has personally grown wiser from singing jazz/flamenco.[37] To further illustrate the point, Ketchup's three female singers are the daughters of classical flamenco singer Tomate [Tomato]. Their catchy and now worldwide successful song, "Aserejé," is nothing but a Spanish version of Sugar Hill's rap song "Rapper's Delight," with a tinge of the Spanish guitar.[38]

Gypsy guitarist and flamenco singer Raimundo Amador (b. 1959) shares with Hughes and Lorca his love, respect, and devotion for his own folklore, culture, and tradition, but at the same time, he is as innovative and open to other musical manifestations as both writers were. Like Lorca—a poet Amador both respects and sings[39]—once he heard black music, he could not but feel the rhythm of flamenco running through the veins of the blues. As with Davis or Iturralde before him, Amador is a pioneering gypsy singer who combines cultures and music, a fact that has led to some severe criticism from the so-called purist flamencologists. When asked how he felt about it, Amador answered:

> Well, to put it boldly, I don't care. I didn't listen to my own father (who did not want me to play the blues), nor to my friends nor the critics. I listened to nobody because that blues/flamenco fusion was what I liked most. I could have chosen the easiest way then. I was already playing the guitar with a great and most respected flamenco family, the Montoyas. I am respected now because I have worked hard. Besides, I do not have to spend my whole life convincing people that I am a flamenco artist, that I play flamenco. I am not lost, as some people might think. But flamenco is not the only thing for me. I am not going to get trapped there, in the hands of flamenco because, thank goodness, I have been playing the blues for over twenty-five or thirty years now. And I am going to take advantage of that experience. Besides, I like flamenco blues.[40]

Raimundo Amador has been instrumental in blackening flamenco music with a tinge of blues,[41] and his creative pioneering attempt at blending flamenco and blues has also brought him critical recognition, both in Spain and abroad, as well as the respect of B. B. King. Amador's veneration for the blues and his mastery in making his guitar, Gerundina, sound with the feeling of the blues songs has made an impact on other Spanish musicians, composers, and bands. Following Amador's passion for blues, numerous gypsy bands now look to black music for inspiration.[42]

Raimundo Amador's professional career is not the product of improvisation and/or studio commercialization. Born and raised in Andalusia, Amador learned to play the guitar during his childhood. As art ran in his family, he lived and breathed flamenco. Amador's father worked at the U.S. military base in Rota (Cádiz), and, as he indicates in the interview, it was there, when in contact with black American soldiers who sang and played blues and jazz music, that he first became familiar with the heartbreaking sound of black music:

> The guy next door, a black soldier, played jazz, and I loved it. To tell you the truth, at that time I could not understand that music, and I did not know as much as I know now, but I could see the man could play. He played the piano, I think, and then a sax player came, and then a trumpet player joined them, and that music sounded just great.[43]

Later, Amador's family moved to Seville. Amador started playing and singing in the streets and he spent much of his early youth busking for change with his songs on street corners and in bars. It was in the flamenco bar *Los Gitanillos*, the equivalent of a blues jukebox, that Amador met legendary flamenco guitarists such as José Camaron or de Lucía. Years later, and thanks to Kiko Veneno,[44] Amador was once again exposed to blues and rock music:

> Before I heard about B. B. King, I had listened to Jimmi Hendrix and his blues *Red House*, and later, when I listened to B. B. King I was just blown away with his blues. Basically, I first listened to Jimmi Hendrix and then I just went all the way back, back [in the history of the blues], and I listened to John Lee Hooker, with his acoustic guitar (and tapping the beat with his foot); I listened to Magic Sam, I listened to Big Bill Broonzy . . . some of the best.[45]

It was after he sent *Blues de la Frontera* [*Frontier Blues*] to B. B. King that Amador's solo career took an unpredictable turn. On listening to *Frontier Blues*, B. B. King agreed to work with him. This is what B. B. King thought once he first heard Amador:

> The rhythm moves so good! When I heard the music in my mind I saw the dancers. In my mind I see the stories that they are telling either with their feet or with their mouths. I hardly know how to explain this, but there is, I think, a kinship between flamenco and blues. For example, when I play with Raimundo I can catch him. We are both performers. We have lots in common as people. So I think I want to say that Spanish music—flamenco—and American music—blues—is a marriage.[46]

Amador, who could not but thank B. B. King for his invitation to play together, stated that the fact that neither B. B. King nor himself spoke each other's language posed no problem: Their guitars spoke for them. *Gerundina* (1995), an album named after Amador's Spanish guitar, which echoes B. B. King's electric guitar Lucille, was the product of that probing and poetic partnership. Since this first encounter, B. B. King and Raimundo have shared the stage at numerous jazz, blues, and flamenco festivals. Referring to his first performance with B. B. King, Amador proudly says:

> I always feel great playing with B. B. King. At the very beginning I was shitting it. Before my own concerts I always panick for a while. But, later, when I get on stage and I play the first notes, I feel great. At the very beginning, I felt a great respect for B. B. King. He is a great star. He is a great person. He is a great musician. Everything is great about him. But, if you are not good too you simply cannot play with B. B. King because it wouldn't sound any good.[47]

For his album *En la esquina de las Vegas* [*At a Corner in Las Vegas*], Amador continued to blend flamenco and blues. For example, the lyrics of "Hoy no estoy pa' nadie" are reminiscent of traditional empty-bed blues when Amador sings about broken hearts and lonely nights.[48] Undoubtedly, *Noche de Flamenco y Blues* [*Night of Flamenco and Blues*] is most representative of Raimundo Amador's own veneration for blues and his long-lived idea that it can walk hand in hand with flamenco. It contains a recreation of the mythical *Blues de la Frontera*, which started B. B. King's and Amador's collaboration, plus a reworking of Robert Johnson's *Love in Vain*. Significantly enough, Jimmi Hendrix's *Little Wing* is one of the pieces included. One has to add only to this the presence of B. B. King on stage, playing *Bolleré*, together with Amador, and the resulting live concert crystallizes B. B. King's and Amador's emotional compatibility, thus forging a link between tradition and innovation when fusing flamenco and blues. Both B. B. King and Raimundo Amador have been criticized for respectively adulterating a traditional folk expression. However, their explorations into each other's music only made them go back to their blues and flamenco tradition with more reverie and respect for their own traditions than ever. As such, neither B. B. King nor Amador break completely with tradition. When playing this new modern acoustic sound of guitars and the traditional blues and *cante jondo*, both still play the music of their respective origins. Furthermore, the ancient songs are brought to life by the sheer newness of their approach to the sensuous sounds of their music. According to Amador:

> I always learn from B. B. King. Yesterday, for example, he was opening with some improvisations I haven't heard from him before. . . . He was playing with a Spanish tinge, flamencolike, because we have already played together in more than twenty live concerts. . . . But B. B. King was not playing blues notes but flamenco. I think he is borrowing from my flamenco notes as I am borrowing from his blues notes. After all, the two musics are not that far apart.[49]

Hughes and Lorca shared a passion for their respective rich folklore tradition: Both could see beauty and poetry where others just saw primitive popular songs. Both writers were vilified for raising the vernacular to the category of art. Hughes felt instantly attracted to flamenco because it reverberated with echoes of the blues, and to gypsies because of their long-lived struggle to survive despite the odds. Lorca was intuitively struck by the social reality of blacks in the United States and fascinated by blacks' proclivity to dancing, singing, and performing, and, especially, by blacks' blues and jazz music. Both Hughes and Lorca felt flamenco and blues shared a common history: Both artistic expressions grew out of the need to communicate the most intimate and intense of personal sentiments; they could not exist without the *feeling*, in the case of the blues, or the *duende*, in the case of flamenco. Miles Davis could neither get the *Concierto de Aranjuez* out of his mind once he first heard it, nor could he resist the haunting appeal of a flamenco show with singers and dancers. A most sensitive musician and a consummate trumpet player himself, Davis painstakingly and superbly reworked the Spanish notes of a *soleá* and a *saeta*, the most revered *cante jondo* songs, into an intimate and passionate jazz composition that redefined the connections between flamenco and jazz. This also led to a darkening of Rodrigo's composition by Davis's superb black soul.

Iturralde's experimentation with jazz-flamenco was accidental, and he never experienced Davis's obsession, but once he got started, he devoted time and energy to producing a consistent body of work that responded to his new creative impetus.

Raimundo Amador shares his veneration for black music with Lorca. Having grown up surrounded by flamenco, Amador could not ignore the heartfelt blues. At the same time, he is well aware of blacks' and gypsies' alienated lives. When asked whether he could see any connection between the way blacks have been discriminated against in the United States and gypsies in Spain, Amador responded:

> . . . gypsies did not have to work in the cotton plantations. But we gypsies have suffered from racism too. That is the reason why I wrote *Gitano de Temporá*.[50]

And:

> We are alike. . . . We share many things. The singing is . . . how could I explain it? Very moving. Flamenco and blues are very emotional. Jazz, for example, is much more open. Blues has fewer notes, and it talks about their troubles and trials, about love and pain. Flamenco deep songs [*cante jondo*], like *siguiriya* o *soleá*, basically sing about the same stuff.[51]

True to his new interest, Amador immersed himself in the history of the blues by literally listening to any singing black person at hand. His encounter with B. B. King seems only natural in view of the historical and fruitful tandem, blacks-gypsies, woven by Lorca and by Hughes. B. B. King's and Amador's mutual admiration for each other speaks volumes for the common chords that flamenco and blues touch. As B. B. King stresses:

> Blues is not only about pain. Some blues, like Spanish dancers, like the songs Raimundo plays, I enjoy it! When I was a boy, and I was growing up, many days I didn't have food. I didn't have good shoes. So, blues is all of it. It is not all the slaves songs. They sing about many things. They sing about slavery. So today when somebody says blues . . . Yes, you can be blue if you want to . . . But if I don't want to, I can boogy. Blues is a part of all of it. Just like your music. Flamenco tells stories about the life we are living. It tells stories about the life we wish we could live. Just like the blues.[52]

Both B. B. King and Amador come from a persecuted people who had been forced to live on the margins of society; both have a history of oral tradition, passed from one generation to the next. Neither singer can possibly utter a sound without the vibrant presence of the *duende* and the *feeling*. Most importantly, however, both B. B. King and Raimundo Amador respect and admire each other's musical traditions. As a result, their natural, spontaneous, vibrant, syncopated, and hot musical combination in which each singer and player gives heart and soul sparks a pure and heartbreaking magic—a unique and innovative blend of flamenco and blues. Taking off from where King and Amador have left it, a young, vibrant, and innovative generation of flamenco singers and players who are also fascinated and infatuated with blues is now experimenting with a fusion of flamenco and blues with a twist of rock and roll. As with King and Amador before them, the *duende* permeates their music.

Notes

1. Of the three thousand American soldiers who enrolled in the International Brigades, 80 percent were black, and most of them were college educated. See Arnold Rampersad, *The Life of Langston Hughes, Volume I: 1902–1941: I Too Sing America* (New York: Oxford University Press, 1986).
2. Ottmar Liebert, *Nouveau Flamenco* (Ventura, Calif.: Creative Concepts, 1997).
3. In Spanish, it is politically correct to refer to *gitanos* as gypsies.
4. Although flamenco can be sung by gypsies and nongypsies, in this essay I am associating gypsies with flamenco because it was originally sung by them.
5. Among the extensive bibliography, see, for example: Bernard Leblon, *Gypsies and Flamenco: The Emergence of the Art of Flamenco in Andalusia* (Westport, Conn.: Bold Strummer, 1995). Meticulously researched, Leblon's work traces the rise and development of flamenco music following the gypsies' long migration from India to Spain. Donn Pohren's scholarship is useful here, too. He is a passionate and respected American flamencologist and a guitarist. His book is considered, by some, the Bible of flamenco. Like Leblon, he is an authority in his field. Donn Pohren, *The Art of Flamenco* (Dorset, England: Musical New Services, 1984).
6. Henry Kamen, *Spain in the Later Seventeenth Century, 1665–1700* (London: Longman, 1980), 282.
7. In August 2002, eight gypsy families were expelled from a camping resort where they had spent their summer holidays for the previous ten years after a total of two hundred families complained they would not use shower facilities and the swimming pool with gypsies. Aymí Oriol, "Ruidosos o Racistas," *El País*, 16 August 2002, 20.
8. Giles Oakley, *The Devil's Music* (New York: Capo Press, 1997), 6.
9. Ian Gibson, *Federico García Lorca: De Nueva York a Fuente Grande, 1929–1936* (Barcelona: Grijalbo, 1987), 30. My translation.
10. Félix Grande, *Memoria del Flamenco* (Madrid: Espasa, 1979), 113.
11. An extensive literature on the history of the blues and on blues musicians exists already. For the purpose of this essay, see, for example, Oakley, *The Devil's Music*, where the author traces the history of the blues from its African roots to B. B. King, and Lawrence Cohn, ed., *Nothing but the Blues: The Music and the Musicians* (New York: Abbeville Press, 1999), an impressive and well-documented series of essays, which includes bluesmen's photos and first record illustrations. On flamenco, a field of studies that is increasingly gaining more aficionados and flamencologists, see, for example, José Caballero Bonald, *Luces y sombras del flamenco* (Barcelona: Lumen, 1975); Grande, *Memoria del Flamenco*; and Angel Alvarez Caballero, *El cante flamenco* (Madrid: Alianza, 1994). The last offers a chronological and rather sketchy study of *cante* and *cantaores*, whereas Grande's book is a personal, moving, opinionated, but quite well documented story of flamenco from its inception to guitarist Paco de Lucía.
12. On flamenco's *duende*, there are numerous theories and differing opinions. See, for example, Federico García Lorca, "Juego y teoría del duende," in *Federico García Lorca*, ed. Miguel García-Posada (Barcelona: Círculo de Lectores, 1997), 150–62. See also Timothy Mitchell, *Flamenco Deep Song* (Yale: Yale University Press, 1994). Most flamencologists devote a section to that complex and evasive term.
13. Tracing the origins of the Delta deep blues, Palmer asserts: "Blues was so disreputable that even its staunchest devotees frequently found it prudent to disown it." Robert Palmer, *Deep Blues* (New York: Penguin, 1981), 17. This disreputable beginning can be applied to flamenco, too. Thus, it is only very recently, in 2002, that the Opera Palace has welcomed flamenco concerts.
14. As translated in J. L. Gili, *Lorca: Selected Poems* (London: Penguin, 1960).

15. For Lorca's restless stay in New York, see his own "Nueva York en un poeta," in *Federico García Lorca: De Nueva York a Fuente Grande, 1929–1936*, ed. Ian Gibson (Barcelona: Grijalbo, 1987), 9–82. In particular, see the section titled "Primeros pasos por el 'Senegal de las máquinas,'" 18–34.

16. With composer and maestro Manuel de Falla, Lorca organized a festival of *cante jondo* in Granada in 1922, which, no doubt, helped to dignify the flamenco singers and the genre. Deep inside Lorca thought, as he highlighted on the occasion of the opening, "by revealing its ancient song, we are trying to discover the soul of Andalusia." Gili, trans., *Lorca: Selected Poems*, xx. The same could be said of Hughes and his poetical explorations and celebration of the black vernacular and the blues.

17. García-Posada, *Federico García Lorca*, 482.

18. Gibson, *Federico García Lorca*, 134.

19. Federico García Lorca, "Arquitectura del cante jondo," in García-Posada, *Federico*, 35–52.

20. García-Posada, *Federico García Lorca*, 166. My translation.

21. Ibid., 167. My translation.

22. Ibid., 167. My translation.

23. Gibson, *Federico García Lorca*, 28. My translation.

24. Helped by Rafael Alberti and Jorge Guillén, Hughes started translating Lorca's play *Bodas de Sangre* and the collections of poems *Cancionero Gitano* and *Un Poeta en Nueva York*. Furthermore, and according to Rampersad, Hughes lectured on Lorca. Rampersad, *The Life of Langston Hughes*, 341–55.

25. Arnold Rampersad, ed. *The Collected Poems of Langston Hughes* (New York: Vintage, 1994), 201.

26. Interestingly enough, Lorca also showed a profound admiration for Pastora Pavón and her unique performance of the *siguiriya*. Lorca, "Arquitectura," 37.

27. Langston Hughes, *An Autobiographical Journey: I Wonder as I Wander* (New York: Hill and Wang, 1956), 332–33.

28. Donn Pohren, *Lives and Legends of Flamenco* (Madrid: Society of Spanish Studies, 1988), 115.

29. I am borrowing here from Hughes's own words when referring to the Harlem Renaissance.

30. The fact that both Hughes and Lorca helped revitalize interest in blues and flamenco respectively has not gone unnoticed. For a personal, readable, and well-informed work on Lorca, Hughes, and Guillén, see Carlos A. y Fco. Javier Rabassó y Rabassó, *Granada-Nueva York-La Habana* (Madrid: Ediciones Libertarias, 1998). For a study of Hughes as a bluesman and blues writer, see Stephen Tracy, *Langston Hughes and the Blues* (Urbana: University of Illinois Press, 1988).

31. Previous to *Sketches of Spain* (1960), Davis had already improvised his haunting version of "Flamenco Sketches" in his much praised *Kind of Blue* (1959). Only one year later, John Coltrane's *Olé* is heavily indebted to Davis's experimentation with and interest in flamenco music. Miles Davis, *Sketches of Spain*, Columbia, 4606042, 1967; Miles Davis, *Kind of Blue*, Columbia/Legacy, CK 64935, 1997; John Coltrane, *Olé*, Rhino 8122799652, 2000.

32. Nat Hentoff, in Miles Davis, *Sketches of Spain*, Columbia 460604 2, 1967. Liner notes.

33. *Saetas* are powerful and hair-raising religious songs that deal with the Passion of Christ. They are sung without accompaniment during the *Semana Santa*, or Holy Week, all around Spain, but most specifically in Andalusia. When the Blessed Virgin or Christ is slowly carried through the streets, a singer (man or woman) spontaneously starts a *saeta*, and the procession stops while the *saeta* is being sung. See Allen Josephs and Juan Caballero, eds., *Federico García Lorca: Poema del Cante Jondo y Romancero gitano* (Madrid: Cátedra, 1981), 165–73. See also Edward Stanton, *The Tragic Myth: Lorca and Cante Jondo* (Lexington: University of Kentucky Press, 1977).

34. As a result of this flamenco-jazz encounter, Iturralde produced three albums: *Flamenco Jazz*, which includes poems written by García Lorca ("Veleta de tu Viento," and "Vito"); *Jazz Flamenco*, which includes flamenco songs such as *soleá* or *peteneras*; and *Flamenco Jazz 2*, with the collaboration of well-known jazz musicians. Pedro Iturralde, *Flamenco Jazz*, SABA 15146, 1967; Pedro Iturralde, *Jazz Flamenco*, Blues Note, 8539332, 1968; Pedro Iturralde, *Flamenco Jazz 2*, SABA 15146, 1968.

35. www.rutamusical.com/entrevistas/josemerce/index.shtml (26 February 2003).

36. www.flamenco-world.com/artists/sorderita/entrevista.htm (26 February 2003).

37. www.flamenco-world.com/artists/espefdez/esperanza.htm (26 February 2003).

38. Pablo Albadalejo, "Un Aserejé bien aprovechado," *El País Tentaciones*, 12 July 2002, 6.

39. The album *Pata Negra* includes a version of Lorca's *Bodas de Sangre*.

40. Raimundo Amador, personal interview with the author, tape recording, Plaza de Toros, Salamanca, Spain, 19 July 2002.

41. I am playing here with Jelly Roll Norton's thesis on the origin of jazz. He emphasized the influence of Spanish rhythms in early jazz, which he called "Spanish tinge."

42. Bands such as Ketama and Cañaveral followed where Raimundo Amador left off. Ketama (which has been defined as a cutting-edge flamenco-blues-rock group) talks about how complicated it was at first to be accepted because of their pioneering *mestizage*. In response to critics' complaints, Antonio Carmona, one of the members, argues: "I can tear off my shirt for an old *cantaor*, but I have shared the stage with Prince, I have played with him, and that makes the difference. That is something the Habichuelas [his clan] never experienced." Diego Manrique, "El triángulo Ketama," *El País Semanal*, 18 August 2002, 34–39. Ketama's albums include *Pa gente con alma* (1991), on which they fuse flamenco and Latino music, and *Songhai* (1994), on which they play with African musician Toumani Diabate from Mali, mixing African instruments and Spanish guitars. Their newest release is *Dame la mano* (2002).

43. Amador, personal interview.

44. Raimundo Amador's first band, Veneno, and subsequently Pata Negra (with his brother Rafael), represent turning points in his career when he moves from flamenco to flamenco blues.

45. Armado, personal interview.

46. B. B. King, personal interview with the author, tape recording, Plaza de Toros, Salamanca, Spain, 19 July 2002.

47. Amador, personal interview.

48. Note that Manuel, the protagonist of the song, listens to Camaron in the morning and to B. B. King at night, thus making blues and flamenco compatible.

49. Amardo, personal interview.

50. Raimundo Amador y B. B. King, *Noche de flamenco y blues*, Universal, UMD, 76162, 1998.

51. Amador, personal interview.

52. King, personal interview.

9
Monsieur Hip-Hop

FELICIA McCARREN

In a Paris dance studio in the now-hip district of Ménilmontant, just down the boulevard from Belleville, a young man wearing the latest dancewear, with a bandana headscarf, teaches a class how to point in the manner of Uncle Sam's "I WANT YOU": "Stop before the elbow is straight," he says. "Stop the gesture in motion. Otherwise you'll look like a beginner."[1] The teacher is a professional dancer in the hip-hop style; he is French—Parisian—but his parents or grandparents came from the Côte d'Ivoire. While pointing the finger attributed to the U.S. icon, appropriated by U.S. hip-hop as a gesture of anger, of accusation, he mimes the rage of working "for the man" and masterfully performs a theatricalization of black America.

Does this gesture translate into French? Does it mean the same thing in a Paris dance studio or concert stage as it does on the New York vacant lot or highly produced video? Does it mean the same thing when worked into a choreography with a modern dance movement vocabulary, a commissioned score of nonrap music, danced by dancers of all different colors?

This dancer is not the "Monsieur Hip-Hop" of my title, but he might be: one of the many figures of the crossover of a popular cultural form, originating in the United States, imported into and diffused in France, and developed into an art form with funding from national and local structures. My title refers to a *fonctionnaire* in the Ministry of Culture responsible for such funding and so nicknamed by a French research team studying the elaboration of this new form.[2]

157

My research for this essay is part of this team's larger project, titled "La transfiguration du hip-hop; Elaboration Artistique d'une expression populaire" under the direction of Roberta Shapiro.[3] The road to professionalization of hip-hop dancers; their "insertion" into the economy; the network of agents helping to develop dancers and choreographers, from professional producers to social (welfare) workers and youth leaders with no experience in choreography or theater production; and the transformation of a popular form into an art by performers, agents, and critics/journalists developing an aesthetic vocabulary[4] have been studied by this team of French sociologists and economists which I joined for fieldwork in Paris in 2001.

French histories of "le hip-hop" usually begin with the arrival of African American dancers—"the pioneers"—in Paris in the early 1980s.[5] There followed the diffusion of a movement, music, and graffiti culture from U.S. inner cities via TV and video, with both popular and institutional support. A famous photograph of President François Mitterand posing with hip-hoppers, sporting a backward baseball cap on his noble brow like a laurel crown, became an icon for his administration's enthusiastic promotion of youth culture. Embraced by Mitterand and the so-called "gauche caviar" led by his culture minister, Jack Lang, French hip-hop dance differs not only in its content and in its rhetoric from the United States but also in its connection to state arts policies. Hip-hop companies, festivals, workshops, choreographic development, and research like ours have been supported by programmers and officials like "Monsieur Hip-Hop." The state's "politique culturelle" has often been criticized as the "recuperation" of hip-hop artists as a quick fix for deep-seated social problems, including racial tensions. However, in France, the rhetoric promulgated by the funding and programming structures—as well as the dancers and companies—is one of inclusion. Discourses articulated in the ongoing debates surrounding hip-hop always engage the vocabulary of social action, antidiscrimination, cultural cultivation of the working class, and elaboration of a popular form into art, revealing dance's place in French culture as something crucial to political and social well-being, capable of doing social good and worthy of tax dollars. With a very different ambience from U.S. rap music and its commercial culture, it provides a site for reflection and discussions about race and class, opportunity and work, and professionalism and the right to artistic self-development; and it is only now beginning to be exploited for its commercial possibilities.

Hip-hop remains rooted in the *banlieue* but has become a highly visible art form. It is taught in modern and jazz dance studios in cities like Paris as well as in the multifunctional rooms of youth centers, gyms, and community theaters across France. It has a well-defined movement vocabulary, steps with names and variations, and a range of styles. It is being integrated into choreographies by well-known contemporary choreographers and taught in master classes at places like the Centre Nationale de la Danse. The possibility of a state diploma is now under debate.

In France *le hip-hop* or *la danse urbaine* is a site where "academies" of all kinds and the French version of "the streets" overlap. French hip-hop dance is linked to institutions of the state and the culture industry; it is surrounded by and generates texts of all kinds, and thrives in a culture of debate and discussion. It is a manifestation of the fact that in France dance can have a political or civic (what the French would call "social") content and give its dancers a political profile. French hip-hop dance differs in its content and in its rhetoric from the United States—where there is almost no equivalent to speak of—because of state arts policies and because of broad visibility, serious funding for dance performance, and historic respect for performers. Hip-hop dancers, after an initial stable engagement, can attain the status of "intermittant de spectacle" and receive unemployment benefits when they are not working in the theater. Hip-hoppers are being hired to appear with groups like the Cirque du Soleil, to appear in Olympic or other festivals and parades, to dance on television (à la American advertising and music videos), and even to dance with the corps de ballet in opera productions, in the 2001 production of *Le Chauve-Souris* at the Opéra de la Bastille, for example. *Danse* is only the first of the impressive list of forms of "urban culture" ("*Danse Théâtre Musique Expos Multimédia Vidéos Débats Ateliers Librairie*") included on the poster for the annual La Villette festival in Paris, now called the *Rencontres des Cultures Urbaines.*[6] Discourses of "authenticity" closely linked to a U.S. original are giving way to questions about professionalization, about artistic quality of choreography (beyond U.S.-style competitive championships or casual local circles), about contact with dancers from other countries, and about global dance traditions.

Hip-hop often serves to represent globalized U.S. culture; like bell hooks, Robert Stam and Ella Shohat have pointed out that hip-hop music, in spite of its origins in U.S. urban, ghettoized counterculture, has been diffused by U.S. multinationals and become a signal element of global culture: "A highly Africanized diasporic music, hip-hop has become the international lingua franca. . . . The same U.S. based and multinational corporations that disseminate inane blockbusters and canned sitcoms also spread Afro-diasporic music around the globe."[7] Yet in the domain of hip-hop dance, cultural differences distinguish its practice on two sides of the Atlantic. Commissions, unemployment compensation, and the politics surrounding hip-hop—including the omnipresent "question" of Africa—give the French dancers artistic goals, social profile, and political visibility. While signing globalized gestures of youth culture in movement, clothing, and gesture, hip-hop arguably has a different significance (and significa-tion) when produced on French stages in these contexts.

In the translation of hip-hop to France, a certain draining of content takes place—akin to what Pierre Bourdieu and Loic Wacquant have called "dehistoricization."[8] Bourdieu and Wacquant have complained that U.S. cultural studies theorists impose a black/white binarism in their study of other cultures, an impoverished analytic approach that is a vestige of the historic particularity of American segregation. Yet, although a certain naiveté in the face of U.S. black experience,[9] and its language of expression, facilitates this French development of hip-hop into something else, it is not entirely the "neutralization" that Bourdieu and Wacquant claim emerges from the circulation of ideas when academics theorize culture. Rather, it is the French artists themselves who pin their cause to the struggle of a peo-ple and art ghettoized in the United States, even as their situation in France is far from that of the U.S. countercultural heroes they embrace, and in many ways still further from the commercialism that has used their art to very different ends.[10]

Investigating what makes French hip-hop different, this article con-siders two features unique to the form: first, the political significance and social importance of dance in France, a historical fact being replayed cur-rently; and second, the signifying of dance's distinct, nonverbal language in its translation to a different culture. The state's *"politique culturelle"* during the last two decades—not unlike that of Louis XIV, turning swords into ploughshares via dance—has often been criticized as "recuperation." In Jean-Pierre Thorn's 1996 film, *Faire Kiffer les Anges,* one hip-hopper com-plains that this cultural politics has used young artists as a kind of "medicament social" or "social band-aid."[11] Yet hip-hop dancer and chore-ographer Stephanie Nataf, codirector of the company Choream, uses the same metaphor in a positive way, explaining in a recent interview that the company's classes for youth help them like good medicine.[12]

If funding for urban dance is sometimes seen as a "recuperation" that threatens the rebel nature of this art, it is also ambitiously sought after by dance companies who seek to sow the seeds of, rather than suppress, an "authentic" hip-hop. Mixed in with the discourse of rebellion heard at many hip-hop events, such as round-table discussions at the festival of *Rencontres* at La Villette, is the complaint that the state is not doing enough, either artistically or socially, for the body of youth involved in the "mouv." In events I attended, hip-hoppers' demand for funding suggested that for them such funding is a right, a sign of respect for citizens; its absence or diminution are indicative not simply of the administration's abandonment of arts and artists, but of the *banlieusards* themselves, immigrants, or youths "in danger."

Second, this article considers the fact that although a wordless form, French urban dance thrives—in part because of its political status—at the center of intense debates. In France, hip-hop dance events are rarely unaccompanied by some form of discussion or text, always open to the public and free. Discourses articulated in the many events surrounding hip-hop dance (panels, debates, and round-table discussions organized around performances, film screenings, and showings of works in progress) always raise and address questions about race and class, opportunity and work, and professionalism and the right to artistic self-development.[13]

Although technically wordless—extralinguistic—French hip-hop is not, ultimately, a silent form, but its "sound track" is more than American rap. Although dance and music are often cited as the truly "universal" forms because of their transcendence of language differences, and rap is marketed as a global music, dance's nonverbality allows it to bypass a certain American "content"—for example, expressed in rap lyrics—and commercialism while remaining at the center of discussions of the social and artistic development of an entire generation.[14] I will argue that in the rhetoric surrounding French hip-hop as well as its choreographies, the "content" of U.S. hip-hop culture is reinterpreted, rather than simply reproduced, in dance. The spirit and practice of inclusion, manifested in the rhetoric of the movement, is expressed choreographically in the concert dance that the hip-hop movement is now producing in France.

In Paris in 2001, *le hip-hop* was both nostalgically familiar to me and alienating, maintaining a closer connection to its late 1970s pop-culture roots and jazz dance forms, funk and R&B music, but transposed into a France with a different relation to African roots. In France, a particular social-political situation emerges from issues of immigration, as well as what could be characterized as a particular naiveté about the African American experience in white America, the specificity and homogeneity of the U.S. ghettos, and the failure of U.S. urban welfare programs.[15] The diffusion of hip-hop represents another chapter in France's twentieth-century romance with African American forms such as jazz, almost always understood as essentially "African" as well as "American."[16] While jazz, funk, and hip-hop dance developed in the United States from popular forms referencing the black American experience, the French elaboration refers to "another" Africa. Dancers of North African origin represent the majority "minority" in French urban dance companies,[17] and French hip-hop encodes the difficulties of Maghrebian and sub-Saharan first- or second-generation immigrants for whom the African continent represents a problematic, if not distant, origin quite different from the Africa often idealized in U.S. hip-hop culture.

Hip-hop serves as a prime example of multicultural urban France and its pluriethnic society in stark contrast to ghettoized U.S. inner cities and also to what is often described as the assimilationist model of French nationhood.[18] In *Deconstructing the Nation: Immigration, Racism and Citizenship in Modern France*, Maxim Silverman describes the ongoing conception of two distinct models of nation in contemporary France, the first based on the right of communities such as ethnic minorities (an Anglo-Saxon or Eastern European model) and the French model of individual adhesion.[19] In the debates surrounding the definition of "What is a nation?" Stam and Shohat emphasize that the "French model does not recognize 'race' as a valid conceptual or institutional category" and in France, the assimilationist model reigns: "The very idea of multiple models is excluded."[20] Yet Silverman argues that the "universalism, assimilation and individualism" of the French model are not opposites of the "particularism, difference and collectivity" of the Anglo-Saxon. Analyzing the contradictions of the French model, Silverman investigates not the differences between "race" and "nation" or "racism" and "nationalism," but the "articulations between them in the development of the modern nation-state."[21]

In France, the rhetoric promulgated by the funding and programming structure—as well as the dancers and companies—is one of inclusion. In Steve Cannon's phrase, this puts French hip-hoppers "well in advance of the forces of the official left"; their movement "has the potential to raise the colors of the 'flag of unity' way beyond its initial audience in the banlieues."[22] Adopted, in Cannon's view, from Africa Bambaata's model of "positivity,"[23] this discourse counters the use of the term of "exclusion" to describe the French equivalent of "underclass."[24] In France, this "positivity" so permeates the "mouv'" that terms like "posse" take on a communitarian, even familial tone, losing their connotation of outlaw justice or breakaway, sectarian individualism. In the first full-length book by an academic on the movement in France, ethnolinguist Claudine Moïse writes: "In the beginning, in the hip-hop movement, there is the posse: a kind of extended family to which each member feels attached, through their home territory, and also by affinities. An allusion to a North-American mythology about the solidarity of a sort of troop of justice-seeking cowboys, the posse is a term without marked connotation, harmoniously resonating with the possibility of freedom, and letting everyone find his own place . . ."[25] In opposition to U.S. rap music, with its commercial culture and its growing equivalent in France,[26] hip-hop dance creates an atmosphere closer in spirit to the French movement of May 1968 than to the American 1980s. This positive tone, whether inspired by U.S. hip-hop's origins or ignoring much of its later content, animates the debates and round tables, organized by the funding structures and also by collectives such as Mouv'N Action.

In the spirit of this mixing, French urban dance adopts images and ideas from black America as one part of the mix. In the more general case of French hip-hop culture, Cannon notes the "specific character of their appropriation" of rap[27]: not the black nationalist or separatist, but a pluriethnic variety that rises from the French suburbs, which have nothing like the homogeneity of U.S. urban inner-city ghettos. In the wake of decolonization and immigration, the denizens of hip-hop in France have stronger links to Africa than their U.S. counterparts but also access to an America that is in many ways, for them, more mythic: The use of the word *black* in contemporary parlance,[28] rather than *noir*, aligns those described by it with America rather than the region referred to as *l'Afrique noire*. Yet as the tripartite title of one of the first French urban dance companies *Black Blanc Beur* indicates, the term functions not in a binarism imposed by the segregated U.S. model, but in sync with postcolonial France and its *verlan* backslang coinage of *beur* for *arabe*, inventing new labels for French of African birth or descent.

In spite of the admiration for American rap music and its constant presence in urban dance classes, the language difference ultimately means that the crucial content of U.S. rappers' songs and their critical messages are ignored or read as inspiration, as the spirit rather than the letter of "gangsta" law. French parents take their young children to learn funky moves in hip-hop dance classes where the recorded musical accompaniment often features explicit lyrics in English of which they seem to be blissfully ignorant.[29] Although in the world of French hip-hop, the concern with authenticity includes using American words as a touchstone, they are only one of many codes in the movement. Nearly as omnipresent as French *verlan* are the official acronyms for the "zones with priority for urbanization" (ZUP), from which hip-hoppers come, and the agencies supporting immigrant families, such as the FAS (*fonds d'action sociale pour les travailleurs immigrés et leurs familles*), the third of the three partners (the other two are the Ministry of Culture and the Parc de la Villette) sponsoring the biggest annual hip-hop dance festival.

In addition to the citation of American words, an entire poetics—beyond *verlan*—is generated around French hip-hop. In one conversation, dancers remarked on the difficulty of using French institutional vocabulary (drawn from classical, contemporary, or jazz dance) for teaching hip-hop, which the establishment of a diploma would necessitate. American words remain crucial in the teaching of French hip-hop, but they are often not the same words as those used on the other side of the Atlantic.[30] Certain dance steps, for example, have a different name in French: The "electric boogie" was referred to as "le smurf"—a term borrowed from white-glove-wearing cartoon characters, *les schtroumpfs*. The range of texts available on hip-hop, including children's how-to manuals, include lexicons and define the names and steps using both American and French slang.[31] But—as in the case of "posse"—they often provide definitions, giving words a different resonance than in the United States.

Far from simply imitating an American model, French hip-hop mixes and invents. And unlike the American model, in French hip-hop, the discourse of inclusion has not erased the possibility of individual multiethnic individuality. Such pluralism is now being explored choreographically through the incorporation of moves from traditional or ethnic dances. Articles on urban dance published in 1996 used the vocabulary of *mélange de genres, métissage, liberté,* and *intercommunalité culturelle*.[32] For many of its performers, hip-hop remains rooted in the *banlieue*, but in practice it has become a highly visible and varied art: The choreographic content of French hip-hop has expanded significantly in the last five years, with movements from *la danse orientale*, Brazilian *capoeira*, pan-African dance, and a whole range of traditional dance forms as well as modern dance. The promotional materials for a 2002 festival that promised a work by choreographer Mourad Merzouki—filmed by Jean-Pierre Thorn some years earlier stating that the essential for dance was rage—staged a work on his company *Käfig*, "sur une musique originale arabo-andalouse."[33]

This spirit of mixing marks hip-hop choreographies against a background of discussion of "authenticity." Because it promotes art with a message of *métissage*, hip-hop can be understood as promulgating a kind of "authentic" ethnic, minority identity while mainstreaming it. With access to national stages, hip-hop now injects high-art culture with the popular as much as it detours the marginal, destining it for another audience. In the *Suresnes Cités Danse* festival, at a theater just outside of Paris, for the past ten years, hip-hoppers have danced for contemporary choreographers; at the former festival of urban dance now under the rubric of *Rencontres des Cultures Urbaines*, at La Villette, since 1996, many hip-hoppers have been supported in their choreographic development. The 2000–2001 season featured the work of choreographers who began as dancers and who—with support from the festival, the Parc de la Villette, and its linked center for choreographic development, the Fondation de France's "Initiatives d'Artistes en Danse Urbaine"—have succeeded in booking some of the biggest stages for contemporary dance. Their contracts are impressive, equivalent only to the major U.S. touring companies.[34]

While this breed of hip-hop mixed into modern dance is traced, in a recent article by Rosita Boisseau and Dominique Frétard in *Le Monde*[35] to U.S. influences such as the Urban Bush Women and Doug Elkins, some of the U.S. modern dance companies able to integrate hip-hop into their repertories, including Elkins and Rennie Harris Puremovement, have found crucial funding from French structures.[36] Although by the time American hip-hop music arrives in France and its marginality has been marketed, French dancers still remain surprised that the great dancers they revere as the "pioneers" have never been recognized or funded—and work, for example, as pizza deliverers.[37] The French artists and social workers inspired by U.S. hip-hop both ally themselves with the marginalized and are themselves the agents who mainstream this popular culture, albeit differently than in the United States, as they deftly use (and allow themselves to be used by) French institutions.

Although French respect for concert dance sometimes threatens the development of new forms, and hip-hoppers sometimes see the possibility of a diploma, for example, as destructive for the "authenticity" in the form, these choreographies (for example at Surenes, La Villette) bring to dance performances people who would otherwise not go to the theater. Hip-hop dance is in some ways only now beginning to be exploited for its commercial possibilities; thus far, many companies have been focused on live stage performance rather than television or film work. A warm dance public seems guaranteed for this dancing, forged out of the already existing public interested in modern and classical dance and in the youth culture of hip-hop. In the past decade, hip-hoppers have been solicited by producers and choreographers of concert dance to bring "life" to the proscenium stage.[38]

Thus far in French hip-hop, institutional funding has neither aimed nor succeeded at erasing the notion of authenticity. Assimilation and individual integrity or ethnic identity, in the world of French urban dance, are not contradictory. French institutional money can "buy" authenticity, in the form of subventions to dance companies—such as *Käfig*—bringing U.S. hip-hopper "Clown" to perform with them as they did for *Dix Versions* in 2001, or to film productions privileging the form's African American precursors. Choreographer Christine Coudun, cofounder of *Black Blanc Beur*, writing in 1996, argued that improvisation is the best working method for the elaboration of choreography and defines good sense as the "harmony between an authentic style of hip-hop (preserved in the group over ten years) and artistic sensibility."[39] Yet in many cases, rhetoric about "authenticity" seems to complement rather than describe choreographic projects. Companies such as Choream, with dancers rooted in hip-hop practice and style, do not worry about it: Stephanie Nataf states in a recent interview that she and José Bertogal, codirector of Choream, don't care any longer if the label hip-hop is attached to their work.[40] The tendency toward eclecticism in hip-hop choreographies, imported through contact with dancers from other traditions or even cultural tourism, as in Accrorap's 2000 and 2001 collaborations with Brazilian or Indian dancers, does not efface the hip-hop "content" in their choreography.

The example of French hip-hop dance thus contradicts Bourdieu and Wacquant's critique of the globalization of imperial U.S. culture, defying stereotypes even while recycling them. It is both supported by the centralized state and municipal funding agencies and studied by academics. It is both popular and a recognized art form, now coming onto the biggest dance and theater stages in the country, and touring (*Käfig*, for example) to New York with the best-known modern dance companies. While prestigious theaters, including the *scènes nationales*, and avant-garde festival directors rival each other to program the best new hip-hop, contemporary choreographers work with hip-hoppers and vice versa, youths keep coming up from the *cités* inspired by an "American" original, and companies such as *Käfig* hire U.S. dancers to appear with them. Paris's annual hip-hop festival at La Villette, the *Rencontres*, has been a primary supporter not only of French but also of fledgling American concert dance companies with hip-hop roots such as Rennie Harris Puremovement.

With many minority groups identifying as marginalized across the globe, French hip-hoppers subscribe to black U.S. culture to articulate their own differences. French hip-hop is inspired by African American culture and continues to valorize it, but draws its strengths now from current multiethnic urban France and reflects not only source cultures of its dancers identified as "issus de l'immigration," but also the presence of "high art" concert dance and classical ethnic dance forms highly visible in cities like Paris. French hip-hop dance exists because it has been cultivated in a culture in which a dancer can be an upstanding citizen, and in which those wishing to speak out against social and political problems and for themselves can use dance to articulate their citizenship. Its success in France makes the U.S. alternatives of ghettoization and commercialization of dance pale in comparison. It has taken a different course in France because the state as well as its subjects understand that art can do civic work, and that dance and the discourses surrounding it have political power that both have been savvy enough to deploy.

Notes

1. Fieldwork done at the studio Georges Momboye, La Maroquinerie, Ménilmontant, Paris, 2001.
2. See Roberta Shapiro and Marie-Christine Bureau, "Un nouveau monde de l'art? Le hip-hop en France et aux Etats-Unis," *Sociologie de l'art* 13 (2000): 13–32; Roberta Shapiro, "La

transfiguration du hip-hop," in *Vers une sociologie des œuvres*, vol. 2, ed. J. O. Majastre and A. Pessin (Paris: l'Harmattan, 2001), 81–119.

3. Roberta Shapiro (LAUA/Laboratoire d'Architecture, Usage, Altérité), Marie-Christine Bureau (CEE/Centre d'Etudes de l'Emploi), and Isabelle Kauffmann (doctoral candidate, Université de Nantes). Our project title is "La transfiguration du hip-hop: élaboration artistique d'une expression populaire," funded in part by the Ministry of Culture, Mission du Patrimoine Ethnologique. See Roberta Shapiro, Isabelle Kauffmann, and Felicia McCarren, "La danse hip-hop; apprentissage, transmission, socialisation," Rapport pour la Mission du Patrimoine ethnologique, Ministère de la Culture et de la Communication, January 2003.

4. Roberta Shapiro has analyzed how this critical discourse has influenced and directed the actions of the many agents producing hip-hop and how these agents preceeded this critique. Roberta Shapiro, "Note sur la critique artistique de la danse hip-hop," *Sociologie de l'art* 2 (nouvelle série) (2002).

5. This was the case with a documentary film that I have not seen, commissioned for the *Rencontres Urbaines* and screened during the festival at La Villette in 1999; see also Claudine Moise, *Danseurs du Défi* (Montpellier: Indigènes, 1999).

6. "Dance, Theater, Music, Exhibitions, Multimedia, Videos, Debates, Workshops, Bookstore."

7. Robert Stam and Ella Shohat, "French Intellectuals and the U.S. Culture Wars," *BlackRenaissance/Renaissance Noir* (2001): 90–119. In their response to Pierre Bourdieu and Loic Wacquant's critique of U.S. academic multiculturalism, Robert Stam and Ella Shohat use hip-hop to characterize a great divide between Anglo-American and French intellectuals. Cultural studies have made important inroads in the United States and the United Kingdom in the exploration of such popular forms: "But in France there seems to be a gap between the highly miscegenated streets of Paris and Marseille and the theorization of culture by intellectuals, who seem invested in conventional hierarchies, at least in the realm of high culture and theory"(112). For Stam and Shohat, this is a gap within France that the case of hip-hop music exemplifies. Emphasizing what they type as "French" misunderstanding of a left intellectual undertaking in what they—ironically—argue should not be typed as "Anglo-Saxon" intellectual milieus, and defending the integrity of an intellectual field (multiculturalism) against what they characterize as Bourdieu's and Wacquant's dismissive summary of a "marketing gimmick promoted by Routledge" (113), Stam and Shohat argue that important work is being done, for example, on French hip-hop and *banlieue* culture in the United States and United Kingdom, sometimes by French-speaking scholars. Whereas hip-hop is usually studied as a global phenomenon, for Stam and Shohat it is a site revealing differences between traditions—in this case "French" and non-French analyses, and "theory" and the streets. In fact, the difference to be found in French hip-hop dance is in how it negotiates this divide, not only in its manifestations in theory, but in its artistic practice.

8. Pierre Bourdieu and Loic Wacquant, "On the Cunning of Imperialist Reason," *Theory, Culture and Society* 16 (1999): 51.

9. At one round table during the *Rencontres* at La Villette 2000, discussion suggested some historical confusion among the speakers and public regarding the specifics of segregation in the United States.

10. The French adoption of American hip-hop takes on an added dimension when considered in the context of French governmental control of U.S. cultural imports (for example, in cinema). In addition, the importation and development of hip-hop follows in some ways the patterns established by modern dance in France—eventually institutionalized alongside classical ballet. Thus rather than a form of cultural imperialism, this importation might be viewed as an often-repeated pattern of French absorption of avant-garde or foreign forms into its cultural institutions.

11. Jean-Pierre Thorn, *Faire Kiffer les Anges*, La Sept Arte, Agat Films & Cie, 1996. Documentary film in French, ninety minutes. When asked whether he viewed his commission from a municipality as such a "recuperation" at a round table at La Villette 2000, one grafitti artist replied in anger not that he (or his art) were being recuperated, but that he was recuperating the municipality.

12. Stéphanie Nataf, "Ce que je crois, par Stéphanie Nataf," *Le Monde*, 11 January 2002, 27. "Notre danse est une sorte de médicament qui peut faire du bien, un bien qu'elle nous a apporté."

13. In my observation, such debates were organized around the social or political issues surrounding hip-hop, including the right to artistic freedom and development, but rarely touched on questions of aesthetic form or "content" of choreographies.

14. Recognized patterns of the global diffusion of rap, its marketing and message, do not hold in the case of French hip-hop dance. Discussing the commercialism of rap and its relation to French urban dance, Philippe Mourat, whose title is "chef de projet à l'Etablissement public de la Villette, Directeur des Rencontres des cultures urbaines," said in an interview: "La danse a été protégée de ça" ("Dance has been protected from that"). In "Le Hip-Hop est-il récupérable par l'Etat?," *Mouvements* 11 (Septembre-Octobre 2000): 67.

15. Loic Wacquant has underlined the noncomparability of U.S. urban ghettos and the French suburban *cités* where hip-hop reigns. Loic J. D. Wacquant, "Pour en finir avec le mythe des 'cités-ghettos'; les différences entre la France et les Etats-Unis," in *Les Annales de la recherche urbaine*, ed. Serge Paugam (September 1992): 20–30. For Wacquant, the "underclass" is a nonexistent group created by journalists and academics in the United States to hide current conditions of crisis and the failure of social programs for the urban poor. See also Loic J. D. Wacquant, "l'underclass urbaine dans l'imaginaire social et scientifique americain," in *L'exclusion: l'etat des savoirs* (Paris: La Decouverte, 1996), 248–62.

16. A 1995 film program, under the aegis of the Cinémathèque Française, showed films from African American dancers like Josephine Baker to African dance captured in ethnographic films. See the program for "Rythmes et Continents Noirs," a film series at the Cinémathèque de la Danse on 13, 14, and 15 January 1995. In this programming, as in documentaries linking African American jazz dance to African dance forms, the programmers seem to be influenced by the aesthetic of the French review *Documents*, whose two issues from the 1930s juxtaposed ethnographic documents from Africa with photographs, film stills, and reviews of the performances of African Americans. On Paris as a meeting point for African Americans and Africa throughout the twentieth century, see Tyler Stovall, *Paris Noir: African Americans in the City of Light* (New York: Houghton Mifflin, 1996). Films screened at the *Rencontres* urban dance festival have also included archival footage of African American dancers, including the Nicholas Brothers and cakewalk dancers.

17. Whereas in his study of French rap, "Panama City Rapping: B-Boys in the Banlieues and Beyond," in *Post-Colonial Cultures in France*, ed. Alec G. Hargreaves and Mark McKinney (London and New York: Routledge, 1997), Steve Cannon has remarked on the paucity of Maghrebian rappers (155), other commentators have remarked on the omnipresence of Maghrebian performers in all the arts in France. See also David A. McMurray, "La France Arabe," in the same volume, 26–39. For the particular case of cinema, see, also in this volume, Carrie Tarr, "French Cinema and Post-Colonial Minorities," 59–83.

18. See David A. Blatt, "Immigrant Politics in a Republican Nation," in Hargreaves and McKinney, *Post-Colonial Cultures in France*, 40–58.

19. Maxim Silverman, *Deconstructing the Nation: Immigration, Racism and Citizenship in Modern France* (London: Routledge, 1992), 4.

20. Stam and Shohat, "French Intellectuals and the U.S. Culture Wars," 106–7. Others have argued that multiple models and differences are necessarily present and incorporated into an ideology of assimilation.

21. Silverman, *Deconstructing the Nation*, 5, 8.

22. Cannon, "Panama City Rapping," 164.

23. Ibid., 161–62.

24. Bourdieu and Wacquant, "On the Cunning," 49. Underlining the differences between the U.S. and French situations, Bourdieu and Wacquant speak of the French use of the term "exclusion" to describe the marginalized equivalent of the American "underclass." Although not ghettoized to the same extent as in America, and in an infrastructure far from its American counterpart, the French "underclass" is for Bourdieu and Wacquant "a fictional group, produced on paper by the classifying principles of those scholars, journalists and related experts in the management of the (black urban) poor who share in the belief in its existence because it is well-suited to give renewed scientific legitimacy to some and a politically and commercially profitable theme to mine for the others" (49).

25. Moïse, *Danseurs du Défi*, 88. In the texts on sale at the book exhibit as part of the La Villette festival, ranging from children's how-to manuals to scholarly studies of the movement, the lexicons almost always included in the books uniformly list "posse" as unmarked term of collectivity.

26. See, for example, André J. Prévos, "Le Business du Rap en France," *The French Review* 74, no. 5 (April 2001), 900–21.

27. Cannon, "Panama City Rapping," 161–63.
28. The word *black* is listed in the *Dictionnaire bilingue de l'argot d'aujourd'hui; Bilingual Diction of Today's Slang* (Paris: Presses Pocket, 1996), 364, as a standard, nonslang term for a "black person."
29. Since French rap groups such as NTM do use explicit language, the French public cannot be assumed to be naïve about hip-hop lyrics, yet the same suspension of judgment seems directed toward rap lyrics in English as to Anglophone rock and roll. Songs by Lou Reed or David Bowie containing explicit references to drugs and sex are being played regularly in their original versions on the sound track of the Monoprix stores.
30. In classes in which the teachers give the names of the steps and insist on their importance in the professional practice of hip-hop, English names are almost always used; other names seem to have been invented in French as the steps themselves may have been. In one ninety-minute class, I practiced the following steps and learned their names: le "pimp walk," le "scoobeedoo," le "chamadoo," le "pace" (a movement referring either to punching the time clock or hitting the drummer's cymbal), le "scoobot" (a step in which the dancer imitates starting the scooter with one hand and braking with the other), and "le stop and go" (a step similar to the walking steps of the American dance the "bus stop"). Although in this regard a certain Americanism reigns, French invention and mispronunciation make the vocabulary less American overall.
    In another class I attended regularly in 2001, I rarely heard the teachers use the name of a step, although they sometimes used the vocabulary of classical or modern dance (such as "first position"). Yet when trying to teach me "la coupole"—the move in break dancing where the dancer, down on the floor, kicks up into a spin on the upper back—they reverted to broken English, in no way comparable to my command of French. Having said to me earlier, "This dance comes from there [the United States]," the teacher may have felt I could better understand how to perform it in my native language or in the language of its invention.
31. See, for example, Marie-Christine Vernay, *La Danse Hip-Hop* (Gallimard: cite de la Musique, n.d.) in the series *Carnets de Danse*, which includes modern, jazz, and classical dance manuals for children. This book, priced at approximately fifteen euros, includes a music CD commissioned from Franck II Louise and helps the children who can afford it not only learn the steps, but also choose their clothing, organize hip-hop dance parties, and speak the lingo.
32. "Danser la Ville," *Territoires* (la Revue de la démocratie locale) 372 (Novembre 1996): 18, 27.
33. See *Programme* for the 2002 festival in *Suresnes Cités Danse, Le Monde*, January 2002, iv.
34. These include "Drop It!" by Franck II Louise, later contracted for a run at the Palais de Chaillot. The dancers' contracts include provisions for snacks in the dressing rooms, publicity and contract materials, courtesy of Franck II Louise and the Fondation de France, Parc de la Villette.
35. Rosita Boisseau and Dominique Frétard, "Dix Coups de Cœur pour fêter les dix ans de Suresnes Cités Danse," *Le Monde*, 11 January 2002, 26.
36. Although Rennie Harris was first signed by the Parc de la Villette, the Suresnes Cités Danse festival presented his *Rome and Jules* in January 2001. Other U.S. companies using hip-hop movement vocabulary or dancers include those of New York choreographers Maya Claire Garrison, Jane Comfort, and Ralph Lemon.
37. Conversation with Olivier Sergent, "administrateur" (manager for the company) Melting Spot, at La Villette *Rencontres Urbaines*, November 2000.
38. Several commentators have noted an "Arab" rejuvenation of the various performing arts in France. See David A. McMurray, "La France Arabe."
39. Christine Coudun, "La companie Black-blanc-beur: du désir au besoin," in *La Hip-Hop Danse; de la rue à la scène, Rue des Usines* 31–32 (Winter 1996): 50.
40. Nataf, "Ce que je crois, par Stéphanie Nataf," 27.

10

Rap, Rebounds, and Rocawear
The "Darkening" of German Youth Culture

CATHY COVELL WAEGNER

German youths saunter through the shopping malls wearing Fubu crop tops and baggy Ecko pants; they dance to the rhythm and blues of R. Kelly in the clubs, rap along with Shaggy on their ghetto blasters, and greet each other with elaborate hip-hop hand gestures; young athletes wear bandanas or "raised" Rocawear hats and thick gold necklaces while playing streetball or counting rebounds in televised NBA games or attending breakdance workshops at local youth centers; cornrows compete with dreadlocks as popular unisex hair styles; and teenagers of both sexes maintain their summer tans in fitness studio solariums. Young people flock to Lauryn Hill concerts to hear her open confession of faith, and Christian youth groups conduct church services based on gospel singing and Martin Luther King, Jr. speeches. African American (women's) novels, notably those of Toni Morrison, are now staples of school and college syllabi, with courses in African American studies very much in demand. The European MTV programming is dominated by black groups, Denzel Washington and Will Smith are but two of countless top black movie star idols, and sitcoms focusing on African American families abound. Newspapers feature huge photos of Michael Jordan or Venus and Serena Williams or Tiger Woods in full sports action. "Mr. Deutschland 2002" is a 28-year-old African German Lufthansa pilot. Any teenage conversation is dotted with slang perceived as African American, such as "man," "to diss" (meaning to criticize), the omnipresent "cool," or the affectionate greeting "Whassup nigga?" For the young people in Germany, "black" is undeniably *in*.

This article will offer some reasons for this striking phenomenon, based on a small-scale survey of young Germans. A common assumption that the darkening results largely from the increasing Americanization of German popular culture will be tested with an eye to German television programming. An analysis of the powerful hip-hop marketing mechanisms will prepare the way for the outline of a theory of "cultural adulation" to attempt to account for the Germans' double-edged fascination with all things black, and to point out the risks involved in their foregrounding of blackness. We will look at the recent historical background of this phenomenon, focusing on the twenty-year evolution of the magnetic German hip-hop scene with its "freedom-fighting" grafitti artists and popular freestyling rappers. Some attention will be paid to the complex interweaving of African, Caribbean, and African American influences, as well as to the legitimizing of hip-hop culture through the anchoring of rap texts in the school curriculum.

Why are black influences so marked? Interviewed on possible reasons for their admiration of black America, students point to the "charisma and exoticness" of black cult figures, often having grown up in disadvantaged circumstances, like the black rapsters who have "dared to develop their own styling and their own way of using words" despite ghetto dangers or mainstream pressure toward conformity.[1] The defiant individuality and enviable success turn the performers into role models: "The African American style makes the young people feel as self-confident and cool as the singers and sports stars appear on TV." Some interviewees see the blackening in universal or generational terms ("the grass is always 'blacker' on the other side" or "every generation has to find a way to rebel against its elders"). Others emphasize the German *adaptation*, not copying, of black habits, trends, and language, reflecting the creativity of the fans of black, a feature that has predominated in the German hip-hop/rap scene. One thoughtful respondent pointed out that the postwar generations of Germans have a particular sensitivity for historically oppressed minorities. A large number of interviewees, however, consider the darkening simply as a result of media imperialism, a strand in the "daily Americanization taking place in TV, movie theaters, and the music scene." Some of the better-informed interviewees were aware that the African American influence on the *American* youth culture, and thus indirectly on the German scene, far exceeds the extent that population statistics would lead one to expect.

This hypothesis of darkening through Americanization can be roughly tested by glancing at the blackness of TV programming in Germany. Both the segments taken over directly from American television (such as the core of MTV, the dubbed sit-com series like Will Smith's *Fresh Prince of Bel Air*, the *Oprah Winfrey Show*, the synchronized feature films) and the German productions, including the German MTV sequences and the VIVA and VIVA-plus music channels, reveal a strong black presence, with the German productions featuring many black faces and voices not of African American origin. African German commentators, show hosts, and MTV announcers now receive top ratings and are greatly sought after, like the Austrian/German/Ghanese talk show host Arabella Kiesbauer, with high household-recognition ratings.[2] The widely viewed coverage of media awards shows was drenched in blackness in 2002: Not only did the American Academy Awards highlight African American stars, with Denzel Washington as "Best Actor" and Halle Berry as "Best Actress," but also the Berlin Media Prize Awards (Bambi Awards) featured engagé American soul singer Macy Gray ("Sexual Revolution") as the "shooting star of the year." British black Craig David was declared "Best R&B Singer" during the MTV Europe music awards, whereas for German rap fans, the dark Samy Deluxe stole the show as "Best German Artist."[3] The New York R&B singer Alicia Keys was crowned "Grammy Queen" in February 2002. The sports coverage of American football and basketball with their largely black teams has increased dramatically on such sports channels as DSF, just as the African or black South American soccer stars are particularly visible in televised German games. One telling example reflects the powerful interrelationship among television, sports, and black attractiveness: In one of his regular guest appearances on the popular RTL *Champions League* soccer report program, the beloved emcee Günther Jauch of the German *Who Wants to be a Millionaire?* show unabashedly drew on the erotic fascination with the black body—and an objectification of it, linked to a subtle racism, as we will discuss later. During a live interview with the handsomely muscular Ghanese German national player Gerald Asamoah, Jauch invited the TV audience to win a prize by calling in with the estimated circumference of Asamoah's upper thigh. After an exact, suspenseful, on-camera measurement with a tape band, Jauch determined the winner—a young woman who screeched with joy—out of the astonishingly wide range of answers. No African Americans were involved in these sports media high jinks.[4] Indeed, the African or African European component in television broadcasting is, as we have seen, strong and appears to be growing. It seems, then, that a direct "Americanization" process, although undoubtedly powerful and pervasive, does not supply a full explanation for increasing "darkening."

Before considering the concept of "cultural adulation," which relates to indirect Americanization with regard to the phenomena of "ethnic intimacy" and "decorative racism" and might shed some further light on the darkening in Germany, we need to look at the way blackness is presented and sold—in other words, at *marketing*. Few of the young informants in the survey on reasons for the blackening specifically mentioned marketing, which perhaps shows the sublety or simply taken-for-grantedness of its mechanisms. In a follow-up survey of other students, the issue of hip-hop marketing was directly addressed and yielded a spectrum of attitudes.[5] Some interviewees felt that the antiestablishment nature of hip-hop music, "dynamic and different from the usual smooth radio fare," makes purchasing its striking consumer articles—from skullies and muscle shirts, sneakers and sunglasses, du-rags and platinum jewelry to caps and skateboards— "both a political and an aesthetic statement"; for these enthusiastic students, the professional marketing of hip-hop is insignificant: "Hip hop would be popular even without marketing." For them, African American music groups seem less "designed or built up" by professional music producers deliberately "trying to meet the needs and desires of a specific mainstream target group with a certain amount of spending money" than other popular rock and pop groups. Other informants felt that the consumerism has encouraged "a fixed style and specific accessories," which have become a type of "uniform," thus undermining the "subversive" thrust of hip-hop. These students tended to view the hip-hop merchandisers as "color blind," selling "new American products and fads on the European market, no matter what the cultural source"; capitalizing on—and to a certain extent creating—the longing of many young people to be close to America, even if only through purchasing its products. These radical skeptics claimed that young Germans' fascination with African American culture and merchandise is purely the result of media/marketing influence, not the quality of the tangible and intangible products, and these skeptics reject the consumer influence on principle: "I never feel the need to dress like the person whose song I'm listening to!"[6] A minority of interviewees simply categorically dislike rap music and the accompanying hype: "No marketing strategy could ever persuade me to buy a hip-hop CD!"

In fact, the marketing gives deeply mixed signals to young consumers: The wealthy glitter of gold chains of the successful rappers *and* tough lyrics and tattoos of the disadvantaged ghetto are simultaneously communicated to the young. Using the rapper Busta Rhymes, highly visible in Germany, as a small case study, we see that his charisma as a role model and the thoughtfulness of his direct television addresses to the German MTV public, as well as the playful ones of his team, are inextricably linked to his image as a tough gangsta with shocking language and ostensible misogyny in his rap texts. Busta Rhymes is frequently featured on *Fett* [in hip-hop English "phat" = "cool"] *MTV*, the late-night segment focusing on hip-hop. He often recapitulates his rise from the ghetto, his career of adventuresome creativity, and his values of industriousness and family. His partner group, Flipmode Squad, touts his CDs on *Fett MTV* by jocularly specifyin' on each other and the German audience ("If you haven't heard of 'Busta Rhymes,' I don't know what *rock* you've been livin' under!"). Busta's website[7] is a masterful high-tech product, with dark wallpapers highlighting the inviting menu points, including the opportunity to "meet and greet" Busta himself—if the website visitor's CD number on his or her Busta Rhymes *Genesis* album, readily available and prominently displayed in music stores, is the lucky one. Busta's performance tour in Germany was advertised in ticker-tape text running throughout the coverage of a live concert by Missy Elliot, the high-profile female rapper. The text extolled him as a versatile, "charismatic personality in the hip hop biz: musician, producer, actor, label boss, bandleader, style-setter, PR man, father, role model." For the youths who attend his concerts or purchase his CDs, which often include fellow rappers in guest appearances, the rap texts laced with "nigga," "sh—," "bitch," and "f-"words might shock at first, but soon meld into the overall hip-hop scene. After all, Missy Elliot says "bitch" and "motherfu—" nearly as much as Busta. The European promotion of the tough but high-achieving Busta is targeted, sophisticated, and thorough—little wonder that he is a cult star for young Germans.[8]

In exploring the German young people's fascination with blackness, I find myself developing a theory of *cultural adulation.* Unlike the emulation of all things French in the eighteenth century—language, literature, art, style, "savoir faire," and sophistication of the aristocrats—by the upward-striving scions of the European bourgeoisie, this current adulation involves a kind of "cultural slumming." The music, language, and dress of the Bronx block parties originally propagated by the economically and socially powerless black youth of the urban ghettos in the 1970s[9] captivate not only the German minority teenagers in similar economic circumstances, but also—and now perhaps chiefly—the offspring of middle- or upper-middle-class families. In the United Kingdom, the phenomenal rise of Caribbean creole slang among the London school children provides a gemlike example of "downward" adulation: Despite the bleakest of future prospects for disadvantaged young blacks in such areas as Brixton, where black unemployment is sky-high, their jargon has been embraced by their white fellow students; each school district even sports its own street-talk vocabulary items, making the insider/outsider line a linguistic more than racial or class one. Although in the larger British society, black talk is the least prestigious, on the streets black English is the most privileged and admired variety. As the cultural linguist Tony Thorne of King's College London puts it, in contemporary Britain "those who have least in material terms and in terms of power possess linguistically what is most prized—amongst young people at any rate."[10]

An earlier version of this downward cultural adulation can be seen in the rise of literary and lifestyle bohemianism in the nineteenth century. The "Trilby" mania provides a particularly spectacular example of a trend arising from an underclass, captivating both sides of the Atlantic and involving blatant commercialism: George du Maurier's serial *Trilby*, first published in the United States in *Harper's* in 1894, was the story of a Parisian laundress, Trilby, who becomes an artists' model for three penniless bohemian painters because of her large but perfectly proportioned feet. The painters from well-to-do British families were "slumming" in choosing to immerse themselves in the Paris underworld—as were, vicariously, the chiefly middle-class readers. The internationally best-selling novel not only reflected a middle-class fascination with deliciously "forbidden" bohemianism, however; it also "engendered a national foot fetish," complete with such consumer fad articles as new lines of "Trilby shoes," silver scarf pins in the shape of Trilby's nude foot, and even ice cream molded in the same form.[11]

The clearest precedent of cultural adulation, perceived as "downward" by most of the casual admirers, is of course the Harlem Renaissance, during which all things of African (American) blackness fascinated the white public. Harlem was invaded on Saturday nights by well-to-do young whites looking for erotic black jazz.[12] The ghetto tourists jammed such jazz centers as the Cotton Club, to which, ironically, black patrons were denied entry. Although the discrimination against African Americans, both in the North and the South, escalated during the 1920s and 1930s, with lynchings reaching an all-time high, jazz was adulated and emulated, entering the white mainstream music culture in countless ways. Even the language of jazz began its striking influence on standard American English at this time. By the 1940s, for instance, Helen O'Connell, a white singer with Jimmy Dorsey's band, was singing the refrain, "Man, that's groovy!,"[13] which was echoed in the spectators' and radio listeners' speech. An additional twist in this downward/upward pattern was the adoption of jazzy black jargon, including "cool" and "heavy," by largely white marginal groups, such as the beatniks and the hippies, which was in turn popularized by such (British) working-class music groups as the Beatles and the Rolling Stones—then appropriated by young people of all classes everywhere.

Houston Baker's concept of cultural "marronage"[14] provides a clever, albeit radical, theoretical tool for this discussion. He sees the emergence in the 1920s of a visibly influential African American expressive culture, which embraced strategies of hybridity, deformation, masking, and inversion, to be analogous to the guerilla warfare of the maroon communities of fugitives and runaway slaves, which dotted the pre–Emancipation Proclamation South and served to undermine and subvert the established order. In Baker's understanding of the influence of the Harlem Renaissance, the focus is not on the white adulators' adoption of black culture, but rather on the blacks' agency in infiltrating and even triumphing over white expressive forms. In the case of our current hip-hop mania, however, a focus on either the white consumer-adopters or the black "gangsta" warriors makes short shrift of a crucial mechanism: the marketing machinery, which we have just seen at work in the Busta Rhymes promotion. The largely invisible marketers behind global MTV, hip-hop merchandising websites, and CD and video distribution, as well as international music-group tours, provide the interface and encourage the ostensibly unmediated interaction between the African American idols and the European adulators.

Homi Bhabha warns against allowing this marketing mechanism to dominate cultural interchange; in his *Location of Culture*, this warning is addressed to cultural analysts, but his admonition would equally apply to the local warriors and consumers on either side of the Atlantic: "Any transnational cultural study must 'translate,' each time locally and specifically, what decentres and subverts this transnational globality, so that it [i.e., the cultural study] does not become enthralled by the new global technologies of ideological transmission and cultural consumption."[15] This "transnational globality" is taking on subtle forms, however, which involve its own deliberate decentering and subversion. The marketing of the master rapper Busta Rhymes in Germany shows the power of those "new global technologies," the enthrallment on the part of many youthful consumers, and the attempt by the marketers to erase their tracks, giving a sense of direct connection between gangstas and fans. The performance style of the internationally performing rappers and hip-hop groups reinforces this sense of interconnection and familiarity, even intimacy; as one student fan in our survey put it, "the hip-hoppers are working with the audience, which is part of the performance and thus part of the hip-hop family." Sophisticated marketing has assured the sale of all available tickets to a Missy Elliot concert, but when she comes down from the stage to walk through the vast audience, and arms of all colors reach out to make contact with her, she, with the help of her handlers, has—at least from the point of view of the young spectators—successfully "translated" global consumption into local and ethnic intimacy.

Another warning in connection with the European adulation of blackness can be found in a Harlem Renaissance novel that has only recently begun to receive the critical recognition it deserves; in the chapters set in

Denmark, Nella Larsen's *Quicksand* depicts a subtle form of racism among liberal whites. Their cultural adulation of the exotic mulatta Helga Crane constantly foregrounds her ethnicity. In a kind of "decorative racism,"[16] her Danish aunt and uncle lavish clothing and accessories upon her, all of which correlate to *their* notions of Africanness; they even select her outfits, often inappropriately brightly colored and daringly low cut, for various social events in order to flaunt her dark skin. The mongrel Helga is, paradoxically enough, treated like an expensive purebred pet, which is viewed only in terms of its bloodline and the features of its breed. The Danish relatives are deeply disappointed by the failure of their matchmaking attempts when Helga refuses to marry a white artist they have selected for her; he is also chiefly attracted to Helga because of her exotic appearance and cannot comprehend her rejection of him. This form of adulation, in which the skin color is viewed positively but is nonetheless the key factor in categorizing the Other, reinforces the superior status of the adulator. The ethnic subject becomes objectified, put on display in a cage, as it were, whereas, in this metaphor, the adulators are either zookeepers, like Helga's Danish relatives, or unabashed tourists at the zoo. The German coach of a third-division soccer team reflects the marketing ramifications of this ethnic tourism among present-day young Germans when he claimed, as quoted in a regional newspaper, that the number of stadium spectators would rise dramatically if the team could afford to literally "purchase" another attractive black player.[17] This admiration of blackness by young Germans and the population at large as spectators is often divorced from practical matters literally close to home, however, such as housing. The head of student services at Cologne University announced on a recent radio broadcast that difficulties in new students' finding apartments to share or rent in the Cologne area are directly related to the degree of darkness of skin color.[18] It also seems that blacks from certain countries of origin are more "decorative" than others; Africans in Germany tend to perceive a difference between the way they are treated in the community or by officials and the way lighter-skinned comrades from the Americas or Europe are received.[19]

With its combination of adoration and objectification, the current German double-edged adulation of blackness has its twentieth-century roots in Germany's scramble to obtain African colonies in the late nineteenth century. The few black immigrants to Germany, mostly tribal aristocrats, from its four colonies[20] were considered desirable and able to be civilized, even occasionally marrying into upper-class German families. The ideology and blatant discrimination that accompanied Hitler's rise to power transformed this frequently patronizing fascination into pure racism. Hans-Jürgen Massaquoi's recent autobiography of a Liberian German

growing up in Nazi Germany movingly depicts the painful daily humiliation of being stared at and deliberately pointed out as an inferior Other,
particularly by schoolteachers, even though Massaquoi had been born and
raised in Hamburg by his German mother and, as a young school boy,
joined his classmates in worshipping Hitler, even sporting a swastika.[21] As
a recent documentary shows, the few blacks who escaped the concentration camps were forced to take on demeaning jobs, such as portraying
primitive natives in the propaganda films of the Hitler years.[22]

The postwar occupation of Germany by the Allied troops placed American black soldiers firmly in the midst of the German population, where
these "Joe Louises" fascinated with their music, bubble gum, and exotic
appearance. Little wonder that Massaquoi chose to "pass" as an American
whenever possible in postwar Germany and eventually found himself
sought after as a sax player in Hamburg jazz bands, more for his skin color
than his musical ability.[23] The generation of African German children that
emerged from soldier-civilian encounters was followed by further mixed-
blood offspring as the military presence continued, particularly in Bavaria
and Hessia, until the present. Fascination did not in fact replace racism,
however, in the German society at large, and the African German offspring
experienced considerable prejudice in the civilian communities. That
racism and fascination can go hand in hand is shown by an incident recorded in Mary Wertsch's interviews of children who grew up in military
families. A black child named Olivia recalls walking down the street in a
German town with her high-ranking African American father. Wertsch recounts Olivia's story: " 'An old German lady came over to us, frowning and
saying something. She put her hand on my father's face and tried to wipe
his color off. That made a lasting impression on me.' [Olivia's] father held
his temper, stepped back and walked around the woman with quiet dignity
and military bearing."[24]

Whatever discrimination the young African Germans experienced, they
came into their own among their all-white peers—apart from those associated with the unsettling proliferation of neo-Nazi groups—in the early 1980s
when the first wave of hip-hop culture washed over Germany. Break dancing
and rap jams were incomplete without some darker faces, and rap groups
sought interculturality as they introduced black tropes into their music and
stage presence. The way had been paved by reggae, which was a popular music
genre in Germany in the 1970s, probably even before its mixing of Caribbean
rhythms and protest with the New York rap scene migrated to Germany.

African Germans moved toward self-empowerment, organizing them-
selves into support groups such as the ISD (Initiative Schwarze Deutsche/
Initiative Black Germans) and the ADEFRA (Afrodeutsche Frauen/African
German Women).[25] Today the deliberately highly visible and articulate

African Germans have become a force influencing young people and even social politics. The Brothers and Sisters Keepers is a case in point. Founded by the Cologne reggae star Adé after the murder of a Mozambican by skinheads in Dessau, June 2000, this group of well-known African German singers, DJs, and producers from the rap, soul, and reggae scenes made public statements against racist violence and produced a best-selling album of songs explicitly condemning racism at all levels in German society.[26] Even a partial list of members reads like a *Who's Who in Black German Music* and reflects a colorful multiethnic and geographic mix: Xavier Naidoo, from Mannheim, South African mother, father of Indian ancestry; Afrob, an East African from Stuttgart; D-Flame, a Jamaican German born as Danny Kretschmar in Frankfurt; Meli, whose father is from St. Kitts, mother from Germany—Meli was born in the United Kingdom and lives in Stuttgart; Bintia, born in Magdeburg of an African father and German mother, and lived in the Caribbean; DJ Tomekk, Polish mother and Moroccan father, born in Krakow and lives, like Bintia, in Berlin and Tyron Ricketts, rapper and actor who grew up in a small Austrian town with his Austrian mother and Jamaican father, now lives in Cologne. To meet the burgeoning needs of the African German music scene, in 1997 Ricketts founded Agentur Panthertainment, an agency for music artists of African ancestry who consider Germany their home. He has also produced a short film called *Afrodeutsch*, portraying his experience with right-wing violence in Germany and Austria; it was featured at the Sundance Film Festival in Salt Lake City in January 2002 and released in German cinemas the following September.

In the late 1970s, when American rap songs began to be distributed in Germany, they quickly achieved cult status with a small percentage of German youths. The African American origins were preserved purely, accompanied by such side effects as the establishment in Germany of a branch of the Zulu Nation, Afrika Bambaataa's antidrug, propeace organization focusing on hip-hop as a common bond. Quickly, however, German hip-hop took on its own personality, following the lead of the rap group Advanced Chemistry, made up of three second-generation immigrant youths (Haiti, Ghana, Italy) from Heidelberg.[27] Born in Germany and possessing German passports, they nonetheless felt the sting of racial-ethnic discrimination. Their highly successful song, "fremd im eigenen land" ("foreign in our own country"), with such lines as "Is it so strange when an Afro-German speaks German—and doesn't have a pale face?," integrated music and frank social protest in the tradition of the best of the Bronx rapsters. The figures of the rappers and their respective "scenes" were foregrounded, the personal protest arising from their own experiences, living conditions, and social context. Break-dancing contests and rapping jams grew more and more popular; graffitti became high and forbidden art, particularly painting train cars in the densely developed German railroad network. A whole new vocabulary of "Anglicisms" arose ("Wholecar," "Wholetrain," "Window-Down-Wholetrain," "Top to Bottom," or simply "T-to-B"), and the thrill of outsmarting the alert trainyard guards, particularly in Berlin, gave the entire hip-hop movement adrenalin and a sense of New York ghetto adventure and defiance of the police. The rap groups were localized, every city having its own distinct scene, not unlike America with its regional East Coast, West Coast, Midwest, and the new South as well as St. Louis rap.

The second generation of hip-hoppers moved decidedly farther away from the African American origins. The break into mainstream music was achieved by the German rap group Die fantastischen Vier (the Fantastic Four), whose songs, especially "die da?" ("her? over there?") became household standards for German teenies. In the beginning of the 1990s, this group brought the rap music genre to the attention of major labels and recording studios, and instead of protest, the theme of young love reigned, albeit provocative in several senses. The underground rapper scene became solidified in seeing the Fanta Four, disrespectfully so-called by the undergrounders, as their commercialized target for barbs and mockery.

The current third hip-hopping generation places the most value on freestyling, which is carried out to a fine art in huge "battle rap" sessions that range from local parties to large media events attended by thousands of youths. The hand gestures, which seem to aid the rappers in finding the rhyme beat, are particularly reminiscent of African American rappers, although to some extent moving beyond their gesture conventions into a type of rapping sign language. Although the released rap texts have remained strongly autobiographical, symbolic body language accompanies the performance, pushing the specific autobiography into the realm of metaphor. In the televised version of the German/French hip-hop festival in Saarbrücken—called "Saar-Brooklyn" during the concert—in the summer of 2001, an intensive but mock fight between the white German rapper Thomas D.,[28] covered with black zigzag tattoos, and his wildly dreadlocked African guitarist, dressed in white, took place to a rhythm of mimed jab and blows accompanied by a staccato of electric guitar chords. The enthusiastic European spectators were not experiencing this performance as an Americanization of their culture or as a substitution for fulfilling the dream of actually traveling to America one day. The metaphorical battle, like most archetypal theater, was depicting a ludic contest between equally matched competitors—no signs of white or American superiority in this here-and-now, both playful and urgent postmodernist confrontation with its displaced aggression.

The underground character of rap is being both capitalized on and undermined by the plethora of schoolbooks that integrate rap into the school curriculum, particularly in music, German, and English classes. Some of these books, such as Loh/Verlan's *HipHop Arbeitsbuch* (workbook),[29] even relate the rhythms and themes of hip-hop to German literary classics such as Johann Wolfgang von Goethe, Joseph von Eichendorf, and Thomas Mann. In addition to drawing on the appeal factor of rap to enliven the often dry teaching of German literature, this anchoring of rap texts in the curriculum serves to legitimize hip-hop culture. The textbooks are accompanied in the popular press by a plethora of survey or introductory books and hip-hop lexica, including an English-German dictionary with the ambiguous title *Explicit HipHop*.[30]

A newly released DVD shows the technical sophistication of the current German hip-hop scene and its media experts. *Battlemönche* (*Battle Monks*) recounts the giant Hamburg "Flash 2001" rap festival, with the DVD format permitting the viewer to edit and recut his/her own rap film or audio CD.[31] The break dance and rap *battles* are versions of the traditional African American ritual boasting contests, like "playing the dozens" and "specifying," although some rappers are more aware of the connection to African American roots than others, as the interviews in *Battlemönche* reflect. Indeed, two opposing directions in the ever evolving German hip-hop scene are represented by the fundamentalist rappers who want to return to the basics of (German) hip-hop and preserve the underground, even confrontational character of its origins on both sides of the Atlantic, and the either more experimental or smoother ones, who produce eclectic rap and generally seek commercial success. Perhaps the most representative figure of the future of German hip-hop would be a multicultural, multilinguistic, and multitalented young star like Denise M'Baye. This rapper/ singer/actress boasts German, Senegalese, Indonesian, and Dutch immediate ancestry; she is a native speaker of German and French, also fluent in English, rapping in a mixture of hip-hop, jazz, and soul sounds in all three languages with the D-Pfunk band on her first album, released in spring 2002. It is easy to understand why she is avidly admired by the German youth as a proponent of sophisticated blackness, relating the African American hip-hop strategies to global interculturality.

The enthrallment of the German youth with all things black is a complex mixed blessing. On the negative side, it makes them vulnerable to global marketing wiles and the tendency to use skin color as an essential(ist) category. However, it involves an opening up to creative ethnic impulses that encourage salutary multiethnic protest and tolerance. It has also tempered the Americanization of the media and marketing landscape with intercultural influences from the Black Atlantic, Africa-direct, and Europe itself. The 1900s have often been called the "American century"; if the predilections of the German youth allow international prognoses, all signs point to the twenty-first century becoming that of the "African American"—with a strong dose of healthy cultural hybridity.

Notes

1. Approximately fifty students in the English department at the University of Siegen/Germany gave their opinions on the reasons for "darkening" in Germany.
2. Kiesbauer, who has conducted her successful talk show *Arabella* since 1994, was the addressee of a letter bomb attack by right-wing radicals in June 1995. She made headlines in July 2002 with her public announcement she might give up her daily 2:00 P.M. show in favor of starting a family, and was thus featured on the covers of TV magazines.
3. Because of this award and other forms of success and his reactions to them, Samy Deluxe has been disowned by the underground hip-hop scene; see, for instance, the interzine "Vorlaut," www.laut.de/wortlaut/artists/d/deluxe_samy/biographie/index.htm (31 January 2002).
4. After an oral version of this article was presented at the MESEA (Multi-Ethnic Studies: Europe and the Americas) conference in Padua, June 2002, a member of the audience rightly pointed out that the titillating but defused eroticism of such media gags can be seen as contributing to a cultural sanctioning of serious sexual exploitation based on color—the sexual tourism of European men in Southeast Asia or European women in the Caribbean or the involuntary prostitution of black women in European cities are cases in point.
5. About sixty media studies students were interviewed. For the full texts of some of their statements, see the University of Siegen student website titled "Media and Economy of North America," www.fb3.uni-siegen.de/sisib/seminars/ENA/home.htm; click on "hip-hop marketing" (17 October 2002).
6. These students use the website marketing of hip-hop brands as an example of blatant commercialism, for which blackness is merely a commercial ploy. A prime example is www.hiphopcloset.com (15 October 2002), which features approximately thirty hip-hop brands, including Tommy Hilfiger, Wu-Wear, Ecko, Rocawear, Fubu, Baby Phat, No Limit, Bushi, and Snoop Dogg. It is worth noting that Spike Lee's controversial film, *Bamboozled* (released in 2000; synchronized as *Showtime* in German), satirizes the Tommy Hilfiger brand, calling it "Timmi Hilnigger," because of its supposed strategy of encouraging low-income/ghetto youths on both sides of the Atlantic to buy its expensive products.
   A new development is the touting of luxury articles in rap songs and hip-hop videos. The rising sales of Courvoisier cognac, Louis Vuitton bags, and even Bentley convertibles after their association with rap stars reflect how far hip-hop marketing has moved beyond low-income youths. P. Diddy, the notorious "king of hip-hop tastemakers," has caused $295 Prada sneakers to become a "hot item." Johnnie L. Roberts, "The Rap of Luxury," *Newsweek International* (7 October 2002): 58.
7. www.bustarhymes.com (1 October 2002).
8. Busta Rhymes was selected "Best Male" in the "International Hip-Hop" category during the "German Black Music Awards" in Oberhausen, October 2002, selected by Internet votes. The white rapper Eminem, however, perhaps overtopped Busta, winning "Best Single," "Best Video," and "Best Album." Internet participants had been specifically permitted to cast their votes for Eminem although he is *white*. This was justified by the young Germans' feeling that "in Eminem's white body there is a black soul"; see, for instance, the biography on the popular music news site, www.laut.de/wortlaut/artists/e/eminem/index.htm (31 January 2003).
9. The Caribbean/reggae underclass component is significant; the disc jockey Kool Herc, who immigrated to New York from Jamaica in 1967, was the main figure in the sound system battles of the early Bronx block parties of the 1970s, combining reggae flair with new techniques of "break beat." The ancient sources of rap in the villages of West Africa before the slave trade time are described in numerous handbooks, such as Sebastian Krekow, Jens

Steiner, and Mathias Taupitz, *HipHop-Lexikon: Rap, Breakdance, Writing & Co: Das Kompendium der Hiphop-Szene* (Berlin: Lexikon Imprint Verlag, 2000), 10.

10. Quoted in Simon Elmes, *The Routes of English, Parts 1–4* [with four CDs] (London: BBC, 2000), 100. In this fine new four-part textbook, Thorne presents an example of British schoolchildren's street talk with its "hundreds" of words meaning "great/excellent/ace": "One school may say *dark* or *det* or *wicked* or *shuysty* and then the next school will have some of those words but they may also favour the words like *fat* and *tick* and *def* and *chris*" (98).

11. Michael Soto, "The Bohemianization of America (and the Americanization of Bohemia)," in *Literature on the Move: Comparing Diasporic Ethnicities in Europe and the Americas*, ed. Dominique Marcais, Mark Niemeyer, Bernard Vincent, and Cathy Waegner (Heidelberg: Universitätsverlag Carl Winter, 2002), 30. Soto's article provides a colorful analysis of the Trilby phenomenon in his larger discussion of the often only symbolically aggressive relationship between bourgeois society and avant-garde movements.

12. The cultural attractiveness of Harlem has been reconfirmed by the recent opening of a grand musical, *Harlem Song*, written and directed by the black playwright George C. Wolfe, at the newly renovated Apollo Theater in Harlem. A revue/review of the past one hundred years in Harlem, it "asserts the district's inarguable status as black America's creative mecca," as a critique in the *Financial Times* (European edition) stressed. The article also points to the economic advantages of the event with regard to tourism: "Foreign tourists have long enjoyed the neighbourhood's gospel music and soul food; now they can discover the Apollo, too" (8 August 2002), n.p.

13. The example is mentioned in a British textbook: Robert McCrum, William Cran, and Robert MacNeil, *The Story of English* (London: Faber and Faber, 1992), 241. The chapter "Black on White" (209–50) has an excellent discussion of the influence of African American talk on standard English.

14. Houston A. Baker Jr., *Modernism and the Harlem Renaissance* (Chicago: Chicago University Press, 1987), particularly chapter 8.

15. Homi K. Bhabha, *The Location of Culture* (London: Routledge, 1994), 241; he draws on Carol Breckenridge and Arjun Appadurai, *The Situation of Public Culture* (unpublished manuscript).

16. With regard to the French admiration of Josephine Baker in the 1920s, see Günther Jacob, "HipHop—Folklore wider Willen: Das Ghetto als Disneyland," *Die Zeit* 37 (9 September 1994): 80.

17. *Siegener Zeitung*, June 2002, n.p. This same regional newspaper reported on, and included a large photo of, an (African) "victory dance" ("Siegestanz") performed by the team's two black players, one from Senegal and the other from Guadaloupe, after a decisive goal. The Senegalese player was labeled a "black pearl" ("schwarze Perle") in the article (2 May 2002, n.p.). Similarly, in a big color photo, the *Westfälische Rundschau* featured the two black Brazilian players of the Dortmund First Division club giving a cheer after a successful goal; caption: "black-yellow joy" ("schwarz-gelber Jubel"), only ostensibly referring to the colors of the club's uniforms (19 November 2001, n.p.).

18. WDR 5 broadcast aimed at new students, 28 September 2002.

19. Based on conversations with African students at various locations, 2002.

20. Deutsch-Südwestafrika (now Namibia), Deutsch-Ostafrika (now Tanzania, Burundi, Ruanda), Cameroon, Togo.

21. Hans Massaquoi, *Destined to Witness: Growing Up Black in Nazi Germany* (New York: HarperCollins, 1999).Translated German edition: "*Neger, Neger, Schornsteinfeger*": *Meine Kindheit in Deutschland* (Zürich: Verlag Fretz and Wasmuth, 1999). The German title is more telling: "*Neger, Neger, Schornsteinfeger*," a common children's rhyming taunt that haunted Massaquoi's childhood: "Negro, negro, chimneysweep."

22. This movement from exotic desirability to demeanment, particularly with regard to the German film industry, is excellently presented in the 2002 German documentary *Pagen in der Traumfabrik: Schwarze Komparsen im Deutschen Spielfilm* (*Pages in the Dream Factory: Black Extras in German Film*), broadcast on Arte, 1 March 2002.

23. Ironically enough, when Massaquoi indeed immigrated to the United States in 1950 and was promptly drafted, he experienced strict segregation in Southern army camps. He found it appalling: "It was utterly ludicrous that a nation that prided itself on its democratic traditions and looked down on the Nazis for their racial attitudes would segregate soldiers who

served in the same army and who were expected to fight the same enemy" (*Destined to Witness*, 428).

24. Mary Edwards Wertsch, *Military Brats: Legacies of Childhood Inside the Fortress* (New York: Harmony Books, 1991), 338. American authorities felt no responsibility for illegitimate "brown babies" born in Germany, as they were German citizens. There has been progress in cooperation on such matters, as the recent Congress of African-American and Black German Communities on 7 April 1997 suggests.

25. The name of ISD was recently changed to Initiative Schwarze Menschen in Deutschland/Initiative for Black People in Germany to open it up to African students and asylum seekers. ADEFRA was founded in connection with the publication of a key work encouraged by Audre Lorde: Katharina Oguntoye, May Opitz, and Dagmar Schultz, eds., *Farbe Bekennen: Afro-deutsche Frauen auf den Spuren ihrer Geschichte* (Berlin: Orlanda Frauenverlag, 1985) [English edition: *Showing Our Colors: Afro-German Women Speak Out* (Amherst: University of Massachusetts Press, 1991)]. Other recent works have followed that seminal collection of autobiographical essays, such as Ika Hügel-Marshall's *Daheim unterwegs: Ein deutsches Leben* (Frankfurt: Fischer, 2001) [English edition: *Invisible Woman: Growing Up Black in Germany* (New York: Continuum, 2001)]; Thomas Usleber, *Die Farbe unter meiner Haut: Autobiographische Aufzeichnungen* [*The Color Under My Skin: Autobiographical Notes*] (Frankfurt: Brandes & Apsel, 2002). There is also an engagé project called *AfroDeutsch* sponsored by the Verband binationaler Familien und Partnerschaften/Society of Binational Families and Relationships.

Two recent scholarly works that analyze the situation of African Germans in the twentieth century are Katharina Oguntoye, *Eine Afro-Deutsche Geschichte: Zur Lebenssituation von Afrikanern und Afro-Deutschen in Deutschland von 1884 bis 1950* (Berlin: Hoffmann & Hoyer Verlag, 1997); Susan Arndt, Heiko Thierl, Ralf Walther, eds., *AfrikaBilder: Studien zu Rassismus in Deutschland* (Münster: Unrast Verlag, 2001).

26. Roughly thirty German stars are taking part in this German branch of the international Brothers Keepers. The title of their first album, *Lightkultur* (released in December 2001), was a pun on the controversial government integration policy advocating a "Leitkultur" (dominant culture). The right-wing scene reacted strongly to Brothers Keepers' criticism, sabotaging the singers' website, www.brothers-keepers.de (13 October 2002)—the guestbook still remains closed. A second album is planned nonetheless.

27. Torch from Haiti, Dofi the Linguist from Ghana, and Toni the Cook from Italy. The video version of the song, filmed on the legendary Heidelberg bridge, can be viewed in the German documentary *Lost in Music*, 1993, which was awarded the Adolf Grimme prize.

28. Thomas D. is a member of the Fantastic Four who has created his own separate image as a daring, engagé rapper.

29. Hannes Loh and Sascha Verlan, *HipHop; Sprechgesang: Raplyriker und Reimkrieger; Ein-Arbeitsbuch—Materialien für den Unterricht* (Mülheim: Verlag an der Ruhr, 2000).

30. See for instance David Dufresne, *Rap Revolution: Geschichte, Gruppen, Bewegung* (Zürich: Atlantis Musikbuch-Verlag, 1997) [French original edition: 1991]; Sebastian Krekow and Jens Steiner, *Bei uns geht Einiges: Die deutsche Hiphop-Szene* (Berlin: Schwarzkopf und Schwarzkopf Verlag, 2000); Sebastian Krekow, Jens Steiner, and Mathias Taupitz, *HipHop-Lexikon; Rap, Breakdance, Writing & Co: Das Kompendium der Hiphop-Szene* (Berlin: Lexikon Imprint Verlag, 2000); Niels Robitzky, *Von Swipe zu Storm: Breakdance in Deutschland* (Hamburg: Backspin, 2000); David Toop, *Rap Attack: African Jive bis Global HipHop* (Planegg/Munich: Hannibal/Verlagsgruppe Koch, 2000) [English original edition: *The Rap Attack: African Jive to New York Hip Hop* (Cambridge, Mass.: South End Press, 1985)]; Sascha Verlan, ed., *Arbeitstexte für den Unterricht: Rap-Texte* (Stuttgart: Philipp Reclam, 2000); Sascha Verlan and Hannes Loh, *20 Jahre Hiphop in Deutschland, 1980–2000* (Höfen: Hannibal/Verlagsgruppe Koch, 2000). Bernhard Schmidt's English-German dictionary (*Explicit HipHop, Englisch-Deutsch: Das Rap-Wörterbuch* [Norderstedt: Books on Demand, 2001]) is cleverly decorated, designed to attract youthful readers.

31. Andreas Hoepfner and Tim Löhr, directors, *Battlemönche: Flash 2001*, Dartclub, 2002.

11
A.R.T., Klikk, K.A.O.S., and the Rest
Hungarian Youth Rapping

ÉVA MIKLÓDY

One of the main purposes of this book is to present a variety of evidence that African American culture has left indelible marks on the cultural productions of European countries. Considering, for instance, former and recent, well-known and popular pieces of various genres of the performing arts such as music, dance, and even film produced in countries of Western Europe, this task seems to be an easy one; "blackness" saturates rhythms, rhymes, melodies, images, styles, and gestures created by Western European artists. It seems, however, a much larger task to locate the sociohistorical, cultural, and even psychological roots of this intriguing phenomenon for Europe at large. Even with recent efforts to create a united Europe, the countries in Europe have always been sharply divided by the diverse ways of their historical and cultural developments. One of the consequences of this division is that American "blackness" is not imitated, drawn upon, or incorporated into cultural creations in a uniform way in Europe. This seems to be of particular interest when considering the African American cultural influence on countries of the former Eastern Bloc, as will be shown in the discussion below, with Hungary as its main focus.

Hungary's case indeed can be regarded as an intriguing one. It has been bearing an especially heavy burden of a singular kind of historical and cultural detachment as its historical and cultural development has always been largely defined by its peculiar geographical position. Being a kind of a borderland between the East and the West, Hungary's role as a cultural mediator needs to be emphasized: It has often functioned as a sort of a junction at which both oriental and occidental cultures could meet and intermingle with each other.[1]

A significant outcome of Hungary's specific geographical situation, as well as of its unique historical development for the study of the relationship between African American and Hungarian cultural expression, is the fact that it has never had a black population as many of the Western countries have had. Therefore, the youth and people in general in Hungary have mostly received mediated information about black Americans, their condition, and their culture. A good example of such mediated transference of cultural products can be the musical forms of the blues and jazz. Hungarian jazz and blues musicians are more likely to have drawn on the domesticated white versions of the blues and jazz than on their indigenous black counterparts.

My goal in this chapter is, thus, to show how African America has influenced Hungary's cultural development: a country regarded as a remote one from the earlier Eastern Bloc by reason of its historical and cultural detachment and, besides, a culture most often neglected when Eastern Europe has been highlighted in any number of contexts. Therefore, I am certain that Hungary's example of drawing on works of art by African Americans will serve well to underline the presence and popularity of black American culture in this part of the world.

How, then, has African American cultural expression become a significant presence in Hungary recently? Before World War II, Hungary's interest in African America must have been purely cultural and restricted to productions in music. During the period of communist rule, the situation changed to a considerable extent: Because one of communism's basic policies was to express sympathy to all "oppressed" peoples in the world—hypocritical as this attitude was because communism was also an oppressive system—the Hungarian people started to receive historically and politically valid information about the plight of the black population of the United States. This is especially true of one of the most turbulent periods of black history, the 1950s and 1960s. Accordingly, there were regular news reports, for instance, about the lynchings committed by the Ku Klux Klan, murders, race riots, the Civil Rights Movement, Martin Luther King's activities and his assassination, the role of the Black Panthers, and so on. Although book publishing was highly censored in those times, at least the major works of Richard Wright and Ralph Ellison were accessible to the general reading public in translation. In addition, a whole generation grew up on the music performed by Bessie Smith, Billie Holiday, Louis Armstrong, Duke Ellington, Ella Fitzgerald, Charlie Parker, and Miles Davis. Furthermore, spirituals and gospel songs were not only favored by, but were also included in the repertoire of numerous choirs. Ever since the fall of communism, there have been no obstacles of any kind—political, economic, or technological—for African American cultural products to either enter Hungary or take roots there.

Thus, in response to the central query of this chapter, I have chosen to present Hungarian rap as a form of expression that would have the closest and strongest links with black America. The fact that in Hungary other musical genres originating in black culture—such as the blues, various jazz-based forms, and rock and its numerous offshoots—have also flourished, however, necessitates further clarification of this choice. My two main reasons, thus, are the following: On the one hand, it is rap's timeliness and subsequent immediacy that can validate it as the focus of this essay; on the other hand, this is the only form of expression that has emerged from a common socioeconomic background in the two cultures, as will be explained later.

Taking the vast geographical, historical, cultural, and, not less importantly, linguistic differences that exist between African America and Hungary, the mere idea of Hungarian youth rapping may seem bizarre to many. Still, it is an unquestionable fact: Hungarian youth do rap. The most striking evidence of this is the existence of approximately *three hundred* rap groups from all parts of the country, out of which about 50 can be considered as enjoying a wide-ranging popularity and about 150 have been registered on an Internet rap homepage.[2] One can only guess that the total number of Hungarian rappers might even exceed this sum. Three hundred is, undoubtedly, an astonishing number, especially if the present demographic state of the country is taken into consideration: Out of ten million people, more than half can be classified as elderly. This is important to consider because rap is basically popular with the younger generation. Thus, it seems to be an undeniable fact that rap is doing surprisingly well in Hungary, and it also underlines my choice of this type of creative expression in explicating the "blackening" of Hungarian culture. Added to this is the fact that rap in Hungary is not only an exceptionally popular musical genre but also constitutes a considerable segment of the recent and present Hungarian youth subculture.

The most irking question, however, remains. How and why could rapping become a significant mode of Hungarian youth's musical and verbal performance despite the fact that it is an indigenously African American cultural practice with roots stretching as far as the oral and musical traditions of West Africa? How could Hungarian youth adopt and "naturalize" what rap is in all its complexity? In other words, what do Hungarian youth have to do with what is described as

> ... a unique U.S. inner-city fusion of funk, technified reggae, teen-to-teen "hardcore" rock, and the early '70s' "poetry of the black experience" of Nikki Giovanni, the Last Poets, etc. [which] has, since its late-70s delivery at the record-scratching hands of Africa Bambaataa and his Zulu Nation, Sugar Hill Gang, Kool Herc and his automated Herculords, and Grandmaster Flash, always had its real roots in the Neighborhood, the black gang-banger Underground, like trees over septics. Black music, of and for blacks.[3]

Difficult as it is to find a satisfactory answer to this query, this specific cultural phenomenon can be explained as the transcultural adaptation of an originally black musical form, the basic impulse of which can be sought in the nature of black music itself. It has become a commonly accepted fact by now that youth in many different countries and societies have found in black music—in addition to appealing musical qualities, including tonality and rhythmic structures—a language and a set of symbols with which to give voice to their own age, feelings, experiences, and reactions to the social and human world surrounding them. What else would account for the fact that in Hungary alone, with few exceptions, all the musical forms regarded as indigenously African American have been adopted, naturalized, and practiced? Some groups or soloists even gained world fame: The Benko Dixieland Band, for instance, had been, at one time, announced as the world's best. Or the name of the double-bass player Pege Aladar would ring familiarly in the ears of many jazz enthusiasts. Consequently, it can be seen that all black musical traditions have had an important and useful interpretive resource for the creative work of Hungarian groups.

The crosscultural adaptation of any art form, though, may cause anxiety about issues concerning artistic appropriation, authorship, originality, artistic integrity, intertextuality, or even the anxiety of influence. When Mark Costello quotes that rap is "of and for blacks,"[4] it can only be hoped that he does not repeat the erroneously exclusionist concept of the black nationalists of the 1960s, according to which black art was meaningful only for blacks because no other people could identify with their specific "black" experience. In this age of globalization, such an idea is untenable as it has always been because it deprives the artwork of its universal validity and usefulness. Without violating the unity of form and content, any art form including rap can be borrowed and applied in different sociocultural circumstances.[5]

This, clearly, also holds true for the rappers in Hungary. In this connection, it is the function of black musical tradition as *interpretative* resource that needs to be emphasized. In other words, Hungarian rap by no means should be understood as a one-to-one adaptation of its black counterpart. Culture that travels undergoes major degrees of transformation as soon as it settles. This is, in fact, how it is made to be meaningful in its new home as well as how it is made to function in its new sociocultural environment. When cultural production is not accommodated to different circumstances, it is not adaptation, but rather imitation or appropriation that seems to be the case.

How could, then, Hungarian rap be assessed? A general reading of a variety of rap lyrics suggests that it is a response to Hungarian conditions in the first place, and reflects on rapping itself as an already naturalized Hungarian form in the second. It can, therefore, be also looked upon as another example, besides jazz and the blues, of the creative adaptation of black American musical styles, images, and oral forms. Many rap songs, for instance, accentuate Hungarian rap's dissociation from the rap of black America in lines such as "This is Hungary and not America,"[6] "This is Szolnok County and not Chicago,"[7] "This country is not New Jack City"[8]— a pun on New York City—, or "From the middle of Central-Europe, it's Budapest speaking,"[9] while celebrating both global and Hungarian hip-hop culture.[10] In an intriguing way, despite the emphasis on local differences, many rappers point to a sense of unity created by the ever expanding global use of rap. "One for everyone, everyone for one; Nonsense for the unity of hip-hop" recites Animal Cannibals, emphasizing the potential power of rapping to unify.[11] Rap in Hungary is thus regarded as a common (musical) language embracing both local and global characteristics. According to the rap group K.A.O.S., "Graffiti or break—buddy, the style is the same, it's called hip-hop—it's a terrible virus; What's the difference between East and West?; Do you have five hands, or you have your ass on your neck?"[12]

Rap seems to have become a genre naturalized to the full by its Hungarian practitioners. In other words, rap has been turned into an expressive tool in Hungary to create a broad spectrum of topical local meanings. Hungarian rappers have actually created a characteristic "Hungarian" brand of rap by simultaneously relying on black rap's indigenous form and content and by transforming it to fit peculiarly Hungarian conditions. Consequently, what both black and Hungarian rap commonly express is, in the first place, a kind of rap "feeling" coming through its free rhythmic recitative and characteristically "cut 'n' mix" style music. Furthermore, rappers in Hungary also seem to have been able to intuit the kind of textual content that could be successfully matched with the music and form of black rap as well as with the specific sociocultural environment into which it has been transferred. This also underlines the conscious use of this art form by Hungarian musicians. The socioeconomic and cultural roots of black rap, for instance, are often referred to. The rap group Klikk, for example, instructs, "And the ghetto which is not good for anyone; that's black fate; the crux of everything; hip-hop is a style of life."[13] Another rap group,

PLUSIDE, claims that "Rap is a black sheep"[14] by which they allude not only to the black origin of rap, but also to the oppositional stance out of which they create and sing. PLUSIDE even turned parts of two of Martin Luther King's famous speeches, "I Have a Dream" (1963) and "I've Been to the Mountaintop" (1968), into a meaningful message on the brotherhood and freedom of mankind.[15] The Hungarian practitioners of authentic rap, however, not only borrow rap as a musical genre from African American culture, but also its underlying subtext of sociopolitical resistance. This legitimizes rap in present-day Hungary as a salient product of youth subculture, which, in this era of general accommodationism, seems to be here the sole "subcultural sound."[16]

It also seems important to emphasize that in general, Hungarian rappers used the lyrics of black rap songs only initially. The oncoming dominant use of the Hungarian language had, in fact, very simple practical reasons: Some groups, for example, could not borrow any of the textual devices from black songs for the pure practical reason that they did not understand black English, let alone black slang, to the extent that could have enabled them to do so.

A peculiarly Hungarian feature of rap performances resides in the way rap groups appear on the stage. Rap singers usually have a particular style in dressing, which is manifested in their insistence on wearing carefully chosen outfits manufactured by certain fashion designers. For instance, they prefer a specific style of leather garments or type of shoes. Their choice of accessories, however, does not necessarily correspond with the "obligatory" frills of baggy pants, bandanas, thick gold necklaces, dreadlocks, and so on. Some rappers claim not to have the financial means to obtain these articles. In this way, they do not aspire either to look like "classic" rappers or to imitate blackness. More emphasis seems to be placed on the achievement of a complex audiovisual effect by their performance in which the style of music and props need to create a sense of harmony.

Consequently, Hungarian rap does not directly reproduce black rap in all of its aspects. Rap as an art form, in any case, cannot be regarded as a fixed and unchangeable end product, but rather a flexible form that can be adjusted to various needs. Its emergence in Hungary can easily be viewed as a cultural-historical necessity because it is via the world cultural media that rap was first introduced in this country as a cultural commodity. Hungarian rap is, thus, an example of what Paul Willis terms "symbolic creativity." As he argues, "Most young people's lives are not involved with the arts and yet are actually full of expressions, signs and symbols through which individuals and groups seek creatively to establish their presence, identity and meaning."[17] In this symbolic creative process, the cultural materials and resources that the youth utilize are cultural commodities that are mostly supplied by large commercial cultural industries and media for profit.[18] That is to say, in symbolic creativity, production is preceded by consumption, in which the process of consuming should be looked upon as an empowering act because the various uses, meanings, and effects of cultural commodities expand and develop symbolic creativity. Therefore, as Willis points out, cultural commodities are catalysts, and consumerism is an active stage in cultural affairs; it is "itself a kind of self-creation."[19] Hungarian rap is the effect of this complex cultural exchange in which the various types of electronic media, such as television, videos, film, advertisements, and magazines, have the lion's share. Some rap songs themselves reveal rap's dependence on the media as well as rap's subsequent commodification: "Now you're the latest show; the topical sensation; because you're the commodity; the brand-new puppet; you've borrowed your talent; your image has been stolen for you from TV by someone; whose pocket is full is of money . . . ," as is wittily summed up by PLUSIDE.[20]

The development of Hungarian rap is, however, not only closely bound up with the advance of media technology, but also with the overthrow of the communist economic and political apparatus. Hungarian rap's very beginnings, in fact, date back to the early 1980s, when no such thing as rap had yet existed in Hungary. Odd it may seem, but the forerunner of rap arrived in Hungary in the form of break dancing through German mediation. That is to say, hip-hop paved the way for rap to seep into the country.[21] In 1983, a popular Hungarian rock star, Fenyő Miklós, fascinated with the break dancing he had first been introduced to in West Germany on a visit, simply brought it home with several German and Turkish break dancers and created a break piece performed as the accompaniment to vigorous break dancing. The next year brought a rap album in which he recreated the Sugar Hill Gang type of funny, entertaining, but rather meaningless, rapping. On Miklós's part, however, rap seems to have been a short-lived engagement only. He returned to rock music and never composed another rap song again. But his dancers' performance of break was sufficiently captivating to call attention to the genre itself and to spread it among the Hungarian youth.

This disrupted attempt, however, could not curb the popularity of break dancing. A documentary titled *Stílusháborúk* (*Battle of Styles*), shown in 1984, initiating the public into all the tricks and mysteries of break dancing, as well as a pamphlet with the telling title, *Jön a break, itt a break* (*Break Is Coming, Break Is Here*), had confirmed the overriding success of break dancing in the country.[22] The popularity of *Break 1* and *Break 2*, shown in 1989 on MTV, testified to the fact that break culture had taken hold.

What could be called the first real rap song was created in 1986 by a group known by the rather farcical name Turbo Break Company (TBC)(!), who not only did rap, but also prepared videos with guidelines for break dancing. In order to draw a full picture of these first years of the history of rap, it is also important to make note of the fact that by 1991, Hungary could also boast of a substantial graffiti culture. It is not only the abundance of graffiti on public buildings, on the garden walls of private residences, on railway wagons, bridges, overpasses, and so forth, that attests to its literally *indelible* presence, but the introduction of graffiti competitions as well. With break dancing, graffiti, and rap introduced and practiced, the beginnings of the 1990s thus saw the advent of a real hip-hop culture in Hungary.

Nevertheless, African American rap obviously arrived in Hungary with a considerable delay, which can be accounted for by the different socioeconomic and political development of the two countries. Whereas in black America, rap appeared at the end of the 1970s, in Hungary, as we have seen, it became a cultural practice only at the beginning of the 1990s, in the years when Hungary had started out on the road of market-oriented, capitalist economic development. Introduction to the Western type of capitalist consumerism and high-technology entertainment thus seems to have served as a basic condition for the emergence of rap in Hungary for two main reasons: (1) The kind of attitudes, feelings, and experiences that are echoed in rap are symptomatic of a capitalist economic order; and (2) After decades of relative isolation from the network of world media because of the self-protective policy of communist hegemony, Hungary not only opened its doors, but also started its own image-making entertainment industry. Consequently, the real breakthrough took place between 1988 and 1990, when the Hungarian media also hooked onto satellite channels such as MTV, SKY, or Super, thus opening the doors for rap to pour into the country.

It took, however, Hungarian rappers a few years to establish a style of their own. Some of the first groups and solo rappers (for instance, Dopeman or the group Drop) started out by imitating American rappers and writing their texts in English. Dopeman believed in the imitation of American rap to the extent that he even aspired to make a career in America.[23] Drop intended to express similar feelings about the hopelessness of their situation in Hungary, as the rappers had done in America. Ganxsta Zolee enforced the legitimacy of black ghetto themes in a Hungarian context and wrote the Hungarian version of Grandmaster Flash's "The Message." Megasound System literally translated black rap into Hungarian rap, producing strikingly rough and tough lyrics by which they became a signpost for other rappers: They were imitated, rapped against, or simply ignored. The overriding influence of black rap at this initial stage is also recognizable in the almost exclusively English names of groups: Last Players, Real

Crew, B-Jack Rappers, Boyz In Da Getto, JFK, Hip Hop Boyz, and so on. Later on, when it became more important to convey messages to the audience as well as to testify to their linguistic skills and not just let them know that they were rappers, rap groups did so by also giving themselves sharp names in Hungarian: Az Árral Szemben, Firma, Hasznos Holmik, Suhanc élet, Klikk, Bőgő Machine.[24]

It is roughly the mid-1990s that can be considered the beginning of the heyday of Hungarian rap, which has not yet ended. The best Hungarian rap groups today would be Megasound System, Dopeman, Idő Urai (Lords of Time), Hátsó Sor (Back Row), Subways Monster, Dózis, Muppet Show, Hősök (Heroes), Hybrid, Fürkésző Elemek (untranslatable), and Raptorz (untranslatable). In 1994, for instance, a popular folk group, Vizöntő (Aquarius), turned out a song titled "Replika," which can be considered one of the most artistic accomplishments in rap because of its masterful application of Hungarian folk material to a rap structure.[25] But besides, since 1998, numerous rap groups have sprung up and many new rap home pages have been included on the Internet.[26] Amateur rap competitions, hip-hop festivals, and rap parties have been organized from 1996 on (Hip Hop Zóna Kamion, Hip-Hop Day—Sziget Fesztivál, Rap Fiesta—Hegyalja Fesztivál, RAP JAM PARTY—Coca Cola Beach House, BEE Hip Hop Zóna 2002, Summer Jam 2002). RAPERTOART is the name of a talent scout for hip-hop and rappers. On the radio, one can listen to Radio DeeJay and a variety of online hip-hop stations or can even volunteer on the radio for simultaneous rapping within the program "Rock Steady Beat," in which the DJ star GYÖREMIX[27] invites listeners to join in. Ko/Média (Comedy/ Media) is a radio station popular even beyond Hungary. If one aspires to get educated in rap, one can consult *The Rap Dictionary*.[28] There are numerous hip-hop stores specializing in paint for graffiti and loose-fitting clothes (Burner Hip-hop Store is run by GYÖREMIX in Budapest). The magazines *Backside*, *BeatBox Magazine*, and *Write Core Graffiti* inform those who are interested in news related to hip-hop and rap. The growing number of rap groups also seems to be unstoppable. Some musicians, among them Köházy Ferenc, a member of the rap group FankaDeli, fear that nowadays anybody can claim to know how to rap, something which has already started to lead to the dilution of this form of performance.[29]

Regarding the musical background, at the start, most performers relied heavily on the music of foreign groups. It was not until about the mid-1990s that Hungarian rap stopped imitating foreign rappers and discovered the potency and power of Hungarian language for rapping. On the other hand, with the improvement of musical technology, the rappers could also "cut 'n' mix" music to their own character and taste. Rappers must have awakened to the fact that they did not have to go abroad for topics either: Hungarian reality offered just as much to turn into meaning-ful messages. Rap, however, should not be mistaken for a mouthpiece to be used solely for political purposes. It is strictly an art form, and rappers express feelings, wishes, or details of reality in the first place, and allude to social or economic problems rather than address them directly. In other words, they rap about the human consequences of timely existential problems, such as the lack of prospects for a meaningful future, the search for ends in life, the quest for identity, how to live an uncorrupted life, and how to simply sur-vive in the chaotic era of the twenty-first century.

When viewed within a socioeconomic and political context, however, a significant parallel can be drawn between black and Hungarian rap as far as the content and the intent of their expression are concerned. African American rap's division into hard-core and commercial rap and the New York– and Los Angeles–centered hard-core rap corresponds with the sim-ilar development of Hungarian rap groups into underground and main-stream branches. Accordingly, when compared with black rap's similar ramifications, it is the so-called Hungarian *underground* rap that would be closest to hard-core rap's focus on cultural resistance, which for black rap-pers also serves to promote a specific kind of political agenda. American commercial rap largely overlaps what Hungarian rappers term *mainstream.* According to a general notion, authentic rap is produced by its under-ground representatives. Those made into stars by the media are regarded as "traitors" in Hungary because they allegedly abuse rapping for career rea-sons and money, of course. K.A.O.S., for instance, labels them as "fashion rappers," and criticizes them for using "the pistol of others as a weapon" as well as for having their "pocket full of money," but "their heads full of nothing."[30] The group Rap-ülők (which can mean both "those who fly" or "those who 'ride' rap"), for instance, parodied black commercial rap stars by wearing exaggerated outfits consisting of enormous plastic neck-laces or sunglasses and lushly colored clothes.

In view of the shared aspects of authentic African American and Hun-garian rap, I propose to look at these cultural productions as acts of sym-bolic resistance against the pressures of a capitalist ideology. They both are subcultural phenomena in which the performers or actors express their need for autonomy from these pressures in symbolic gestures such as clothing, language, and music. The need and the gestures expressing it thus are similar; it is the pressures that are different. Black rap receives its basic impulse from ideological racism and discrimination in capitalist America. For instance, among the targets of resistance in hard-core gangsta rap is "the black nationalist focus on Africa by politically minded rappers, the government's role in the international drug trade, the racist hypocrisy of capitalism, the success of the black middle class, and the problem of police brutality."[31] Hungarian rappers respond, in the first place, to the dire social, cultural, and human consequences of a newly established, rough, capitalist economic system, such as the alienating focus on money and lucrative careers, the power of consumer goods, or the uncritical mimicking of Western lifestyles. Meanwhile, they diagnose the symptoms of the spiritual and emotional barrenness as well as the meaninglessness of contemporary human existence both within a Hungarian and a worldwide context. This is not to say that Hungarian rap has no political implications. Some of the rap texts openly criticize the malpractice or impotence of the government and of the political parties in power as does PLUSIDE in their "Who Protects Us from Ourselves?," reciting the following lines: "It's hate and chaos everywhere; the parties are loud but say little; this country follows the wrong line—you're brainwashed; if you know too much, you're silenced . . ."[32] or in their "Make Way for the Truth," by asking, "Mr. Minister, how much worth does truth have for you?"[33] In terms of the meanings and the ways in which they are created, the overall palette of Hungarian rap shows a large complexity and a wide spectrum of shades. Some, Országos Cement Club, for instance, create philosophical thoughts, whereas PLUSIDE is concerned with current political events. DEEGO is an authentic chronicler of Hungarian reality; so is Funk'n'Stein, who rap about the barrenness of life on housing estates. Kicsi Tyson, one of the Roma rappers, seems to be, with his criminal background, the odd man out. He is found to be a prototypical Hungarian ghetto rapper using authentic street slang in his songs. A highly controversial rap musician is Ganxsta Zolee ÉS A Kartel, who is described as looking down on hip-hop, writing shockingly rough lyrics, and even expressing misogynistic attitudes. In general, Hungarian rappers emphasize and celebrate the rhythm, the dynamism, and the freedom of expression that rap allows them. They also make use of the indigenously instructive nature of rap by calling young people to listen to them to learn about (their version of) truth and reality. Animal Cannibals, for instance, emphasizes that "There're more voices, more purposes, and the styles vary; But we reflect true reality . . ."[34] These rappers also claim that rap is a tool for them to express a new and rebellious attitude and meaning. In one of the rap songs, for instance, rap is defined as "verbal graffiti," and the rapper is the artist who paints life with words.[35] Many Hungarian rappers seem to have succeeded in elevating their rap lyrics into poetry. They all share the thought that very few, if any, young people read poems nowadays and thus view themselves as surrogate "bards" of the twenty-first century.

Both African American and Hungarian rap contain significant aspects of a cultural resistance against the hegemony of mass media products, which manifests itself in the creation of specific conventions regarding the use of various idioms, including dress, dance, posturing, and language, of which, I believe, language is the most important. For instance, the black urban youth—by incorporating a specific kind of black dialect into hip-hop culture, which was the sign of blackness used earlier by mass media to rationalize the oppression of African Americans—have given overt expression of their resistance to the cultural hegemony of mass media.[36] Hungarian rappers also use language in an idiosyncratic way to express their opposition to, and the rejection of, the meaningless idiocy of the syrupy lyrics of popular songs and advertising slogans. "Only pump up the volume—my text will explode; All we want is a happier tomorrow; I will also say what's wrong and noisome; We don't play the same old horseshit . . . the music of PLUSIDE will never be nice; Because we don't want to satisfy popular taste . . ." is how PLUSIDE cries out.[37] With the aim of creating a deliberately ironic effect, Hungarian rap songs often contain bits and pieces of texts that they strive to invalidate. For instance, the brand names of overadvertised consumer goods, of fast-food restaurants, and of various western products (such as Mars, Milka, Nintendo, Budmil, Benetton, Adidas, Puma, Barbie, Marlboro, Big Mac, Pizza Hut, McDonald's, Irish Coffee, Porsche, and so forth) are incorporated in many texts. In some cases, the media is addressed in an unshrouded way, especially the radio and television. Thus, what one can witness here is, actually, how subcultural expressions are generated. Commodities produced by industries of cultural hegemony can be appropriated by subordinate groups who reapply them with oppositional meanings that, in turn, express their resistance to hegemony. The postmodern label, therefore, also applies to rap as a manifestation of subcultural activity in the sense that it attempts to create small islands of meaning as well as to provide sustenance in the postmodern world of chaos and meaninglessness. The main subject of many rap songs is the validation of the rapping itself as the only true mode/form of expression against the tide of "garbage" pouring out of the various organs of mass media. "Don't believe all that shit the media emits," warns PLUSIDE, and makes TV as the major target of their criticism: "Idiotic programs—Hollywood garbage; they're looking for sensation, that's all they want; They're false and just as bad as the magazines are; . . . You're brainwashed—the pictures are vibrating; . . . Ads, films—the rich and the poor; idols from soap operas."[38]

Rap music, in fact, is essentially and inherently oppositional, as is indicated by its main technical and structural device "cut 'n' mix." By "scratching, sampling, and remixing" records to create new meanings, rappers not only aim at overturning earlier musical and textual conventions, but also at breaking the ownership of black music by copyright laws. "Cut 'n' mix," therefore, can symbolically legitimize the adoption of indigenous African American forms of expression by other cultures. As Dick Hebdige explains:

> The hip-hoppers "stole" music off air and cut it up. Then they broke it down
> into its component parts and remixed it on tape. By doing this they were break-

ing the law of copyright. But the cut 'n' mix attitude was that no one owns a rhythm or a sound. You just borrow it and use it and give it back to the people in a slightly different form. To use the language of Jamaican reggae and dub, you just version it. And anyone can do "version."[39]

And that is what, I think, Hungarian youth also do: They create a Hungarian version of African American rap by reflecting Hungarian reality— as they view it—and by cutting and mixing basic elements of black rap with the idiosyncrasies of Hungarian musical and linguistic traditions. My initial query was how the Hungarian youth could adapt a musical form that is originally "of and for blacks." Milan Kundera, in *The Book of Laughter and Forgetting*, renders an appropriate answer by stating that "The most complex music is still *a language*."[40] And, I think, anybody can learn a foreign language.

Notes

1. It would be a mistake to "blame" only the past fifty years of communist rule for the historical and cultural state of present-day Hungary. We need to go back much further in time than that. For instance, the salient role of the country's geographical situation can be well exemplified by the Tartar (1241–1242) and Turkish (1544–1664) invasions, during which Hungary functioned as an "end post," thus saving the rest of Europe from major "occidental" influences. The 120 years of Turkish rule, however, had an impact upon Hungary's administrative system, its economic and cultural growth, and, not negligibly, even on the development of the Hungarian language as well. In addition to this "Eastern" influence, the period of Austrian rule from the end of the Turkish rule in 1699 until the end of World War I in 1918 signifies Western social and cultural intervention. It is, however, the Trianon Peace Treaty (1920) that can be seen as a more immediate cause of Hungary's present socioeconomic, cultural, and political state, as a consequence of which the country lost two-thirds (!) of its territory and more than half of its population. With this, Hungary has gained a new type of geopolitical significance, as a result of which it could easily be used and even sacrificed by the rest of Europe to keep its balance of powers. The communist rule, also sanctioned by the West in order to maintain the political status quo in Europe, is one of the best examples of the dire consequences of Hungary's situation on the borderline.
2. The following is just a very short excerpt from a list of current Hungarian rappers: Akus-Tica, Ammóniaszökevények, Amps, Animal Cannibals, A Nyugat Hirnökei, A.R.T., A Sráco, Aza, Az Idö Urai, Battlejuice, BBD, Beatkillah', Beszélö Jelen, Big-Laca G., BKA, Black Lords, Black Sheep's Projekt, Blades of the Little Town, Bloose Broavaz, Blow-up Ice, BobaKrome, CoCkRoAcHeS, Community, C.O.N.E.R., Cool Caffee, CostCab, CPF (Captives to the Future), crazy east crew, Csiszolatlan Gyémánt, D12 Break dance, DA CRU, Da Posse, Dark L&ERS, Dark Side, Deego, Fuckin Killah, Funk'n'Stein, Fuzio Budacolor, Gangbusters, Ganxsta Zolee És a Kartel, GodDamn, Guttersnipe, H-40, Hálózati Brigád, Hangyász Kft., Három az Egyben, Hasznos Holmik, Metró Teljes Felelöséggel, Mikrofon Party, Miskolc Hangja, MOCSKOS DÓZEREK, Muppet Show, Nat Force.
3. Mark Costello and David Foster Wallace, *Signifying Rappers: Rap and Race in the Urban Present* (Hopewell, N.J.: Ecco Press, 1990), 21.
4. Ibid., 21.
5. Human culture abounds in examples of this kind, as there has always been an interchange within the world of artistic creativity. Art forms, styles, concepts, and so forth, be they literary, musical, or of the fine arts, have always been borrowed, drawn upon, adopted, and adapted, with constructive rather than destructive intents.
6. K.A.O.S., "Cool Side, Sunny Side," www.tar.hu/lordkeri/lyrics/kaos2.txt (25 November 2002).
7. Ibid.

8. Animal Cannibals, "Everybody," www.Tar.hu/lordkeri/lyrics/mindenki.txt (25 November 2002).
9. Ibid.
10. All quotations from Hungarian rap songs have been translated into English by the author of this essay.
11. Animal Cannibals, "Everybody."
12. K.A.O.S., "Cool Side, Sunny Side."
13. Klikk, "Know Yourself," www.tar.hu/lordkeri/lyrics/klikk12.txt (3 December 2002).
14. PLUSIDE, "Stop Me If You Can," www.tar.hu/lordkeri/lyrics/ps3.txt (3 December 2002).
15. This is one of the few rap songs performed in English. PLUSIDE, "MLK," www.tar.hu/lordkeri/lyrics/ps/.txt (3 December 2002).
16. Here I draw upon the title of Mark Slobin's book, *Subcultural Sounds: Micromusics of the West* (Hanover, N.H.: Wesleyan University Press, 1993).
17. Paul Willis, *Common Culture: Symbolic Work at Play in the Everyday Cultures of the Young* (Buckingham: Open University Press, 1990), 1.
18. Ibid., 17.
19. Ibid., 18.
20. PLUSIDE, "MLK."
21. Because of a lack of written sources, all data and information in connection with the history of Hungarian rap that follow are based on a telephone interview with Győrő Győző—one of Hungary's most popular DJs, the "emperor of hip-hop culture" as he is often referred to, known as GYŐREMIX in rap circles—which took place in December 2002. Two written sources that do exist are Katalin Molnar, "Különös Stilusházasság: a folklór és a rap," *Modern Filológiai Közlemények* II, no. 2 (2000), 63–82, and Gábor Gánóczi, *Rap* (Sátoraljaújhely: self-published, 2001).
22. *Jön a break, itt a break* (Budapest: Ifjúsági Lap és Könyvkiadó, 1984).
23. See PLUSIDE, "Stop Me If You Can."
24. Translations of the names of some of the Hungarian groups: Idő Urai (Lords of Time), Hátsó Sor (Back Row), Hősök (Heroes).
25. The word "replika" is a pun on rap: the first syllabus is a transcript of the word *rap*, and the whole utterance expresses the act of verbal retort. The closest English equivalent would be "replication."
26. For example: hiphop.hu (The Hungarian Hip Hop Site); RAP HOMEPaGe; RapNet; EGERSZEGI Homepage; jOIes rap linkjei; rApOnLinE. On the Hungarian web, there are 12,607 web pages on rap at present.
27. See PLUSIDE, "Make Way for the Truth," www.tar.hu/lordkeri/lyrics/ps6.txt (3 December 2002).
28. *The Rap Dictionary*, www.rapdict.org/.
29. I conducted a telephone interview with Kőházy Ferenc in December 2002.
30. K.A.O.S., "Fashion Rappers," www.tar.hu/lordkeri/lyrics/kaos2.txt (25 November 2002).
31. Tommy L. Lott, *The Invention of Race: Black Culture and the Politics of Representation* (Malden, Mass.: Blackwell, 1999), 102.
32. PLUSIDE, "Who Protects Us from Ourselves?," www.tar.hu/lordkeri/lyrics/ps8.txt (3 December 2002).
33. PLUSIDE, "Make Way for the Truth."
34. Animal Cannibals, "Everybody."
35. Questworld, "The Microphone Is in My Hand," www.tar.hu/lordkeri/lyrics/quest7.txt. (5 December 2002).
36. Lott, *The Invention of Race*, 101.
37. PLUSIDE, "First But Not Last," www.tar.hu/lordkeri/lyrics/ps6.txt (3 December 2002).
38. PLUSIDE, "Ko/Media," www.tar.hu/lordkeri/lyrics/ps7.txt (3 December 2002).
39. Dick Hebdige, *Cut 'N' Mix: Culture, Identity and Caribbean Music* (London: Routledge, 1987), 141.
40. Milan Kundera, *The Book of Laughter and Forgetting* (New York: Alfred A. Knopf, 1981), 178.

12

"But I Ain't African, I'm American!"

Black American Exiles and the Construction of Racial Identities in Twentieth-Century France

CH. DIDIER GONDOLA

The French could entertain the idea of me because they were not immersed in guilt about a mutual history—just as white Americans found it easier to accept Africans, Cubans or South American Blacks than the Blacks who had lived with them foot to neck for two hundred years. I saw no benefit in exchanging one kind of prejudice for another.
—Maya Angelou

Maya Angelou, like many black American artists activists, and writers—such as Richard Wright, James Baldwin, Josephine Baker, Alex Haley, Angela Davis, Eldridge Cleaver, among other willing *émigrés*—chose France in her attempt to escape racism at home and trace back her roots to the African motherland. In their own words, France was portrayed as an oasis of freedom tucked in the middle of an interminable and humiliating wilderness; a temporary harbor between Scylla and Charybdis, between America's smothering racism and Africa's unfathomable and inaccessible "otherness." Yet, the privileged treatment of the small black American community in France is not to the credit of a French liberalism as widely assumed—a liberalism that is neither supported by indisputable evidence nor ascertained under closer examination. What is revelatory is the historical context of intimacy stressed by Angelou and the guilt it implies. To mask this hegemonic history threaded by a sort of original sin, or what Albert Memmi has identified as the "Nero complex,"[1] dominant groups have always assigned those under their thumbs the status of "nigger." In the United States, blacks, Latinos, Italians, and Irish,[2] to name a few, have fallen under that category. In France, colonial history has constructed Africans as "niggers" and Europeans as victimizers. Once this "nigger" status has been created, Europeans need to guarantee their status as usurpers. To that end, they use other minorities as auxiliaries to create a fiction that race does not matter and that culture is, in essence, what sets subjects apart from citizens, victims from victimizers. The auxiliary is constructed as the deracialized alter ego and naturally pitted against the "nigger." Or, to put it differently, the process of "othering" and indexing "niggers" can only operate with unmitigated success through the use of a liminal, *deus-ex-machina* group. In this schema, racial characteristics are obliterated while their cultural and social features are overemphasized. In early-twentieth-century France, black American *émigrés* served as liminal figures. They were thrust in what Shelby Steele calls "a nirvana of complete freedom,"[3] a world that was yet to define the racial and cultural arsenal that would in later years enhance whiteness at the expense of African immigrants.

Black Americans' passion for France did not begin with the First World War but the social turmoil unleashed by emancipation. It can even be traced to the 1790s when news about the Haitian revolution reached the plantations of the American South and acquired powerful symbolism of black liberation. According to James Sidbury, who has examined the impact of this great revolution on the American South, "Frenchness became a trope for freedom and a non-racist vision of revolution."[4] Several activists, such as Frederick Douglass, Booker T. Washington, and Mary Church Terrell, as well as artists, such as the painter Henry Ossawa Tanner,[5] among other luminaries of the day, and a considerable number of black American entertainers came to France seeking an illusive color-blind society which postbellum America had denied its black minority. They experienced what Tanner described in the following terms: "Here in France, no one judges a man by his color. The color of the face neither helps nor hinders."[6]

Very early on, for the mixed-blood New Orleans elite whose children were excluded from the best schools, France became a convenient and idealized place of refuge and opportunity. Before the First World War, black Americans in France represented an elite, and the crossing of the Atlantic, for the burgeoning black bourgeoisie, was often the threshold of a golden exile.

The arrival *en masse* of black American soldiers in France during the First World War evinced a radical change in France's cultural image by promoting the image of a liberal France, faithfully upholding her revolutionary motto, "Liberty, Equality, Fraternity." These, according to Countee Cullen (who lived in Paris during the 1920s), were not only words, but expressed the "spirit of which Paris is made."[7] Experiences such as the one expressed by one black American soldier were indeed common: "These French people don't bother with no color line business. They treat us so good that the only time I ever know I'm colored is when I look in the glass."[8] Being integrated into French units did not necessarily mean that black soldiers were exempt from Jim Crow laws that white Americans vigorously maintained on French soil; however, here in France their humiliating treatment was met with protests from the French authorities and citizens. Fearing the serious implications that might develop from treating black American soldiers as equals, especially after their return to the United States, Colonel Linard, commander of the colonial troops of French Equatorial Africa, laid it quite forthrightly in a set of instructions called "Secret Information Concerning Black American Troops." The document was obviously intended to mollify American military officials by asking the French parliamentaries "*qu'elles ne gâtent pas les noirs*"[9] (not to spoil blacks), but it drew instead a strong opposition in the *Assemblée*, where it was debated in July 1917. A majority of the deputies were so outraged by the Linard instructions that they responded with a resolution guaranteeing equal rights and treatment of black American troops. Another incident that occurred in April 1919 at the port of Saint-Nazaire (Loire) illustrates the protected status black Americans enjoyed in France. There, the local French community publicly rebuked Anglo-white American soldiers on the grounds that they insulted a French woman seated at a restaurant with a black soldier. Likewise, at Grandvillars (Franche-Comté), an arrogant group of white American troops, acting like conquerors, were driven out by the inhabitants who, through their mayor, asked for the return of the "true Americans," that is, the black soldiers of the 370th American regiment who had endeared themselves to the French villagers because of their courteousness.[10] In Cherbourg (Normandy), American officers failed in their vigorous attempt at segregating brothels. Military police were posted around these houses of ill repute to enforce the color bar. However, the same group of prostitutes impishly operated in the two houses, thus offering their service to both black and white male clients.[11]

After the First World War, another chapter of a new migration era opened, that of the writers, intellectuals, and some black American students for whom Paris became a site of literary pilgrimage.[12] In the 1920s, the writer James Weldon Johnson noted in his autobiography, "From the day I set foot in France, I became aware of the working of a miracle within me. I became aware of a quick readjustment to life and to environment. I recaptured for the first time since childhood the sense of being just a human being."[13] For many succeeding writers, France became what Chester Himes described as ". . . the opportunity to write without the barriers imposed by race, politics, . . . state of health, finances, or . . . appearance. The color of a person's skin holds no advantage in France; most French people never notice it, unless it is beautiful."[14] Paris became the literary center of black America and, with the possible exception of New York, Tyler Stovall explains, ". . . no city in America could rival the collection of black literary talent along the banks of the Seine."[15]

Perhaps the most important impact black Americans had on the Parisian cultural scene came with the popularity of jazz, which became so significant in the interwar period that according to one observer, "No American city has had more jazz orchestras to visit it than has Paris. . . . Perhaps there is no Negro musician of any note, whether instrumental or vocal, who has not given a concert in France."[16] The excitement spurred by the Black Renaissance seemed to have been livelier in Paris than in Harlem. For many years Harlem served as a launching pad for American artists and musicians who would finally end up in France. Harlem may have given to modern black culture its cachet, but it was Paris that nurtured and fostered it.

The encounter with the French republican ethos transformed black America. Nourished by the numerous accounts of black American writers and artists, the idea of a tolerant, generous, and color-blind France assumed mythical qualities. In the eyes of many black Americans, France served as a substitute for the mythical Africa of Marcus Garvey and W. E. B. Du Bois, the ancestral but distant land of their untraceable roots. Unlike Africa, which, in the eyes of so many black Americans, remained shrouded in the dark mantle of primitivism,[17] France had something tangible to offer—liberty. Even if millions of colonized people in the French empire were deprived of it, the paradox of liberty is something that few black Americans chose to bear witness.

In France, black Americans found an identity that was cultural, and not racial—an identity that even the Civil Rights Movement in the 1960s achieved only imperfectly. "In Paris," wrote James Baldwin, "the American Negro . . . is very nearly the invisible man,"[18] a reference to the celebrated novel of Ralph Ellison who had also visited Paris during the 1950s.

Influenced by this mythical France, and before actually living there, Richard Wright has written, "For a reason I don't know, I've always felt that France would mean something to me, and that I'd live there. So I'm honor bound to see France."[19] Wright's search for an antidote to American Jim Crowism led him to uphold and propagate the virtues of a "color blind" France. The acceptance of black Americans in Parisian social circles, I argue, was cleverly cultivated by the French official discourse and emotionally embraced by black Americans. Blacks' purported "emotional defection"[20] vis-à-vis America contrasts with their garrulousness in upholding France's color-blind virtues. In Paris, there is such an absence of "race hate," Wright wrote to a friend, that it seems a bit unreal, "For the first time in my life [he wrote upon arrival in France in 1946], I stepped on free land. If you are not black you will never know how heavy weights seem to fall off your body."[21] Wright went so far as to proclaim in his acute Francophilia, "There was more freedom in one square block of Paris than there was in the entire United States."[22] Running counter to his blissful experience in France, Wright's account of his first encounter with Africa in 1953 might as well have been penned by a well-meaning French colonialist blinded by racism and imbued with racial superiority:

> The kaleidoscope of sea, jungle, nudity, mud huts, and crowded market places induced me in a conflict deeper than I was aware of; a protest against what I saw seized me. As the bus rolled swiftly forward I waited irrationally for these fantastic scenes to fade; I had the foolish feeling that I had but to turn my head and I'd see the ordered, clothed streets of Paris.[23]

Uncanny as it may be, Wright's words are a testimonial not only to the emotional chasm between black Americans and Africa but also to France's liminal position, mediating their relationship to Africa as a site of alienation and longing. Black Americans were indeed sheltered from both French xenophobia and racism. With the intermittent eruption of anti-American sentiment in France, black Americans were considered a special case, contrived as victims themselves of the same American bigotry and supremacy expressed in the anti-American French poster campaigns.

However, France did not offer this safe haven and newfound liberty to all black people who found themselves on her soil. Already during the first half of the twentieth century, colonial subjects, with the exception of those who had "successfully" assimilated, were typically not treated with the same respect as black Americans. Several factors explain France's immense interest in and seemingly color-blind treatment of black Americans throughout the twentieth century, on the one hand, and its simultaneous xenophobic and racist treatment of Africans on the other hand. From the primitivism of the 1920s to the anti-American sentiment of the postwar years, the French attitude toward black Americans was refracted through a vision of both themselves and the changing world around them. As Petrine Archer-Straw has aptly noted, the primitive and savage tropes of black people deployed by the French tell us more about the French than about blacks.[24] The presence of black Americans in France allowed the French, especially the liberal fringes of society, to have a vicarious, "sanitized" African experience, affording engagement with so-called "African primitive culture" without that uncomfortable intimacy. This infatuation with

African culture, mediated by black Americans, can best be exemplified by Nancy Cunard's involvement with the black American musician Henry Crowder. A wealthy shipping heiress, Cunard was a tireless promoter of *l'art nègre* and an influential patron of the Parisian avant-garde artists of the 1920s. Her love affair with Crowder revealed her wayward, zealous negrophilia. According to her biographer, Cunard often expressed the wish that Crowder ". . . had a blacker skin, or that he behaved in a more primitive exotic manner. 'Be more African' Harold Acton remembers Nancy saying to Crowder one evening. 'But I ain't African, I'm American,' Crowder replied mildly."[25]

As Crowder's example shows, black Americans were constantly battling, not so much French racism, but a more a subtle, yet vicious attempt to control their image and identity. His example may not be as notorious as that of Josephine Baker but remains still telling. The metamorphosis of Baker's persona from an uncouth and libidinous entertainer to a symbol of success and integration constitutes yet another testimony to France's alleged liberal virtues. Baker arrived on the Parisian music scene in the 1920s as the incarnation of an exotic colonial sexuality at once abhorred and adored by metropolitan France. Countess Riguidi, a jet setter and Paris's foremost trendsetter in the interwar period, describes her show as animal copulation, "Blacks, sweating, stamping their feet, apocalyptic beings bumping against one another, rubbing and wiggling their hips in a hideous semblance of a rut."[26]

Even negrophiles' accounts of Baker's debut in *La Revue Nègre* tended to frame her performance as well as her persona in stereotypical images rooted in colonial thinking. Paul Colin, who witnessed Baker's show and would later portray her in numerous sketches, later wrote, "I sat gaping at the stage. The contortions and cries, [her] sporty perky breasts and buttocks, the brilliant coloured cottons, the Charleston, were all brand new to Europe."[27] During the 1930s, and especially after the Liberation, Baker was vaulted into the limelight of the Parisian music hall scene. She was not merely a celebrity but the embodiment and a public affirmation of France's civilizing mission that had supposedly transformed her from a lewd banana-skirt dancer into a civilized and sophisticated lady.[28]

More than any other group, the left-bank French intelligentsia fancied itself as being too preoccupied with cosmopolitanism to be negrophobic and strove to criticize American racism in the spirit of a maligned French liberal-mindedness. As black American journalist and author Roi Ottley wittily noted, these black Americans were not ". . . a social or economic threat to the Frenchman in Paris or elsewhere within metropolitan France, so the average Frenchman can afford racial liberalism."[29] But once he had broken out of this cocoon, the black American, heartthrob of all of Paris, became an ordinary black at the mercy of a racism that is also ordinary. James Baldwin experienced it at his own expense during a routine police racial profiling. A French police officer demanded to see his I.D. Baldwin had left his *carte d'identité* at home and, hesitatingly, presented the officer the English edition of his first novel, *Go Tell It on the Mountain* that had his picture on its cover. "*Oh, vous êtes écrivain, monsieur!*"[30] the officer apologetically addressed Baldwin, suddenly sparing him the humiliating treatment to which he was ready to subject other Africans caught in the net of police arbitrariness.

French liberalism, to be sure, appears to be a myth that has had severe consequences in the way African identities have been shaped in France, and it is certainly at least as pernicious as discriminatory American laws. Lured by this amiable façade, the majority of black Americans fell into the trap of French liberalism without noticing colonial racism.[31] Or, if they did, they were resolute to paint a prejudice-free image of France, not out of a myopic and naïve vision of French double-edged negrophilia or even by conscious mendacity, but because their victimization in the hands of Jim Crow as well as their longing for racial equality at home had marked their identities as exiled. Even the radical Marcus Garvey spared the French when he accused the white race in *The Negro World*. Du Bois, then editor of *The Crisis* magazine (published by the NAACP), fervently advocated sending black troops to France. He extolled the integration of black Americans in the French regiments at Verdun without denouncing the treatment of Senegalese infantrymen that the French officers sent to the front lines without adequate training. Mary Church Terrell may have been inspired by the same convenient francophilia when she affirmed upon visiting the Bourbon Palace in the company of Senegalese deputy Blaise Diagne, "Nobody who has a drop of African blood in his veins can fail to honor and love France on account of the way she treats her black subjects when they live on her soil and mingle with other citizens of the great Republic."[32] In reality, the Frenchman, to borrow Ottley's apt expression, is "*Monsieur* Jim Crow,"[33] a Janus-faced liberal who showed black Americans a liberalism that did not cost him anything, but saved the worse treatment for those colonized in Africa and elsewhere. Few black Americans have excoriated this double-standard treatment meted out to blacks, but those who did so used unequivocal statements to express their sentiments. Black literary critic Addison Gayle, for example, pinned down French double-edged liberalism: "The French don't bother me, don't get into my hair. Not because they are so damn moral. But you see they have their niggers in the Algerians, so they don't annoy me."[34]

Returning to Angelou's notion of "guilt about a mutual history" and her refusal to "exchange one kind of prejudice for another," one could easily dredge up French racism from the vestiges of French liberalism and gaze at French ambivalent racial tolerance. This notion came to Angelou as an epiphany while attending a reception in Paris. It suddenly dawned on her why the French made such a sharp distinction between her, a black American, and the "Africans from Africa." Some of her costars who were also in the musical *Porgy and Bess* were unable to join her, so she was escorted to the reception by two elegantly dressed Senegalese men. As soon as the three made their appearance, the hostess greeted them:

> "Oh, mademoiselle. How it is kind of you to come." She offered me her hand, but gave her eyes to my escorts. They bowed smartly. "And your friends you brought. Who of you is the Porgy?"
>
> I said, "No, madame." It was hard to wrest her attention from the two men. "No, madame, they are not with *Porgy and Bess*. These are friends from Africa."
>
> When the import of my statement struck her, the smile involuntarily slid off her face and she recovered her hand from my grasp.
>
> "*D'Afrique, d'Afrique?*" Suddenly there were no bubbles in her voice.
>
> M'Ba bowed formally and said in French, "Yes, madame. We are from Senegal."
>
> She looked at me as if I had betrayed her. . . . She turned and left. I never saw madame again.[35]

Another black author who demystified French complacency toward his compatriots is West-Indian activist Claude McKay, who arrived in France in 1923. In his novel *Banjo*, one of the most clear-sighted works of fiction that deal with the race question in France, McKay brought to light the mechanisms and intricacies of French racism toward Africans in post–World War II Marseilles. To demonstrate how this racism operates and reaches its objective, McKay uses the foil of one of the protagonists from *Banjo* in the following manner:

> The whites would treat Negroes [i.e. black Americans] better in this town if it were not for the Senegalese. Before the war and the coming of the Senegalese it was splendid in France for Negroes. We were liked, we were respected, but now.[36]

Thus it is possible to observe two completely different treatments of black people in France, starting already during the First World War: Black Americans disembarking in France as soldiers would return home covered with laurels, not only for fighting with bravery but also for introducing France to jazz, a musical style that came to express Paris's interwar cosmopolitanism. Thanks to jazz, black Americans had the opportunity to mix with *le tout-Paris*, as later during the 1950s black American novelists and intellectuals would frequent the literary salons and cafés of the Left Bank. Simultaneously, popular racism turned against North Africans, the *Arabes*, in full-fledged pogroms. In the spring of 1917 at Dives-sur-Mer,

Versailles, Brest, Dijon, and, above all, Le Havre, *Arabes* were hunted down. In Le Havre, about fifteen Moroccans were massacred by the city's inhabitants in the aftermath of a brawl on 17 June 1917.[37]

I argue that the preferential hospitality accorded black Americans in France served an officially sanctioned discourse proclaiming the absence of race discrimination and negrophobia. Within these terms, any mistreatment of Africans was not connected to race but simply to *immigration*, an equally pernicious semantic construct used euphemistically in French official discourse in lieu of race. As I will demonstrate, *immigration* serves as a cipher for xenophobia and racism. Contrary to the common claim that recrudescent numbers of immigrants create race-based discrimination, I argue that the deepening xenophobic sentiment in France today has nothing to do with the growth of the immigrant population[38]; instead, it is linked to the regional and racial origins of the immigrants in question, many of whom now come from North Africa and sub-Saharan Africa.

In the pre–World War I period, many foreigners lived in France; some acquired French citizenship and identified as French. Already around 1880, before the 1889 Naturalization Law, the jurist Daniel de Folleville estimated that France housed "a multitude of individuals who, having lived here for generations, have not actually become naturalized, but enjoy nonetheless the benefits of being French. . . . They can be found holding public offices or seated in parliament or in municipal councils due to an electoral mistake, everyone believing they are French."[39]

During the First World War, when black Americans became a visible presence in Paris, more than one million foreign workers were integrated into the French labor market. This first migratory wave of the twentieth century cast a large net that reached as far as the French colonial territories in Indochina and Madagascar.[40] France's status as a country of immigration, outdistancing even a historic land of immigration such as the United States, did not coincide with the arrival of Africans. For example, in 1930, France had, of all the countries, the largest proportion of foreigners on her soil: 515 foreigners for every 100,000 French citizens, whereas the United States only had 492 per 100,000.[41] Despite bouts of popular xenophobia and a strong eugenic strand within French right and far-right circles— a strand that would finally triumph during the Vichy Regime[42]—these foreigners, whom the conservative *Le Figaro* regarded as "*la vermine du monde*" (the world's vermin), benefited from the new naturalization law passed on 10 August 1927.[43]

It is during the first wave of immigration during the First World War that working-class France discovered "another" foreigner—the North African (Kabyle). In the decades to follow, the Kabyle represented the *Arabe* stereotype in France for whom the most elaborate lexicon of degrading terms was developed. *Arabes* would be called *Sidis* beginning in 1918 and later *bicots*. According to public opinion, largely shaped by the French media (from the conservative daily newspaper *Le Figaro* to the radical *L'Humanité*), they were dirty, clumsy, obscene, lazy, vindictive, and unstable. Gradually, they came to be viewed as dangerous criminals, as child molesters, and even as carriers of syphilis, tuberculosis, and leprosy. The neighborhood of *Les Grésillons* in Paris became, according to detractors, a replica of the most sordid slums of Algiers. In the popular press of the prewar period, they constituted a perpetual menace for the purity of the French race. As the communist daily newspaper *L'Humanité* reports, "They eat dogs, cats and rats. . . . Soon they will be eating human flesh. When a crime, rape, theft or whatever offense has been committed, don't hesitate: go after the *Arabe*."[44]

Arabes evoked an irrational fear among the French working class, and this was clearly unrelated to their numbers and belied the fact that until 1954 most of them had been granted French citizenship. As census numbers of the time show, the North African *Arabe* constituted less than 4 percent of the total immigrant population and had the highest rate of repatriation. For example, the 1931 census indicates that from the total of 2,890,000 foreigners, only 102,000 were North Africans, and Europeans dominated this immigrant population with 808,000 Italians, 507,800 Poles, 351,900 Spaniards, 253,700 Belgians, 98,000 Swiss, 71,900 Russians, and 71,700 Germans.[45]

France thus counted almost three million immigrants, mostly Europeans, without the immigration issue becoming the source of all evils and without the authorities evoking public hostility toward foreigners. As I already claimed above, the deepening xenophobic sentiment and racism that characterize France today have nothing to do with the growth of the immigrant population, but are linked to the regional and racial origin of the immigrants. This holds also true for the second half of the twentieth century, when most European countries closed their doors to immigrants. Just as in previous decades, the majority of migrants flooding into France were still Europeans, including Italians, Spaniards, and Portuguese. In 1975, sub-Saharan African nationals constituted less than three percent of the 3,442,415 foreigners present in France.[46] Whereas the number of immigrants in France has remained about the same since the 1920s, it is, however, the composition of newly arriving immigrants that has varied since the 1980s, with the arrival of "new foreigners," sub-Saharan Africans, Southeast Asians, Turks, and the increasing numbers of *Maghrebins*. There are between 300,000 to 400,000 sub-Saharan Africans legally living in France today, and there is an estimated undocumented population of about 200,000 individuals. But even then, together they make up less than five percent of the foreign population in France.[47]

The institutionalized xenophobia toward Africans in France is even more disconcerting given that demographic analyses indicate an increase in the number of African immigrant families in France. Up until the 1970s, the African population was very different from the French population: It was more masculine, most immigrants were adults, and they comprised few women, children, and elderly people. Africans, for the most part, were "migrant workers" (*travailleurs immigrés*). Of late, thanks to couples and families being reunited, and to the birth of children, the two population pyramids are obviously converging. Will it be this convergence that creates a renewed racism toward Africans? Paradoxically, the single immigrant, passing through France, living in housing projects for migrant workers, and sending remittances home every month was the subject of public hostility during the interwar period but is viewed today with a very tolerant eye. Now, however, racism turns toward immigrant families that live in the same building, send their children to the same school, and are admitted to the same hospital. Though this situation increases the chances of a more rapid integration of the African population in France, it also fosters unfounded hatred. Using the term "odor" (*les odeurs*) as a metaphor for race, Jacques Chirac, then prime minister, suggested nothing other than the pervasive notion that an immigrant invasion is corrupting the purity of French culture in all aspects. On 19 June 1991, he went on public television telling France of the abuses of certain polygamous *immigrés* who are on welfare and receive compensations on account of having twenty children under their care. Further, Chirac claimed that the last straw inflicted by this foreign invasion on the hard-working French families is the "unbearable" and "strange" odor that pervades the halls and the staircases in the apartment complexes that these *immigrés* share with the French.

This racist discourse evidently omits how active the *immigrés* have been in the building of France's economy and prestige. It focuses on the liability to the point of caricature. Thus, France has reaped the profits generated by cheap labor and enriched herself with the cultural and social contributions of Africans but refuses them their due place in the purported French melting pot. Even those thought to be well assimilated, such as Kofi Yamgnane, former secretary of state for integration and socialist deputy of Finistère (in Brittany), are criticizing the *lepénisation* of France. "There will never be another Kofi Yamgnane," has become his favorite quip. As he writes:

> What other African immigrant having studied in France today can climb the ladder of success as I have done? Today, I would have been quickly thrown out. . . . Today I would never have received a *carte de séjour*. I would have become undocumented; I would have been caught in the metro. I would have been deported.[48]

Yet, France is indebted to this Togolese-born mining engineer who landed in Brest in 1964, was naturalized as French in 1975, and designed most of the highway bridges in Brittany. Africans' achievements in France have always been overlooked or, more accurately, obscured by a discourse of intolerance that is passively accepted by sections of France's white population. Today, Africans living in France fall prey to arbitrary laws and are subjected to bullying and all sorts of humiliation.

I have stressed the potency of racial "othering" that compartmentalized black American, sub–Saharan African, and North African migrants in France from the primitivistic negrophilia of the 1920s to present anxieties about the future of France's race relations. In so doing, I have shown how these three groups of "others" have been racially indexed and assigned identities that were not only based upon race but also upon class and culture.[49]

What emerges from this is that France's treatment of these groups was not intended to construct blackness but was preoccupied with forging and delineating a national identity that conflated race with citizenship. In this respect, foreign immigrants afforded France to create a racial identity: "Frenchness" or "whiteness." These terms do not overlap *de jure*, but remain, *de facto*, interchangeable in popular parlance. As in the United States, certain European immigrants (e.g., Italians and Portuguese) were not assimilated painlessly and without tension. They managed, however, to assimilate as part of the French identity above all because *Arabes* and Africans have paid the cost of this "racial" and economic integration.

Several authors have pointed to the leveling-down effect of immigration in France. Late arrivals in France were "othered" and relegated to the lower echelons of society.[50] They were willing to accept the lowest paid and least desirable jobs, allowing French workers and the older immigrants to move up the social ladder.[51] What is less known is that twentieth-century immigration to France facilitated the emergence of a racial identity in which those who are French "by origin" as well as the European migrants could join together in relegating Africans and *Arabes* to a status of *inassimilables*.[52] Africans who are naturalized French citizens, just as those born in France, have acquired, it is true, legal French citizenship, and thus have become *intégrés*. But it is commonplace to say that France will continue to deny them as she has denied *Antillais*, who have been French for several generations, the social and emotional wage that accompanies *Frenchness*. In order words, they can be *intégrés* but not *assimilés*. To be French in France is, above all, "to be white," a privilege bestowed upon certain people by virtue of their origins. Duval, Regiani, or Bogossian, Da Souza, Poniatowski, and the like, have become French.[53] As for Abdallah or Touré, who might be French for four generations and whose grandfather might have been a *tirailleur*, who plausibly died French and for France at Verdun, he is regarded as an occasional and versatile citizen—French when he mounts the podium, but Malian or *Arabe* when he zips through the suburb of La Courneuve or Sarcelles on a stolen motorbike.

Previous versions of this essay were delivered at two annual meetings of the African Studies Association, and I would like to thank the participants for their insightful comments and questions. I am grateful to many friends and colleagues who have at various stages offered to read the paper and made some valuable criticisms and suggestions, especially Peter Bloom and Nina Gondola. I also thank Peter Rachleff, Joëlle Vitiello, Sarah Manyika, Monroe Little, Bennetta Jules-Rosette, Paul Krause, Adell Patton Jr., and Larbi Oukada.

Notes

1. See Albert Memmi, *The Colonizer and the Colonized* (Boston: Beacon Press, [1957] 1996), 52, in which he exposes the colonizer's obsession with power and control. "He endeavours to falsify history, he rewrites laws, he would extinguish memories—anything to succeed in transforming his usurpation into legitimacy."
2. See Noel Ignatiev, *How the Irish Became White* (New York: Routledge, 1995).
3. Shelby Steele, "The Age of White Guilt and the Disappearence of the Black Individual," *Harper's Magazine* (November 2002): 35.
4. James Sidbury, "Saint-Domingue in Virginia: Ideology, Local Meanings, and Resistance to Slavery, 1790–1800," *The Journal of Southern History* LXIII, no. 3 (1997): 547.
5. He settled in Paris in 1891 and died there in 1937. Most of his paintings were acquired by the French government and exhibited at the Luxembourg Museum. Tanner was one of the many black Americans (along with Josephine Baker and James Baldwin) to have been decorated with *La Croix de la Légion d'Honneur* in recognition of his talent and work.
6. Michel Fabre, *From Harlem to Paris: Black American Writers in France, 1840–1980* (Urbana and Chicago: University of Illinois Press, 1991), 35.
7. Ibid., 81.
8. Excerpt from a letter sent by a black American soldier to his mother, cited in Tyler Stovall, "The Color Line behind the Lines: Racial Violence in France during the Great War," *The American Historical Review* 103, no. 3 (June 1998): 766f.
9. Linard's main argument vindicated American military officials' Jim Crowism by stressing that the presence of fifteen million blacks in the United States posed a serious threat of "race mongrelization" in that country while their marginal numbers on French soil meant that French could afford to treat them without prejudice; see Arthur Barbeau and Florette Henri, *The Unknown Soldiers: Black American Troops in World War I* (Philadelphia: Temple University Press, 1974), 114–15.
10. Tyler Stovall, *Paris Noir: African Americans in the City of Light* (Boston and New York: Houghton Mifflin, 1996), 35–36.
11. Roi Ottley, *No Green Pastures* (London: John Murray, 1951), 76.
12. This tradition has captivated many black American fiction writers to this day, as shown in Shay Youngblood's latest novel, *Black Girl in Paris* (New York: Riverhead Books, 2000), which revisits the mythology of Paris as a literary sanctuary that has called out to black American artists.
13. James Weldon Johnson, *Along this Way* (New York: The Viking Press, 1933), 209.
14. Fabre, *From Harlem to Paris*, 215.
15. Stovall, *Paris Noir*, 182.
16. Shelby McCloy, *The Negro in France* (Lexington: University of Kentucky Press, 1961), 229 and 232.

17. Richard Wright, *Black Power* (London: Dobson, 1954), 10.
18. James Baldwin, *The Price of the Ticket: Collected Non Fiction 1948–1985* (New York: St. Martin/Marek, 1985), 36.
19. Michel Fabre, *The Unfinished Quest of Richard Wright* (Urbana and Chicago: University of Illinois Press, 1993), 297.
20. Randall Robinson, *The Debt: What America Owes to Blacks* (New York: Dutton, 2000).
21. Constance Webb, *Richard Wright: A Biography* (New York: G. P. Putnam's Sons, 1968), 245.
22. Ibid., 247.
23. Wright, *Black Power*, 37.
24. Petrine Archer-Straw, *Negrophilia: Avant-Garde Paris and Black Culture in the 1920s* (New York: Thames and Hudson, 2000), 10.
25. Ibid., 164.
26. Gérard Noiriel, *Le creuset français: Histoire de l'immigration, XIXe–XXe siècle* (Paris: Éditions du Seuil, 1988), 266–67.
27. Archer-Straw, *Negrophilia*, 117.
28. What made Baker the heartthrob of the Parisian public was first and foremost her adoption of French citizenship in 1937 ("I was proud to become a French citizen," she would later confess), not to mention her role within the French resistance during World War II while her two "rivals" on the Parisian music hall scene, Mistinguette and Maurice Chevalier, lost their credibility and popularity by supporting the Vichy regime and performing in Nazi Germany.
29. Ottley, *No Green Pastures*, 109–10.
30. Fabre, *From Harlem to Paris*, 206.
31. The myth of a tolerant and liberal France is still alive and well in contemporary black America, as exemplified by a recent article in the *Washington Post*, written by black American journalist Gary Lee, which approvingly lends credence to the age-old myth that Parisians may snub their "less racially sensitive countrymen from the provinces," but would racially accommodate blacks and other foreigners; Gary Lee, "An African American in Paris: A Sojourn in the City of Light, in the Footsteps of Black Expatriates and Cultural Icons," *Washington Post*, 19 January 1997, E1.
32. Fabre, *From Harlem to Paris*, 40.
33. Ottley, *No Green Pastures*, 70.
34. Quoted in Fabre, *From Harlem to Paris*, 283.
35. Maya Angelou, *Singin' and Swingin' and Gettin' Merry like Christmas* (New York: Random House, 1976), 184.
36. Claude McKay, *Banjo* (New York: Harcourt Brace Jovanovitch, Inc., 1929), 199–200.
37. Stovall, *Paris Noir*, 752–56.
38. In 1996, the immigrant population in France represented 6.4 percent of the total French population, whereas in 1931 the percentage was slightly higher (6.7 percent). Between 1992 and 1995, the number of foreigners authorized to reside in France plummeted from a high of 110,669 to 50,387; see INSEE, "Les immigrés en France," in *Contours et caractères* (Paris: INSEE, 1997), 29.
39. Noiriel, *Le creuset français*, 78.
40. As many as 222,793 non-European workers—including 78,556 Algerians, 48,995 Indo-Chinese, 36,941 Chinese, 35,506 Moroccans, 18,249 Tunisians, and 4,546 Madagascans—were incorporated into the French metropolitan labor force; see Bertrand Nogaro and Lucien Weil, *La main-d'œuvre étrangère et coloniale pendant la guerre* (Paris: Les Presses Universitaires de France, 1926), 25.
41. Noiriel, *Le creuset français*, 21.
42. See William H. Schneider, *Quality and Quantity: The Quest for Biological Regeneration in Twentieth Century France* (Cambridge, Mass.: Cambridge University Press, 1990), 231–55.
43. Between 1927 and 1933, nearly 200,000 foreigners were granted French citizenship thanks to a liberal policy that reached its peak in 1933 (24,763 naturalizations); see Patrick Weil, *Qu'est-ce qu'un Français? Histoire de la nationalité française depuis la Révolution* (Paris: Grasset, 2002), 79–80.
44. Quoted in Neil MacMaster, *Colonial Migrants and Racism: Algerians in France, 1900–62* (New York: St. Martin's Press, 1997), 127.
45. Bernard Granotier, *Les travailleurs immigrés en France* (Paris: Maspero, 1970), 43.

46. INSEE, *Les étrangers en France* (Paris: INSEE, 1994), 17.

47. See Jean-Paul Gourévitch, *L'Afrique, le fric, la France* (Paris: Le Pré aux Clercs, 1997), 238.

48. Quoted in Béatrice Bantman, "Kofi Yamgnane, le modèle se rebelle," *Libération*, 27 November 1997, 5.

49. One could argue, for example, that before the 1970s, racist sentiment in France against sub–Saharan Africans was relatively marginal, not merely because there were few Africans in France but because most of them were students and had unreservedly embraced the French culture. See Jean-Pierre N'Diaye, *Enquête sur les étudiants noirs en France* (Paris: Éditions Réalités africaines, 1962).

50. The ghettoization of *Arabes* and Africans into the projects (*HLMs*) that sprouted in the suburbs of Paris, Lyon, and Marseilles has played a critical role in both their social marginalization and racial demotion; see Hervé Vieillard-Baron, *Les banlieues françaises ou le ghetto impossible* (La Tour d'Aigues: Aube, 1994).

51. Noiriel, *Le creuset français*, 309.

52. Although other Europeans, Jews, and Armenians were also branded *inassimilables* in the 1930s and under the Vichy Regime, eugenic debates about their dubious "racial purity" gave way to their total admission into what eugenics expert René Martial dubbed la "race française" (the French race) once the numbers of Africans and *Arabes* in France had increased; see Weil, *Qu'est-ce qu'un Français?*, 84–85, 115–17.

53. This opinion is echoed in Chirac's aforementioned racist outburst on French public television on 19 June 1991, which he prefaced by saying, "Foreigners are not the problem. There is a real overdose. It is true that having Spaniards, Poles, and Portuguese creates less problems than having Muslims and blacks."

13

"Heroes across the Sea"

Black and White British Fascination with African Americans in the Contemporary Black British Fiction of Caryl Phillips and Jackie Kay

ALAN RICE

There can hardly be a more substantial iconographic African American male spokesperson than the filmmaker Spike Lee. Yet his profound ignorance about black British history is revealed by his response to questions from an audience when he visited Britain in 1999. I want to quote the encounter in full to show the flavor of an almost arrogant, condescending, neocolonial response to European blacks. In reply to a question about the difficulties facing black British actors and asking whether he might be able to do anything for them, Lee answered, "I've been coming here since 1986 and every time I come I get asked this same question. Spike, What can you do for us? Nothing's changed. How many years have black people been here? Fifty?"[1]

Lee's willful ignorance here (there has been a black presence in Britain since Roman times) is very revealing and is commented on by the exiled African American Tara Mack, who admits to having had similar prejudices herself. Her further comments, however, are pertinent to the relationship of black Britons to African Americans. She says, "It always amazes me how much black people in Britain seem to know about and identify with black Americans. Sometimes I want to say, you do realise that black Americans are barely aware you exist."[2]

This essay will address the mid-twentieth century as key to the development of the fascination of those diasporan Africans in Britain with an African American culture that has an exoticism and dynamism that is in marked contrast to their own more liminal presence on European shores. This partiality to African American culture did not occur in a monocultural vacuum, however, but was related to the arrival of substantial numbers (more than 130,000) of black American troops in Britain from 1942 to 1945, which had a profound effect on the white British population, too. Jackie Kay and Caryl Phillips, respectively, address black and white fascination with African Americans in *Trumpet* (1998) and *Crossing the River* (1993).³ Crucially, both concur that Spike Lee is wide of the mark in his limited knowledge about the presence of blacks in Britain that long predates his late twentieth-century blinkers.

In my study *Radical Narratives of the Black Atlantic*,⁴ I trace some of these black historical presences in Britain: from Scipio Kennedy in Ayrshire in the early eighteenth century through the brief sojourn of Sambo in Lancashire in 1736 and the London mendicant Joseph Johnson, who begged with a ship on his head in the early nineteenth century, to Pompey, major-domo to Wilfred Scawen Blunt, who lived in rural Sussex from 1866 to 1885. Such lesser-known figures are set alongside characters like Olaudah Equiano, Robert Wedderburn, and Mary Prince, whose radical interventions helped to define and make a place for a black British presence that thoroughly undermines Lee's crass generalization about black Britons being a recent phenomenon. Historical black figures are constantly being discovered in the most obscure corners of Britain in communities that have generally been thought of as completely white. Of course, this should not surprise us, as trading relations between Britain and the West Indies in the slave trade and afterward meant that people were moved as well as goods. For instance, in the small coastal town of Wigtown in southwest Scotland, a black lady, Margaret McGuffie, the daughter of the provost no less, lived between 1841 and 1894 in the big house, then called Barbados Villas, named for her birthplace. Her presence is attested to by still extant legends about the "dark lady of the big house" and by her name on the family obelisk in Mochrum churchyard, several miles northwest.⁵

Paul Gilroy, in his epochal 1993 study *The Black Atlantic: Modernity and Double Consciousness*, describes a different litany of names that stand for the complexities of the many dynamic African diasporan lives that have all too often been occluded in traditional histories of the circum-Atlantic. His monograph attempted more, however, than a discovery of hitherto marginalized figures, indicating a paradigm shift beyond the narrow nationalisms of much African diasporan history to posit an interconnected internationalist narrative. By focusing on "routes" rather than "roots" actually explicates the multifarious reality of lives lived in the diaspora; as he explains, "cultural historians" should "take the Atlantic as one single, complex unit of analysis in their discussions of the modern world and use it to produce an explicity transnational and intercultural perspective."[6]

Such an approach challenges the nationalist approach to history with its search for a univocal purity of expression that is linked inexorably to a single defined point of origin. Thus it makes imperial histories and their legacies problematic and likewise interrogates Afrocentric historical paradigms. With its positing of an in-between space of encounter and meaning, Gilroy's theory designates new spheres of cultural activity that exhibit "an inescapable hybridity and intermixture of ideas."[7]

Jackie Kay and Caryl Phillips are acutely aware both of this history of black British presence, which predated the Windrush generation (so-called after the SS *Windrush* that brought the first postwar boatload of West Indians across in 1948), and of the need, in the wake of Gilroy, to tell a more complicated intercultural story of Britishness and black Britishness. It is to their fiction I want to turn in order to interrogate the interaction of a black British literature imbued with knowledge of a sustained historical tradition that is always dovetailed, however, with a fascination with their sophisticated African cousins across the sea in America.

Kay establishes the long tradition of black presence in Britain as her starting point:

> I think the history that children are taught in schools, British history or Scottish history or English history, doesn't really include black people, and yet black people have been part of this country's history long, long before the *Windrush* that everybody seems to talk about as a marker date.[8]

Likewise, Phillips wants to "work against an undertow of historical ignorance," stressing the need to "debunk the idea that this is the story of the advent of black people in Britain. Black people have been continuously present here for five centuries; the first wave connected with slavery, the second with Empire."[9]

Despite both authors' avowed intent to foreground black British presence in their landmark novels, Phillips's *Crossing the River* and Kay's *Trumpet* are just as concerned with investigating pivotal moments of African American intervention in British culture. The final section of the former novel examines the arrival of black American troops in a small white Yorkshire community during the Second World War; the latter is concerned, in part at least, with the liberational possibilities of the African American form jazz in a British (and black British) context.

As someone who was born in the aftermath of the Second World War, Phillips is fascinated by the welcome given to black American troops by many Britons whose generally humane treatment of these fighters for democracy was in such marked contrast to the segregation and racial prejudice they faced at home. In an interview with Alan Taylor, he remarks:

> Can you imagine yourself as an eighteen-year-old black kid from Alabama and you suddenly find yourself in East Anglia where nobody is calling you nigger? You think to yourself: "Well wait a minute." It completely turns your whole world picture. It goes whoop and you think: "I thought the world was black and white." But when you get these little old ladies inviting you in for cheese and biscuits and what have you and you wonder what is going on. Then you get the pub landlord putting signs in the window saying we'll serve American soldiers as long as they are colored. Black people were treated with a certain degree of decency and civility.[10]

This experience in Norfolk was repeated in many other locations as the white British in general reacted tetchily to white American attempts to impose a color line and treated black American troops as equals. Between 1942 and D-Day in 1944, the number of nonwhite troops based in Britain rose from 7,000 to 130,000, and although this put strain on the relations between the white British and the African American troops, they were generally convivial. They are probably best summed up by stories about black Americans that "probably had their origins in truth but assumed the status of popular myths."[11] The most widely told was from a West Country farmer who, when asked about the visitors, replied, "I love the Americans but I don't like these white ones they've brought with them."[12] As this anecdote illustrates, the greatest strains seemed to come with the presence of white American troops and officers (particularly Southerners) who could not stomach the conviviality between the white British and the African Americans. As Maggi M. Morehouse, who gathered many firsthand testimonies of black troops, attests, "Generally the only time black soldiers ran into blatant discrimination was when they encountered white American soldiers."[13]

In racial incidents that developed into riots in Cosham near Portsmouth and Bamber Bridge in Preston in 1943, it was white British bystanders who generally supported African American troops against the racist American military police. Emboldened, the black troops fought back with a black sergeant telling the military police at the Cosham incident that, "we ain't no slaves, this is England."[14] Phillips is so interested in resurrecting this almost forgotten history of African Americans in Britain because it illustrates how white British fascination with African American troops, despite its sometimes condescending nature, was key to the questioning of a racialized ideology that the British Empire had left as one of its most pernicious legacies. His own and other black British writers' fascination is linked to the timing of this "invasion" as a prelude to the Windrush generation migration that would happen after the war. By dwelling on the surprising nature of general white welcome for the black presence, Phillips can complicate a narrative that claims that the British were uniquely susceptible to a racism that was unwelcoming to blacks—after all, they had just reacted in a generally favorable light to the billeting of a large number of black troops on their shores. As we shall see later in this essay, the presence of African American troops was not always greeted with pleasure by the native white population, but progressive whites who were engaged in a life-or-death struggle with fascism are shown to be willing to question received racialized opinions about nonwhite abilities and capacities.

An exemplary case of this liberal process at work comes in part four of Phillip's novel, titled "Somewhere in England," and tells the story of a white British woman, Joyce, who escapes a loveless marriage with a petty-minded bigoted black marketeer through an intense relationship with an African American soldier, Travis. Joyce tells the story in a series of flashbacks, which reveal that the arrival of these exotic strangers had a profound effect on the narrow, constricted working-class British worldview of the war years. Phillips's decision to use the white Yorkshire woman as the narrative voice for this section of his novel adds a piquancy as he empathizes with her position as oppressed woman, discovering her voice through his own native tongue. Finding the truth through her voice simultaneously foregrounds his own Yorkshire heritage. As he says himself, "Joyce speaks a Yorkshire dialect I grew up speaking. But it's probably the most painful thing I have ever written."[15] In foregrounding his Yorkshire past, Phillips moves away from an essentializing discourse to emphasize his hybrid identity as both regional Englishman and black Englishman. The complexity of his position here undermines glib generalizations about Phillips as simply a black British writer—he has other loyalties and allegiances. His fascination with African Americans adds to a melange of identities Phillips mediates.

Phillips uses Joyce's narrative voice to highlight both her own and a typical white American response to the arrival of the "colored" troops. A white officer comes to the shop she runs and tries to explain the potential difficulties of dealing with such men. He outlines how "(a) lot of these boys are not used to us treating them as equals, so don't be alarmed by their response."[16] His description of them as "not very educated boys" needing "time to adjust to your customs and ways"[17] is typical of white American officers' liaison attempts as detailed in official documents about the stationing of African Americans in the war. For instance, in a War Office briefing by the American military in August 1942, it was asserted that

"British civilians needed to be educated out of their hospitableness towards black Americans."[18] Such attempts to guide the white British civilian response to African American troops were legion during the war by both the American military and certain sections of the British establishment worried about miscegenation. Thus, despite official attempts to police and contain white British fascination with the African American troops, Phillips shows how Joyce refuses to kowtow to such pressure. Philips has Joyce questioning each of this officer's seemingly irrefutable statements, thus highlighting the fact that the white British response to the "colored" troops was far more enlightened than the narrow segregationist attitudes of the American military. Joyce mocks the hubris of the officer "lazily blowing out smoke" from his cigarette[19] and determines to make up her own mind about the troops. In common with many British women, her first close encounter with the "coloreds" was to happen at a dance. She narrates how two soldiers invite her while in her shop:

> And then they asked me to a dance they are having on Saturday. Asked me politely. Well, I can't dance, I told them. You'll learn, said the tall one. He smiled. We've got our own band ma'am, said the other one. You hear us play, you can't help but dance.[20]

At the dance, Joyce is the one who makes the first move to dance with the soldiers and is complimented by Travis, her dance partner, as being different from the others, "not act(ing) like them in some ways."[21] An outsider in her own community, Joyce is immediately more receptive to the marginalized African Americans. Phillips is empathetic with her because of his own outsider status in contemporary Britain. Joyce is emboldened by contact with these African Americans into actions that begin to assert her independence from the narrow provincial mores of her home village. Not used to being treated as an equal herself in the sexist culture of wartime Britain, she is transformed by contact with these soldiers (and Travis in particular) to a position in which she questions the dictates of patriarchal society, including the sham of her marriage. Phillips here reflects the change black soldiers wrought on small-town English culture. This was attested to by both the indigenous population and the black troops. For instance, an anonymous respondent from Wiltshire commented that the blacks were "better dancers. Some of them took over the band during the evening and we had some real swing and jitter bugging."[22] A former black GI, Cleother Hathcock, remembers:

> At that time the Jitterbug was in and the blacks would get a buggin' and the English just loved that. We would go into a dance hall and just take over the place because everybody wanted to learn how to do that American dance, the Jitterbug. They went wild over that.[23]

The importance of popular culture and particularly music as an enabler of interracial exchange is foregrounded in such arenas and through such cultural forms that the authorities find very hard to police. Vernacular modes are seen as threatening by white cultural policeman on both sides of the Atlantic; however, they have a potency, which is partly a result of their liminality and marginality, that enables them to cross geographical and cultural boundaries with ease. Gilroy's description of these modes as "insubordinate racial countercultures"[24] is apposite here, as it foregrounds the radical nature of such interventions in seemingly monocultural societies like wartime Britain. The sublime difference of modes like the jitterbug, with their physicality and eroticism, meant that British women like Joyce were captured in a kind of erotic fascination that Phillips illustrates through Joyce's excitement at the exotic mores of these African American troops. He shows this in his descriptions of Travis's everyday differences, his Lucky Strikes, candy, and most sensually, his distinctive hair: "His hair is well-combed, with a sort of razor parting on the left. It's short like thin black wool, but he puts some oil on it because it shines in the light. Quite bright actually."[25]

Phillips describes Travis through Joyce's eyes; however, his own fascination with the exoticism of the African American shines through this and other descriptions of the black American troops. The smart, rich, and suave African Americans are as fascinating to the Yorkshire man, the author, as they are to his character.

Joyce's fascination with Travis encourages her to ask him out for a walk. Yet, the outcome of this mixed-race assignation has a decidedly American denouement when he is beaten up by the American military police in a racist attack because of his "uppity" behavior in walking out with a white woman. The potential for new kinds of relationships away from segregationist America is undermined by the racist nature of the American army. There is much firsthand testimony to this racism in correspondence from African American troops. Probably the most poignant is a letter from an anonymous black soldier to Eleanor Roosevelt in November 1944:

> We were told that there was no serigation [*sic*] in England, it isn't from the people, they are fine, only from our officers. We are receiving blurring rumours of reports they put out. We are forbidden any recreation that might cause us to mix as a whole with the people. We are a negro unit, I do hope you can help us in some way.[26]

Phillips draws on evidence of racism such as this and incidents like those at Bamber Bridge and Cosham to show the iniquity of American race relations and their effect even on this side of the pond. As he details, many British people railed against this racism, especially in the context of a war against the pernicious evils of Nazism. As one British soldier wrote:

During the summer of 1942 there was that Army order about keeping aloof from coloured troops to avoid the risk of rows with white troops. That I'm glad to say, was very unfavourably received by the troops. . . . It savoured of Hitlerism. "Just like Hitler and the Jews" was one typical reaction to the order, I remember.[27]

Phillips highlights the effects of such racism and opposition to it through the military's attempts to influence Joyce against the black soldiers. He does this in order to show that British good feelings toward and ultimate fascination with the African Americans during the war continued despite official attempts to police the relationship by the British and American governments and military.

Eventually Travis is sent to Italy to directly fight fascism. Here, black troops' marginality to a white imperial media is highlighted by Joyce's comment that the newsreels "never showed the coloureds."[28] Joyce and Travis marry when Joyce is pregnant, but there is a constant refrain, "We couldn't live together in America, it wouldn't be allowed."[29] Before they can even try, Travis is killed in Italy, leaving Joyce widowed. She decides to give up her son, Greer, for adoption. This decision was by far the most common by the British mothers of the one thousand or so mixed-race babies from the immediate postwar period, as detailed in Smith's exhaustive survey.[30] Phillips, rather than overromanticizing his character, has Joyce commit an awful act of abandonment that complicates her heroic status. Her choice, though, is in keeping with that of the majority of the actual white mothers of "brown babies" in the immediate postwar period.

The narrative is completed when Greer locates Joyce and visits her in 1963. Now a housewife with a new family, she struggles to give the moment the right resonances: "I took a deep breath and turned to face him. I almost said make yourself at home, but I didn't. At least I avoided that."[31] Joyce struggles to make him feel truly at home but fails in the end. But it is not with the relationship to her son that Phillips completes his tale, but with Joyce as a crucial player in his diasporan tale being designated as "my daughter" by the African father who links the four tales in *Crossing the River*. As Phillips himself says, "it seemed emotionally correct. She grew up without a dad, and what binds her to the others is that lack."[32] What Phillips points to here is an emotional attachment that transcends racial difference. As a Yorkshire woman, she exhibits a crucial aspect of Phillips's own hybrid identity and exemplifies Phillips's tendency to a nonessentialized rendering of black Britishness. Joyce's reaching out beyond her narrow background allows her to empathize with a diasporan people fatherless like herself.

But Phillips also has Joyce exemplifying the many British people whose welcome to African American troops undermined the racist white British solidarity that was needed in order for segregation to continue. Phillips,

2

5

5

though, also shows how the arrival of the Jim Crow army meant new perspectives for white British people whose horizons had up until then been limited by the restrictions of a class-ridden imperialist culture of Spam sandwiches, anodyne tea parties, and warm beer. The wartime period, in which ordinary white British people seemed to welcome diasporan Africans, seems an almost lost utopian moment of racial harmony in comparison to the racist face Britain showed Caribbean migrants over the next fifty years. Phillips revels in this moment but realizes it is created by the strange historical nuances of the war.

Specific incidents of fascination with the African American troops reached their climax in one related by Graham Smith in his study *When Jim Crow Met John Bull*. He details a telling anecdote from a *Sunday Pictorial* report of August 1945 that shows how the presence of African American troops had dynamically changed sexual and racial mores in Britain. It relates to an event in Bristol at the end of the war:

> Hundreds of screaming girls aged 17 to 25 besieged the barracks where black soldiers were preparing to go back to the US, singing a Bing Crosby hit "Don't Fence Me In." Barriers were broken down and later the gates of the railway station were rushed. "To Hell with the US Army color bars! We want our colored sweethearts" was the cry while one rain-soaked 18-year-old said, "We intend to give our sweeties a good send off. And what's more, we intend going to America after them."[33]

This news report shows how Phillips's description of Joyce's liberation from restrictive British mores through her relationship with an African American soldier is representative of many such encounters during the war years, attesting to a white British fascination with African Americans that had the consequence of liberalizing British society. The incident has its own particularly pertinent sound track that accompanies the white British girls' performative direct action prescient of the rock-and-roll hysteria of the mid-1950s. This could be seen as an example of Gilroy's "insubordinate racial countercultures," which interpellates these white British women as actors in a wider drama of hybridization and the mixing of cultures.

Just as these women's world—and indeed Joyce's—is completely changed by the arrival of black troops in the 1940s, so Millie Macfarlane, the white Scots woman in Jackie Kay's novel *Trumpet*, is blown off her feet by the jazz music played by her African Scottish lover Joss Moody in the 1950s. Almost all the reviews and academic criticism on this novel have concentrated on the sensational story at its center—that Joss Moody was born a woman, Josephine Moore, and hid this from his adopted son and his fans until it was revealed at his death. Kay brilliantly resituates the true story of the life of the white American pianist Billy Tipton to tell the similar cross-dressing story of the fictional black Scottish trumpeter Joss

Moody. This is such a fascinating scenario that it was bound to engage critics of the book; however, I want to concentrate on what the novel can tell us about the tiny black community in Scotland in the middle of the twentieth century and afterward, about the racial dynamics in that small Celtic country and the relationship of Britain to an African American culture that was in the 1950s extending its global reach through its most successful global export, music. Joss's dual parentage, half Scottish/half African (like Kay herself) is revealed in Millie's early description of him having "skin . . . the colour of Highland toffee."[34] However, Joss exhibits his identity principally not through Scottish or African cultural forms but through American music. Joss and Millie's wedding is not played out to a sound track of Scottish ceilidh music or even British pop tunes, but to the fresh tunes coming from America and principally from African American forms such as blues and jazz. Just as Joyce in *Crossing the River* and the Bristol girls in the *Sunday Pictorial* article find African American culture at the dance hall, so Millie is portrayed jitterbugging at her wedding with her Scottish African lover to sounds from across the Atlantic:

> Joss takes me up in his arms and kisses me. Everyone claps and hoots. Then we dance. A circle of people, a human wall, swiftly forms around us. All gamblers' eyes on us. Joss takes my hand and we spin. I twirl under his arm; swing under his legs. He lifts me high in the air. He jumps enjoying himself now. It is the 28th of October 1955. . . . We dance for ages. We dance as if we are in a movie. Everyone grabs the limelight as if their dance was a solo spot. "Shake, Rattle and Roll," "Bill Bailey," "Take the A Train," "Why Don't You Do Right?," "Blues in the Night". . . . The Moody Men are in their element changing music all the time.[35]

The complex and different generational nature of this adoption of African American musicking is exemplified by Millie's mother's reaction to it. Millie describes her mother dancing with the bridegroom:

> My mother dancing with Joss is quite a picture. If she only knew. The Moody Men start singing songs that have just come in from America like new trains arriving, steaming at the station. Old Mason Dixie line. It is not my mother's idea of wedding music.[36]

Mrs. Macfarlane's narrow prejudice is not just exposed in her reaction to the foreign music played at the wedding. She had not been happy about her daughter's choice of husband. Kay's description of this racism is told through Millie's narrative and illuminates a Scottish racism that undermines the mythology of welcome encapsulated in Robert Burns's signal Scottish phrase "A man's a man for all that." This racism comes not out of proximity to a large black presence but from a generalized absence of different races in some of the provinces in Britain. Kay brilliantly dissects such racism:

> When I told her I was marrying Joss, she said she had nothing against them, but she didn't want her own daughter. People should keep to their own. It wasn't prejudice, it was common sense, she said. Then she said the word, "Darky." I don't want you marrying a "Darky."[37]

This description works as an incisive exemplar of racialized thinking. Mrs. Macfarlane is unable to finish her sentences, unable to mouth the prejudice she feels. These fragments show her fighting to maintain her dignity in the face of her prejudice. She cannot utter the fully racialized thoughts because she realizes they come from an ignorance her bourgeois aspirations make her disdain in others. Yet, her horror at her own daughter's future miscegenation emboldens her to say what she thinks and to utter the word "Darky." In a sense, Mrs. Macfarlane's horror is the flip side of her daughter's fascination. The delight in difference that attracts Millie is the horror of the other that repulses Mrs. Macfarlane. This polite racism that hides behind elision and feigned politeness is so powerful when written because it is still typical of many places in Britain in the twenty-first century. Kay relates how many Scots still find it hard to acknowledge their own black citizens. In conjuring the historical racism of the 1950s, Kay speaks to her own experience growing up in Scotland in the latter half of the twentieth century. She feels like a stranger in her own land because of the questioning of her origins. As she explains it, in Scotland, "Everyone kept asking me, 'Where are you from?' even though my accent sounded exactly like theirs."[38] An anecdote she tells illustrates her point:

> I went to sit down in this chair in a London pub and this woman says, "You cannae sit doon—that's ma chair." I said, "Oh, you're from Glasgow aren't you?" And she said, "Aye, how did you know that?" I said, "I'm from Glasgow myself." She said, "You're not, are you, you foreign looking bugger." . . . I still have Scottish people asking me where I am from. They won't actually hear my voice, because they are so busy seeing my face.[39]

Joss Moody has a similar problem of finding his identity in a Scotland that has no place for an African presence, that builds its Scottish identity in part at least through a racialized mythology of Celtic whiteness. Joss searches and discovers identity through his art form, jazz music. A Scots African person uses an art form intimately associated with African Americans to mold his identity in a predominantly white Britain. As Colman, his adopted son, rather disparagingly narrates, Joss is enthralled by his heroes across the water:

> All the Black guys his father loved to talk about were Americans, black Americans. Black Yanks. . . . You spend your whole time worshipping black Yanks: Martin Luther King, Louis Armstrong, Fats Waller, Count Basie, Duke Ellington, Miles Davis. Black Yanks all of them.[40]

Moody plays the music of black America with his own signature because black America with its large population and dynamic homegrown cultures has a cultural cogency far removed from the marginality of black Europeans in the 1950s and 1960s. It is while playing African American musical forms that he comes to terms with the ambiguities of his seemingly schizophrenic identity. But it is not only his gender ambivalence that he plays out, not even particularly that, but also his position as a black person on the fringes of a predominantly white Europe. Such a diasporan personality is figured by Kay as being typical of black Scots and other black Europeans, but as not being necessarily problematic: "I like the in-between land and what I am really interested in writing about is how that affects people, when they feel they belong and they don't belong, when they fit in and they don't fit in. A lot of us have that experience, being slightly outside of things."[41]

Kay makes Moody's in-betweenness, his black Atlantic "hybridity and intermixture"[42] explicit in describing how when he plays a solo, he is working out and through his identity, expressing his own specific history and that of diasporan African strangers in an unwelcoming land. Jazz, paradoxically, enables Moody to be at home when thinking about Scotland:

> So when he takes off he is the whole century galloping to its close. The wide moors. The big mouth. Scotland. Africa. Slavery. Freedom. He is a girl. A man. Everything, nothing. He is sickness, health. The sun. The moon. Black, white. Nothing weighs him down. . . . He just keeps blowing. He is blowing his story. His story is blowing in the wind. He lets it rip. He tears himself apart. He explodes. Then he brings himself back. Slowly, slowly, piecing himself together.[43]

Moody here self-invents, but does so on the basis of his own African diasporan identity, of having a home somewhere else that he is in exile from and a home in Europe he is a stranger to. Charlotte Williams succinctly describes this paradox: "Diaspora peoples without a collective historical event to refer to invent one in order to define their presence in their inherited country."[44] Moody constructs his multinational past that inscribes his homeland in his music. His piecing together of himself is done through the narrative he "blows," and the enabling form is a jazz music that is perfect for encapsulating the story of a "stranger in a strange land," as it was developed in America to tell the story of diasporan Africans. It is only natural for a black man in Scotland to use it to tell his own specific and similar story of exile. The tortured histories of slavery and of empire create such fractured personalities as Moody's, but jazz music allows the Scottish African musician to resolve the contradictions of his multivarious identities through this African American art form, as Kay explains:

> When music moves you, it strips you bare, beyond being a boy or girl, black or white, gay or straight, old or young. The music contains so many contradic-

tions, and it doesn't have rigid boundaries, so it is very freeing. In *Trumpet*, jazz becomes a beautiful way of exploring identity, expressing that process of losing yourself, finding yourself, forgetting yourself and remembering yourself, going backwards and forwards.[45]

Joss Moody is engaged in a form of self-invention through improvization. Performing his own specific African Scottish story, but surrounding it with a wider story of diaspora, allows him to claim a wider brotherhood. He explains this to Colman, describing how "you make up your own bloodline . . . make it up and trace it back. Design your own family tree."[46] In the context of a fractured diaspora, such willed invention is essential in order to reconstruct a genealogy that underpins an identity even if it implies the invention of a Fantastic Africa. There is a self-awareness about Joss's invention that he reveals in talking to Millie about his hit, "Fantasy Africa." Millie narrates:

> We never actually got to go to Africa. Joss had built up such a strong imaginary landscape within himself that he said it would affect his music to go to the real Africa. Every black person has a fantasy Africa, he'd say. Black British people, Black Americans, Black Caribbeans, they all have a fantasy Africa. It is all in the head.[47]

This landscape of the mind is a mythological Africa that links diasporan blacks across the Atlantic and is the reason that jazz music has such transatlantic resonance for Africans in Europe and America. However, Kay does not end her novel with constructed genealogies but with Joss's written memories of his African father, which he leaves for Colman after his death. In his notes, Joss describes his father as a stranger who is able to make himself at home in Scotland through the power of music:

> . . . he missed his mother, his country, his mother-country. My father had a wonderful singing voice and could sing from memory just about any folk song I wanted. Every time he sang a Scottish folk song, he'd have a far away look on his face. *Heil Ya Ho boys, Let her go boys, Swing her head round, And all together.*[48]

The faraway look on his face occurs because the Scottish song gives him space to be nostalgic about his other home. His appropriation of it is figured by Kay as an inevitable by-product of the African diaspora that mixed peoples together in new locations. As Gilroy describes, "The history of the black Atlantic yields a course of lessons as to the instability and mutability of identities, which are always unfinished, always being remade."[49] For instance, the folk song has the rhythm of a shanty, the origin of which is in the collision of Celtic folk songs with African American work songs in the ports of the Deep South.[50] Jazz is not the first musical form to have transatlantic resonance, but only one in a tradition stretching back to the slave trade and onward to rap music. Moody's father can be at home in Scotland partly because folk memories are transported across and between cultures.

Seeming disparity can be coalesced through artistic invention, as Paul Robeson's career singing world folk songs in Scotland, Wales, and Russia so amply exemplified. Joss finally reaches for a symbol of continuity and circularity that aptly figures his identity as Scottish and from the African diaspora and describes it thus: "My own father is back by the bed here singing. The present is just a loop stitch. *Heil Ya Ho boys, Let her go boys.* . . . My father came off a boat right enough."[51]

What Kay and Phillips describe is a mobile African Atlantic world where African Americans function as modern heroes to the British, either as soldiers, dancers, or musicians; but as Kay shows most appositely, there are African descended heroes too, and some of these black heroes are in fact just about as British as Spam. The loop-stitch circles constructing links between Africa, America, and Scotland allow Joss's true genealogy to underpin his constructed identity. Transformative mobility is crucially figured by the boat here, as Gilroy's work reminds us. However, it is music, jazz and folk, that provides the sound track to such journeys and is played with memorial vigor once destinations are reached. It is music that seems to offer a performative outlet for questions of diasporan identity for European Africans as seen in Kay's and equally in Phillips's fiction.

Notes

1. Tara Mack, "The US Isn't Great on Race. Are You Brits any Better?," *Observer*, 20 February 2000, 2.
2. Ibid., 2.
3. Jackie Kay, *Trumpet*, 1998 (London: Picador, 1999); Caryl Phillips, *Crossing the River*, 1993 (London: Picador, 1994).
4. Alan Rice, *Radical Narratives of the Black Atlantic* (London: Continuum, 2003).
5. Donna Brewster, *The House that Sugar Built* (Bodmin, England: MPG, 1999), 3–4.
6. Paul Gilroy, *The Black Atlantic: Modernity and Double-Consciousness* (London: Verso, 1993), 15.
7. Ibid., xi.
8. Richard Dyer, "Jackie Kay in Conversation," *Wasafiri* 29 (spring 1999): 58.
9. Maya Jaggi, "Their Long Voyage Home," *The Guardian*, 16 December 1995, 29.
10. Alan Taylor, "Two Way Traffic," *Scotland on Sunday*, 30 May 1993, sec. 2:2.
11. Graham Smith, *When Jim Crow Met John Bull: Black American Soldiers in WWII Britain* (London: I. B. Tauris, 1987), 118.
12. Ibid., 118–19.
13. Maggi M. Morehouse, *Fighting the Jim Crow Army: Black Men and Women Remember WWII* (Lanham, Md.: Rowman and Littlefield, 2000), 200.
14. David Reynolds, *Rich Relation: The American Occupation of Britain 1942–45* (London: Harper Collins, 1996), 305.
15. Maya Jaggi, "Spectral Triangle," *The Guardian*, 5 May 1993, 4.
16. Phillips, *Crossing*, 145.
17. Ibid., 145.
18. Smith, *Jim Crow*, 55.
19. Phillips, *Crossing*, 145.
20. Ibid., 149.
21. Ibid., 163.

22. Smith, *Jim Crow*, 124.
23. Morehouse, *Fighting the Jim Crow Army*, 199.
24. Gilroy, *Black Atlantic*, 200.
25. Phillips, *Crossing*, 167.
26. Smith, *Jim Crow*, 165.
27. Ibid., 61.
28. Phillips, *Crossing*, 223.
29. Ibid., 225.
30. Smith, *Jim Crow*, 180–220.
31. Phillips, *Crossing*, 232.
32. Jaggi, "Spectral Triangle," 4.
33. Smith, *Jim Crow*, 204.
34. Kay, *Trumpet*, 11.
35. Ibid., 28.
36. Ibid., 29.
37. Ibid., 27.
38. Jackie Kay, "Silence is Golden," *Time Out* (3 February 2002): 105.
39. Libby Brooks, "Don't Tell Me Who I am," *The Guardian*, 12 January 2002, 34.
40. Kay, *Trumpet*, 192.
41. Anna Burnside, "Outside Edge," *The Sunday Herald*, 2 April 2000, 8.
42. Gilroy, *Black Atlantic*, xi.
43. Kay, *Trumpet*, 136.
44. Gary Younge, "Congo Boys of Cardiff," *The Guardian*, 1 June 2002, 16.
45. Andrea Stuart, "Performing Writes," *The Independent*, 8 August 1998, 7.
46. Kay, *Trumpet*, 58.
47. Ibid., 47.
48. Ibid., 275.
49. Gilroy, *Black Atlantic*, xi.
50. Rice, *Radical Narratives*, 17–20.
51. Kay, *Trumpet*, 277.

PART III

Turning into Theory for Europe

14

Never Shall We *Be* Slaves

Locke's Treatises, Slavery, and Early European Modernity

SABINE BROECK

Slavery is so vile and miserable an estate of Man, and so directly opposite to the generous Temper and Courage of our Nation; that 'tis hardly to be conceived, that an Englishman, *much less a* Gentleman, *should plead for it.*
—John Locke[1]

To see the histories of slavery and colonialism as a kind of "collective unconscious" of Western modernity is not a new argument in Black Atlantic studies, of course. It has to be observed, however, that even though this insight has helped foster a discourse of postcolonialism in various disciplines, it has not been very pointedly received within and connected to the study of modern philosophy, political theory, or even to many areas within the more recent cultural studies. Nothing in the previously prevailing view of things has prepared scholars who work on, for example, the cultural history of hygiene in France—or food production and consumption patterns in modern Europe, early modern women's writing in Britain, the aesthetics of Renaissance urban representation in Italy, the history of seafaring populations in northern Europe, the vagaries of African "development" policies of the United States during the Cold War, the implications of the Shoah for postmodern ethics, the history of popularization of coffee in Germany, the intricacies of West African subeconomies, the political employment of universal human rights strategies in global conflicts, the culture of gardening, the art of flower painting, the history of sexuality and pornography in

Western culture, the development of political philosophy in Germany—to include in their research horizons the knowledge of the trading in human beings that once occupied and shaped the transatlantic world and most of its transactions in Europe, the United States, Africa, and the Caribbean. On the other hand, scholars have been addressing what has very loosely been called Black Atlantic for some time now, supplementingour view of modern and postmodern Western societies with research of black literatures and cultures in the diaspora, or the travels of black musical cultures, or the intertextual relations in political rhetoric of the postcolonial moment. Gender studies, cultural studies, and postcolonial studies from their respective perspectives have taken on a critique of modernity for its relentless hegemonial insistences. However, the fact that European modernity was intimately connected to—and indeed constituted *within* and to a large extent *by*—a slave trading economy has not become an actively engaged issue.[2]

In this environment, my essay moves toward a rather partial rereading of John Locke's *Two Treatises* of 1689, the most notorious of his attacks on feudal rule. For his sound and far-reaching declarations as the one in my epigraph, which is in fact the very first sentence of the *Treatises*, Locke has come to figure, in all modern and in most postmodern readings, as a pioneer whose philosophical and political arguments for *freedom as self-possession* strategically reject any absolutist voluntarism and boldly advance the rights and obligations of the emerging enlightened subject—as an individual and as a group—and their appropriate political representation. If Locke argued so forcefully for "freedom" though, it was not to secure the gradual realization of a universal ethics, but to find the most effective rhetorical counterpoint to refute Robert Filmer's feudal elaborations in *Patriarcha*. Critical evolutions of Locke's *Treatises* have notoriously disagreed on this point; my own reading approaches the text as a contingent part of political controversy. In my view, Locke's rather local act of political theorizing—by way of the long history of a universalizing philosophical reception—propelled a European post–seventeenth-century discursive tradition in which "freedom" became an object of negotiation, always already in relation to "slavery," as appears most graphically visible in the later Hegelian *master-slave dialectic*. This negotiation, however, becomes effective only in the abstract. The prototypical Enlightenment monologue altogether bypasses the historical experience of lively and angry early modern controversies around the slave trade, slavery, and issues of mastery, ownership, and oppression of human beings; it arrives at a philosophical condensation that does not know the "other" of its speculation, let alone their formulations of "rights" and "freedom." Notwithstanding the influences of older philosophical ruminations on the nature of freedom, Locke's formulations set in motion a specifically modern *political argumentation*, a strident political intervention based on philosophical generalizations. My project then begs the question of how and why "slavery" evolved into such a contentious and productive metaphor for modernity and its articulations of freedom in Europe, whereas any collective recollection of and reckoning with the fact of European slaving and its revenues have been suppressed without leaving hardly any trace at all. Situated within this context, my reading of the *Two Treatises* is meant as a contestation; it wants to trace the progressive abstraction of "slavery," that is, the suppression and cumulative recession of its value as *referent*, in favor of its growing importance as *signifier* for modernity's collective self-genealogies. My approach questions the complacency with which most political or cultural theorists and philosophers have settled on an acceptance of Locke's arguments as untroubled, or marked by a civil ambivalence typical of his time, his class position, and his historical horizon, at best. Because making a distinction between Locke's implementation of the notion of slavery and the factual slavery of New World colonization will be crucial to my argument, I will henceforth put the Lockean concept in quotation marks, and talk about it as "slavery."

I claim that the rebuttal of "slavery" in the Lockean conception had nothing to do with a universal rejection of slavery, but, on the contrary, became a motor of the Atlantic slave trade *and* of early modern bourgeois emancipation in tandem. This thesis gains illustration by, for example, the ire of West Indian planters against the English government being articulated as a refusal to be treated like "slaves." In the year 1744, the Jamaican Assembly (a political body of slaveholders) petitioned the British crown to alleviate metropolitan pressure on the colonies. The assembly demanded "that no laws should be made and attempted to be forced upon them, injurious to their rights, as Colonists, Englishmen, or Britons," and they asked the king to "avert that last and greatest of calamities that of being reduced to an abject state of slavery, by having an arbitrary government established in the Colonies." [3]

"Slavery" here functions, as in Locke's argument, as the most effective signifier to attack what free Englishmen see as oppression of their rights. Thus, a genealogical rereading of the *Two Treatises* feeds into the project of recuperation of the fraught modern Western conceptions of "freedom" and "civil liberty" that philosophers, social scientists, and critical theorists (post–Foucault, gender studies prominently among them) have carried on for a while, but that has largely lacked a connection to the camps of Black Atlantic research. My argument draws on these respective advances; it owes its largest debts, of course, to the historiography of the slave trade and slavery. To examine, from a Black Atlantic point of view, the genealogy of tropes like "civil society," "natural rights," and "universal freedom" across disciplines helps foreground the displaced subtext of slavery in European modernity's knowledge of itself. A scenario of the seventeenth- and eighteenth-century slave-trading economy may only be invoked at this point; space and focus do not permit a thorough historical documentation. Nevertheless, such an invocation articulates the need to question Locke's text—which will function here as a paradigmatic, iconographic moment—from what I suggest to call a *post–Middle-Passage* point of view.[4]

Both European and U.S.-American historiography, as well as African American studies, for a long time used to conceptualize the phenomenon of Western early modern slaving as a system consisting of (a) "the slave trade," a distinguished and rather isolated entity that concerned selected European nations and the United States at a certain *limited* historical moment, and only in a sense of being marginal to the national "grand récits," but mostly, and more imminently, the African communities in the American diaspora, and (b) slavery as also a circumscribed historical entity that mostly occupied American citizens and people in the Caribbean. Only more recently has the transatlantic social, cultural, material, and technological generativity of European slave-trading economies come into view. Only a small number of scholars outside the subdiscipline of slave-trade historians have made the massive social and cultural ruptures, and the immensely productive violence and energies of the slave trade and its implications, the focus of their work, which calls for much more extended response. Even though the extent to which Western economies and societies have profited from the internationally expansive phenomenon of slave trading in terms of monetary revenue remains an object of controversy, slave-trade historiographers seem to have recently come to a basic agreement: Transatlantic modernity was socially, culturally, and economically "made" and mobilized in crucial ways by the slave-trading economy. From the work of those historiographers, the trade emerges as the first incorporated socially sanctioned instance of large-scale modernization on an international level and as such, a defining moment. The implications of this, of course, reach far beyond the notorious argument among historians and economists as to the effective monetary value the trade generated. What is at stake here goes far beyond fiscal figurations. The ubiquity and dynamic character of the trade, its profitability on so many different levels adjacent to the shipping and handling proper, afforded early modern merchant societies and European burgeoning nation-state systems with opportunities of mass social experiment and a form of human laboratory on a scale hitherto unavailable.[5] Seen from a post–Middle-Passage perspective, then, one of the reasons for the rising merchant class's growing political and ideological success in early modern Europe over and against the absolutist system of sovereignty may be found in their transition in status from having been subjects of (and subjected to) local feudal rule to becoming masterful subjects of and over the colonial world. This is a process that an early Enlightenment text like the *Treatises* elaborately inscripts in its almost obsessive preoccupation with every free man's right to property onto and in himself, and the adhering right to make expansive use of that property. One should not misunderstand property here in any late capitalist commodity-oriented sense, or even see it as a preoccupation with private accumulation of land or of other means of wealth. Rather, the free man's right to *own himself*, to be his own person—and thus to be precisely *distinct and distinguished* from slaves who are subjected to some other party's whims and powers—is what Locke, foremost among his contemporaries, articulates. As Crawford Brough Macpherson phrased it succinctly:

> The individual . . . is free inasmuch as he is proprietor of his person and capacities. The human essence is freedom from dependence on the wills of others and freedom is a function of possession. Society becomes a lot of free equal individuals related to each as proprietors of their own capacities and of what they have acquired by their exercise. Society consists of relations of exchange between proprietors. Political society becomes a calculated device for the protection of this property and for the maintenance of an orderly relation of exchange.[6]

Absent in this consideration is the factor of New World slavery that constituted a particular group of humans as exterior to this "exchange of equals" in that they were turned, by force of the violence of European "equals," into the "exchanged" objects of European equality. "Slavery," then, instead of becoming the text's negative horizon of universal rejection, becomes its very particularly indispensable presence. Colonial space and its mercantile and productive possibilities provided English gentlemen as a group with an experience of entitlement to being properly themselves and knowing/owning the world for themselves, hitherto unknown to but a very small number of Europeans—it opened a window on becoming possessors instead of being possessed. The *Treatises* formulate this claim rather obviously, and it is only by way of later repetitions of intellectual displacement that this colonial frame of the text came to be ignored against evidence to the contrary. Colonialism, right from the beginning, was embedded in a controversial discourse, in which radical defenders of the slave trade, for whom "the case of metropolitan complicity in slavery seemed overwhelming"[7] were explicitly adamant about the benefits of the trade and slavery to the motherland's population. Or, as James Walvin remarks, "Proponents of the slave trade made great play of the fact that throughout much of the eighteenth century few of those British statesmen and politicians involved in contemporary debates about political liberties so much as *mentioned* the iniquities and inconsistencies of the slave trade."[8]

Thus, the perpetual modern reconceptualization of Locke's writings as a legitimizing and/or prescriptive "urtext" for *all societies* that lay claim to civilized development—as a blueprint for an implementation of rights, consensual contract systems, and freedom for humankind in the universal sense—seems to consist of a succession of rather willfully invested misreadings. Accordingly, what underlies my contention is a critical movement away from an undisturbed and unpuzzled identification with the Enlightenment as quintessential articulation of modernity toward "hating tradition properly"—to quote Theodor Adorno against himself, as it were.[9]

European modernity and postmodernity have been rooted in an Enlightenment tradition that still functions as a metareferent for framing most issues concerning Western (and beyond) communities' social life—a fact most palpable in the realm of higher education. U.S. undergraduate college anthologies about Western civilization, for example, will return their readers routinely to a perspective of naiveté, ignorance, or displacement. To illustrate my point: The entry on Locke in a rather prototypical college textbook, *Philosophy and Ethics* from 1999, reads as follows regarding "slavery":

> *Curiously,* Locke justified slavery on the grounds that those who became slaves were originally in a state of wrongful war with those who conquered them and, being captive, forfeited their freedom. Apart from being bad history, this argument ignores the rights of the children of slaves. Locke's *inconsistency* here may be mercifully passed over.[10]

Whereas textbook nonchalance might be, indeed, mercifully cast aside as a didactic challenge that places it outside this article's reach, the consistency with which political theorists and philosophers—including feminists— have staged rather melancholic, and fetishistic returns to Enlightenment theories like Locke's may produce investigative puzzlement. For *modern* philosophy in the wake of Locke, freedom from feudalism has been acknowledged as the major progress in European development. It has shaped the contrary *postmodern* impetus, eventually, to focus on the extent to which this social, cultural, and political momentum has always been contingent on—not in contradiction with—the freedom of men to become the "masters" of others. Among others, Zygmunt Bauman, following Foucault, has asserted that "freedom" must be first and foremost seen as a "social relation,"[11] as the establishment of a privilege:

The effectiveness of freedom demands that some other people stay unfree. To
be free means to be allowed and to be able to keep others unfree. . . . Self-
awareness of mastery over one's conditions (mastery inevitably attained at the
expense of someone else's subordination) is articulated as the collective
achievement of mankind: purposeful, efficiency-conscious, reason-guided
conduct is identified with rationalization of society as such.[12]

However, Bauman's "sociogenesis" of modern freedom does not extend
to the problematics of an early modern notion of freedom intricately connected to the interests of European slave-trading-holding economies and
cultures. With Foucault, he traces freedom as mastery back to prototypical
modern phenomena like Jeremy Bentham's *Panopticon* but eschews any
reference to colonial slavery. It obviously does not strike him that the
structures of the panopticon and its technologies of confinement, administration, labor coercion, and surveillance might be directly modeled along
the lines of New World experience, except maybe for some British main-
land improvements in "efficiency." However, the affinity of the structures
Bauman describes to chattel labor plantations invites examination, if
viewed from a post–Middle-Passage perspective. But for postmodern theory, "*mastering* the other" remains mostly a trope without colonial history,
its sign value having become merely allegorical for a host of theoretical
approaches and social movements ranging from white feminism to post-
Marxist considerations. Most of the relatively recent contributions to
an African American critique of modernity also remain invested in texts
like the *Treatises*, trying to mobilize what they see as Enlightenment's paradigmatic political argument against the oppression of free citizenship
to philosophically support African American civil rights.[13] Recourse to the
European Enlightenment as compromised by a slave-trading-holding
economy remains curiously absent from even the most radically critical
considerations.

This oversight, or suppression, is due to the fact that scholars have followed a tradition set up by texts like the *Treatises* in the first place that marginalized the foundational function of slave trading/holding, marked it as a
peripheral aside of state- and nation-building, and consequently instrumen-
talized the notion of "slavery" as an abstraction, as a useful foil. Modernity's
enabling fiction has been to see itself grounded in an advocacy of universal
freedom for humankind, which key texts like the *Treatises* have inscribed
and prescribed far beyond their own historical and geographical moment.

A post–Middle-Passage perspective affords a reading against that particular investment, which even more critical Locke readings perpetuate
by an articulation of the *Treatises*' arguments as "paradox" and "inconsistent."[14] Locke's text does not harbor the inexplicable ambivalence toward

slavery that has arrested radical critics; on the contrary, it will yield a strident articulation of the rights of free men to enslave species on the condition that readers decipher its textual maneuvers against the identification it invites. Accordingly, the by now notorious facts that Locke cowrote the slaveholders' Constitution of the Carolinas and that he had his own money invested in the slave trade—two of the famous "inconsistencies" critics have of late unearthed, only to excuse them as paradoxes—does not contradict his arguments at all, if one cares to read with some measure of disinvestedness. Rather than focusing on these biographical items, however, I will engage the litany of the *Treatises*' paradox that has persistently homed Locke in critical thinking, even if only as a distant paternal authority.

In my opinion, reading the *Treatises* as ambivalent results from a malconception of Locke's terms of address, from a failure to acknowledge the *Treatises*' rhetorical and narrative strategies, and from general disciplinary lacunae as to the implications of the slave trade.[15] The *Treatises* contain, indeed, an aggressive rejection of feudal power, a detailed vision for a society in which a representative government, constituted by consensual contract, has obligation, responsibility, and power to defend free men's life, health, liberty, and *property*, which becomes the first key issue in my reading:

> From all which it is evident, that through the things of Nature are given in common, yet Man (by being master of himself, and *Proprietor of his own person*, and the Actions of *Labour*) had still in himself the *great Foundation of Property*. . . . Now of those good things which nature hath provided in common, every one had a Right to as much as he could use, and had a Property in all that he could affect with his labor: all that his Industry could extend to, to alter from the State of Nature had put it in, was his . . . the *exceeding of the bounds* of his just *Property* not lying in the largeness of his possession but the perishing of any thing uselessly in it. . . . And as different degrees of Industry were apt to give Men Possessions in different Proportions, so this *Invention of Money* gave them the opportunity to continue and enlarge them. . . . Thus in the beginning all the World was *America*, and more so than it is now; for no such thing as *Money* was any where known. . . . But since Gold and Silver, being little useful to the Life of Man in proportion to Food, Rayment and Carriage, has its value only from the consent of Men, whereof Labour yet makes in great part the *measure*, it is plain that Men have agreed to disproportionate and unequal possession of the Earth, they having by a tacit and voluntary consent found out a way, how a man may fairly possess more land than he himself can use the product of, by receiving in exchange for the overplus, Gold and Silver, which may be hoarded up without injury to any one. . . .[16]

The trade in African flesh does not figure in Locke's argument against "slavery"; African bodies and their labor capacity, however, function as the crucial absent presence, the invisible lever in the above-stated argument about the legitimate accumulation of "property." The trading and working of creatures—that is to say, the purposeful ownership of chattel labor— is an *a priori element of property* deliberately built into the Lockean system,[17] which only wants to combat an ownership of and control over persons *as* Englishmen. According to Locke, everything a free man does to safeguard and accumulate his private property is legitimate, provided he does not encroach on another free man's property. This includes the appropriation and possession of formerly common "waste" land beyond a free individual's own possibilities and needs to exhaust its riches as long as this person does not leave land to lie uncultivated. Not to tolerate wasteland requires working it according to one's operational abilities, which are of course determined by one's property status. Because this status includes the potential ownership of chattel as a matter of course, working land productively with this chattel labor force becomes an advantage for the society's healthy development as a whole. The famous phrase "In the beginning, all the world was America"—which in Locke's verbal framework is a synonym for improperly "unused" and thus wasteland, which by its very existence calls for cultivation through labor—effectively contains but also hides the fact of slave labor. Because the *Treatises* emphatically pressure for a productive human state of sociality (as opposed to the conceptually rejected warlike and wasteful "state of nature"), which positively moves beyond "beginnings" and continues to construct "rational" systems of collectivity, the extension of his trope of natural beginning as "America" implies an entitlement to go beyond "America," that is, to cultivate, socialize, and thus make "America" yield individual and common wealth for the cultivators. In this logic, colonialism *by means of* slave labor is clearly implicated as the immediately available and even pressing option.

Locke criticism has essentially not recognized this issue of slave labor. Barbara Arneil's more recent postcolonial reading even credits Locke for his notion of "peaceful colonization by work" as positively different from Spain's politics of violent conquest.[18] Locke's idea of New World colonization is based on cultivation, that means on exploiting (what he calls "improving") the land by means of labor to make it deliver its best potential. Readings such as Arneil's inescapably—by lacking the slave trade, and slavery as referential horizon—repeat the *Treatises* crucial lacunae in that Locke misconstructs and Arneil evades an answer to the urgent question of *who* labors. Absent from such otherwise productive attention to Locke's textual figuration of the colonial scene is the fact that New World cultivation was necessarily and inevitably built on the slave trade and carried out by chattel labor. Locke's swift allegorical narrative, of course, does its best to obscure this fact, presenting to readers a pastoral idyll of private wealth in harmony with social benefit, all produced originally by honest labor upgraded by the practical invention of money.

Generations of critics have looked past the fact that when Locke speaks about "slavery"—as the opposite of "liberty"—he does not allude to actual New World chattel labor. "Slavery"—which does have its own such titled subchapter in the *Treatises*—in his rhetorical repertoire becomes a signifier for the oppression of free gentlemen, and thus an indispensable move to define "liberty":

> The *Liberty of Man, in Society* is to be under no other Legislative Power, but that established, by consent, in the Common-wealth, but what the Legislative shall enact, according to the Trust put in it. . . . *Freedom of Men under Government* is, to have a standing Rule to live by, common to every one of that Society, and made by the Legislative Power erected in it; A Liberty to follow my own will in all things where the Rule prescribes not; and not to be subject to the inconstant, uncertain, unknown, Arbitrary Will of another Man.[19]

The passages in which Locke does speak of "slavery" address a scenario completely different from chattel slavery, namely the capture of individuals in military conquest, which was a medieval practice that had characterized all European societies he could have known at his time. By the time Locke is writing the *Treatises*, factual slavery has been widely erased from major European societies. What remains are extreme forms of servitude for peasants and urban workforce, and the subjection of gentlemen and commoners to the king's and lords' practices of absolute power. So that even referring to "slavery" in the local English context actually already distances the Englishman, the "citoyen" on the rise, from the objects of the chattel trade. Locke's notion here has a corrupt circular, narcissistic logic: Only for the category of the free man (the subject of his address) does oppression of his "natural rights" become a controversial issue; to species who do not figure under that category, the privilege of having a right against oppression does not extend.

What later moderns have taken to be the referent for the "vile and miserable estate" Locke propagates against—New World factual slavery—is not at all the *Treatises'* concern. African chattel slaves figure as property, so "rights" issues do not pertain to them; rather, these human creatures function as a "right to property" issue for English gentlemen. The *Treatises* do not entail an indictment of the inhuman practices of New World slavery, and even less a denial of the power of free men to do what they see fit with their property. The one message the text does deliver is that Englishmen shall not *be* slaves. That they could and did very well own them remains the state of affairs unqualified by Locke's address—it stands commensurate with, and not in paradox to, his notion of freedom. The *Treatises* contract gentlemen's and commoners' abhorrence of servitude into a polemical signification on a state of being that Locke wants a prototypical *Englishman* to be able to transcend. It is only later readings that have transformed this rhetorical, highly metaphorical undertaking into a universal rejection of slavery.

Late-twentieth-century Locke readings seem to have a defensive need to *assume* a Lockean ambivalence toward slavery because their own critical horizons have developed in response to a modern ethical imperative and its use of "slavery" as metasignifier for a rhetoric of antioppression. The reverse logic of this metasignifier at work implies that an Enlightenment discourse put forward against oppression *named as* "slavery" (like the *Treatises* most prominently) must inherently be an argument against slavery. Tied into disciplinary frameworks that starkly restrict or discourage access to a knowledge of New World slave trade and slavery, even radical postmodern critics have shared in the modern complacency of equating "slavery" as in the Lockean repertoire with chattel slavery, though their ethical motivations differ from the late-eighteenth- and nineteenth-century European self-centered acquisitive use of the signifier. In this logic, Locke's textual and biographical investments in slavery must indeed produce wonder and/or disappointment and require critical acts of redemptive compensation.

Political opposition to slavery has known better and militated against Lockean style arguments as early as the first decade of the eighteenth century. Historians have unearthed ample textual evidence for articulate counternarrative. Jack Greene, for example, discusses a 1710 antislavery pamphlet published anonymously whose author "both anticipated most of the objections antislavery writers would make later in the century and called into question the humanity . . . of free West Indian settlers . . . contending that 'life and liberty' were 'hardly things' that could be purchased or sold."[20]

Attentiveness to these voices raises the question of why even postmodern narratives of human rights feel compelled to anchor themselves in propositions of modernity like Locke's (which requires the strange twists and bends of allotting foundational paradox) and not in the testimony of early radical abolition or black diaspora testimony. Metaphorically speaking, one could ask why even radical theory has insisted on critiquing mainstream modernity for a promise made inconsistently, or not (yet) delivered, instead of calling attention to the fact that it was never given in an emphatically "universal" sense. Contemporary philosophical and political defenses of "universal rights" as well as genealogists of modernity may thus be well advised to recuperate traces that do not lead back inevitably to thinkers like Locke. Instead of unwarranted returns to the Enlightenment's projections, I argue for a hermeneutics of epistemological suspicion from the point of view of the desubjectification of African human beings. The "subjectification" of the Enlightenment was contingent on the "desubjectification" of humans who were forced to provide the chattel labor force so indispensable for the slave-trading economy. At a very early point in modern history, the *Treatises'* advances served to inscribe this process for philosophical generations to come by means of a rhetorical strategy that eschews Africans as subjects of chattel labor and focuses all civil attention on a European plight for "freedom" as (self)-possession. As even this very condensed polemics might help to articulate, to witness the Middle Passage as a hitherto ignored or displaced point of departure for postmodern instances of self-reflexivity within and across disciplines may open windows on the genealogies of modernity, which those disciplines have not provided before.

Notes

1. John Locke, *Two Treatises of Government*, ed. Peter Laslett (Cambridge, Mass.: Cambridge University Press, 1988), 141, original emphasis. To my knowledge at this point, only Jennifer Welchman, in her "Locke on Slavery and Inalienable Rights," *Canadian Journal of Philosophy* 25, no. 1 (1995), 67–81, offers a critical reading of Locke's approach to slavery that does not treat the *Treatises'* argumentation as, in Welchman's own words, an embarrassing "error of philosophical judgement" (69). Her argument still differs from my own, though, in the sense that it is a very immanent, philosophical critique of the text and does not contextualize the *Treatises* as one of the discursive moments of early modernity, which actually legitimize the slave trade.
2. For rather typical postcolonial mappings of modernity that do not address the issues of slave trade and slavery, see Couze Venn, *Occidentalism: Modernity and Subjectivity* (London: Sage Publications, 2000) and Uday Singh Mehta, *Liberalism and Empire: A Study in Nineteenth-Century British Liberal Thought* (Chicago: University of Chicago Press, 1999).
3. Jack P. Greene, "Liberty, Slavery and the Transformation of British Identity in the Eighteenth-Century West Indies," *Slavery and Abolition: A Journal of Slave and Post-Slave Studies* 21, no. 1 (2000), 27.
4. See, of course, Paul Gilroy, *The Black Atlantic: Modernity and Double Consciousness* (Cambridge, Mass.: Harvard University Press, 1993), but also the much earlier and mostly neglected work of Hans Werner Debrunner, *Presence and Prestige: Africans in Europe: A History of Africans in Europe before 1918* (Basel: Basler Afrika Bibliographien, 1979).
5. Out of the rich and extensive field of slave-trade historiography and related research, I want to single out a number of works most pertinent for my argument: Robin Blackburn, *The Making of New World Slavery: From the Baroque to the Modern 1492–1800* (London: Verso, 1998); David Brion Davis, *The Problem of Slavery in Western Culture* (Ithaca, N.Y.: Cornell University Press, 1966); Doudou Diène, ed., *From Chains to Bonds: The Slave Trade Revisited* (New York: Berghahn Books, 2001); Hans-Jürgen Puhle, ed., *Sklaverei in der modernen Geschichte*, special issue of *Geschichte und Gesellschaft* 16, no. 2 (1990); Gert Oostindie, ed., *Fifty Years Later: Antislavery, Capitalism and Modernity in the Dutch Orbit* (Pittsburgh: University of Pittsburgh Press, 1996); Eric Williams, *Capitalism and Slavery* (Chapel Hill: University of North Carolina Press, 1944); Jürgen Osterhammel, *Sklaverei und die Zivilisation des Westens* (München: Carl Friedrich von Siemens Stiftung, 2000); Albert Wirz, *Sklaverei und kapitalistisches Weltsystem* (Frankfurt am Main: Suhrkamp, 1984); Immanuel Wallerstein, *The Modern World-System* (New York: Academic Press, 1974).
6. Crawford Brough Macpherson, *The Political Theory of Possessive Individualism: Hobbes to Locke* (New York: Oxford University Press, 1962), 3.
7. Greene, "Liberty, Slavery," 18.
8. James Walvin, *Questioning Slavery* (London: Routledge, 1996), 25.
9. See Theodor W. Adorno, *Minima Moralia: Reflections from Damaged Life*, trans. E. F. N. Jephcott (London: Verso, 1978), 52.
10. James Gordon Clapp, "John Locke," in *Philosophy and Ethics: Selections from the Encyclopedia of Philosophy*, ed. Donald M. Borchert (New York: Macmillan, 1999), 499.

11. Zygmunt Bauman, *Freedom* (Minneapolis: University of Minnesota Press, 1988), 7.

12. Ibid., 46.

13. See, for example, Howard McGary and Bill E. Lawson, *Between Slavery and Freedom: Philosophy and American Slavery* (Bloomington: Indiana University Press, 1992); Tommy L. Lott, ed., *Subjugation and Bondage: Critical Essays on Slavery and Social Philosophy* (Lanham, Md.: Rowman & Littlefield, 1998).

14. See James Farr, "So Vile and Miserable an Estate: The Problem of Slavery in Locke's Political Thought," *Political Theory* 14 (1986), 263–89, and Charles W. Mills, *Blackness Visible: Essays on Philosophy and Race* (Ithaca, N.Y.: Cornell University Press, 1998), 1–19. See also Jennifer Welchman's judgment in "Locke on Slavery," 67.

15. One may notice strange argumentative voids, for example, in James Tully, *A Discourse on Property: John Locke and His Adversaries* (Cambridge, Mass.: Cambridge University Press, 1980) and in Gopal Sreenivasan, *The Limits of Lockean Rights in Property* (Oxford: Oxford University Press, 1995) whose respective monographs, being entirely devoted to the question of property rights, offer no allusion to the status of chattel slaves as free man's legitimate property.

16. Locke, *Two Treatises*, 298–302, original emphasis.

17. Here my argument receives scholarly philosophical support from Welchman's reading of Locke's conceptualization of sub–Saharan Africans: Welchman, "Locke on Slavery," 78–80.

18. Barbara Arneil, *John Locke and America: The Defense of English Colonialism* (Oxford: Clarendon Press, 1996), 9.

19. Locke, *Two Treatises*, 283–84, original emphasis.

20. Greene, "Liberty, Slavery," 8.

15

Make Capital Out of Their Sympathy

Rhetoric and Reality of U.S. Slavery and Italian Immigrant Prostitution along the Color Line from the Nineteenth to the Twenty-first Century

PETER GARDNER

> *They did not know her history,*
> *and she did not tell it,*
> *because she had no desire*
> *to make capital out of their sympathy.*
> —Harriet Jacobs

Fear and racism welcome immigrants to Europe. Italy is no exception. Ignoring warnings that diminished immigration is a threat to the Italian economy, many natives view foreign-born residents as menacing safety, public order, culture, or national identity.[1] From Milan to Palermo, immigrants are associated with the assaults, drunken driving, drug dealing, murder, and prostitution that make up between forty and sixty percent of all reporting on immigration. Such negative reports have spawned a "fear of being invaded."[2] Understandably, young people in the industrial north consider racism "cool," and scarcely a day passes without television and newspaper accounts of aggression committed by or against immigrants.[3]

Racist ideology presumably appeals to many as a makeshift alternative to an economic and political analysis of immigration. In an attempt to contribute to such an analysis, this essay will examine one type of immigration: the foreign prostitute in Italy. I will contend that the representation of the enslaved foreign prostitute is a rhetorical construct that fissures along the color line. In the course of making this argument, I hope to demonstrate that the Italian discourse of the enslaved foreign prostitute, although not univocal, privileges white women by marginalizing the Africans. Current African American feminist theory and Harriet Jacobs's *Incidents in the Life of a Slave Girl* will be proposed as theoretical instruments to explicate the insufficiency of this rhetorical construct.

In addition, I will argue that the rhetorical construct of the enslaved immigrant prostitute is a displaced discourse that diverts attention away from the widespread exploitation of a large number of immigrants to a small number of women who have been forced into prostitution.

Most Italians want to deport not only immigrant prostitutes, but nearly all legal and illegal immigrants.[4] Almost seventy-five percent believed that the country's immigration laws were too permissive before the passage of the current immigration restrictions.[5] This is not surprising. Italian television news has often depicted the landing of illegal immigrants as if they were an invasion. Close-ups of the Italian coastguard cut to footage of a speeding boat, with the illegal immigrants finally scrambling ashore in scenes reminiscent of the Allied soldiers hitting the Normandy beaches, while a reporter announces that the women and children are destined for the prostitution market.

As though an immigrant invasion were not enough, a "well-documented" article in *Le Monde*, widely reprinted in Italy, ominously predicts that zero population growth is leading Italy to "demographic suicide."[6] Qualms about immigration and "race suicide" are unique neither to Italy nor to this century. In twentieth-century America, when Italian immigrants were arriving in ever-increasing numbers, Theodore Roosevelt issued like warnings, pleading for larger families to protect the "Anglo-Saxon race." Today's alarming reports, couched in the militaristic language of landings, invasions, and extermination, make it difficult to remember that immigrants in Italy make up less than 4 percent of the population, a rate that is among the lowest in the European Union.[7]

Many legal and illegal immigrants in Italy are employed in agriculture, construction, manufacturing, and services. Fifty-five percent of these businesses pay employees off the books.[8] Two-thirds of immigrants are paid under the table, catapulting unreported income in Italy to 27 percent, the second highest in Europe. Domestic work is the major source of employment for women from the Philippines, Africa, East Europe, and South America, who occupy more than half of these jobs.[9] Four of out five domestic workers remain unregistered, working off the books without contracts, pensions, or job protection.[10] Just as in the United States, where black women have been so overrepresented in this undervalued occupation as to become synonymous with it, so has the word "Filipina" come to signify a domestic worker in Rome.

Immigrant domestic workers and immigrant prostitutes seem to be unrelated problems. Black feminist bell hooks challenges that assumption when theorizing on the systemic connections of class, gender, and ethnicity throughout *Where We Stand: Class Matters*, arguing that the relative independence of Western women requires the enslavement or subordination of many Third World women.[11] hooks is not alone. Rose M. Brewer construes current African American feminist thinking as the formula of "race × class × gender," expressing "the embeddedness and relationship of race, class and gender and the multiplicative nature of these relationships."[12] This formula is certainly applicable to immigrant domestic workers in Italy today, where darker-skinned women hold most of these low-paying jobs. Immigrant domestic workers and immigrant prostitutes in Italy share a silent and invisible subordinate status. Until the current immigration restrictions were approved by the Italian Parliament, the conservatively estimated 500,000 domestic workers were invisible to the press, despite being seen shopping in the markets, taking children to school, and accompanying the elderly on outings.[13]

The estimated 25,000 immigrant prostitutes, on the other hand, have consistently attracted a great deal of attention from the Italian media, with numerous newspaper articles representing the phenomenon as slavery. The value of each element of Brewer's formula of race × class × gender is conceivably intensified to the highest degree in the representation of the enslaved foreign prostitute, for whom ethnicity, economics, and gender collide.

As early as 1991, a journalist reported on the shipload of Albanian immigrants that landed in Italy, commenting that the abduction of two young Albanian women raised the "suspicion that this incident actually involves slave trafficking."[14] On 20 May 2000, the women's magazine supplement of *Il Corriere della Sera* informed readers that "twenty pretty girls are worth more than a load of cocaine" in Kosovo. In addition, "young women who are little more than children" are "sold at auction" and sent to the "affluent sidewalks of Italy."[15] *La Stampa* of Turin carried an extensive article in June recounting how an eighteen-year-old British girl had been "kidnapped and forced to prostitute herself" in Vicenza as the "slave of two Albanians."[16] In July, the same paper published another lengthy article under the banner "New Slaves: The Numbers of the Sex Market."[17] Because 59 percent of foreign prostitutes in Italy still come from Nigeria, 14.1 percent from Albania, and 10 percent from the former Yugoslavia, and the African prostitutes lining the roads failed to elicit this slavery rhetoric, the public outcry in Italy seems to be determined by skin color. This impression is not refuted by Prime Minister Silvio Berlusconi's recent claim that prostitutes are "victims of the *white*-slave traffic" (my emphasis added) on the same day the news aired the deportation of 124 black prostitutes, representing them not as victims but as defiant criminals.[18] A previous equal opportunity minister created a political flurry by suggesting that some of these immigrants had chosen to be prostitutes, a flurry that caused Parliamentarians Alessandra Mussolini and Francesca Scopelliti, for instance, to insist that "they are all slaves" and that foreign prostitutes were "women lured to Italy by false promises and thrown onto the street."[19]

As rhetoric, these two tropes are interdependent. The newspaper accounts of foreign victims not only confine slavery within the immigrant population but also specify the high fees of Italians practicing the same calling.[20] These newspaper articles formulate a class distinction among prostitutes, ranking foreign women as lower paid and consequently less professional than Italians. Many articles represent Albanian and Nigerian prostitutes as the slaves of Albanian pimps and Nigerian madams, as does an article on the deportation of Nigerian prostitutes in Rome, by emphasizing how they are defrauded of most of their earnings.[21] Remarkably, on the same page of this paper is a another report of a raid on a massage parlor near the Vatican where five Italians and a Polish woman were working as prostitutes. In spite of specifying that "[o]nly a small percentage of the earnings went to the 'masseuses'," there is neither any suggestion that these prostitutes were slaves nor any accusations that the two Italian women who managed the establishment were slaveholders.[22] The two articles differentiate between immigrant and Italian prostitutes, ostensibly reflecting the ongoing debate regarding prostitutes as victims or sex workers. In actuality, they make ethnicity of the prostitute and of the slaveholder the decisive factor as to whether they are represented as slaves or free agents. This play of the factors of race × class subordinates foreign prostitutes to an unskilled level, implying that the stereotype of the unskilled immigrant holds true here as well.

At times Nigerian women are included and at others excluded from the slavery discourse. In an early article of an interview with a Nigerian prostitute, the journalist placed the Nigerian outside the white-slave rhetoric because she knew she was to be a prostitute in Italy, and the innocence of the woman is essential to the white-slave rhetoric. This African prostitute's chronicle of racist slurs from clients and sexual abuse by the police is discredited by the authorial comment: "The stories are all the same, three-fourths lies and one-fourth truth."[23] The reader is told to reject her testimony, just as American slaves' evidence was barred on the basis of their innate untruthfulness.

Excluding the Africans conforms easily to preconceived notions of black sexuality. hooks points out how the commodification of black sexuality is fostered by contemporary films and music videos, "an image which suggests they are sexually available and licentious," the same ones that are seen across Italy.[24] These images, together with blackface performers on Mr. Berlusconi's television network,[25] are then recontextualized in a culture in which darker-skinned women, suggesting the easily accessible sexuality of colonized women, have been used to sell a wide range of products, from licorice and coffee to televisions and air-conditioners. Yvonne Durant, an African American advertising executive in Milan, once identified "these shapely, exotic creatures oozing with sex" as "distorted images of black women," and wondered how this advertising would affect Italian boys.[26] Yet representing black sexuality as animalistic is hardly a new phenomenon. Today's images recycle the cartoons, jokes, and songs popular during the fascist occupation of Africa. Black women conform to these images of sexual availability and bridge the distance from the Italian Army's bordellos in Africa to the streets of Italy in a way that fair-skinned women do not.

Sander L. Gilman's study of the ideologically charged iconography of nineteenth-century images and texts demonstrates how the "overt sexuality" of black bodies has been employed to express the "covert sexuality" of white women.[27] The prostitute-slave rhetoric of contemporary Italy similarly engages white and black prostitutes. Although both Albanians and Nigerians are reportedly enslaved, the tacitly presumed animalistic sexuality of black women casts the shadow needed to highlight the innocence of the white women. In the extended discourse, the white women are constructed as victimized white slaves. The black women are increasingly constructed as prostitutes or, more and more frequently, simply vanish from the discourse altogether. Their marginality in the slave rhetoric and their visibility along the roads silently corroborate the innocence of the Eastern European women.

Former Northern League Speaker of the House Irene Pivetti unwittingly unveiled this fissure during a television talk show on prostitution. A social worker cautioned against regarding immigrant women as prostitutes because so few engaged in commercial sex. Pivetti hurriedly assured him that such was not the case at all and to assume this would be nothing less than racism.[28] Less than a month later, the Northern League's bantam television channel aired a special program about the "immigration problem" in the north. Native Italians were filmed in close-up, concurring with the journalist that there were too many immigrants. As the natives complained about those who did not seek employment, the camera filmed three North African men at a table having coffee. As the interviewees complained about increasing crime, almost a dozen young black women were filmed from behind, with the camera focused below their waists, so annoying them that often they turned angry faces to the camera.[29] These young women were modestly dressed. None was behaving in a manner or standing in a location that suggested prostitution. The camera, cutting from white women's faces to black women's buttocks, aggressively inflected Gilman's thesis; now the "covert sexuality" of black women expresses the "overt sexuality" of white men. This visual discourse, vacillating between public and private, first disclosed the construction of black women as prostitutes and then the incongruity between the public and private discourses regarding immigrant prostitutes.

It is consequently interesting to speculate further on how representing foreign prostitutes as slaves functions in the context of the anxiety provoked by the questions of race and immigration in present-day Italy. This construction appears to bind the issues of immigration, sexuality, and market values, displacing the anxiety of immigration onto constructions of immigrant victims and immigrant villains. In addition to the talk of slave markets, auctions, and the pricing of young women in shipments of cocaine, newspapers at times compare the large number of immigrant prostitutes, and the vast revenues generated, with the supposedly smaller number of Italian women engaging in commercial sex. This presentation of the data draws upon the apprehension of immigrants taking jobs away from the natives. An article on the deportation of Nigerian prostitutes in Rome makes this bluntly clear: The "meager patrol of Italian women . . . will be very happy to get rid of the competition."[30]

In contrast to the representation of the Italian prostitutes' active dislike of their competition is the use of the passive voice to represent African prostitutes. Reports on the arrest of a Nigerian woman for prostitution trafficking told readers how "[m]ore than 200 women were bought and sold as if they were animals. [They] were beaten, threatened with voodoo and forced to walk the streets."[31] "They are women whose wills have been completely broken. . . . They only did what they were ordered to do."[32] The passive voice in these instances determines that Nigerian immigrants are both subjects and objects, consequently excluding Italian clients from any involvement.

This rhetorical construct of slavery brings to mind why free white labor in nineteenth-century America eventually rejected similar rhetoric. Industrial workers learned that calling themselves slaves meant forfeiting their voice in the discourse of industrial capitalism. Applying the slave metaphor to all nonnative prostitutes accomplishes an analogous rhetorical feat today. Slavery rhetoric contains prostitution within the immigrant population by ignoring the Italian men who have created this market. The resulting representation of mindless passivity and the fear of voodoo marginalizes these women even as it includes them. Public sympathy for immigrant prostitutes is won through racist insinuations of cultural inferiority.

Harriet Jacobs's narrative of her life, *Incidents in the Life of a Slave Girl*, published in 1861, challenges the assumption of slavery being synonymous with passivity. Slavery for Jacobs was a legal reality, not rhetoric, yet in her narrative she assumes full responsibility for bartering her sexual favors in the hope her children would not become the property of her lecherous master. Linda Brent, Jacobs's pseudonymous narrator, says: "I have promised to tell you the truth, and I will do it honestly, let it cost me what it may. I will not try to screen myself behind the plea of compulsion from a master; for it was not so. Neither can I plead ignorance or thoughtlessness. . . . I knew what I did, and I did it with deliberate calculation."[33] Although the depravity of her master is itemized, Jacobs not only refuses to be a victim but also refuses to conform to the nineteenth-century ideal of the passive female found in sentimental novels and many slave narratives. Her master "should not, after my long struggle with him, succeed at last in trampling his victim under his feet."[34] "My master had power and law on his side; I had a determined will. There is might in each."[35]

Jacobs's defiance cuts two ways. In essentialist gender ideology, reason and will are masculine attributes. In her introduction to the narrative, Lydia Maria Child, Jacobs's editor, strives to fabricate the feminine ideal with the passive voice describing "my sisters in bondage who are suffering wrongs" that have "generally been kept veiled." Child promises to exhibit the sexual victimization of black women to her white sisters "with the veil withdrawn."[36] Her promise of decorous passivity remains unfulfilled. Jacobs's calculated strategy and willful defiance is not the resistance of the women in Frederick Douglass's narrative, but of Douglass himself.

Incidents in the Life of a Slave Girl consequently contributes to this discussion by bringing the race × gender elements of Brewer's formula to the fore. The defiance of Nigerian prostitutes resisting deportation on the evening news clashes with the representation of these women having been bought, sold, and defrauded of their earnings. The cognitive dissonance created by the texts of their (feminine) victimization and the images of their (masculine) defiance exposes the inept confines of contemporary slavery rhetoric, bound by the stereotypical native-born professional at one end and the foreign victim at the other. Were these contemporary rhetorical constructs applied to the reality of Jacobs's life, they would leave no room for her agonizing decision to take another white man as her lover. Jacobs's "desperate act of free agency, exercised within the limits of a constrained situation," as Gerald D. Jaynes aptly puts it, allows us to make the connection between her narrative and the immigrant prostitutes in Italy today.[37] *Incidents in the Life of a Slave Girl* here acquires important contemporary value by unveiling the distortions inherent in constructing prostitutes as either enslaved victims or free professionals. The resulting oversimplification confuses rather than clarifies such a complex social and economic phenomenon, with a much broader spectrum than an either/or dichotomy.

Brewer's race × class × gender formula has therefore proven to be a useful tool in explicating the rhetorical construct of the enslaved foreign prostitute. Examining the construct as the play of the multiplicative relationships of these factors has clarified the embeddedness of race, class, and gender, and how the interrelatedness of these elements has contributed to the creation of the enslaved foreign prostitute as an either/or dichotomy. Then Brewer's formula has identified the racist underpinnings of this rhetorical construct and how the resultant dichotomy marginalizes the African prostitutes in Italy. Finally, engaging Harriet Jacobs's narrative with the race × class × gender formula renders the distortions of the contemporary rhetorical construct less ambiguous.

Harriet Jacobs further informs this discussion by providing the tools needed to foreground the larger problems of subordination, exploitation, and dependency involved in immigration to Italy. Jacobs insists on locating the limitations of her choices within the larger context of slavery in order to critique that institution, rather than the isolated manifestations of sexual slavery occurring within it. She writes:

> Slavery is a curse to the whites as well as to the blacks. It makes the white fathers cruel and sensual; the sons violent and licentious; it contaminates the daughters, and makes the wives wretched. And as for the colored race, it needs an abler pen than mine to describe the extremity of their sufferings, the depth of their degradation.[38]

Jacobs contexts white licentiousness within the larger institution of slavery, but male sexual desire is curiously absent in the rhetoric surrounding foreign prostitutes in Italy. Although a victim requires a victimizer, Italian men are rarely included in the slave rhetoric. When local police were confiscating clients' cars as a penalty for aiding and abetting prostitution, one man so punished committed suicide. The subsequent howl of protest led the then interior minister to cast doubt on the constitutionality of the practice.[39]

The Italian press points to Albanians, Nigerians, and Yugoslavians as the victimizers of enslaved Albanians, Nigerians, and Yugoslavians, designating immigrants as both victims and victimizers. By detaching commercial sexual activity from the larger economic context, which includes the Italian clients, the enslavement of prostitutes is constructed as a problem confined to immigrants, even when identifying which Italian cities are centers of child prostitution.[40]

Many Italians now favor reopening houses of prostitution, in spite of unrelenting opposition by militant prostitutes.[41] Prime Minister Berlusconi's outrage at seeing scantily dressed prostitutes, and his subsequent public musings on the desirability of reopening brothels, has rekindled the debate.[42] Inasmuch as forcing women into brothels institutionalizes what is simultaneously denounced as slavery, Jesuits have given their blessing to "protected locations" for prostitutes. Carlo Giovanardi, a former deputy speaker of the Chamber of Deputies, applauded the proposal and remarked, "the problem is to reduce the supply of prostitution and not increase it."[43] This logic is remarkably similar to that of the American Thomas Cobb, whose 1858 treatise on slave law reasoned that "the want of chastity among female slaves" was the cause of sexual immorality among white men.[44] By focusing on supply and ignoring demand, the Italian press sidesteps the role of Italian men in creating the market for the immigrant prostitutes represented as enslaved.

This is more than bashful reticence; it is a refusal to acknowledge the economic principle of supply and demand. The unwillingness to recognize the role of Italian men in the exploitation of prostitutes hints at an uneasiness to admit that Italians exploit other immigrants as well. Divorcing the isolated accounts of sexual slavery of foreign prostitutes from the context of the demand for cheap immigrant labor in other areas confuses both issues, rather than rendering them intelligible.

How tangled the questions of immigration and prostitution actually are can be seen in a front-page headline of a free popular newspaper. "Incentives and Repressive Measures against the New Slaveholders" discusses how Great Britain and Italy are fighting illegal immigration through increased border controls in Bosnia and cash incentives for illegal immigrants who wish to return to their native land.[45] The word "slaveholders" in the headline leads the reader to expect prostitutes to be the subject of the report. However, the text includes neither prostitutes nor women, contradicting these expectations by using masculine forms when referring to illegal immigrants.

This article alludes to the fact that illegal immigrants circulate among the estimated five million unregistered workers in Italy.[46] Illegal immigrants cross the border by paying large sums of money to the same criminal organizations involved in the prostitution traffic.[47] What is perplexing, in a country where businesses have petitioned the government for more immigrant workers, is how the 1,875 prostitutes experts consider enslaved in Italy[48] displace the 530,000 immigrants working in the underground economy.[49] Obviously, this does not mean that the brutal reality of enslavement and sexual abuse of these women is to be minimized; it means not to isolate this phenomenon from the context of immigration exploitation in all its manifestations. Setting immigrant prostitution within the larger context of all exploited immigrants suggests that Italians tolerate a certain amount of illegal immigration, giving their unspoken consent to dismiss or deport illegal immigrants who protest their subordinate position. Foregrounding the larger economic context reveals how most immigrants come to Italy to satisfy the demand for cheap industrial labor in the north, agricultural work in the south, domestic service, and building trades, but very few come to meet the demand for commercial sex. Thus, the emphasis on the economic exploitation of enslaved prostitutes is a displaced discourse. The debate on immigration is successfully shifted from factory floors and building sites into bedrooms and parked cars.

This displacement is so persistent that photographs of prostitutes accompany articles on human trafficking, which focus on pedophilia, prostitution, and pornography but avoid mentioning sweated labor in any but the sex industry. Journalists deflect any mention of sweated labor in Italy to the issue of prostitution, as in this example, when the article abruptly shifts from talking about illegal Chinese labor to prostitution, "[I]t costs the Chinese at least $12,500.00 to come to Italy, which is repaid by working no less than eighteen hours a day. Enslaved prostitutes are bought and sold by criminal organizations for sums from $1,500.00 to $10,000.00 and from whom they extort as much as 10 thousand dollars a month."[50] The profits involved in prostitution are itemized, but no hint is given of how Chinese workers repay their debt or what goods and services they provide Italians. These Chinese workers are decontextualized and marginalized by the discourse to the same degree that the immigrant prostitutes are.

One article deplores the estimated twenty thousand underground workshops producing luxury goods in southern Italy, discusses the problem of unregistered Italian workers, but falls silent on the question of unregistered immigrant labor.[51] Similarly, another article fails to include sweated labor in an article on human trafficking by announcing that "[t]here are 200 million new slaves, 2 million victims of child abuse" and then confining the discourse to pornography and prostitution. Only toward the end of this article is there a comment that "criminal organizations have transformed the natural tendency of immigration from poorer to richer countries into a continuously cycling mechanism."[52] Anonymous villains are set center stage to manipulate the supply of illegal immigrants, but both articles fail to conceal the behind-the-scenes demand for illegal immigrants in 55 percent of industrial, retail, service, construction, and agricultural businesses.

It will be very difficult to stop the traffic of prostitutes without also cutting off this supply of cheap labor that satisfies the needs of the Italian economy. Illegal immigrants toil at off-the-books jobs without health-care benefits, union protection, or pensions. But the public discourse on slavery does not include these illegal immigrants until the Italian police raid a sweatshop and arrest a Chinese manufacturer for enslaving his Chinese workers.

Each culture develops its own rhetorical strategies of containment, inclusion, or exclusion to articulate the anxiety produced by immigration. In Italy, splitting the representation from the reality severs the connections between the women and men working in fields and factories, cleaning homes, caring for children, and aiding the elderly in the twilight of the underground economy and those forced to walk the streets. Current African American feminist theory, expressed in the formula of race $\times$ class $\times$ gender, and Harriet Jacobs's *Incidents in the Life of a Slave Girl* critique the insufficiency of the rhetorical construct of the enslaved foreign prostitute by setting sexual slavery within this context of immigrant exploitation. Displacing the discourse on immigration onto the estimated 1,875 enslaved prostitutes alleviates the discomfort of exploiting more than half a million illegal immigrants. The immigrant victims of coerced prostitution are pitied while the rights of other immigrant workers are denied. The enslavement and subordination of many Third World women necessary for the privileges of Western women, posited by bell hooks, is masked by the rhetorical construct of immigrant prostitutes as slaves, gaining sympathy for a few while capitalizing on many others.

I am deeply indebted to M. Giulia Fabi for her insights on Harriet Jacobs and for many other points throughout this essay. My thanks to Giovanna Carlo, Frances Eubanks, Heike Raphael-Hernandez, P. A. Skantze, Susan Tomlinson, and Victoria Quandamatteo for their wise suggestions.

Notes

1.   "Immigrati, quella legge sa di spot," *La Repubblica*, 8 giugno 2002, 7. See also "Sanatoria e dritto di voto per gli immigrati," *La Stampa*, 8 giugno 2002, 7.
2.   Marco Lollo, "Invaso dallo straniero, così la percezione degli italiani," *La Stampa*, 18 febbraio 2001, 8.
3.   Carlo Macri, "Gli italiani & gli immigrati 2," *Il Corriere della Sera*, 11 gennaio 2002, 19.
4.   "L'immigrato fa sempre più paura: il 60% degli italiani: fermiamo anche i regolari," *La Stampa*, 24 febbraio 2001, 6.
5.   "Le paure degli italiani," *L'Unità*, 21 luglio 2000, 8.
6.   "Italiani a rischio d'estinzione," *Leggo*, 19 febbraio 2002, 3. See also Fillipo Ceccarelli, "Allarme crescita zero: Gli italiani sono in via d'estinzione," *La Stampa*, 12 febbraio 2002, 13.
7.   *Rainews24*, RAI 3 (Rome), 13 January 2002.
8.   "lavoro: dossier carabinieri, 1 azienda su 2 occupa in nero," www.ansa.it/rubriche/topnews /2003–01–14_1238271.html (14 January 2003).
9.   Christopher Emsden, "Immigrant Labor Fuels Economy but Not the State's Tax Coffers," *International Herald Tribune*, 7 March 2001, Italy Daily, 2. See also "Economia in nero, Italia da primato," *Il Sole-24 Ore*, 27 aprile 2002, 17.
10. "Un rapporto Eurispes fotografa il cambiamento," *La Repubblica*, 5 febbraio 2002, www. politicainsieme.it/tema/alcuni_articoli_della_stampa_sull'immigrazione.htm (9 July 2002).

See also "Rassegna Sindacale n. 6, del 19 febbraio 2002," www.lomb.cgil.it/sanita/blocknotes/ n.3_2002.htm#5> (9 July 2002).

11. bell hooks, *Where We Stand: Class Matters* (New York: Routledge, 2000), 109.
12. Rose M. Brewer, "Theorizing Race, Gender and Class: The New Scholarship of Black Feminist Intellectuals and Black Women's Labor," in *Theorizing Black Feminisms: The Visionary Pragmatism of Black Women*, ed. Stanlie M. James and Abena P. A. Busia (London: Routledge, 1993), 13–30.
13. Virginia Piccolillo, "Immigrati, assalto alle poste per i moduli," *Il Corriere della Sera*, 29 agosto 2002, 1+.
14. Claudio Gerino, "La grande fuga Brindisi, indagine sui ritardi di stato," *La Repubblica*, 13 marzo 1991, 7.
15. Roberta Ruscica, "Al mercato del sesso," *Io Donna*, 20 maggio 2000, 88–92.
16. Alessandro Mognon, "In vacanza premio, rapita e costretta a prostituirsi," *La Stampa*, 4 giugno 2000, 11.
17. "Nuove schiave i numeri del mercato del sesso," *La Stampa*, 12 luglio 2000, 13.
18. Roberto Zuccolini, "Cofferati torni a trattare, lo invito a cena," *Il Corriere della Sera*, 11 luglio 2002, 5. See also *TG2*, RAI 2 (Rome), 10 July 2002.
19. Anna Maria Sersale, "I gesuiti: 'Per le prostitute meglio riaprire le case chiuse,'" *Il Messaggero*, 15 dicembre 2000, 10. See also "I gesuiti: luoghi protetti per la prostituzione Bellillo: ma c'è anche chi si vende per scelta," *Il Corriere della Sera*, 17 dicembre 2000, 17.
20. Luca Fazzo, "La notte a luci rosse dei campione dell'Inter," *La Repubblica*, 31 gennaio 2001, 30.
21. Massimo Lugli, "Prostitute, nuova offensiva, rimpatriate in poche ore," *La Repubblica*, 13 marzo 2001, Roma Cronaca, III.
22. "Chiuso il centro estetico a luci rosse a poche centinaia di metri dal Vaticano," *La Repubblica*, 13 marzo 2001, Roma Cronaca, III.
23. Maria Noella De Luca, "Ecco le nuove schiave a luci rosse 'io nigeriana prigioniera del racket,'" *La Repubblica*, 1 maggio 1990, 18.
24. bell hooks, *Black Looks: Race and Representation* (Boston: South End Press, 1992), 65.
25. *La Corrida*, Canale 5 (Milan), 25 January 2003, www.mediasetonline.com/news/scheda/ 4990.shtml (31 January 2003).
26. Yvonne Durant, "Racism Among the Chic," *Yes Please* (September 1991): 10.
27. Sander L. Gilman, "Black Bodies, White Bodies: Toward an Iconography of Female Sexuality in Late Nineteenth-Century Art, Medicine, and Literature," in *Race, Writing and Difference*, ed. Henry Louis Gates Jr. (Chicago: University of Chicago Press, 1985), 223–61.
28. *Omnibus*, La 7 (Rome), 10 May 2002.
29. *Speciale: immigrazione*, TelePadania, 1 June 2002.
30. Lugli, "Prostitute, nuova offensiva, rimpatriate in poche ore," III.
31. "Traffico di immigrati, Fermata 'Iron Lady': sfruttava centinaia di prostitute nigeriane," *Il Messaggero*, 24 febbraio 2001, Roma Città, 33.
32. Massimo Lugli, "In un negozio dell'Esquilino l'Iron Lady delle nuove schiave," *La Repubblica*, 24 febbraio 2001, Roma Cronaca, IV.
33. Harriet Jacobs, *Incidents in the Life of a Slave Girl* (New York: Oxford University Press, 1990), 83.
34. Ibid., 83.
35. Ibid., 130.
36. Ibid., 8.
37. Gerald D. Jaynes, "Identity and Economic Performance," *Annals of the American Academy of Political and Social Science* (March 2000): 4.
38. Jacobs, *Incidents*, 81.
39. " 'Era un buono,' il paese è con Antonello," *La Stampa*, 10 settembre 2000, 11.
40. Cristina Mangani, "Italia, mercato di piccoli schiavi," *Il Messaggero*, 11 luglio 2002, 8.
41. Allessandra Longo, "Che nostalgia per mamma-maitresse," *La Repubblica*, 1 luglio 1990, 19.
42. "Togliere le prostitute dalle strade," *Il Corriere della Sera*, 6 gennaio 2002, 15.
43. Marco Politi, "I gesuiti: sì alle case chiuse," *La Repubblica*, 15 dicembre 2000, 32.
44. Christina Accomando, "'The laws were laid down to me anew': Harriet Jacobs and the Reframing of Legal Fictions," *African American Review* 32, no. 2 (summer 1998), 8.
45. "Incentivi e repressione contro i nuovi schiavisti," *Metro* (Roma), 5 febbraio 2001, 1.

46. Giovanni Tagliapietra, "Gli italiani? Apatici e fatalisti," *Il Tempo*, 27 gennaio 2001, 5. See also Giovanna Casadio, "Italia, casa degli Oblomov 'pigra, egoista, antiquata,'" *La Repubblica*, 27 gennaio 2001, 5.
47. Lirio Abbate, "L'Onu cancella i paradisi-rifugio dei boss," *La Stampa*, 13 dicembre 2000, 2.
48. Franscesco Carchedi, "la prostituzione straniera in Italia: analisi dei risultati della indagine sulle protagoniste e i modelli relazionali," in *I colori della notte: migrazioni, sfruttamento sessuale, esperienze di intervento sociale*, ed. Francesco Carchedi, Anna Picciolini, Giovanna Mottura, and Giovanna Campani (Milano: FrancoAngeli, 2000), 136. See also "Numeri e problemi di una piaga sociale," *La Stampa*, 6 gennaio 2002, 7.
49. Emsden, "Immigrant Labor Fuels Economy," 2.
50. Giovanna Casadio, "I trafficanti di uomini sono come mafiosi," *La Repubblica*, 1 marzo 2001, 29.
51. Gian Antonio Stella, "La fabbrica dell'eleganza? È nascosta nei vicoli di Napoli," *Il Corriere della Sera*, 3 marzo 2001, 1+.
52. Rita Di Giovacchino, "Tratta delle schiave: 186 straniere uccise," *Il Messaggero*, 1 marzo 2001, 11.

16

Blackening Gypsy Slavery
The Romanian Case

MIHAELA MUDURE

My mother and my father were no longer slaves,
but they were poor.
To make a living they did the hard manual labor for the farmers.
—Petre Copoiu[1]

For centuries, both Romanian Roma (Gypsies)[2] and African Americans have occupied a problematic space in their respective societies: They have been a negative other on which the majority could throw most of their fears. The Roma and the African American problems have had a common cause: enslavement of an outsider group coupled with visibly racial otherness. For both groups, the legal status of slavery ended in the mid-nineteenth century, and since then, both groups have had to fight for full emancipation and full respect in their societies, which they still do not enjoy. Even if these two communities have grown in different historical environments—the Romanian rural society lacking strong democratic traditions and the U.S. highly industrialized society having a democratic tradition—attempts at solutions are strikingly similar: mutual efforts both by the minority and the majority for fullest emancipation at all levels of society.

A reading of the Romanian Roma situation in comparison with the African American experience facilitates two different kinds of comparisons. On the one hand, I will discuss the historical reality that the Roma situation was often indeed read in Romanian nineteenth-century history through the African American lens, with the appropriate nuances, of course. On the other hand, I claim that in contemporary circumstances, the African American community has accomplished a lot more in its effort for full emancipation and acceptance at all levels of society than the Romanian Roma community. By reading the situation of contemporary Roma through African American lenses and comparing the two groups at the beginning of the twenty-first century, I hope to point to some possible solutions for the still very problematic position of the Roma community in Romanian society.

The Romanian intelligentsia of the nineteenth century followed with great interest and empathy the evolution of the abolitionist movement in the United States. Their interest raised the question of the problem of Gypsy slavery in Romania, a question they became acutely aware of through Masonic channels. Already during the eighteenth century, the idea of the Gypsy and black slaves' manumission appeared in the Masonic Lodge of the Nine Muses. This lodge, among whose members were Benjamin Franklin and Marquis de Lafayette and whose president was the French revolutionary Jacques Pierre Brissot, focused both on the black slaves of America and on the Gypsy slaves of the Old World. Because many of the important Romanian militants of the 1848 revolution were Masons, they got particularly sensitive to this issue.

One of these intellectuals influenced both by the nationalist and abolitionist ideas was Mihail Kogălniceanu (1817–1891). He offered one of the most consistent and thorough Romanian perspectives on the Gypsy problem at that time. In 1837, as a student in Berlin, Kogălniceanu wrote a presentation of the Gypsies at the request of Alexander von Humboldt. Interestingly, Kogălniceanu complains about the momentary and biased interest in the nineteenth-century slaves, yet, on the other hand, he criticizes the "lack of civilization" of this "miserable" group.[3] Kogălniceanu mentions the peculiarities of the Gypsy slave situation in Moldavia. The owner has no right over the slave's life or over his property unless the slave does not have heirs. But if a slave runs away, the owner has the right to follow the fugitive slave.[4] Slaves are allowed to have a home, a garden, and a little store, but they cannot have a farm or an estate.[5] The owner has to feed and clothe the slaves who work on his estate or in his household. In Wallachia, the situation is almost the same, except that some slaves are allowed to wander all over the country, practicing their trade and paying their owner certain dues. Interestingly, slaves were not only owned by private individuals, but by monasteries and by the Crown as well.[6]

During the Middle Ages, no legitimate union between a free person and a local slave was allowed. A free individual who married a slave became a slave too. But slaves coming from other countries became free if they married a free person.[7] If two slaves decided to marry, they needed the approval of the owner. If they belonged to different owners, usually an arrangement between the two owners had to take place. The couple was to live on one of the estates only, and a compensation or another slave was offered to the other owner. If the owners could reach no agreement, the couple was separated. Under the influence of the Enlightenment ideology, this began to change. In 1743 Alexandru Mavrocordat, then prince of Wallachia, forbade the separation of the slave spouses and ruled that the offspring of a slave and a free person were free. Yet, in Moldovia there was great opposition to these changes. In 1766, priests were forbidden to marry a slave to a free person, and in 1785, there was a return to the medieval custom: The offspring of a slave and a free person were slaves as well.

Kogălniceanu also describes the various forms of punishments that the owners had a right to use—punishments that are impressively cruel. The most frequent ones were the whip and the "falanga." Slaves were taken in chains or obliged to wear an iron horn on their forehead and chains around their necks.[8] In another essay dedicated to the Gypsies, but published later, in 1891, after emancipation, Kogălniceanu describes, in retrospect, the pain of slave families that were separated.

However, in spite of his good intentions, Kogălniceanu's approach to the Gypsies is from a superior and paternalistic position imbued with the ordinary stereotypes about the so-called "inferior" groups. For instance, his description of the Gypsy women alone shows that he is in tune with well-known stereotypes about the representation of marginalized groups. Women belonging to these groups are usually associated with nature and considered more potent or more sexually accessible than the "civilized" groups. The same stereotype has held true for African American women throughout history. The Gypsy woman is an icon of attractive and subversive sexuality and fertility, often represented as an insinuating flower girl. Kogălniceanu claims that Gypsy women are very accessible sexually[9] and hypersexual.[10] And indeed, the stereotype of the attractive Gypsy woman has had a glorious career both in Romanian literature and Romanian painting.

This paternalistic attitude leads Kogălniceanu to fail seeing the causes for the misery and the solutions for this community, although he intends to describe Gypsy status in fairness. He claims, "If the Gypsy steals something, he does not steal big things, but he usually steals clothes and food."[11] Yet he does not suggest at all that this is caused by an extremely marginal way of life at the limit of survival. His solution is purely moralistic and assimilatory. "The Gypsies have vices, but if we succeed in uprooting them from their hearts, they will be extremely useful for Moldavia and Wallachia, mostly working as workers in the factories."[12]

Sympathy from a paternalistic perspective had been a peculiarity of Romanian mainstream intellectuals in general ever since *The Gypsiad*,[13] the mock-heroic epic by Ion Budai Deleanu (1763–1820), the first significant literary work in which Gypsies appear. Written with a lot of humor and benevolence, *The Gypsiad* actually reinforced the stereotypes against the coward Gypsies, interested more in feeding their bellies than in the actual fight for Wallachia's independence and in their equality. And as Gypsies had not developed a written culture to respond, stereotypes had all the chances to develop further.

In addition to these writings by Romanian intellectuals, the Romanian press often included articles on slavery in America and on the abolitionist movement. Already in 1853, only one year after its publication in the United States, Harriet Beecher Stowe's *Uncle Tom's Cabin* was published in translation—*Coliba moşului Toma*, translated by Teodor Codrescu. Kogălniceanu wrote a preface for this translation. Commenting on this publication, the Romanian press did not fail to establish a relationship between the American and the Romanian circumstances. For example, *Gazeta de Moldavia* includes an article "Sfadă de la Unchiul Tom" ("Argument Starting from Uncle Tom"), in which the anonymous author talks about the polemical echo of Harriet Beecher Stowe's book in the United States and England and makes a reference to the slaves in the Romanian principalities.[14] In another article published during the same year in *Gazeta de Moldavia*, the author (also anonymous) talks about the success of *Uncle Tom's Cabin* in the Romanian principalities. The author emphasizes "that the Moldo-Romanian reader will find a misfortunate similarity between the fate of the Blacks in America and those from our country."[15] The popularity of the book led, indeed, to the appearance of two almost simultaneous translations of the same best-seller under two different titles: Shortly after Teodor Codrescu's *Coliba moşului Toma*, D. Pop published *Bordeiul unchiului Tom*. Both translations enjoyed great success among the Romanian readership. In the journal *Propăşirea*, Kogălniceanu published an article titled "Dezrobirea ţiganilor" ("The Manumission of the Gypsies"), in which he takes pride in the abolitionist discussions from the Legislative Assemblies of Moldavia and Wallachia as compared with the legislative bodies of the United States and France.[16] Alecu Russo, another prominent intellectual and writer of the nineteenth century, argued in an article published in *Steaua Dunării* in 1855 against slavery.[17] It is interesting that his argumentation follows, without quoting, the argumentation of modern economics according to Adam Smith. Slavery should be abolished because it is better to have a free worker who buys what he wants and contributes to the development of the market than to have a slave owner who only provides for the slave's barest necessities.

Manumission was finally made possible by a combination of ideological and economic factors. On the one hand, in Romanian culture there was a sort of belated continuation of the Enlightenment that relied on the axiom "that all humans are free and equal." The emergence of a Romantic *forma mentis* created a favorable public opinion for the enslaved people. Kogălniceanu himself acknowledged this influence of the ideological humanist tendencies of the time.[18] Into this mindset fits the attraction to the American abolitionist movement. Because of these comparisons with outside models, in this case American slavery, the general Romanian public became more aware of the issue. Having slaves became embarrassing because Romanians were not in tune with the outside, civilized world—a catch-up mentality that still lingers in Romanian culture today. On the other hand, the appearance of machines on the big estates where Gypsy slaves worked led to greater productivity in agriculture and to less need for a large labor force, a factor that also contributed to final manumission.

The emancipation of the Gypsies was a long historical process, which started in 1831 and lasted until the 1850s. In 1831, through the Organic Regulations, both in Wallachia and Moldavia, the Gypsies who were slaves of the Crown were obliged to pay the same taxes as free citizens.[19] They were also encouraged to settle down in a village and till the land like the Romanians. These efforts to gradually turn the Gypsies into free citizens and taxpayers continued during the next years. Landlords could hire Crown-owned slaves if they gave them land and a garden and helped them build a house on the estate—in a word, get them sedentary. In 1832, in Wallachia, the state offered to buy slaves from private owners. In 1840, also in Wallachia, the state intervened to regulate the status of the monastery-owned slaves who were abused. In 1839 in Moldavia, slaves were given the right of "protemisis": When the owner wanted to sell a slave and the slave offered a price that equaled the offer by his prospective buyer, the owner was obliged to set the slave free. In 1844, the marriages between a slave and a free individual were recognized legally. The offspring from such unions were free. Slaves had to pay for their manumission, and if they did not have the money, it was paid from the revenue of the Church. In 1843 in Wallachia, the slaves of the Crown became free. On 31 January 1844, Mihail Sturdza enacted abolitionist legislation in Moldavia, thus the slaves of the Church became free. On 14 February 1844, the slaves of the Crown become free in Moldavia. On 11 February 1847 in Wallachia, Gheorghe Bibescu set free the slaves of the Church without any compensation. In 1848, the proclamation issued on June 11 in Wallachia mentioned the manumission of the Gypsies as a Christian deed. The slave owners would be forgiven by the Romanian people for the shameful act of having held humans in bondage, and they would be compensated for their economic losses as consequences of the manumission.[20] The defeat of the 1848 revolution both in Moldavia and in Wallachia postponed these evolutions. The manumission of the slaves of the private slave owners occurred on 10/22 December 1855 in Moldavia and on 8/20 February 1856 in Wallachia. In Moldavia, the authors of this bill of law were Petre Mavrogheni and Kogălniceanu. In Wallachia it was Prince Barbu Ştirbei who greatly contributed to this progress. He believed that slavery was a "monstrosity."[21] Interestingly, hundreds of owners in both Romanian principalities refused the compensations. One can only speculate about a possible influence of *Uncle Tom's Cabin* in this case.

In any case, the manumission of the Roma gave Romanians a happy conscience that is well expressed in its naïve limitations in the memorial text *Vasile Porojan* (1880) by Vasile Alecsandri. This text reflects the resistance of prejudice under the mask of egalitarian ideology. Alecsandri, the boy of aristocratic descent, and Vasile Porojan, the Gypsy boy, can play together as children, but they will separate as soon as socialization through education occurs. Alecsandri will go to college, but Vasile Porojan will remain at home and become, at best, a baker's apprentice. After manumission, Alecsandri's Gypsy slaves want to leave the estate, but the lack of any professional prospects will make them return and ask to be hired as servants. It is only Vasile Porojan who refuses to return. He starts working in a little baker's shop and prefers to visit his former master only years later, as a friend.

Manumission presented only the beginning of emancipation and the dawn of a new life for Roma because the nineteenth-century manumissions were actually only acts of juridical emancipation. In an agricultural economy, the new free citizens should have been given land. Yet, the *Rural Law* of 1864[22] contains provisions for the Romanian peasants only, who were given the land they had previously worked for the boyars, but does not even mention the manumitted Roma. It was up to the landowner to give land to the former slaves. Some landowners did, others did not. However, in an agricultural country, the lack of land property practically further marginalized the former slaves. No coherent, well-organized social or cultural programs to integrate the new citizens existed. A few singular voices, such as the one of the Romanian writer Gheorghe Sion, for instance, talked about the necessity to offer vocational education to the manumitted Roma,[23] but nothing organized and coherent was done, and the Roma did not have an intelligentsia of their own to represent their own perspective on their emancipation. The origins of present-day economic marginalization of the Roma go back to this period. Prejudice was easily grafted on the image of a group that was often pushed to crime by poverty and lack of opportunities.

Years later, in 1891, Kogălniceanu summarizes in an *Address* to Charles I, then king of Romania, the efforts of the Romanian society to manumit and integrate Roma. One has to wonder if his naïve and/or blind enthusiasm that manumission automatically led to the acceptance of Roma by the Romanian society is either baffling or mere flattery for Charles I or both when he wrote:

> The emancipatory reform soon had its salutary effects: besides the Layash Gypsies who still live partly in camps, and besides the Ursaries who still practice their trade taming beasts, but also till the land, almost all the other groups of Gypsies have blended into the mass of the nation. And one can only differentiate them by their dark Asian face and by the vivacity of their imagination, otherwise we find them in all the classes of our society.[24]

After their manumission the Gypsies were practically forgotten by the Romanian establishment, and today, 150 years after manumission, the Roma community still faces tremendous poverty, racial discrimination, and stereotyping.

In the United States as well, in spite of all the efforts of both the African American community and, mostly, northern intellectuals, African American problems were not solved with the abolition of slavery. Still, in 1963, Martin Luther King Jr. said about African Americans:

> One hundred years later the life of the Negro is still sadly crippled by the manacles of segregation and the chains of discrimination. One hundred years later the Negro lives on a lonely island of poverty in the midst of a vast ocean of material prosperity. One hundred years later he is still languished in the corners of the American society and finds himself in exile in his own land.[25]

And still, even if both groups started their way to emancipation around the same time and in somewhat similar ideological circumstances, in spite of King's 1963 discontent about the few accomplishments made since then, one can claim that the situation of African Americans is much more improved today than the one of the Roma. Looking at the reasons for the African American lead, one can actually find some possible answers for the still miserable and sometimes even worsening Roma situation of today.

Unlike in Roma culture, in African American culture one can find many African American personalities who contributed to the formation of an intellectual, cultural, and literary African American tradition. Frederick Douglass and Booker T. Washington are among the first to have become spokesmen for their people in American society. Frederick Douglass started from the principles of the United States Constitution and the Bill of Rights. He laid claim to the principles of full citizenship enacted in these documents. Booker T. Washington stressed the black community's necessary efforts to surpass the stigma and the moral and material consequences of slavery. Washington was vigorously opposed by W. E. B. Du Bois. Du Bois, whose perspective was highly sophisticated, strongly believed in human progress and perfectibility. He also realized that the black people's organized collective action needed an institutional structure to be effective, so he became the main organizer and coordinator of the NAACP. Today, one can not name the incredible number of African American intellectuals who offer radical and critical scholarship at the highest sophisticated levels in U.S. society. Names such as Henry Louis Gates Jr., Toni Morrison, Cornel West, Barbara Christian, Robin D. G. Kelley, or bell hooks can only serve as symbolic representatives for the already well established and highly respected, and also for a large group of young, upcoming scholars.

The different approaches to slavery by Douglass and Washington; the intellectual arguments between Du Bois and Washington; the two black charismatic personalities of the twentieth century, Martin Luther King, Jr. and Malcolm X; and today's innumerable sophisticated scholars do not have any counterpart in Roma culture or history. If one compares the historical development of the two groups, one realizes that a main difference between them is their intelligentsia. For a long time, the African American community has had many intellectuals who have contributed either to the passing on of a powerful oral tradition or to the formation of a written intellectual, cultural, and literary African American tradition. As one has been able to observe in the African American case, such a tradition has been necessary for the formation of a group identity. And group identity has been a necessary foundation for political organization and activism. Nothing comparable exists in Roma history so far. Although Roma culture comprises a set of specific cultural patterns (language, music, dances, oral literature), it simply has not had the intelligentsia that would have laid a strong foundation necessary for the cultural identification of a group. It is only after December 1989, the breakdown of the communist system, that one can really talk about an emerging Roma intelligentsia that is influential enough to valorize Roma culture through consistent efforts and that carries the potential to become spokespersons for the Roma themselves.

At one point in time, some tender beginning of a Roma elite that could have become quite influential politically and that had the potential to produce powerful spokespersons did indeed exist. During the period between the two world wars, a few Roma were interested in the appearance of journals and magazines and in organizing their minority within the democratic political frames then existent. In the 1930s, two periodical publications appeared, *Glasul romilor* (*The Voice of the Romanies*) and *Neamul Țiganilor* (*The Gypsy Nation*). Yet they were forced to cease their existence in the 1940s because of the specific historical circumstances. Also in 1933, some Roma militants (Gheorghe A. Lăzărescu-Lăzurică, Gheorghe Niculescu, and Calinic I. Popp Şerboianu) organized the General Association of Gypsies in Romania, which, however, quickly splintered into two organizations. One of these splinter groups, the General Union of the Romanian Gypsies, organized the first congress of Roma on 8 October 1933 and elected Lăzărescu-Lăzurică as the "voivode of the Gypsies."[26] Aware that their plight extended beyond the boundaries of Romania and eager to offer a coherent international Roma agenda, the same group organized the first international meeting of Roma in Bucharest in 1934. Another Roma militant, Aurel Manolescu-Dolj, organized a regional organization of Roma in Oltenia. In spite of rivalry and dissensions, the agenda of these organizations was pretty much the same. They were interested in creating educational opportunities for Roma and in offering welfare benefits: a hostel for the homeless, free meals for the poor, and juridical and medical assistance for all Roma. In addition, they were also interested in settling down the nomadic Roma and in improving the image of Roma in the media.

Unfortunately, these efforts to make Roma visible for the Romanian political and cultural scene were terminated by the general disastrous development of Romanian politics in the 1940s. First the authoritarian rule of King Charles II and then the fascist dictatorship of Ion Antonescu stifled any democratic evolution. More than that, in 1941, all these promising efforts were brought to a brutal end by the official deportation policy of Roma. In the xenophobic and anti-Semitic atmosphere of the time, on 6 April 1941, Marshall Ion Antonescu noticed Roma robbing houses in Bucharest during a curfew while American aviation was bombing Bucharest. He ordered that all the Roma be driven out of Bucharest. Then the idea came to deport the nomadic Roma to Transdniestria, a Romanian-occupied territory of the USSR east of the river Dniester, which was turned into a "dumping ground" for the Romanian "aliens"—Gypsies and Jews. Although this was not part of a "final solution" as it was understood in Nazi Germany, it was a campaign to cleanse Romania of "undesirable" ethnic groups. The high crime record among Roma greatly influenced this decision. Initially, only nomadic Roma were deported. Then sedentary Roma were deported if they had a criminal record or if they were considered dangerous. In some cases, individual Roma came to demand to be deported because they wanted to follow their extended families or because rumors spread that land would be given to Roma in Transdniestria. On the whole, between 1941 and 1942, according to some historians, some 25,000 Roma were deported.[27] Lucien Nastasă and Andrea Varga, who published a collection of documents relating to this painful episode in Romanian history, note 24,000 deported Roma,[28] according to the documents from the trial of General C. Z. Vasiliu, who organized the deportation of the Roma.

According to Viorel Achim, the author of the most documented history of Romanian Roma, about half of the deported died.[29] Once in Transdniestria, the Roma were abandoned and hunger and diseases killed many of them.[30]

There is very little written material about this painful episode in the modern history of Romania, except for some references in the documents of Ion Antonescu's trial or in the novel *Şatra* (*The Gypsy Camp*) by Zaharia Stancu, a novel inspired by facts. In addition, in a recent collection of Roma oral histories, one can find some discreet references to this period: ". . . when I was a maiden, the great war started. The Germans came to us, to our country. Then came an order from the king and they took us Gypsies far away, to another country, in Russia, near the river Bug."[31] In 1944, as the Red Army was approaching Transdniestria, all Roma were set free. Until today, no moral or material compensations have ever been offered to the survivors of the Transdniestria camps or to their heirs.

After 1948, Roma did not appear in the public discourse until after 22 December 1989 (the fall of the communist regime). As the Romanian Communist Party encouraged minorities and the underprivileged to join its ranks, some Roma became policemen or even minor party activists, but reference to their ethnicity was never made, and the price for their integration into the communist power structures was their acculturation. In 1989, a Roma (Gogu Rădulescu) was even a member of the political executive committee, the highest structure of the Communist Party. But most Roma lived on the periphery of Romanian society, and they became the concern of the new, post–World War II authorities in a completely different way. The communist regime installed after World War II tried to forcibly integrate this ethnic minority. "But," as Zoltan Barany explains, "the means to realize Romani assimilation were often carelessly chosen and insensitively implemented, and at times resulted in increased exclusion of the Roma."[32] There was a first wave of sedenterization in 1957 and then a second one in 1962, following similar programs in other communist countries. The industrialization process and the collective farms offered jobs to many Roma. Some of them were also given the modest facilities of an apartment. As this kind of "integration" was executed under pressure, it often happened that the nomadic Roma did not appreciate their sedentary dwellings and often destroyed them, which increased the animosities between the Romanian majority and the Roma minority. The authorities of the totalitarian communist regime never consulted the Roma about the way in which they saw their own integration. In 1977, a meeting of the central committee of the Romanian Communist Party was dedicated to the Roma situation, and in 1983, the propaganda section of the central committee of the Romanian Communist Party made a report on the Roma.[33] Free medical care, modest but free housing, guaranteed (but also mandatory) employment, and general education improved the situation of the Roma but with a price that some of them did not want to pay: their acculturation.

Interestingly, communist Romania had its own connection to African American issues. In the 1950s and 1960s, the situation of African Americans was used by the then officialdom to read America as a place of oppression and exploitation, thus especially highlighting the nature of oppression-free communism. Yet the racial problems of communist Romania with its own Roma community seemed not to exist. Following a long tradition of bleaching Romanian history, the communist regime turned a blind eye to the racial problems under the pretext that in communist Romania, discrimination based on ethnicity or race did not exist.

The fall of communism in 1989 gave Roma the possibility to have a public voice of their own, but it worsened their economic situation. The political transition painfully affected the less educated and those who did not have professional skills to survive in the modern world, as most Roma are not formally educated, still cling to traditional ways of life, and are at the bottom of the underprivileged. The marginal way of life of most Roma ensured their physical survival but not their advancement in the modern world.

After 1990, in postcommunist times, freedom has sometimes become anarchy or wild voluntarism. With regard to the Roma situation, it also has implied an increase in prejudice and conflict against Roma that have occurred in reaction to the public articulation of a Roma ethnic identity. The causes of the conflict are rooted both in the social, nonmulticultural ideological heritage of former communist countries in general, in the tremendous economic problems in postcommunist Romania itself—some scholars even called the Romania at the end of the 1980s the "Ethiopia of Europe"[34]—and in the decrease of the prestige of the public authority. Recovering will take time and effort. In postcommunist conditions, the gap between the non-Roma majority and the Roma minority has widened, and stereotyping resulting from racism is getting worse.

Interestingly enough, recently lots of international attention has been paid to the Roma issues both in the press and in academic scholarship. However, most of the newspaper articles and scholarly research focus on more "shocking" aspects, such as ethnic violence or on ethnographic research, but do not offer at all any analytical approaches or any solutions. As I claim above, taking the African American evolution as a model, what is foremost necessary is to help Roma get a voice of their own through their own intelligentsia. Yet, taking the African American situation as example, I also would claim that a lot of analytical and unbiased scholarship is urgently needed.

So far one can find only very few examples of such analytical scholarship by Roma intellectuals themselves. One example is offered by Elena Zamfir and Cătălin Zamfir; their analytical approach to contemporary Roma problems has led them to argue in their work that modernization is a key issue for Roma communities. They claim that any group that does not modernize its way of life automatically tends to become a chronically marginalized and disadvantaged group. Such groups then become kinds of social reservations that are maintained by the dominant community for a variety of reasons, in which "helplessness combines with vague abstract principles about minority rights quickly abandoned at the first conflict with that peculiar minority."[35] Such reservations can be tolerated or protected on condition that they be small, which is the situation in Western countries. But if such communities grow in number, there inevitably arise tensions that prevent the reciprocal accommodation of the majority and the minority. This is very much the situation of Roma in Romania. Therefore, according to the Zamfirs, Roma must modernize their own culture and begin a new tradition.

One such extremely important factor in the process of changing Roma from within, of modernizing their culture, is their attitude toward education. According to some European Roma Center statistics for 2001, the average age for marriage is seventeen for girls and eighteen for boys; the birth rate is presently 5.1 children per woman, whereas Romania's average birth rate is 1.9 per woman; 58 percent of all Roma men and 89 percent of all Roma women have no professional qualifications; 44 percent of all Roma men and 59 percent of all Roma women are illiterate; only 4.5 percent of Roma population graduate from high school; 40 percent of Roma children do not attend kindergarten; only 50 percent of the children attend primary school, and only 7 percent pursue secondary education.[36]

Yet, in the case of education, one can also see the urgent need for analytical scholarship at the highest level as one can find for the African American situation, because the Roma negative mindset toward education is often strongly connected to the racism they have to face in the classroom by Romanian majority teachers, students, and parents. As Teodor Cozma, Constantin Cucos, and Mariana Momanu show, teachers do not pay the same attention to Roma students; these students are seated at the back of the class; and if their grades are lower, it is an excuse for teachers to send them to schools or classes for students with special educational needs.[37]

In addition, poverty is a crucially deciding factor in Roma eduation. According to Romanian legislation, the right to education is guaranteed for every citizen; practically, however, education is often impossible for poor people and particularly for Roma children. Therefore, because of the extreme poverty of many Roma, of the prejudice they have to face, and of a

Fig. 6 Young women from the Laies clan at the Costesti Fair. Photograph: Rareş Beuran.

negative mindset caused by a long history of marginalization, many Roma children drop out of school.

After 1992, the Romanian government tried to do something about this problem by implementing specific positive-discrimination measures.[38] Special seats for Romani candidates were offered at the School of Law, at the schools for police officers, or at the faculty of social welfare assistance at Babes-Bolyai University, for example. At the University of Bucharest, a special department for the study of Roma language and literature was founded. At the level of each county, there is a school superintendent responsible with Roma education. In 2002, an affirmative-action experimental policy was implemented in Bucharest: one hundred Roma students were admitted to the best high schools in Bucharest although their examination grades were lower than those of the mainstream candidates.

Although one must wait to see the effects of these affirmative-action strategies, one also has to observe, at the same time, how the expression of the general public opinion during the 1990s has worsened and stereotypes have often openly ruled public opinions and discussions. Stereotyping and verbal abuse are crucial elements in Roma discrimination and marginalization. To do away with these flaws, awareness about this tendency of the majority to make negative general statements about Roma has to increase. The study of Romanian newspapers alone is relevant in this respect and serves as one example of the imperious necessity to discuss race and racism in Romanian scholarship. By their use of language, Romanian mass media contribute tremendously to the aggressive stereotyping of Roma, which proves the necessity of a politically correct language.[39] It often happens, for example, that within a group of criminals, journalists distinguish Roma specifically, or that the spatial coordinates of a crime are presented like this: "In an area inhabited by Gypsies . . ."[40] It often happens that the Roma ethnicity of the perpetrators of a crime is singled out.[41] And the threat of Gypsy mafia seems to be overwhelming.[42] Most Romanian journalists are not acquainted with the concept of a politically correct language, and freedom of speech is often confused with freedom for verbal abuse. If a public personality is criticized, he or she is often called a "Gypsy." Soon after the execution of Nicolae Ceaușescu in 1989, newspaper articles claimed that his and his wife's families were of Gypsy origin.[43] The poet Mircea Dinescu, a dissident and a leader in the 1989 revolution, was called "a Gypsy with a swine-life face."[44] Politicians such as Ion Iliescu, the current president of Romania, or Adrian Năstase, the current prime minister of Romania, have been labeled "Gypsies" if the journalist wanted to show his discontent with their moral profile. The president of the Humanist Party of Romania has been criticized because he is dark-skinned and he lies on pillows like a "bulibasha."[45] Mădălin Voicu, one of the Romani members of parliament, has been called "the representative of Gypsy music in the Romanian Parliament."[46]

Such labeling that relies on a linguistic practice embedded in Romanian vocabulary and that gives negative meanings to the word "Gypsy" or to its derivatives is connected to the fact that Romanian society lacks any serious discussion of race and of racism at the complex and sophisticated theorizing level that exists in African American culture. In American culture, there is strong awareness that race is "a fundamental organizing principle of social re-

Fig. 7 Old man from the Kalderash clan, at Bratei, Sibiu County. Photograph: Rareş Beuran.

lationships," that "racial meanings pervade US society, extending from the shaping of individual racial identities to the structuring of collective political action on the terrain of the state."[47] In Romanian culture, "race" has been used mostly in the anti-Semitic discourse, in the syntagma "the Jewish race," whereas blackness—although it is a factor of behavioral regulation—was practically never theorized upon because of its obvious visibility. Gypsiness was not discussed in racial terms, but in ethnic terms. Reading the contemporary Roma situation through African American lenses points to the importance of a consolidated democratic environment in dealing with racial issues.

Fig. 8 Nomad Gypsy camp near Timisoara. Photograph: Rareş Beuran.

Yet even with all the problems that Romanian society is facing while on its post-1989 way to truly democratic circumstances and better economic provisions, it is also, historically, the first time that Roma have a chance to be integrated into Romanian society in respectful and fair ways without being forced to give up their own cultural identity. But to accomplish that task, the Romanian society faces a very complex and challenging task. The non-Roma majority has to learn about the multicultural and intercultural nature of modern democracies, and Roma need modernization from within their community to meet the challenges of the twenty-first century.

Interestingly, the emerging Roma intelligentsia and the Romanian government seem indeed be inspired by the African American experience when they together try to combine stratagems to overcome racial labeling and to teach Roma very up-to-date professional skills. For instance, in August 2002, several Roma nongovernmental organizations and the minister of culture organized a Roma summer school at Saturn, a city at the Black Sea. The motto of the school was significant: "Be black and you will be free!" Participants were taught to use computers, to valorize their Roma cultural heritage, and to respond to racial stereotypes by taking pride in their blackness.[48]

The Roma community is not a homogenous group. Politically, a great problem for the Roma community in Romania is its lack of cohesion beyond the extended family. In addition, traditional Roma do not accept marriages outside the group.[49] The Roma defense cultural stratagem was the development of *mageripen* or *mahrime*, a set of interdictions and taboos based on the opposition between cleanliness and uncleanliness (socially and spiritually), very much like the Jewish *kosher*. Naturally, what is inside the group is clean, what is outside the group is unclean. It is particularly since 1990, when international organizations also began paying more attention to Roma issues, that some voices in the Roma community have argued against mixed blood because of the inability of mixed-blood Roma to express the authenticity of the Roma point of view. The fact that for the moment, at least, many of the Roma intellectuals and militants are mixed blood shows the necessity of urgent rethinking of certain traditional attitudes on the way toward modernization and toward economic resources.

But again, in spite of these problems that the Roma have to cope with themselves, the 1990s are historically also the first time where one can see changes—where a Roma intelligentsia is emerging, where Roma become their own spokespeople for their own concerns. For the first time in Romania's history, Roma people have their own representatives in the parliament. Roma have also been included in the restitution policies of the postcommunist Romanian administrations. The Petre Roman administration has returned the gold confiscated from the Roma in 1960 and 1978.[50] Also, a Roma civil rights movement has been developing in Romania under the democratic circumstances after 1990. This movement includes the appearance of Roma political organizations, Roma nongovernmental organizations, and efforts to cultivate the Roma language and culture to prevent further acculturation. In 1997, the SIS-Rrom was founded.[51] The SIS-Rrom is an organization meant to prevent ethnic conflicts. It has three boards (the internal affairs board, the foreign affairs board, the political board) and the sociocultural service. Even if Roma organizations are still far from the prestigious organizations of the black community in the United States—and even if the coronation of Emperor Iulian or of King Cioabă (two elders of rival Roma clans) after 1990 point to the need to replace the more impersonal and less spectacular modern forms of political representation with supposedly more charismatic royalties and traditional forms of authority[52]—one still can claim all these things as necessary to help create or further a sense of communal self-esteem.

The solutions offered by the few Roma intellectuals are also interesting to consider. For instance, Dan Oprescu is mostly interested in the political representation of Roma. To find out the real proportion of this minority within the population of Romania (a very important element in order to charter further minority policies), Oprescu recommends the possibility that a person could claim, in the census, mixed ethnicity, for instance, Romanian Roma or Hungarian Roma.[53]

A new development among the Roma elite is the theoretical discussion of Roma nationalism.[54] A recent seminar in Jadwisin, Poland, became an excellent opportunity to consider Roma empowerment by creating a Roma nationalist ideology. The demand for political recognition led to various possible solutions: a Roma nation in diaspora, a Roma transnationality, or a Roma nonterritorial European minority.[55] Whether this evolution is in the interest of all Roma people or rather in the interest of a more and more active elite eager to get as much power as possible is a very complex and important question. Debates have pointed to the danger of an increasing disparity between the Roma elite and the Roma people. The Roma nationalism discourse will lead to the demand of extraterritorial rights for Roma, which will create frictions within the existing European states. Is this strategy worth it for all Roma? The question remains open. The consolidation of the European Union to the detriment of national sovereignties may lead to and ease the growing awareness of a Roma nation all over Europe. The participants in the Jadswin Seminar came to the conclusion that for the moment, at least, "The Roma nation is an open structure; every group can join it because what binds them together is anti-Gypsy structure."[56] As the Roma success story is only at its very beginning, for the moment, solidarity is the most important value.

Like African Americans, Roma were reified through slavery. After 1990, their economic and social exclusion worsened, but their political and cultural representation improved. The dynamics of marginality have changed, but breakthroughs have been too slow for Roma, until now at least. The example of the African Americans who have been able to have their own elite is relevant, in this respect. Otherwise, marginalization will breed marginalization, and the pattern will continue for the next generations. If neglected, Roma "could become a permanent underclass,"[57] a great challenge for the whole Romanian society.

The understanding of the historical and changing characteristics of Roma marginalization as an open process, in which this minority has negotiated its participation in the public sphere to preserve the private space from assimilatory tendencies, is a must for the majority. More scholarship needs to be done in this respect, with the required nuances. Roma themselves have to develop their group identity beyond professional or clan affiliations through acquaintance with their history, culture, and cultivation of their language. The growth of an elite is a prerequisite in this long process. This elite will help to modernize the Roma community from within by preserving their identity and by negotiating a new identity with both traditional and modern components. From among this elite, politicians and spokespersons for the group will emerge. The Romanian Roma are only at the beginning of this process, but any failure or neglect may result in enormous negative costs, both for the minority and the majority.

I would like to thank Rareş Beuran for having graciously offered the three photos that complete the text of the present article. Beuran is a distinguished professional photographer who has worked for several Romanian and international news agencies. At present, Beuran works for the Resource Center for Roma Communities, Soros Open Network in Cluj-Napoca, Romania. My thanks also go to Heike Raphael-Hernandez for her very helpful suggestions.

Notes

1. All Romanian quotes are translated by Mihaela Mudure.
2. I have used the term *Gypsy* in the title of my article because my work concentrates on the stereotypes about the Gypsies and on the Gypsies' adversarial relations within the Romanian society. *Gypsy* is a rhetorical and stylistic device to stress the issues at stake. At present there are three competing names for this ethnic group in Romania: *Gypsy*, *Roma*, and *Rroma*. The first is the name given to this population by the majority; *Roma* is their autonym and also the scholarly and neutral term; and *Rroma* is a very recently coined term meant to spare certain Romanian susceptibilities because of the closeness of the words *Roma* and *Romanian*. Roma themselves are divided over their autonym. There are Romani people who want to be called *Gypsy* and who take pride in this traditional name.
3. Kogălniceanu talks about "an interest which, unfortunately, will only be transitory, for that is how Europeans are! They found philantrophical societies for the abolishment of slavery in America whereas on their own continent, in Europe, there are four million Gypsies who are slaves and two hundred thousand more who are swamped in the darkness of ignorance and barbarism! And nobody does anything to civilise an entire people!" Mihail Kogălniceanu, *Esquisse sur les moeurs et la langue de Cigains* (Berlin: Librairie de B. Behr., 1837), iv.
4. Ibid., 11.
5. Ibid., 12.
6. For a detailed analysis of the Gypsy slaves' condition, see Viorel Achim, *Ţiganii în istoria României* (Bucureşti: Editura Enciclopedică, 1998).
7. Kogălniceanu, *Esquisse*, 10–11.
8. Ibid., 14.
9. Ibid., 1.
10. Ibid., 11.
11. Ibid., 22.
12. Ibid., 25.
13. *The Gypsiad* was published posthumously between 1875 and 1877.
14. "Sfadă de la Unchiul Tom," *Gazeta de Moldavia* XXV (1853), 101–3, in *Bibliografia analitică a periodicelor româneşti, vol. II. 1851–1858, Partea a III-a*, ed. Ioan Lupu, Dan Berindei, Nestor Camariano, and Ovidiu Papadima (Bucureşti: Editura Academiei Republicii Socialiste România,1972), 1154.
15. Ibid., 1155.
16. Achim, *Ţiganii în istoria României*, 86–87.
17. Ibid., 86–87.

18. "That is why according to the spirit of the century and the laws of humanity, several old and young boyars decided to do their away with their country's shameful slavery." Mihail Kogălniceanu, *Desrobirea țiganilor. ștergerea privilegiilor boeresci. Emanciparea țăranilor: Discurs rostitu in Academia Română la 1 aprilie, 1891* (București: Lito-tipografia Carol Grobl, 1891), 14–15.

19. In Transylvania, there were many fewer Gypsy slaves, mostly Crown property, and their emancipation had started much earlier in the eighteenth century under Emperess Maria Theresa and Emperor Joseph II.

20. "The Romanian people should do away with the inhumanity and the shame of having slaves and manumit the Gypsies of the private owners. Those who have suffered from the shame of this sin of having slaves, are forgiven by the Romanian people, but the country, like a good mother, will pay damages, from its treasure house, to anyone who claims having had losses because of this Christian deed." Kogălniceanu, *Desrobirea*, 16.

21. Achim, *Țiganii în istoria României*, 96.

22. Inaccurately considered by Crowe as the "full emancipation" of the Gypsy slaves that would have occurred "three years after Romania became an independent state." David M. Crowe, "The Gypsies of Romania since 1990," *Nationalities Papers* 27, no. 1 (March 1999), 57. Romania became independent in 1877, which is thirteen years after the *Rural Law* of 1864.

23. Gheorghe Sion, *Emanciparea țiganilor*, ed. Petru V. Haneș (București: Librăria H. Steinberg, 1924).

24. Kogălniceanu, *Desrobirea*, 17–18.

25. Martin Luther King Jr., "I Have a Dream," in *Heath Anthology of American Literature*, vol. II., ed. Paul Lauter (Lexington: Heath, 1994), 2483.

26. Lucian Nastasă and Andrea Varga, *țiganii din România (1919–1944)* (Cluj: Centrul de resurse pentru diversitate etnoculturală, 2001), 16.

27. Donald Kenrick, *Historical Dictionary of the Gypsies (Romanies)* (Lanham, Md. and London: Scarecrow Press, 1998), 169, and Achim, *Țiganii în istoria României*, 142.

28. Nastasă and Varga, *Țiganii din România (1919–1944)*, 21.

29. Achim, *Țiganii în istoria României*, 147.

30. Crowe cites 36,000 dead Roma out of 300,000 Roma before the war, but he does not give any source for his statement. Historians who worked in Romanian archives and used the records of the Romanian gendarmes give figures between 24,000 and 25,000 deported people, out of which it would have been impossible for 36,000 to die. Crowe, "The Gypsies of Romania since 1990," 57. The assessment of accurate figures is difficult because of movements to and from the Dniester, with some deported people returning to Romania and others going to Transdniestria.

31. Petre Copoiu, *Romane Paramìca/Povești țigănești* (București: Kriterion, 1996), 79.

32. Zoltan Barany, "Living on the Edge: The East European Roma in Postcommunist Politics and Societies," *Slavic Review* 53, no. 2 (summer 1994): 326.

33. Unfortunately, the archives of this period are not open yet, and these documents cannot be examined.

34. Nestor Rateș quoted in Crowe, "The Gypsies of Romania since 1990," 57.

35. Elena Zamfir and Cătălin Zamfir, *Țiganii între ignorare și îngrijorare* (București: Editura Alternative, 1993), 25.

36. European Roma Rights Center, *Stare de impunitate: Încălcarea drepturilor oamenilor—cazul romilor din România* (Cluj-Napoca: Centrul de Resurse pentru Comunită țile de Romi, 2001), 282. Barany gives the following figures: 51.3 percent of Romani children go to school regularly, 79.4 percent of the Romani adults have no professional training and only 16.5 percent have modern professions, and unemployment affects 77.9 percent of Roma. Barany, "Living on the Edge," 330.

37. Teodor Cozma, Constantin Cucos, and Mariana Momanu, "The Education of Roma Children in Romania: Description, Difficulties, Solutions," *Intercultural Education* 11, no. 3 (2000): 281–87.

38. European Roma Rights Center, *Stare de impunitate*, 116.

39. See also Barany, "Living on the Edge," 329.

40. n.a., *Național*, 18 November 1997, 3, and n.a., *Național*, 28 February 1998, 3.

41. Sandu Constantin, "Film de groază la Bacău," *România Mare*, no. 572 (29 June 2001): 10–11.

42. See Andreea Moldoveanu, "Mafia ṭigǎneascǎ din Giurgiu face legea nestingheritǎ," *Atac la persoanǎ,* no. 35 (3 September 2001): 4, and Departamentul Anticorupṭie al PRM, "In Strehaia, mafia ṭigǎneascǎ ṭine cǎpǎstrul pe capul Poliṭiei ṣi Parchetului," *România Mare,* no. 574 (13 July 2001): 18.
43. See Crowe, "The Gypsies of Romania since 1990," 57.
44. Alcibiade, weekly column, *România Mare,* no. 574 (13 July 2001): 3.
45. Term for Gypsy clan leader. Alcibiade, weekly column, *România Mare,* no. 574 (13 July 2001): 3.
46. Dan Victor, "Mǎdǎlin Voicu îl fenteazǎ pe Gheorghe Zamfir," *Atac la persoanǎ,* no. 36 (10 September 2001): 17.
47. Michael Omi and Howard Winant, *Racial Formation in the United States from the 1960s to the 1980s* (New York and London: Routledge,1986), 66.
48. Monica Tripon, "Negrii ṣi . . . liberi," *Adevǎrul de Cluj,* 13 August 2002, 6.
49. See Barany, "Living on the Edge," 324.
50. However, there are Roma voices who claim that not all of the gold was returned because part of it had not been recorded.
51. Cǎtǎlina Ciutac and Cǎtǎlin Ciutac, "Structura SRI-ului ṭigǎnesc—SIS Rrom (Serviciul de Informaṭii ṣi Siguranṭǎ)" in *Naṭional,* 24 November 1997, 7.
52. See Barany, "Living on the Edge," 334. Barany argues that the authority of Roma kings or emperors is actually limited to their clan and that they are mostly good at offering a media show than solving the very complex problems of the Roma communities.
53. Dan Oprescu, "Despre romi," *22* (February 1998): 10–16.
54. Barany, "Living on the Edge," 334. He links the survival of the nationalist discourse during the postcommunist transition with a counterevolution, the development of Roma nationalism. But his reference to the nationalist organization "Vatra Românescǎ" ("Romanian Hearth") as anti-Gypsy is not accurate. "Vatra Romaneasca" aims at countering the Hungarian nationalist and irredentist discourse.
55. Project on Ethnic Relations, *Roma and the Question of Self-Determination: Fiction and Reality,* Conference Report, Jadwisin, Poland, 15–16 April 2002, 4.
56. Ibid., 15.
57. Justin Burke, "An Anti-Gypsy Fervor Sweeps East Europa," *Christian Science Monitor* 87, no. 194 (1995): 1.

17

"Niggas" and "Skins"

Nihilism among African American Youth in Low-Income Urban Communities and East German Youth in Satellite Cities, Small Towns, and Rural Areas

HEIKE RAPHAEL-HERNANDEZ

Two groups of young people from two completely different backgrounds, African American youth in low-income, poverty-dominated urban communities and youth in former East German satellite cities, small towns, and rural areas, that have nothing to do with each other, in comparison? Not only do the groups appear not to have anything in common, but were they ever to meet, they might even be mortal enemies.

However, when considering both groups, one can easily find similarities that allow such a comparison. Both are social products of economically heavily disadvantaged communities. Both belong to generations that have grown up in an "afterward," either after the Civil Rights Movement or after German reunification. They both grew up with the new argument of "individual responsibility"—society suddenly offered them circumstances of legal equality for personal advancement at all levels, along with the rhetoric that if an individual just tries hard enough, he or she will succeed. And indeed, for many individuals, that approach has worked. The black middle class has grown during the last decades substantially, and for many former East Germans, reunification has opened personal and professional doors that were closed before. Yet, precisely because so many individuals have been able to follow this new route of legal equality accompanied by individual hard work, it has been difficult to establish the fact that for certain groups, because of complicated societal circumstances, this route still might simply not be possible. Despite some sporadic government-sponsored programs throughout the years, and despite regular, albeit sensational, media attention, these two groups of young people are moving more and more to the very bottom of society—a fact that has created in them a growing, deep-seated sense of despair about their present and their future, an increasing attitude of nihilism, and a relatively ready willingness to use violence. Connected to this violence, one can already observe extreme and dangerous forms of things gone wrong: the high crime rate among young African Americans and the widespread, uncritical acceptance and often practice of right-wing ideology among the young in former East Germany.[1] For the African American group, I would even claim that if one considers facts of their everyday life, they are already being treated as the "human trash" of their society. Jawanza Kunjufu rhetorically supports this thesis when he claims the following in his analysis of African American young men:

> If one of every three White males were involved in the penal system, White America would declare a state of emergency.
> If one of every twelve White males in Washington, D.C., were a victim of homicide, White America would declare a state of emergency.
> If 31 percent of White males in Alabama and Florida were permanently disenfranchised, White America would declare a state of emergency.
> If Whites were 13 percent of the population, but comprised 35 percent of drug arrests, 55 percent of drug convictions, and 74 percent of drug prisoners, White America would declare a state of emergency.
> If Whites were 13 percent of the population, but 50 percent of those waiting on death row, White America would declare a state of emergency.[2]

For the current East German young generation and the ones to come, I recognize so many similarities with the African American situation that I see the dangerous potential of a development in the same direction—of being treated as the "human trash" of their society.

This essay takes African American studies as the lens through which one looks at Europe, thus making African American knowledge primary instead of secondary (as opposed to the usual methods of most European or white American theorists). In regard to the African American youth situation, abundant sophisticated scholarship and high-level analytical discourse has been published during the last decade. For the East German side, an abundance of critical scholarship and journalistic research has been undertaken as well. But I see a problem in that the existing discourse focuses mainly on the actual right-wing ideology and its widespread uncritical acceptance in former East Germany. I understand this widespread acceptance as only the tip of an iceberg—the tip that everybody sees and is shocked about and that national and international media can use for sensational reports about current problems in former East Germany. I argue that it should be understood as an outcry by a generation who, with their parents, were thrown into a new societal system after reunification, yet the system offered its own rules of self-determination, which many of them could not handle. Today they stumble through high youth unemployment rates, geographical group identity problems, group and/or individual self-esteem problems, missing meaningful leisure time offers, and no true options for their future. I argue that if a development of deteriorating economic conditions combined with a nihilistic attitude among these young people in East German satellite cities, small towns, and rural areas continues, Germany is well on its way to creating a "ghetto underclass," with dangerous implications for the future. My assumption is not that far-fetched. As early as 1945, Richard Wright made the connection between African American disadvantaged communities and the rise of right-wing ideology in his introduction to *Black Metropolis*, when he argued:

> Do not hold a light attitude toward the slums of Chicago's South Side. Remember that Hitler came out of such a slum. Remember that Chicago could be the Vienna of American Fascism! Out of these mucky slums can come ideas quickening life or hastening death, giving us peace or carrying us toward another war.[3]

With my application of African American knowledge and concerns in this comparison between "niggas" and "skins," I intend to raise awareness of such possible disastrous developments, yet also to point to some solutions currently discussed for the African American youth problem, thus hoping to contribute to some prevention. I am aware that such an application carries many limitations. For example, both groups' pre–new-society's conditions differed radically from each other. Whereas in pre–Civil Rights time, African Americans were forced to live with tremendous racism and discrimination, many of the East German group in question did not experience any oppression that would be comparable to the African American situation. And in their new respective societies, whereas African Americans still often have to experience racism simply because of their skin color, which clearly marks them as belonging to their group, former East Germans can escape or hide their group adherence. Even if in a new geographical setting, some are comparably marked as not belonging because of their regional East German dialect, their children, as the second generation, do not carry that mark anymore. Still, I think that because of specific similarities in their new societies, an application of the African American lens is to a certain extent possible.

In relation to East Germany, the application of the African American lens has indeed been done before. For example, during the fight for a more liberated society in the 1980s, some East German opposition leaders compared their nonviolent struggle with the Civil Rights Movement in the United States. After reunification in Germany in 1990, as many original high hopes were dashed by reality, and when disappointment about governmental changes and regulations started to set in, intellectuals sometimes compared the situation of post-reunification East Germans to the plight of African Americans during the Reconstruction period. Even the stereotypes have been comparable: As African Americans did when they attempted to enter middle-class America in larger numbers, East Germans had to hear statements like, "They are lazy" or "They don't know how to work hard" or "It is not their fault, but the fault of their education that they are not able to hold higher positions at executive levels." Even genetics was not spared; one could indeed hear statements like, "Genes *do* alter in forty years."

Applying the African American lens to contemporary Germany-East, I see certain satellite cities, small towns, and rural areas heading in the direction of the U.S. "ghetto." I base my prediction on these similarities: a deteriorating economy toward underclass conditions, the departure of many who were able or smart enough to leave, a devastating nihilistic mindset coupled with a widespread feeling of "double-abandonment," and the widening gap between the middle and the working-poor class.

To see such a slow but steady move toward the creation of an underclass, one has to look at the development of economic conditions. For African Americans, the downward development started right at the beginning of the post-Civil Rights era. For example, during the 1970s, the maximum benefit paid by Aid to Families with Dependent Children to a family of four was 63 percent of the federal poverty level. This amount dropped to 40 percent of the federal poverty level in 1980. Forty percent of poor children were cut from welfare benefits from 1973 to 1983. Between 1978 and 1988, there was an 80 percent drop in housing assistance for poor families. Of the twenty-one million jobs created during the 1980s, 44 percent paid less than $7,400, which was 30 percent less than the poverty level for a family of three.[4] Presently, about 26 percent of all African American families live below the poverty line.[5] The unemployment rate for blacks remains more than twice as high as for whites; among young black men in central cities, the unemployment rate is as high as 40 percent.[6] A 1998 Department of Housing and Urban Development study acknowledged that more than five million people in the United States, an overwhelming percentage of whom are black, need housing assistance.[7] And, contrary to the widespread stereotype about people of the underclass in general, most of these people are working every day,[8] some in two or three low-level minimum-wage jobs, so-called McJobs.[9] Furthermore, the modern employment market faces new challenges that have already tremendously contributed to the deteriorating conditions in inner cities and that can only bring worse conditions for the working poor and the underclass in the future: On the one hand, modern technology is more and more rendering unskilled or low-skilled jobs obsolete; on the other hand, in addition to a flight of jobs from urban areas in U.S. cities to suburban areas,[10] the age of globalization has caused the flight of many manufacturing jobs to low-wage countries overseas.

To understand the "ghetto" development in former East German satellite cities, small towns, and rural areas, one has to look at unemployment figures. In Germany-West, unemployment in general right now is stated as 9 percent, but it is 20–22 percent for the East.[11] But if larger cities are excluded and one looks at specific examples of small towns in the East, the numbers are even worse. For example, unemployment in small towns and surrounding rural areas in Sachsen-Anhalt were as high as 26.3 percent in Sangerhausen, 23.7 percent in Merseburg, and 24.4 percent in Altenburg in February 2003, and worse still in Mecklenburg-Vorpommern, where the area of Neubrandenburg recorded 25.8 percent and Stralsund 25.2 percent.[12] And these statistics have to be understood as "corrected" figures, as they do not include "hidden" unemployed people, such as any person unemployed but not officially registered with the government's employment offices, any person who took or was asked to take early retirement starting at age fifty-five, any person who currently holds part-time employment but is actually seeking full-time employment, or any person currently enrolled in some continuous education program. Youth unemployment figures are similar to the statistics above and are also rising at an alarming rate.[13] For satellite cities, it is not so easy to obtain "obvious" numbers, as they are areas that draw the influx of many people—especially the young—who are not registered there. For example, for the satellite city of Berlin-Marzahn/Hellersdorf, the government's employment office gives only the official changes in the number of the registered unemployed by comparing a particular month from last year with the same month this year. While even the officially registered number is horrendous—a rise of 58 percent (in comparison, for instance, the rise of Berlin-Southwest is only 6.8 percent and Berlin-South 4.2 percent)[14]—and leaves room for interpretation of an enormous recent influx, according to social workers' observations in the area, the actual number has to be much higher if one takes into consideration the non-registered young people that are drawn to these satellite cities.

To address youth unemployment, the government created a special program in 1999, JUMP (Jugend mit Perspektive [Youth with Perspectives])—an initiative that promised to help any young person who was seeking some kind of training program or apprenticeship to guarantee him or her that opportunity. If there was no program available in his or her home town, then additional financial support was provided to move to another part of Germany.[15] Originally planned as a one-time initiative, JUMP has been renewed several times since 1999. JUMP is indeed praiseworthy, but one has to read between the lines about its true success for Germany-East. The government itself praises its own initiative, yet other voices, such as the Association of German Employers, point to the fact that although JUMP has been successful for Germany-West, it did not fulfill the high hopes for Germany-East. Young people in Germany-East continue to have negative success in finding any training or employment, and even "public and governmental financial support programs that have been implemented especially for East Germany and that have been increased tremendously during the last years did not change that fact."[16] In addition, it is important to stress that initiatives like JUMP guarantee only training or apprenticeship, but no job afterward—and again, the problem worsens for Germany-East. Because of the lack of employment options, groups like the Association of German Employers have argued vehemently for moving able and employable young people away from these economically depressed areas to the West. Indeed, several financial support programs have been implemented recently that allow able young people to leave Germany-East.

Yet, whereas the encouragement to move is a well-intended idea, the emigration causes another problem for these regions: It creates a community of the "left behind," including the ones who are either too old, not easily employable, or not willing to work. It creates a feeling of abandonment in a double sense—not only being abandoned by the government, but also being abandoned by their own people who have "made it." The abandoned may feel that they must be "dummies" or worthless or simply "human trash."

That such a flight from disadvantaged communities causes a tremendously nihilistic mindset has been observed in African American scholarship. Elijah Anderson, for example, explains that when "many of those who are capable leave," this depletion adds tremendously to the already depressing mode. He describes the downward development in spirits:

> The open-air drug sales, the many pregnant girls, the incivility, the crime, the many street kids, and the diminished number of upstanding (as the residents say) role models make it difficult for old and young alike to maintain a positive outlook, to envision themselves beyond the immediate situation. As neighborhood deterioration feeds on itself, decent law-aiding people become increasingly demoralized.[17]

The tremendous flight of East Germans, especially the young ones, from their areas has indeed already been officially recognized. The Shell Foundation, a highly respected organization in regard to regular youth analysis, argues in its *2001 Youth Report* that one can observe for Germany-East youth two parallel developments: The ones who have already completed higher education or have hope for some higher education decide to move away from their home region, and the ones who stay behind display a growing sense of hopelessness and of missing equal opportunities. Interestingly, the Shell authors record a high rate of mobility among young East German women[18]—something comparable to the upward mobility of African American women during the last decades. And although the government so far has supported special financial programs for young people to move to areas with better employment options, in their recent publications, they recognize the danger of the "flight of the young" and call for action to stop that development, as it will have disastrous effects in the future on these abandoned regions.[19]

One of the major contributions to the ongoing African American debate about solutions is connected to this idea of the negative mindset—something that cannot be measured in statistical figures and numbers. As Wright argued as early as 1945, one has to take such a nihilistic attitude into serious consideration when trying to predict any future development. He writes:

> Social discontent assumes many subtle guises, and a society that recognizes only those forms of social maladjustment which are recorded in courts, prisons, clinics, hospitals, newspapers, and bureaus of vital statistics will be missing some of the most fateful of the telltale clues to its destiny. What I mean is this: it is distinctly possible to know, *before it happens*, that certain forms of violence will occur.[20]

African American scholars after Wright have urged us to see the effect of the nihilistic mindset as a powerful negative force that can indeed cause people to lose or give up fundamental human abilities, such as fighting against negative conditions or seeing chances and opportunities offered to them. bell hooks, for example, argues in this regard in *Class Matters*:

> The result of [the] psychosis for the poor and underprivileged is despair. In the case of the black poor, that nihilism intensified because the combined forces of race and class and exploitation and oppression make it highly unlikely that they will be able to change their lives . . . they do not see the resources they have and might effectively use to enhance the quality of their lives.[21]

In her *The Condemnation of Little B*, a detailed and well-documented research about the young African American underclass at the beginning of the twenty-first century, Elaine Brown argues that their problem is no longer just a matter of "lack of opportunity" but the "loss of self-respect, self-love and personal responsibility."[22] Many other African American scholars have pointed to the tragic power of nihilism for the African American underclass. Perhaps one of the most famous and most quoted articles in this regard is Cornel West's "Nihilism in Black America" in his *Race Matters*. West underlines the profoundly destroying force of "psychological depression, personal worthlessness, and social despair so widespread in black America."[23] He explains his idea of nihilism for deteriorating communities as follows:

> In fact, the major enemy of black survival in America has been and is neither oppression nor exploitation but rather the nihilistic threat—that is, loss of hope and absence of meaning. For as long as hope remains and meaning is preserved, the possibility of overcoming oppression stays alive. The self-fulfilling prophesy of the nihilistic threat is that without hope there can be no future, that without meaning there can be no struggle.[24]

That also explains why such nihilism occurred in post– rather than in pre-Civil Rights Movement times. Whereas before and during the 1950s and 1960s, hope for a changed future was still alive and even possible, contemporary disappointment and despair are based on the lived and experienced disappointment of hope in reality due to "the structural dynamics of corporate market institutions that affect all Americans."[25] As one of many results of this nihilistic mindset, the suicide rate for young black men has tripled over the last fifteen years, "reflecting not rising criminality but increased depression among them."[26]

For the East German nihilistic mindset, one does not have to think of any future development as this development already has happened. One has to talk only to any social worker or youth minister in these areas to hear that fact again and again. According to Rainer Becker, for example, former youth minister in the rural area near the Polish border and now youth minister in Berlin-Marzahn/Hellersdorf, nihilism is cross-generational and so widespread that it feels like being on another planet in these neighborhoods. Regarding young people, one can only be shocked about their already extreme level of hopelessness, their sense of abandonment by parents and by politicians, and the absence of any dreams for their future. The highest aspiration for the majority of them is to "dream" of getting some low-level job such as gas station attendant—indeed a true dream for them, as they are surrounded by more unemployed young people than employed ones.[27]

As another reason for the deteriorating conditions in the left-behind "ghetto," many African American scholars have pointed to the widening gap between the middle and the underclass. bell hooks, for example, argues that many members of the growing middle class have lost any sense of responsibility for the ones left behind, and that to be reminded of their origins by someone is considered a major sin.[28] Yet, middle-class members argue that it cannot be their responsibility to "pull up" people that have had a choice the same way they had. Already famous is Henry Louis Gates Jr.'s statement about choice in his PBS documentary about the class issue in the black community. He states:

> There is nothing natural about feeling compassion toward those people who look like you, but who have not been as successful as you. . . . You see, the causes for poverty . . . are both structural and behavioral. . . . Deciding to get pregnant or not to have protected sex. Deciding to do drugs. Deciding not to study. Deciding, deciding, deciding . . .[29]

Gates's statement displays exactly the widening gap between the two classes—it grossly supports the above-mentioned wrong assumption by mainstream society that most people of the underclass are on drugs, un-employed, and probably even criminal. Yet, as I have already shown above,[30] the developing "ghetto" economy throughout the decades has included many people either working full time, often in several jobs, and still living below the poverty line, or has shut out people willing and wanting to work because the necessary number of needed jobs simply does not exist. Gates argues that it is all about personal decisions. But he offers only decisions *against* something. What about decisions *for* something? So if someone decides *against* getting pregnant, what other significant life decisions are there for her in addition? Did her pregnancy prevent her from getting an executive level position? Or from even just an entry-level but, after all, a full-time job? Was that McJob already there in the first place, just waiting to be filled by someone, waiting for her to decide *for* taking it? Or could she have decided *for* joining the military? Indeed, many individuals have es-caped the "ghetto" via the military, and many have had the chance to de-cide *for* it. But one has to understand that these individuals, as high and laudable as their number might be, still only represent the exception, not the norm. U.S. society simply does not hold the option for every single in-dividual to decide *for* something. One has just to imagine the U.S. military's reaction if all African American underclass young people would show up at a recruiter's office, expressing their personal and free, individual decision to join the military.

I have already argued that the flight away from the "ghetto" and the ni-hilistic mindset have resulted in missing role models for the generations growing up in these conditions. The widening gap of the two classes makes the problem of the role model even worse. Yet, the underclass does need the members of the middle class for many different reasons, be it for teach-ing them about the options that do indeed exist (How do the underclass members know about the tremendous variety of scholarships?), for help-ing them to understand how community politics in the United States sometimes can be influenced from below (How would underclass parents

294 • Heike Raphael-Hernandez

know that there is indeed money for their children's schools if only they would petition for it?), or for showing them simple family economics necessary to get out of the underclass (How does one do a monthly budget, and how does one balance a checkbook, and how does one not live from check to check?). In addition, middle-class members are often also the ones who understand the macro-structure of current society; thus, they are the ones that have the ability to keep the underclass problems and the call for improvement on the government's agenda and on the general public's mind, be it locally or nationwide.[31]

The same argument about the necessary contact of the middle class with the underclass holds true for the East German situation. Yet, the class gap is a more complicated case for former East Germany than for African America. In pre-Civil Rights time, all classes in the African American community were forced to experience white society's racism together, and the shared sense of a horrible history, of ongoing exploitation and dominating racism created at least some form of a cross-class community spirit, even if only in connection to white society. Such a cross-class spirit has never existed for East Germany. In general, historically and culturally, Germany is a class-obsessed country. And Marxist/Leninist ideology practiced in East Germany did not propagate class equality at all. While lip service was often paid to an obscure idea of equality, it was made very clear in ideology and everyday practice that East Germany celebrated the "dictatorship of the working class," and middle-class members had to accept a life and daily treatment of second-class citizens. East Germany even invented a new class, the so-called i-class (the intelligentsia class). The "dictatorship of the working class" was manifested in many different forms, such as privileging working-class children over middle-class or i-class children when they applied for the already limited number of slots at colleges or universities. After the reunification, it was definitely the middle or the i-class that gained from the new system—in fact, their children are the true winners of the reunification—whereas the working class lost "old" privileges and did not really gain as much as the middle class. Shortly after the reunification, a cross-class spirit comparable to the African American one existed because of general second-class treatment of East Germans by West German society. Yet, the 1990s stabilized conditions for many, be it because of a geographical move or because of some found niche. Today second-class treatment by West Germans is not so stereotype-dominated anymore as it was in the early 1990s. But since the idea of "personal responsibility" has dominated the discourse of the new Germany, the widening class gap is now one between the class "who made it" and the one moving more and more toward described underclass conditions. To close such a gap in Germany seems to be as complicated as it is in African America.

My thesis is that this widening, perhaps even antagonistic gap between classes in Germany-East, together with a growing sense of nihilism and a feeling of double-abandonment caused by deteriorating economic conditions, is creating "ghetto-type" communities with a large underclass. This gap should be recognized, and the widespread uncritical acceptance of right-wing ideology, especially among the young, should be seen as one urgent sign of the danger to come. I am not saying that right-wing fascination and right-wing activities are correct as long as they occur among East German disadvantaged young people. Right-wing violence should be called a crime and should be punished as such; right-wing ideology should be dealt with in any way possible so as to eliminate it from young people's minds. Yet, when trying to look at solutions, my impression is that right-wing activities among the young in Germany-East are singled out in the government's effort and are often focused upon, for example, as former East Germany's failure to teach modern-day democratic forms of multi-cultural attitudes. My impression is that the widespread fascination among young people in former East German satellite cities, small cities, and rural areas is not taken as the dangerous tip of the iceberg it is—as the sign hinting at other things to come, as the outcry of something different. It is the same official view of the high crime rate among young African Americans. Instead of seeing the high crime rate as a symptom of urgent problems, official legislation has treated it only on the surface, as criminals committing crimes. The treatment introduced was the "three strikes and you're out" program.

Yet, any society that treats certain groups that way, as small as these groups may be, has also to be aware that these groups carry the potential to be ticking time bombs. My prediction for the German future and my application of the African American lens to the East German situation is frightening—especially if one considers that often in African American history, riots have erupted when people became too desperate in their conditions. The last riot happened as recently as last year, 2002, in Cincinnati, Ohio.

However, that same lens I apply to show a possible frightening future development can also be applied to look at possible solutions. I do not claim that the African American situation is already out of the danger zone—on the contrary, my example of last year's race riot in Cincinnati proves the still-urgent need for radical changes. But the African American situation allows us to talk about some hope for future improvement. During recent years, one can observe a tremendously growing debate with diverse voices that come from the African American community itself and that seem to have the honest intention of truly wanting to change the situation without any self-serving political agenda in mind. Many voices even vehemently disagree among each other about reasons and solutions for the underclass: The debate about structural constraints versus behavioral impediments, and the question of responsibility of the middle class for the underclass serve as just two examples here. Still, a powerful and widespread debate is going on in search of possible solutions. And a strong debate can only push forward arguments, ideas, and policy maker's actions as long as it stays active and alive.

One specific part of this highly active, ongoing African American debate has to be mentioned in particular and can perhaps become "transportable" to Germany-East. During recent years, there has been a growing initiative among the younger African American generation itself that has done excellent work in regard to analyzing African American urban youth conditions and contemplating solutions. It is impossible to mention all these initiatives, but I would like to mention three very different examples—a book, a website, and a nonprofit organization—to show the rich variety of the young generation's move to pick up the work themselves:

- Bakari Kitwana's *The Hip Hop Generation: Young Blacks and the Crisis in African-America.* He offers a wealth of ideas that, if all were taken into consideration, would probably bring radical changes.
- www.sistaspace.com. Among many different items, they offer <Nommo>, a forum that publishes excellent essays regarding the African American young underclass.
- LISTEN (Local Initiative, Support, Training, and Education Network), Washington, D.C. Founded in 1998, they state as their mission for the twenty-first century the task "to develop leadership and strengthen the social capital of urban youth ages 14–29 for civic engagement and community problem solving."[32]

Such a widespread and heated ongoing debate among diverse participants—including academics, journalists, religious leaders, policy makers, social workers, leading intellectuals, artists, writers, members of the young group in question themselves, and "simply concerned" people—does not exist so far in Germany-East. Of course, many politicians have made Germany-East their agenda, but one cannot lose the impression that these are self-serving, vote-collecting efforts. In 2000, a chance for the beginning of such an ongoing debate was there—the city of Leipzig held a conference at which about three hundred youth studies experts came together to discuss the tremendous problem of right-wing fascination in Germany-East and to look for possible solutions. Yet, as one contributor to the conference volume concludes, the enthusiastic idea of exchanging E-mail addresses in order to start an ongoing debate and ongoing cooperation was never executed.[33]

To show this difference of debate—the diversity, complexity, and sophistication of the African American debate versus the weakness and rarity of the East German debate—I want to single out the "education" discussion. In the African American search for solutions, one of the most heated discussions is connected to education. Two different aspects are important in this regard: On the one hand, young African Americans have to give up their attitude that education is "uncool," that striving hard to achieve academically is "acting white." They have to come to understand that modern society's reality offers fewer and fewer jobs for unskilled or semiskilled workers and moves more and more toward offering jobs that require at least some level of higher education. In innumerable oral and written discussions, African Americans drive this change of attitude home, hoping that it reaches the target group. One can find some material about this education attitude in so-called academic scholarship, but it is actually important that the discussion is heard by the target group—a group that does not read such academic material. In this regard, an awareness drive has been undertaken in many different cities. Schools now regularly invite people who have "made it" because of education; church leaders, social workers, youth ministers, members of the Big Brothers/Big Sisters initiative, to name a few, try on a continual basis to show a different perspective on what many young blacks call "uncool white education." And written material that is clearly intended for these young people or their parents as a kind of self-help literature has been published.[34] Yet, on the other hand, in all the important discussion about changing attitudes toward academic achievement, these voices also clearly express the responsibility of the government toward struggling substandard schools, which are forced to attempt to educate their students with fewer books, fewer qualified teachers, fewer supplies, fewer or no field trips, overcrowded classrooms, deteriorating school buildings, and broken science equipment. The newest idea to meet that challenge, a voucher system for gifted students to enable them to attend private schools, already seems not to work as intended and is already hotly debated: A few inner-city students meeting many privileged suburban children in the classroom creates new problems of missing material outfits, missing privileges, and missing self-esteem. In addition, instead of helping the underclass children as a whole group and improving the whole school system, only individuals get the chance to participate in flight and escape again—the same phenomenon described above. And the African American debate warns about another dangerous development that has already started. A plethora of voices warn that in an economy that is developing toward globalization and the demand for high-skilled jobs that require at least some higher education, current education standards of inner-city schools simply fail to prepare their students for such a changing future.[35]

The debate for Germany-East's young "soon-to-be-lost" generation, however, does not really focus on the specifics of education. Currently,

Germany discusses education in general for the country at large because of some poor results in international comparative tests, but again, any specific implications for the future of certain young groups in former East Germany do not yet officially exist. Yet, interestingly, one would assume that such a debate has forced itself on the public agenda because the government itself confesses that the JUMP program has failed so far for Germany-East, among other reasons precisely because of education standards. The government's short discussion for the future sounds more like a joke. Because they discuss high rates of youth unemployment only in regard to providing employment, but not in connection with education, they see two possible solutions for the youths not able to move away with the help of the government-sponsored "mobility program." On the one hand, the idea of "two sharing one job" has been introduced—companies are encouraged to convince older employees who will retire during the upcoming years to work part-time, thus sharing his or her job with a young, otherwise unemployed person. On the other hand, the government also states quite boldly that a large number of currently employed people in Germany-East will retire in 2006, so there is hope for unemployed youth as long as they hold on until then. But is there any mention of post-2006 demands for higher-skilled jobs? Any mention of jobs that require some kind of higher education? Any mention of the disappearance of the large number of low-skilled jobs that still would pay decent salaries in the twenty-first century? Any mention of globalization? Not in the government's discussion. As one can see with the example of education alone, Germany-East urgently needs the diverse and powerful African American debate conducted by its own members.

One of the problems in finding solutions for Germany-East is that the majority of critical and analytical scholarship still focuses only on the micro-context (the actual right-wing fascination or violence among the young) without placing it into a larger macro-context (to see it as the tip of the iceberg of something connected to the special situation of people who were transported from one political system to another overnight, without learning how to live in that new system, and who have had to face tremendously difficult economic challenges). Such limited micro-context analysis in search of solutions for the right-wing problem has concentrated on topics such as the personal experience of violence in abusive homes, the high rates of single motherhood and absentee fathers in former East Germany, and the results of the East German early-life day-care center practice.[36] Other limited micro-context analytical approaches deal with former East Germany's denial of existing right-wing ideology[37] or consider the missing multicultural awareness of former East Germans responsible for the development. For example, the German Youth Institute in Munich, a highly respected organization that does analytical youth research, holds such a limited multicultural view in its annual report for 2002, thus offering "workshop" solutions. The report suggests four points as the main solutions: teaching of tolerance, teaching of cosmopolitan thinking, promotion of democratic behavior, and promotion of civil engagement.[38] Indeed, numerous official youth politics initiatives for Germany-East go in such a "workshop" direction. At the Leipzig conference, too, one can find all the aforementioned ideas about workshops and education and the individual family among the suggestions; however, the majority of speakers did not move beyond the sole focus on right-wing ideology, thus missing the chance of placing the problem into a larger social context.[39]

Such a focus on the right-wing topic and its connected ideas for solutions often seems something like a proof to the world that "one is very active in doing something" rather than a means for amelioration. This can be seen with the example of Hildburghausen, Thüringen. In 1995, its local *gymnasium*—a high school that prepares its students for college—received, as the first high school in Germany-East and as the second high school in Germany at all, the award "Schule ohne Rassismus" (School without Racism), which also carries the duty to teach multicultural awareness during the following years. While its students and faculty have been busy since then in innumerable workshops and activities, many citizens of Hildburghausen and its surrounding villages have more and more allowed right-wing ideology to enter their minds and their talks; right now Adolf Hitler's *Mein Kampf* is uncritically recommended as something to read if one wants to know more about the foreigner and the unemployment problems.[40]

Somehow, one cannot lose the strange feeling that all those "busybody" activities of educating the young in Germany-East happen more in order to stay out of the international media—Germany does not want to be perceived as a foreigner-hating and -mistreating country again. After all, how influential can an African cooking workshop be in turning around a skin?

A few voices, however, have been calling for that larger macro-context. For example, one presenter at the Leipzig conference, Klaus Breymann, district attorney at the Higher Court Magdeburg, offers an excellent analysis in this regard.[41] The Shell Foundation researchers, too, argue in their *2001 Youth Report* that one definitely has to take the difference between Germany-East and Germany-West into consideration. According to their findings, right-wing young people expressed fear about their own actual or possible unemployment and about society's nonexisting equal opportunities. Therefore, the report claims that it would be the wrong approach to try to debate or discuss ideology with right-wing young people but a better solution to create programs for jobs and training for them—it is "rather a question of resources than of ideology."[42]

These few recent voices allow hope that someday such a strong, diverse debate, already going on in African America, will exist among East Germans, too. Perhaps even the young themselves will find their own strong voice in that still-missing debate. One such young voice recently entered the public debate: Ingo Hasselbach, who was one of the leaders of the East German young, organized Neonazis during the 1990s and who has become an outspoken opponent since his break with right-wing ideology.[43]

I claim that a look at the East German situation through the lens of the urban African American experience can offer better understanding and possible solutions. In regard to "rather a question of resources than of ideology," such a lens could generate the following specific questions for Germany-East: Could a much better-funded school system that would tremendously improve the standard of education in their communities help, thus providing better chances for young people to become marketable for higher employment? Could it help to make these young people aware of the need for higher education for tomorrow's limited employment options? Could the U.S. initiative of the Big Brother/Big Sister program be an idea for East Germans to counter the nihilistic mindset? Or could a specific cultural youth movement of their own help them to overcome a deadly attitude of nihilism? Could something comparable to hip-hop help them to find their own generation's self-esteem? Or could it be that these young East Germans urgently need a strong lobby of famous intellectuals like the African American urban youth seem to have, especially since the 1990s?

Whatever the answers to these questions are for Germany-East, the main idea is clear: Young people in these growing "ghetto communities" do need that heated, but strong public debate that would place them on the public agenda. The hope remains that during the next decade, the young generation itself will enter the public debate in powerful ways and numbers, as has been the case with African America in the 1990s.

Many friends and colleagues have offered valuable suggestions and ideas for this essay. While I am indebted to all of them, I would like to especially thank Wendy Pfeffer, Nathan Schwartz, Hildegard Storek, Don Hernandez, Derek Bembry, and Cathy Covell Waegner. Many of my students in my African American literature classes have discussed with me my ideas of this essay; among them I would like to specifically mention and thank all the participants of Term 3/2003's "African American Fiction in the 20th Century." Academic scholarship often proves "truth" with academe-defined, correctly documented material, yet for my essay I base a lot of my "truth" on innumerable talks and personal observations with many East Germans during the thirteen years after reunification—my own family, other relatives, friends, people I met, youth ministers—who shared with me their own experiences, their thoughts, their hopes, and their disappointments in post-reunified Germany-East. I express my thanks to all of them.

Notes

1. The term "skins" that I use in my title for this specific group of young East Germans has to be understood differently than the term "skinheads." Skinheads consider themselves one specific form of youth subculture, one that intends to provoke but does not necessarily imply right-wing ideology, as widely assumed. For more information, see Klaus Farin, ed., *Skinheads—A Way of Life: Eine Jugendbewegung stellt sich selbst dar* (Bad Tölz: Tilsner, 1999). The term "skins" in this essay refers to Germany's general and undifferentiated usage of the term for *all* right-wing young East Germans regardless of their hairstyle or their dress code.
2. Jawanza Kunjufu, *State of Emergency: We Must Save African American Males* (Chicago: African American Images, 2001), 1–13.
3. Richard Wright, Introduction, in St. Clair Drake and Horace R. Cayton, *Black Metropolis: A Study of Negro Life in a Northern City* (Chicago: University of Chicago Press, [1945] 1993), xx. I would like to thank Shelly Eversley for pointing this out to me.
4. Osagyefo Uhuru Sekou, "Poverty, Priests, and Popular Culture," *Spike Magazin* www.spikemagazin.com (17 November 2001), 2–3.
5. Osagyefo Uhuru Sekou, *urbansouls* (St. Louis: Urban Press, 2001), 73.
6. Elaine Brown, *The Condemnation of Little B* (Boston: Beacon Press, 2002), 79.
7. Ibid., 75.
8. Ibid., 75.
9. In her well-documented *No Shame in My Game: The Working Poor in the Inner City*, Katherine Newman, for example, disproves such an assumption. She explains that in 1996, for instance, from all Americans "whose annual income put them below the official poverty line . . . 58 percent of them worked full-time" (41). She argues against the widespread assumption of most poor people being on welfare, saying that such an assumption is "misleading because in fact the largest group of poor people in the United States are not those on welfare. They are the working poor whose earnings are so meager that despite their best efforts, they cannot afford decent housing, diets, health care or child care. The debilitating conditions that impinge upon the working poor—substandard housing, crumbling schools, inaccessible health care—are hardly different from those that surround their nonworking counterparts" (40). Katherine Newman, *No Shame in My Game: The Working Poor in the Inner City* (New York: Vintage Books, 1999).
10. See, for example, William Julius Wilson, *When Work Disappears: The World of the New Urban Poor* (New York: Alfred A. Knopf, 1997).
11. www.arbeitsamt.de (6 March 2003).
12. Ibid.
13. Ibid.
14. Ibid.
15. www.bundesregierung.de (28 February 2003).
16. www.bda-online.de/ (28 February 2003). Translation mine.
17. Elijah Anderson, *Code of the Street: Decency, Violence, and the Moral Life of the Inner City* (New York: W. W. Norton, 1999), 146.
18. www.shell-jugendstudie.de (8 April 2002), 17.
19. www.arbeitsamt.de (6 March 2003).
20. Wright, *Black Metropolis*, xxvi–xxvii.
21. bell hooks, *Where We Stand: Class Matters* (New York: Routledge, 2000), 126–27.
22. Brown, *The Condemnation of Little B*, 10.
23. Cornel West, "Nihilism in Black America," in Cornel West, *Race Matters* (Boston: Beacon Press, 1993), 13.
24. Ibid., 14–15.
25. Ibid., 17.

26. Brown, *The Condemnation of Little B*, 120.

27. I would like to thank Rainer Becker for the personal interview (9 March 2003).

28. See especially her chapter "Class and Race: The New Black Elite" in hooks, *Where We Stand*, 89–100.

29. Henry Louis Gates Jr., interview, "The Two Nations of Black America," *Frontline*, PBS, 1997.

30. See note 8.

31. One example of such a collaboration of middle-class members, their knowledge, and their honest engagement—together with underclass members in regard to keeping the underclass's urgent need for improvement on the local and the nationwide agenda—is the Urban League. As one can see with the case of Louisville, Kentucky, in their annual report for 2001, they cite not only meticulous details for specific conditions for Louisville, including details about actual accomplished improvement, but also existing problems and concrete ideas for short- and long-term solutions. They address the debate about structure and personal responsibility as they, in a very detailed way, call to action local policy makers as well as the members of the underclass. www.lul.org (15 June 2002).

32. Bakari Kitwana, *The Hip Hop Generation: Young Blacks and the Crisis in African-American Culture* (New York: Basic *Civitas* Books, 2002); www.sistaspace.com; LISTEN: www.lisn.org.

33. Heiner Wichterich, "Gewaltprävention: Vernetzung und Kooperation," in *Rechtsextreme Jugend: Eine Erschütterung der Gesellschaft? Ursachen, Ausdrucksformen, Prävention und Intervention*, ed. Stefan Danner, Nina Dulabaum, Peter Rieker, and Christian von Wolffersdorff (Leipzig: Stadt Leipzig, 2001), 147.

34. See, for example, Jawanza Kunjufu, *To Be Smart or Popular: The Black Peer Group* (Chicago: African American Images, 1988); Anthony Davis and Jeffrey Jackson, *"Yo, Little Brother . . .": Basic Rules of Survival for Young African American Males* (Chicago: African American Images, 1998).

35. For the globalization and the high-skilled future jobs demands, see, for example, Kitwana, *The Hip Hop Generation*; Brown, *The Condemnation of Little B*; Wilson, *When Work Disappears*; Anderson, *Code of the Street*.

36. The German Youth Institute, for example, did several studies with the University of Munich and the University of Jena in regard to domestic violence. They came to the conclusion that youth unemployment might be one factor for right-wing violence, but is not the essential one. According to them, the experience of early domestic child abuse should be given much more weight than unemployment. Their suggestions for the future are to become aware of these children as early as possible, hopefully already in kindergarten and in elementary school, and to offer help to them. www.dji.de (12 April 2002).

37. For an analysis made already at the beginning of the 1990s, see, for example, Karl-Heinz Heinemann and Wilfried Schubarth, eds., *Der antifaschistische Staat entläßt seine Kinder: Jugend und Rechtsextremismus in Ostdeutschland* (Köln: PapyRossa Verlag, 1992).

38. www.dji.de (8 March 2003)

39. See their conference papers: Stefan Danner, Nina Dulabaum, Peter Rieker, and Christian von Wolffersdorff, eds., *Rechtsextreme Jugend: Eine Erschütterung der Gesellschaft? Ursachen, Ausdrucksformen, Prävention und Intervention* (Leipzig: Stadt Leipzig, 2001).

40. The school's website is www.gym-georg.de. My thanks for this specific information goes to a former student at the Gymnasium Georgianum, who is personally known to me, and to his family, who still resides in the area.

41. Klaus Breymann, "Soziale Prävention statt Kriminalprävention," in Danner et al., *Rechtsextreme Jugend*, 73–87.

42. www.shell-jugendstudie.de (8 April 2002), 20. Translation mine.

43. He has published two somewhat different autobiographies since then. Ingo Hasselbach/Tom Reiss, *Führer-Ex: Memoirs of a Former Neo-Nazi* (New York: Random House, 1996); Ingo Hasselbach/Winfried Bonengel, *Die Abrechnung: Ein Neonazi steigt aus* (Berlin: Aufbau Verlag, 2001).

Contributors

Sabine Broeck is Professor of American Studies at the University of Bremen, with a major emphasis on Gender Studies and African American Studies. She published two books, *White Amnesia—Black Memory? American Women's Writing and History* (1999) and *Der entkolonisierte Koerper: Die Protagonistin in der afroamerikanischen weiblichen Erzähltradition der 30er bis 80er Jahre* (1988), as well as various articles in *Amerikastudien/ American Studies*, in American journals, and in German and American anthologies. Her current research focuses on comparative aspects of the black diaspora in the "New World" and Europe, particularly in Germany, and on American-African-European transatlantic literary and cultural relations in the modern and postmodern context.

Samir Dayal is Associate Professor of English at Bentley College, Massachusetts. He is the editor, with an introduction, of Julia Kristeva's *Crisis of the European Subject*, François Rachline's *Don Juan's Wager*, Lucien Gubbay's *Jews under Islam*, and Patricia Gherovici's *The Puerto Rican Syndrome* (forthcoming), among other books. He has contributed chapters to several edited collections and articles in journals, including *Amerasia Journal, Angelaki: A Journal of the Theoretical Humanities, Colby Quarterly, College English, Bulletin of Concerned Asian Scholars, Contemporary South Asia Review, Critical Asian Studies, Cultural Critique, Genders, The Journal of the Midwest Modern Language Association, L'Infini, MELUS, Postmodern Culture*, and *Socialist Review*. He has also published some short fiction. Currently he is writing a book about contemporary South Asian fiction and film.

Dorothea Fischer-Hornung is Senior Lecturer in the English Department at Ruprecht-Karls-Universitaet Heidelberg, Germany. Among her book publications are *Women in the United States* (1990); *Women and War* (1991), co-edited with Maria Diedrich; *Holding Their Own: Perspectives on the Multi-Ethnic Literatures of the United States* (2000), co-edited with Heike Raphael-Hernandez; *EmBODYing Liberation: The Black Body in American Dance* (2001), co-edited with Alison Goeller; and *Sleuthing Ethnicity: The Detective in Multi-Ethnic Crime Fiction* (2003), co-edited with Monika Mueller. Currently, she is project co-director for the American Cultural Studies Online project (www.acs-onweb.de) in cooperation with the universities of South Australia, Adelaide; Heidelberg and Stuttgart, Germany; Padua, Italy; and St. Petersburg, Russia. She is a member of the executive board of MESEA (Society for Multi-Ethnic Studies: Europe and the Americas).

María Frías is Professor of American and African American Literature at the University of La Coruña, Spain. She is the author of *"Marriage Doesn't Make Love": El discurso del matrimonio en la obra de Zora Neale Hurston* (2000).

Peter Gardner worked in theatre in New York City before he moved to Italy in 1988. He currently teaches at the University of Rome "Tor Vergata" and at the Saint Mary's College Rome Program.

Paul Gilroy is Professor of Sociology and African-American Studies at Yale University. Until recently he was Professor of Sociology and Cultural Studies at Goldsmiths College, University of London. He is the author of *Against Race: Imagining Political Culture beyond the Color Line, The Black Atlantic: Modernity and Double Consciousness, There Ain't No Black in the Union Jack: The Cultural Politics of Race and Nation,* and *Small Acts: Thoughts on the Politics of Black Cultures.* Paul Gilroy is widely recognized for his critical commentaries on black music and vernacular culture, and his work has been an inspiration to the resurgent black arts movement in Britain. His work has been translated into ten languages.

Ch. Didier Gondola is Associate Professor of African History at Indiana University in Indianapolis. He has devoted extensive years to the study of popular cultures and published numerous articles on fashion, music, gambling, and sports. He is the author of *Villes Miroirs: migrations et identités urbaines à Brazzaville et Kinshasa, 1930–1970* (1997) and *The History of Congo* (2002), and is working on an archive-based project on political protest and messianic movements in colonial Congo.

Johanna C. Kardux is Director of American Studies and Associate Professor of English at Leiden University, The Netherlands. Kardux has taught American literature and cultural history at Leiden since 1986, after earning a doctorate degree in English from Cornell University. In recent years, she has published mostly on the politics of historical memory, with a special focus on African American and postcolonial literatures. She is co-author (with Eduard van de Bilt) of *Newcomers in an Old City: The American Pilgrims in Leiden, 1609–1620* (1998; second ed. 2001), and co-editor (with Rosemarijn Hoefte) of *Connecting Cultures: The Netherlands in Five Centuries of Transatlantic Exchange* (1994). At present, she is writing a book on the African diaspora and the production of cultural memory.

André Lepecki is a New York–based essayist, dramaturg, and critic. He is an Assistant Professor at the Department of Performance Studies at New York University.

Felicia McCarren, Associate Professor in the Department of French and Italian, Tulane University, has taught as visiting faculty at UCLA, the University of New Mexico, and NYU–Tisch School of the Arts. She is the author of *Dance Pathologies: Performance, Poetics, Medicine* (1998) and the forthcoming *Dancing Machines: Choreographies of the Age of Mechanical Reproduction*, and translator of Michel Serres's *Rome: the book of foundations* and Philippe Lacoue-Labarthe's *Musica Ficta: Figures of Wagner* (all from Stanford University Press). She has published articles in *Critical Inquiry* and *L'Esprit Créateur* as well as in France, and spent 2000–2001 in Paris working on a collaborative project on French hip-hop, organized by Roberta Shapiro and Marie-Christine Bureau and funded in part by the Ministère de la Culture, Mission du patrimoine ethnologique.

Éva Miklódy currently teaches African American and American literature at the University of Debrecen, Hungary. She was awarded a university doctoral degree in 1993 in American literature. She has published numerous articles on African American women authors and African American literary theory.

Mihaela Mudure is Associate Professor in the English Department of Babes-Bolyai University, Cluj-Napoca, Romania. She is interested in American ethnic studies and the intersection between gender and ethnicity, as well as in comparative multiculturalisms. Her publications include articles, a collaboration at *Encyclopedia of Postcolonial Studies*, edited by John Hawley and published at Greenwood Press (2001), and four books. Her two recent ones are *Feminine* (2000) and *Coveting Multiculturalism* (2000). She is the translator of Donald Kenrick's *Historical Dictionary of the Gypsies* (2002) into Romanian.

Irina Novikova is Associate Professor in the Department of Culture and Literature, University of Latvia, and Director of the Center for Gender Studies at the same university. She taught as a Visiting Professor at the University of Helsinki (2002–2003). Her research interests are American women's literature; gender in literature and film; and gender, ethnicity, and citizenship. She is editor of the volume *Contemporary Feminist Theories* in the Latvian language and author of numerous essays in literary, gender, and cultural studies. Currently, she is writing a book on comparative aspects of contemporary women's literatures (autobiography and Bildungsroman).

Heike Raphael-Hernandez is Professor of English at the University of Maryland University College in Europe. Among her publications are *Holding Their Own: Perspectives on the Multi-Ethnic Literatures of the United States* (2000), co-edited with Dorothea Fischer-Hornung, and several articles on contemporary African American writers. She is a member of the executive board of MESEA (Society for Multi-Ethnic Studies: Europe and the Americas).

Jed Rasula is Helen S. Lanier Distinguished Professor of English at the University of Georgia, having previously taught at Queen's University in Canada and at Pomona College in California. He is author of *The American Poetry Wax Museum: Reality Effects 1940–1960* (1996), *This Compost: Ecological Imperatives in American Poetry* (2002), *Syncopations* (forthcoming), and co-editor, with Steve McCaffery, of *Imagining Language: An Anthology* (1998). He has published widely on modernism in poetry and fiction, and on jazz, including contributions to *Jazz among the Discourses*, edited by Krin Gabbard (1994) and *The Cambridge Companion to Jazz*, edited by Mervyn Cooke and David Horn (2002).

Alan Rice is Senior Lecturer in American Studies and Cultural Theory at the University of Central Lancashire in Preston. His Ph.D. thesis was on Toni Morrison and jazz music, and he has published widely in African American studies. His work on Frederick Douglass's 1845 visit to Britain was published in a jointly edited volume (with Martin Crawford) *Liberating Sojourn: Frederick Douglass and Transatlantic Reform*. He has edited a special volume on *Issues of Blackness and Whiteness in the Fiction of Saul Bellow* for the *Saul Bellow Journal* and has just completed his first monograph, *Radical Narratives of the Black Atlantic* (Continuum, 2003). He is joint editor (with Angela Leonard) of the *Encyclopaedia of African American Relations* to be published in 2004–2005.

P. A. Skantze received her Ph.D. in European theatre and English from Columbia University. During her tenure as Assistant Professor at the University of Michigan, Ann Arbor, she taught courses on performance studies, early modern theater, Shakespeare, and "world" drama. She works as independent scholar and directs theater in Rome, Italy. Currently a Fellow at the Italian Academy of Columbia University in 2003, she was a Fulbright Senior Research Fellow in 2002, working on a project on the European Union, transnational identity, and theater festivals. She is the author of *Stillness in Motion in the Seventeenth-Century Theatre* (2003).

Cathy Covell Waegner has been on the English faculty of the University of Siegen in Germany since 1977 and has published on William Faulkner and Toni Morrison, literary historical topics, African American culture, and comparative ethnicities. Her current research fields include hybridity in literature and film, contemporary German Jewish identity, and instructional uses of the new media. She recently co-edited *Literature on the Move: Comparing Diasporic Ethnicities in Europe and the Americas* (2002).

Index